From Papa.
He and Stephen Bonsal were
friends when he was studying
at the Beaux Arts in the late 8[...]

HEYDAY IN A VANISHED WORLD

Stephen Bonsal

HEYDAY
in a
VANISHED WORLD

by Stephen Bonsal

W · W · NORTON & CO · INC · *New York*

Copyright, 1937, by
STEPHEN BONSAL

FIRST EDITION

PRINTED IN THE UNITED STATES OF AMERICA
FOR THE PUBLISHERS BY THE VAIL-BALLOU PRESS

TO

R. M. B.

NAME CHILD AND VOTARY OF

ST. RITA

TIRELESS ADVOCATE OF SEEMINGLY UNATTAINABLE

BLESSINGS—WITH THANKS

. . . .

So they hunted, and they holloa'd till the setting of the sun;
And they'd nought to bring away at last when th' huntin' day
was done,

Look ye there!

Then one unto the other said, "This huntin' doesn't pay
But we've prowli't up an' down a bit an' had a rattlin' day,

Look ye there!"

OLD ENGLISH SONG

CONTENTS

HEYDAY IN A VANISHED WORLD

1. FIRST GALLOP

I HAD come a cropper when the mare, carrying our hopes and our money, had left us in the lurch at Sheepshead Bay. There was no particular reason why I should return to Maryland, and it would have been absurd to follow the horses, because I had no money to play with; and besides my confidence in my knowledge of horseflesh had received a rude jolt. It would have been quite natural in the circumstances if, like the hero in *Under Two Flags*, at the time my favorite reading, I should have sought glory and forgetfulness on the tented field, and I did dally with the thought of joining the Foreign Legion, under an assumed name, of course. But the recruiting stations that led to this romantic career were in faraway Paris, or Oran, and my resources were at a very low ebb; besides I had in my slender baggage a manuscript dealing with the epic days in the Balkan Peninsula, of which I had a high opinion. This secret manuscript decided me to enter upon the field of journalism where, as I well knew, the goddess of chance also ruled and might prove more propitious than she had upon the race track.

On the morning after reaching this momentous decision I left the St. James Hotel and I left it in style, which as I knew was so important in New York. "Ed" Hill and some of the race-horse men came out from the lobby and wished me better luck next time. The hackman started to drive me to the Desbrosses Street ferry, he knew the route I was likely to take; but when we had gone a few blocks I diverted him and soon we were bumping over the cobblestones of the Bowery. I had him stop at a convenient place, and charging him with the custody of my bag I entered Simpson's, the famous pawnbroker under the sign of the Three Balls, and in a minute I had parted, temporarily I hoped, with my precious Wesley

9

Richards shotgun, and had five ten-dollar bills in my pocket.

I was determined that the new life I was entering upon was to have a sound economic basis. I told the good-natured hackman, who understood the situation perfectly, to drive west, and he deposited me at a convenient corner on Wooster Street where the uptown horse cars of that day halted as they traveled along with incredible slowness. Soon, keeping close watch over my bag, I was on the front platform of a car and discoursing with the driver about the rather obvious ailments of his nags.

At last we emerged from the narrow business street where our progress had been greatly retarded by the many trucks that sprawled over the tracks as they were unloaded, and came out into Washington Square. We skirted the great gray stone building on the east, then as now a famous hall of learning, and pursued our leisurely way up University Place. The tired horses just naturally came to a halt at Ninth Street and at the same moment my eyes fell upon two private residences on the right side of the street which were somewhat superficially joined together by a sign which read "Hotel Martin." Over all waved a brave new tricolor flag of France. I knew from my student days in Paris that this sign and these colors connoted good food and reasonable prices, so with a word of cheer to my friend the driver I got out. The hotel that I now entered had been opened only the day before, but I was not the first guest to arrive. I had been preceded by several hours by Dr. Zaldivar, still, as he maintained, the Constitutional President of the Republic of El Salvador, who after a narrow escape from his dissatisfied countrymen in an open boat had managed to reach New York. The Doctor-President could not speak English, and at the time very little French, and with him I brushed up my Spanish while listening to his views on Central American politics.

My idea from the beginning had been to get a job on the *New York Herald*, but first off I was, at least I thought so, quite rudely rebuffed. Then I wrote some articles on the political situation in Southeastern Europe, with which I thought I was quite familiar, for Mr. S. . . . of the *World*. I was not surprised that they were immediately published but I was astonished in those, the days of my innocence, to see them appear as cablegrams under the Vienna date line. Of course I wrote a lot more of them but finally Mr. S. . . . explained that, while they were of absorbing interest, he could not publish one every day, and yet at the rate of pay I received that was what my financial situation demanded. "I must give our readers a balanced ration," was his decision, which my eloquence failed to shake.

Mr. Bowers, the able city editor of the *Tribune*, a paper which, at the time, was famous in Printing House Square for its high standard of thought and extremely low rate of pay, offered me, evidently impressed by the glib way I explained my deep knowledge of the turf, the position of racing reporter, but, honest fellow that he was, he made one condition and that was extremely unpalatable. "I imagine you suspect that I know nothing about horses, and you may be right, but at the same time I must tell you that I always assign myself to cover the big stakes and the Cup races." So I decided not to play second fiddle even to such a charming chief as this man undoubtedly was.

I then resumed my plotting to secure a place on the *Herald*, and by persistence and with the backing of a chance acquaintance, met at the Hoffman House bar, whose name escapes me but whose friendly face I shall never forget, I succeeded. The *Herald* was a paper with world-wide range and it offered scope for my languages which, while easily surpassed by any waiter in a cosmopolitan restaurant, were rather unusual in the newspaper offices of those days. Fortune favored me from the start. My account of the arrival of a Supreme Chief coming in haste from one of the Latin-American republics—good Dr. Zaldivar put me on to that—attracted the attention of Junius Henry Brown of the editorial staff, indeed our chief editorial writer at the time, and he gave orders that I should always be assigned to welcome gentlemen of this ilk, and happily they kept coming in considerable numbers and no one of them was so obscure or so coy as to escape my welcoming pen. Soon I was taken off "space," of which I was appropriating too much, and put on salary—a very small salary to be sure but it carried with it stability and even prestige. Undeniably I was on the upgrade.

One evening the fickle goddess, favoring me most generously, led my footsteps to the *stamm-tisch* upstairs in the Vienna café next door to the ultra-conservative Grace Church. Here many interesting people foregathered. They were doubtless "misfits and remnants" as they were called in a book written a few months later by a member of their circle, but they were all of absorbing interest to me at the time and none more so than Helena von Racowitsa, known to us all as the "Red" Countess, and her husband Serge Shevitch. They had come to America together from Switzerland some years before, unmarried, but almost immediately, as soon as they learned the custom of the country, they had been married three times: once in New Jersey by a Justice of the Peace, at the City Hall in Manhattan, and then at the Greek Church on Eighth Street.

The first time I saw this remarkable woman was in a smoke-filled cellar restaurant of the Reds on the East Side. She was listening now with tears and now with smiles to the "comrades" as they sang the marching song they had dedicated to their dead leader with whom the Red Countess had been on such friendly terms, and she indeed, quite unwittingly of course, had encompassed his death. Helena came into the world as the daughter of an impoverished Junker family of East Prussia and, when barely seventeen, she met the popular orator and tribune Ferdinand Lassalle, the man who inspired in the great Bismarck feelings of envy and perhaps of malice. Helena threw herself at the feet, and perhaps into the arms, of the middle-aged leader, and he was flattered and ensnared by her flashing eyes and her gorgeous golden hair. Twenty years after this mistake, which cut short a great political career, I could well understand how it happened and how inevitable it must have been.

For this and other reasons the family of Helena arranged a marriage for her with a *Boyar* or prince from Roumania, a man of large means named Yanko Racowitz who was destined to play a capital part in the drama by which the development of socialism in Germany was set back for at least a generation. Chance played havoc with the worldly-wise plans of the parents. They took Helena to Berne for a change of scene but by accident or by arrangement Lassalle was there and in broad daylight Helena went to see him in his hotel. Father Dönniges challenged the tribune because, as he maintained, he had compromised his daughter; but he was old and infirm and on the field of honor the young Roumanian was substi-

tuted for him and in the duel Lassalle received the wound which a
very few hours later put an end to his promising career.

On this fortunate evening, after a light dinner at the round table,
we talked of this and that (but certainly not of the fatal duel) when
suddenly Shevitch urged the Countess to go home. "You have
fought on quite enough barricades and been in the midst of too
many riots," he said. The Countess was far from well and yielded,
though with evident reluctance.

As we wandered along, escorting her to the humble apartment
where the couple lived, Shevitch explained that the Social Democratic groups of the party in New York, of which he was an outstanding leader, had called a meeting for that evening to denounce
recent dynamite outrages in London which had even endangered
Westminster Hall, the home of the Mother of Parliaments. "Of
course we don't approve of the English Parliament," he stated,
"but, on the other hand, until something better takes its place we
should hate to see it blown sky high. Now John Most in the *Freiheit*
has announced that he and his comrades will attend and, if they cannot outvote us on the resolution, he will break up the meeting."

"Why don't you ask for police protection?" I suggested in my
innocence.

"Because Russians never appeal to the police," was his proud
reply.

After leaving the Countess we continued on foot to Concordia
Hall on Avenue A which, in the light of subsequent developments,
was certainly misnamed. It was up three flights of rickety and winding stairs over a beer saloon, and was crowded with noisy foreigners,
mostly Germans, when we arrived. I stayed on the platform with
Shevitch as he introduced his quite moderate resolution of disapproval rather than censure of the dynamiters, but this fair proposition strangely enough had a most infuriating effect. Chairs and beer
glasses came hurtling on to the stage and several of Shevitch's men
were badly hurt.

My sense of duty (at least I hoped it was that!) led me to leave
the stage at this juncture and push my way as best I could toward
the corner from where John Most and Justus Schwab were direct-
ing the riot. It took time but I got there at last. I knew exactly what

Shevitch had in mind and now I wanted to know what Most was planning. As I got through I saw several men being carried away on benches that had been converted into stretchers, and then someone downstairs with the best of motives put in an ambulance call. It was apparently in this roundabout way that the police learned of the pitched battle that had been in progress for nearly an hour. Someone also succeeded in turning off most of the feeble lights and the battle continued in a smoky twilight. Even when the unfortunate *Wirth* of the establishment appeared in the gallery, and through a megaphone announced that the floor was giving way under the pounding of hundreds of excited feet, the fight went on faster and more furiously. After my talk with Most I endeavored to return to my friends on the platform, but was not successful and unfortunately was standing by Most's side when Captain McCullagh and about fifty policemen arrived and began to clear the hall with their night sticks. Over the turmoil was heard the cry, "Remember the Haymarket," an allusion to the alleged police murders in Chicago for which half a dozen anarchists were hanged. There were also shrieks of "Dynamite!" and "Look out for bombs!" but while several suspicious-looking containers were hastily dropped out of the window I believe nothing more deadly than bad beer kegs was discovered. We were all rushed to the stairs by the police, and beaten with night sticks as we were pushed down them. Near the bottom I evidently fell, and must have been unconscious for a minute or two. When I came to the uproar continued but it came now from the street. Captain McCullagh was standing over me and saying, "I'm sorry, but you were in bad company." I now noticed that one of my trouser legs was strangely missing and that I could hardly walk. All I asked of the good Captain was to get me a hack, and thanks to him I reached the office shortly before midnight. Of course the other papers learned what the police knew of the riot, but that was very little. McCullagh described it as "just a lot of foreigners having a fight and we gave them a belly full." But for the *Herald* it was a complete and practically an exclusive story, and they kept me writing it until the paper went to press. As the dynamite outrages had occurred in London the yarn had a foreign angle and it was cabled abroad, and of course the *Herald* preened its feathers most amusingly about its exclusive and therefore, of course, important information, on a subject of which its "Steemed contemporaries," as we called them, were profoundly ignorant.

From then on the attitude of those in authority in the city rooms was quite different. If I frowned when advised of my assignment for the day it was generally changed to something more to my liking. Jim F. . . . congratulated me; indeed all did. I was regarded as a coming man though nothing happened to change my status and no effort was made to replace my trousers which undeniably had been ruined in the line of duty. And there was a cloud on the horizon which at times depressed me. I had a wretched handwriting and the Commodore * would not permit typewriters on the premises. When I complained to Jack Henderson, head of our composing room, with some bitterness of the substitution of "looming" for the more appropriate word "leonine" with reference to Schwab's head, which I held had disfigured my riot article, he told me frankly that there were only three men upstairs who could set up my copy, "and unfortunately," he added, "they are all three past middle age."

In the course of a few weeks I went ballooning, a sport in which the *Herald* was the pioneer, and I made a trip in a submarine around New York harbor, perhaps an epoch-marking experience in those days. I spent six weeks in Haiti "covering" a revolution, and on my return I was given complete charge of two or three sensational murder stories which I handled at least to my own complete satisfaction; but to my surprise none of these exploits excited comment of any kind. However, I kept on writing and at last produced a story which was in the office generally pronounced to be a "peacherino." It dealt with a fracas on board a canal boat anchored in the North River. It was full of fight and gore and the police had intervened. In the style of the *Herald* of that day you had to read fifteen hundred words before you learned that while men were involved as accessories it was really a dog-fight, but as the desk men said, "interest and uncertainty were sustained to the very end."

* The title by which James Gordon Bennett, the owner of the *New York Herald*, was generally known. In Europe it was assumed that he had played a naval role in our Civil War. As a matter of fact, the title was based on the rank he held in the New York Yacht Club.

A month later as I came in the office I saw that my yarn was posted on the bulletin board marked "good" in the Commodore's blue pencil. This happened every now and then when an article caught the wandering eye of our vagrant chief. Sometimes praise was accompanied by an order that the prize story should be paid double rates—though in my case this did not happen. But of course there was additional prestige and, as Jim said, "now he knows your name —and that is all to the good."

And this was true. When another month had passed there came a cable which read "Send Bonsal to London. I think I can use him and his languages over here."

I was in the seventh heaven of delight and so were my good friends, but, of course, I was not allowed to remain in ignorance of the many distressing experiences that had overtaken men who for a moment had basked in the favor of our mercurial chief. Reick, while he congratulated me, let drop words of warning which coming from this source it was difficult to shake off. "Remember," he said, "that once over there I can do nothing for you. No more than can 'Jimmy' Williams or 'Tommy' Namack the office boy—perhaps not as much." But I was not afraid, and sailed confident that my star now in the ascendant would never sink below the horizon.

2. PARNELL AND KITTY O'SHEA

FOR THE next six months I lived in London; and now, although he was generally thousands of miles away, I was in direct communication with the Commodore. Perhaps to try me out, but more probably for his amusement, he would send me cablegrams from Leghorn or Djibouti, from wherever he had cast anchor, asking my opinion on this and that and urging me to express it freely by wire. "Did I think the tension apparent over the Dardanelles would prove serious?" or "Should the concert of Europe order the Bulgars out of Roumelia or would it be wiser, in my judgment, to let sleeping dogs lie?" Of course he may have had his tongue in his cheek when he put these inquiries on the wire, and certainly that was the position of my tongue when I answered many of them.

The intervals of silence were pleasant, too. The Commodore on the *Namouna* was cruising in distant waters, beyond cable communications, and I remained alone and as I thought supreme in London, on the top of the world. Perhaps I was not living as an Ambassador, like de Blowitz,* but at least I emulated in some respects the scale of a Minister Plenipotentiary of a minor power and I had very comfortable bachelor quarters within a stone's throw of St. James's Palace to which, at least in a news sense, I was accredited. I enjoyed myself hugely, though I did miss the sun. I rarely got to bed before

---

* I am asked by a very wise reader to "identify" de Blowitz—*sic transit gloria mundi*. In my day this Franco-Polish correspondent was the most famous purveyor of Continental news to the English press. Those who liked him not, and their name was legion, asserted that he was an apt pupil of Villemessant, the founder of the *Figaro* and of modern French journalism who insisted that when there was no news his young men must create it. It was, however, conceded that de Blowitz's views on the questions of the day were generally plausible and that his dispatches were always readable.

five in the morning, and when I arose to face my active duties again, what sunlight there had been had disappeared.

But I was in daily contact with interesting people. I had been received by Gladstone several times at Dollis Hill, I had sat at the feet of Charles Bradlaugh, and paid court to Annie Besant, so often with him, and listened enraptured as this remarkable tribune of the people with his great organ-like voice discoursed on the future of democratic institutions. It was thrilling, too, to listen to Eleanor Aveling, a daughter of Karl Marx, whose tragic end was so near, as she talked about the coming of the world revolution, which was a brand-new topic in those distant days.

On the whole the most wonderful of my new experiences was a chance meeting with Stepniak, the mysterious author of *Underground Russia*, a man whose marble-white face verified the rumor that he had lived for months in a cave-like cellar with three companions, digging their way to the railway, under which they placed the bombs that came so near destroying the Emperor Alexander and his suite. As a matter of fact, this meeting swept away all the bounds of prudence and frugality which the business office so often inculcated. Right off the bat I cabled five thousand words in regard to Stepniak, his exploits and his plans, and thereby earned and richly deserved my first reproof.

"I do not say it was not a good 'story.' It was a good story and has attracted considerable attention," wrote the news editor, "but you have made us incur an unnecessary expense. As you dashed them off you should have stopped to think that each one of those five thousand words cost the paper a quarter of a dollar and that the total was a considerable sum. You had better have sent it by mail."

By mail! When all Russia was seething with revolution and revolt! When any day the throne of the Autocrat might be sent tumbling into the scrap-heap of discarded things! What have we men on the firing line almost always had to contend with in the shape of those penny-wise news editors! The man was incredibly stupid, and of course I decided not to give his bleat a second thought. And then his absurd suggestion that I withdraw Stepniak from the public gaze and keep him on tap when wanted! Isolate Stepniak! the greatest revolutionist in the world, the most romantic figure in London!

Of course I did what I could. Stepniak was in dire financial distress and he gave me Russian lessons every morning at eight-thirty, the only hour he had available. The rest of the day he was engaged in the British Museum, gathering material for his great tome on Tsarist Russia. Not seldom I was totally unprepared for my lesson; generally it seemed to me I had but just gotten into bed when he came prancing into my dark lodgings, and then he was rude, but I soon found a way to divert his righteous anger. I had only to mention Vera Zasulitch or Sofia Figner, his companions in many a revolutionary exploit, and he was off. Nothing could stop his flow of thrilling reminiscences—now in Italian and now in German—but the lunch hour. It was, perhaps, in one of these trances that some months later the unfortunate man walked directly into an express train coming towards him at great speed near Surbiton on the Thames. The engineer blew his whistle in alarm, but to his amazement Stepniak continued to walk towards him and was killed. He was thinking, probably, of his underground heroine, with whom he came so near to encompassing the Tsar's destruction. Last year, more than a generation later, I saw his portrait and that of the woman he adored in the Revolutionary Museum at Moscow where all the heroes and heroines of the unsuccessful battles are celebrated by the victors of today. It was in the place of honor under his real name which I do not recall. To me he will always live as Stepniak.

Jim O'Kelley, the famous *Herald* correspondent, then an Irish Member of Parliament, who had represented our paper in many foreign wars, took me to see Parnell in a little hotel on Victoria Street. O'Kelley talked and Mrs. O'Shea, who was there, talked, and Parnell said never a word.

"But some day he will talk," said O'Kelley, "and then—"

"Ah, yes, then—"

And so for a time, with a clear conscience, I returned to the fascinating Russians. Often in the evening with Prince Kropotkin and Stepniak I journeyed out to the garden house of William Morris in Hammersmith and listened to that wonderful spinner of words as he painted the beauties and the pleasures of a world reborn, and pictured the horizon that would be unfolded to mankind once our eyes were opened. "Yes," was Kropotkin's comment, "how wonderful life would be if things were a little different—and also people."

Sometimes we would go to a tavern in the East End and listen to a man who, though his name was never mentioned, was Lvoff Hartmann, the hero of many a daring exploit of the Nihilists. Often the erstwhile prince and actual philosopher would say, "We must be patient. We must persist! Still we must go down to the villages. We may yet open the eyes of the somnolent peasants!" and then the burly Hartmann would explode. His black hair would turn to bristles and his beady eyes would blaze. "No," he would shout, "we must throw bombs; only with bombs can we destroy the tyrants and smash the shackles of the enslaved!"

The debates in Parliament on the proclamation of the Land League, the Crimes Act, and the other episodes of the campaign in Ireland were of thrilling interest. I would not willingly have missed one of them. It was worth a great deal to watch Gladstone's mastiff head, to hear his roar of indignation as he sprang into action and, as a matter of fact, I shall hear it as long as I live. Some have thrown stones at this great leader and charged him with inconsistency and indeed many other and more serious political misdemeanors, but to me he always was and always will be, I think, the greatest orator, speaking in our tongue, I ever heard.

While in these days the foreign correspondents received no recognition from the authorities of the press gallery in the House of Commons, I had gotten around this obstacle and strange neglect very easily. There was a bluff, blond sergeant of the police guard with whom I struck up an acquaintance, and for a paltry five shillings he never failed to get me a seat in the Strangers' Gallery, where I would sit as Mr. Snowball from Linlithgow, or as Mr. Smithson-Robinson from Peterborough, and in these disguises I sat through the world-shaking debates and passed on to my paper what I thought they would care for—and they cared for a lot of it. Sergeant H. . . . of course suffered from qualms of conscience; dynamiters mostly from across the Atlantic were all about, indeed a bomb had been recently set off in St. Stephen's Hall; but still the two half-crowns loomed large on the policeman's horizon and he found comfort in saying, as he passed on the ticket, "Anyone can see that you have not been away from the old country a long time," while as a matter of fact, judging from my personal appearance, no one would have assigned my ancestry to the Anglo-Saxon strain.

But truth to tell I did not have to look far afield for a revolution. According to some authorities worthy of consideration, serious trouble was developing right under our noses, quite apart from all the dangers that flowed from the perennial Irish problem. The unemployed were assembling in great numbers every afternoon in Trafalgar Square. "Honest John" Burns * (who would have thought that he would end his days as a Right Honorable!) and Cunninghame-Graham were there haranguing the people and telling them of their inalienable right to bread and work, and when one evening the police failed to clear the Square, the High Sheriff, in white wig and gorgeous red regalia, having read the riot act at which everybody hooted, called out the Horse Guards. While they charged and many were wounded, a German Marxist by my side announced, "Ze Queen he's tottering on ze throne." He did not know the English!

You might imagine that with all these live topics I had my hands full, but not at all; we were veritable gluttons for work in those days. I had many other irons in the fire, and I was paying particular attention to that fanatic from Minnesota, Ignatius Donnelly, who had come to London with his Baconian cipher theory and was doing his best to demolish "Immortal Will" and his works, the noblest heritage of the English-speaking and indeed of all civilized races. Of course, as Donnelly was an American, I gave him a fair show, but I was a stern defender of the Bard of Avon and many Shakespearean scholars furnished me with extremely valuable information to buttress our cause; one even traveled up from Oxford to stand by me

---

* I should note here that John Burns was not the only man who rose to higher things out of the fracas in Trafalgar Square. In the police court, where with battered heads Burns and Cunninghame-Graham were haled, a young and at the time undistinguished barrister of the name of Herbert Asquith made an eloquent but unsuccessful plea for their liberation. Five years later the young unknown became Home Secretary and, as almost his first official act, he insisted on throwing open Trafalgar Square to popular demonstrations. In 1908 Asquith became Prime Minister and in 1915, in the dark days of the War, his appearance in behalf of the alleged rioters was one of the very few amusing things we had to talk about.

and I had valued support from Frederick James Furnivall, the great English scholar, and from that outstanding Shakespearean, Horace Howard Furness of Philadelphia.

The present world, rushing ahead upon its amazing course, is so forgetful of the past that it may be well to recall here the main features of the Irish situation at this time. Under a Protestant leader Catholic Ireland was presenting a tremendous problem to the British Empire. Parnell's parliamentary tactics were sweeping away all opposition in the Emerald Isle, and what was more disastrous to the Tories they were winning increasing favor and support in England. To stem this rising tide of nationalism, early in 1887 the *London Times* began the publication of a famous series of articles under the caption of "Parnellism and Crime," with the purpose of demonstrating that the campaign within the law was merely a blind and that Parnell was the real leader of the Fenians and the Invincibles who, under his inspiration, were responsible for the hideous crimes that had recently been committed in Ireland, and for the many dynamite outrages of which the United Kingdom was the scene. The belief was general that this campaign was sustained by the contributions of Irish-Americans.

It was certainly through no choice of mine that I became involved, although merely as an insignificant pawn, in what the Tory papers, following the leadership of the *Times,* insisted upon calling "Parnellism and Crime." I was still immensely interested in the Russian situation and fascinated by both Prince Kropotkin and Stepniak. This was new stuff while the Irish question with its many complications had begun to pall on me and, as I thought, upon our readers. But Jim O'Kelley, now a Member of Parliament after having represented the *Herald* in many parts of the world, was continually dropping in; and there also came, not infrequently, letters from McGarrahan in New York which intimated that many there thought I was neglecting the Irish. This was not the fact, but I recognized that it would not do to have this impression spread, so when O'Kelley offered to take me once again to see the silent leader of the most garrulous people in the world I consented—willingly. He did not have to tell me that a statement from Parnell on the Irish situation would be the biggest kind of news.

Before he returned to the Emerald Isle and entered politics as a home ruler O'Kelley had marched with Maximo Gomez during the first Cuban revolution, and his book *In Mambi Land* has never been superseded as a picture of guerilla warfare. His pen gave able support to the patriots and so did, I fear, his sword and pistol. He was a modest man and while his exploits were many and daring I only heard him indulge in one boast, and that was to the effect that the Spanish Captain-General had placed a higher price upon his head than upon that of the other daredevil correspondents of his day. After participating in several of the Soudan campaigns, in one of which he narrowly escaped the sad fate of the gallant O'Donovan, Jim entered Irish politics and it was only then that he learned, as he often said, how cruel war could be. Parnell was still living under his own name at the dingy little hotel in Victoria Street where I had first seen him, and without any delay we were ushered into his presence. The visit was short and formal. Parnell's manner was as cold and forbidding as was the dark little sitting room in which he received us. "But at least we have broken the ice," asserted O'Kelley, and we followed this first visit up with four or five others spaced at intervals of two or three days. In all of them warm-hearted Jim talked with his wheedling brogue, I talked, and Michael Davitt, who dropped in not seldom, talked. Parnell said never a word but he did seem more human when Mrs. Kitty O'Shea, who was frequently there, prattled on about some amusing incident of the day.

I was disappointed, of course, at the apparent failure of our plan, but reasonable about it. I could even see Mr. Parnell's point of view. Powerful influences were at work, the most unscrupulous in the world seeking for a chink in his armor, to bring him low, even to hamstring him by a disloyal stroke if necessary. It was the wisest course for him to remain on the silent defensive, to wait and see. In the meantime it was interesting and also amusing to view the Irish situation from the side lines to which I now seemed definitely relegated. Night after night I sat in the gallery and listened to the debates on the Land League and the other phases of the struggle. The man who had to face the Irish onslaught was a certain Colonel King-Harman, a magnificent specimen of the English soldier. He was tall and handsome and deep-chested. He seemed built for the ages, but by their badgering and heckling the Irish members brought him down. In ten weeks he looked and was a sick man, and in three months he lay dead, a victim of Irish wrath.

And then Lord Salisbury put in his place as Under Secretary for Ireland his nephew, a callow youth who at the time looked for all the world like the Verdant Green of the English classic. "Tim" Healy, who strangely enough in the whirligig of time became the Governor-General of the Irish Free State, the official link between the Crown and the Nationalists, both of whom in the stormy days he had denounced in unmeasured terms, called him "a stick of yellow toffy" on the floor of the House, and, as I recall, this was the least offensive term that was applied to the new arrival on the parliamentary scene. For the most part the Irish members roared with delight as this dainty morsel was placed before them. A few, it is true, in private expressed pity for the poor lad so unfitted for the role in which by nepotism of the rankest character he had been cast, but of course they would demolish and devour him, because that was their duty.

The first time I saw Arthur Balfour, as he was led to what we all were confident would prove for him a slaughter-pen, I was sorry for him, too. There he sat, apparently timid and diffident on the Treasury bench. He was tall and ungainly, broad at the hips and narrow at the shoulders. He was goggle-eyed, pale and sallow. He was always engaged in tying his hands and fingers into inextricable knots and winding his long shapeless right leg around the left; apparently he was double-jointed and could perform this feat half a dozen times and there was always some two or three feet of leg left over to swing nervously in the air. But this time Lord Salisbury had not placed his money and his hopes upon the "wrong horse." The more the Irish roared the more softly and courteously the youngster answered them. It was soon apparent that the convolutions of his brain were as elastic as his legs, and at the end of the month the Honorable "Tim" was reported down with nervous prostration. The more the Irish roared the more imperturbable became the Right Honorable Arthur J. Balfour.

It seemed to me on the whole that my relations with "Parnellism and Crime" were quite sufficiently complicated when a cable came which put me in touch with the man who was directly responsible for the persecution of the Irish leader that only a few months later resulted in the most famous State trial of the century. The cable was from the Commodore and dated Port Said. He instructed me to get in touch with Dr. MacDonald, the editor of the *Times*, and to suggest to him an exchange of proofs before publication; his agent in New York to have the run of the *Herald* office and I to be given similar facilities in London. Later this practice of news exchange became quite common between the great papers, but so far as I know this was the first time it was attempted. I was not a diviner but the unmentioned purpose of my chief was by no means obscure. "It jumped to the eyes," as the French have it. He wanted to have the first show at the "Parnellism and Crime" articles which were creating such a furore, the better to combat and ridicule them, of course, to the delectation of the Irish servant girls in America who poured such a constant stream of wealth into the *Herald's* coffers.

I immediately wrote Dr. MacDonald, outlining the proposition and asking for an appointment to discuss the details, and two days later a note came acceding to my request. I started for the City at ten in the morning, and after strange experiences in the anterooms and the corridors of the *Times* building I finally reached the editorial sanctum about one o'clock. The office was an embattled fortress and I as an American was undoubtedly "suspect." Within a few days bombs had been placed in the immediate vicinity of the printing establishment and I had, in the free and easy style of New York journalism, neglected to bring with me the note which doubtless would have made my entrance smoother. First and last I was examined and even adroitly searched by about twenty "bobbies," and when I reached MacDonald I was at least two hours late for my appointment.

I explained as politely as I could that the delay was no fault of mine, and as MacDonald expressed his regret at the inconvenience I had suffered I ventured the remark, "I shall not give the matter a second thought—but I don't see how you maintain contact with the public." This drew the characteristic reply, "Why bless my soul! Why should we want to keep in touch with the public?"

MacDonald, after these preliminaries were out of the way, was very civil and rather more friendly to the exchange idea than I had anticipated. He explained that owing to the friendship between Mr. Walter and Mr. Childs of the *Ledger*, the *Times* had for many years been committed to Philadelphia as its American base. "But I recognize that news is traveling faster than it did formerly and the New York arrangement would prove perhaps mutually advantageous." Then he made an inquiry which it seemed to me displayed considerable ignorance of American geography. "Would it not be possible," he suggested, "for our Philadelphia man to hop over to New York every evening and have a look at your proofs?" I told the Doctor that this was feasible but hardly practical, and then after a few generalities he explained that he would take the matter up as soon as the new foreign editor of the paper arrived from India (Sir Donald Mackenzie Wallace whom I was to meet later in the Balkans) and then give Mr. Bennett a definite answer. I did not hear from him during the few weeks that elapsed before I was transferred to the Continent and so I do not know what came of the proposition which afforded me this curious experience. It was not long, however, before the case against the Irish leader collapsed, the High Court rendered its verdict and, rather than face the libel suit that was brought, the *Times* paid Parnell twenty-five thousand dollars and withdrew all the substantial charges that were advanced in the "Parnellism and Crime" articles.

It was inevitable, of course, that MacDonald, who had led the paper into this adventure that cost a million and as a high authority asserted "reduced its prestige to the lowest ebb of its history," * should be retired. He was succeeded by Moberly Bell, a Levantine Englishman, long a correspondent of English papers in Cairo where he had sat at the feet of Lord Cromer and become an ardent apostle of Imperialism. He, more than any other journalist, insisted upon the Boer War which cost the nation hundreds of millions. But in this instance the *Times* came off scot free. It was the taxpayers who had to meet the expense of this folly.

In later years I have often thought of MacDonald and the penalty he had to pay for his poor judgment. Curiously enough, in the single interview I had with him he made the same impression upon

* *Encyclopædia Britannica.*

me that Parnell did. There was the same anxiety in both their faces. To neither of them was the future clear. They both feared the outcome of events they had initiated which had now passed out of their control. I have often seen MacDonald as I saw him first and last that day in the *Times* office. Restless and ill at ease, there he sat in his shabby black coat speckled over with dandruff, surrounded by police, but he was, I think, assailed by thoughts that no cordon of guards could shield him from. It seemed to me that he had already begun to fear that the terrible indictment he had broadcast to the world against the idolized leader of a nation had been based on lies. Parnell, too, for all the frigid composure he displayed in public, was always ill at ease and nervous when I saw him in private and face to face. The tension under which they lived, the ordeal which they had to face, was playing havoc with the lives of the great adversaries, Parnell and MacDonald.

One foggy morning Davitt and O'Kelley reappeared. They were beaming. They reported that all hesitation had been removed, all doubts dispelled. Parnell had agreed to take the world into his confidence. He was now ready to tell the story of his persecution and the *Herald* was to be the medium for this world-shaking communication. I had not moved a finger and yet this opportunity had dropped into my lap. My good fortune was all the more welcome because I recognized that it was wholly undeserved. I had only one anxiety. I feared that in recognition of this achievement the Commodore would make me news editor, and of course I preferred to be footloose and roam the world.

But truth to tell, when I re-entered the damp and draughty little sitting room and faced the uncrowned king of Ireland, confidence began to ooze out from my finger tips. For perhaps an hour Parnell listened with evidently flagging interest to what his ardent followers, who wished to give him a winning lead, had to say, and then, abruptly, he excused himself. He had an important engagement which could not be postponed. Frankly I was discouraged—not so Davitt and O'Kelley. They assured me that in view of the circumstances and the character of their leader we were making notable progress.

The next day but one we had a longer talk and to my delight

some headway was made. Davitt wanted a paragraph inserted warning the Irish-Americans against the Extremists. Suddenly Parnell
flushed and said, "I'll go farther than that, I want to say and I want
you to emphasize it—that the Invincibles and the Dynamiters, while
doubtless meaning well, have done more harm to the Irish cause
than all the Tory squires and all the Birmingham manufacturers
that ever lived. And that General Mellon!" * Here Parnell threw
up his arms in disgust, and then he added, speaking slowly, "He is
a madman, a dangerous one I fear."

Looking at the situation in retrospect it may seem strange that
while in the talks that were now in progress I was doing my best to
help Parnell parry the blows of the *Times,* I did not suspect for a
moment that his real destroyer was to be the blithe and charming
lady who so often sat by his side. But no one at all in touch with the
social-political conditions that prevailed in London at the time will
be surprised. Many distinguished men who represented the government on the Treasury bench, or who led Her Majesty's Opposition
in Parliament, were notoriously involved in marital triangles or
even quadrangles. These were broadly hinted at by Nelly Farren
and Marie Lloyd in the music halls—even the Italian soubrette at
the Alhambra would sing, smiling knowingly the while, *"cosi fan
tutti."* But as long as these matters were "corked up" and kept out
of court, as long as the injured party was complaisant or sophisticated, the public did not care a hoot.

In these days my Lord H. . . . could practically live at the
little "God-given" hotel in Ryder Street, St. James's, with the
stately duchess of Germanic origin, and the frequent sojourns of the
Earl of D. . . . with Lady M. . . . at the Star and Garter, while
not unnoticed, were viewed with complete indifference; so why
should I fash myself as to the relations between Mrs. O'Shea and
the grandson of Commodore Stewart, U.S. Navy, who was now the
hope of Ireland? Of course I was not unaware of the tremendous
influence that this charming woman exerted over the cold dour man
who was the idol of Ireland, perhaps because he had not a single
Irish trait. Of course I noticed that Parnell's harsh voice softened

* An Irish-American who from France, it was alleged, directed the dynamite
campaign in England.

when he greeted this frequent visitor and I could not fail to see how his cold green eyes glowed when they rested on her fair face. She was gracious to me and I was grateful when, as was often the case, she ranged herself in support of O'Kelley and Davitt when my article began to take shape and the advisability of publishing it came under discussion. She always listened intently as I read paragraphs of the proposed statement and when once she interrupted with "O! I say Charles, that *is* well put," I thought Mrs. O'Shea was a very intelligent woman. But Parnell only said "Go on."

We must have worked over the article for two months: not every day however; there were frequent intervals during which Parnell made hasty visits to Ireland or was otherwise engaged. And then when the picture that I wished to present across the Atlantic took definite shape there came from Parnell, in his cold, suspicious voice, definite objections, and it often had to be refashioned, here toned down and there given a deeper splash of belligerent color.

But we made headway and even the methods of transmission had been discussed. Parnell came out with emphasis against using the cable and with equal insistence against leaving the title of the article to the editorial desk—as was customary. He insisted that in the cable office there might be a leak and further by inadvertence or design an important sentence might be garbled. Just as it left our hands, without the change of a comma, the article must be printed. I agreed, of course, and in anticipation I enjoyed the tremendous effect that the arrival of this epoch-making document would have as it came into the office on the wings of ordinary postage!

I sat up one night and wrote out the article slowly in my own hand; it must have run to eight thousand words. We either had no typewriters in those days, or, as now, I did not know how to use one. I also made a copy, laboriously, in my best handwriting. And on the following day as agreed we read it over—aloud. Only O'Kelley and Parnell were present this time. O'Kelley, bless him! was loud in his approval and most generous in his praise. This was mail day, Friday from Liverpool I think, and I was anxious to get it off.

"It seems correct. You have made the changes I suggested," said Parnell, and then, "Perhaps it will do no harm." "It will do a lot of good," said O'Kelley, and for emphasis he thumped on the table. "It will hearten our people in America from coast to coast—and here all but the most shameless of your traducers will be silenced."

Parnell nodded and then said slowly, "You are probably right—but I want to sleep on it." My hopes fell! another mail day missed and in all probability another examination of my work with pitiless microscope! O'Kelley voiced my dismay and for a moment Parnell seemed to relent. Then he hardened and with more than his usual animation said, "I have an idea. I want to sleep on it and then in the morning I can send the article to the General Postoffice by a special messenger and by paying the late mail fee it will catch the steamer at Queenstown and reach New York—just as if it had been posted today."

"Splendid!" said O'Kelley, and I breathed more freely. Parnell put the article back in the addressed envelope in which I had hoped to carry it myself to the post office, and then, "By the way," he said, "let me have the copy. You see the article may be cabled back and—I shall want to keep tab on those cables." That sounded reasonable. It *was* reasonable and I gave him the duplicate. "Cabled!" said O'Kelley. "It will be cabled to the ends of the earth." And with that we bowed ourselves out.

"You have done a fine job for the *Herald*," said the generous Irishman as we walked out into Victoria Street. "You have done a fine job for your old paper and for the cause," I countered, and O'Kelley was pleased.

Ten days of restless scrutiny of the shipping news followed. It was the old *Baltic* that as I thought carried the precious document. She arrived in New York and hourly I expected a whoop of joy and congratulation, but nothing came but the most routine messages. Finally I wired, using our code word for the Irish leader, "What have you done with the interview?" Almost immediately the word came back, "Not received."

When I recovered and could face the situation with something like equanimity I had difficulty in getting in touch with O'Kelley. He, unlike his leader, certainly had no permanent place of abode. When at last I cornered him he was not a little embarrassed. "He slept on it and in the morning decided 'better not.' We should not fire our broadside until they have used more of their ammunition. But the chief is grateful. You will hear from him."

I did not until another week had passed, and then by messenger a great blackthorn walking stick was left at my lodging. To it was attached a blank card on which was scribbled, "Thanks, best wishes," and the initials C.S.P.

While the High Court convened by Act of Parliament in 1888 to investigate the activities of the Irish leaders did not issue its report until early in 1890, the case against Parnell collapsed when the *Times* withdrew the forged letter and agreed to the payment of heavy damages. Parnell consented to this expeditious settlement because matters of more vital importance were calling for his whole attention. The conferences with Gladstone at Hawarden Castle were in progress, the Home Rule bill that the Liberal leader had agreed to present to Parliament was taking shape, indeed all the difficulties had been ironed out at these momentous meetings, victory was in sight, soon Ireland would enter into the comity of nations, the long battle was won and then came the bolt out of the blue; Captain O'Shea who, apparently, had been a complaisant husband for eight years, decided that after all he was a cave man!

When O'Shea brought suit for divorce from the charming Kitty, Parnell did not appreciate the gravity of the situation. Publicly he said all the pother was simply "a tempest in a tea pot" and that it would as quickly subside. The sequel, even before the Gladstone-Morley correspondence was published, demonstrated that he was mistaken and that, as the success of Home Rule for Ireland depended upon the Non-Conformist vote in England, the uncrowned king of Ireland would have to abdicate or he would be deposed. The United Kingdom and Ireland rang with the wrongs of O'Shea, and by a majority vote the Irish Members of Parliament demoted their leader—one might with but a little exaggeration say the creator of their party. Of the twenty-six members who, when the split came, remained faithful to Parnell, there was not one who did not believe that the *Times* was responsible for the disaster. They were confident that after having failed even with the expenditure of a million dollars and with all the perjured evidence that it produced, to ruin Parnell politically, the *Times* by granting O'Shea a small annuity accomplished its purpose. Of course this charge was difficult to prove and so far as I know no attempt was made to do so.

A year later, in the summer of 1891, I saw the fortunate-unfortunate pair (as you will have it!) for the last time. A weakening illness that I brought back with me from my Morocco journey had laid me low, and for a few days I sat in the sun on the Parade at Brighton and watched the world go by. And suddenly out of the crowd of trippers appeared the once gay and charming Kitty. Evidently broken in health she sat in her wheel chair as it was pushed along the waterfront. Her tired eyes rested with fixed attention upon the restless waves. By her side, crippled with rheumatism, Parnell hobbled along looking, as it seemed to me, with staring eyes into the blackness that was ahead. When three months later death came to him I am confident Parnell welcomed the scythe-bearer.

3. THE PRINCE AND THE PUGILIST

As I MOVED entranced in this paradise of perplexing problems, or disported myself, an enthusiastic hero-worshiper of twenty-two, in this ever-renewed and ever-changing gallery of important or fascinating people, there came one morning a cable from the news editor.

"John L. Sullivan, champion of the world, sails for England in a few days. He will fight anyone who presents himself. You should meet him at Liverpool and stay right with him. He is, as you know, the idol of Americans, church-goers as well as all others. Keep right with him to the ringside or wherever he goes. As to the Irish debates and other political developments, for the present we shall have to depend upon the A.P."

Depend upon the Associated Press! Well, in those days, their service was less than nothing. I was not a prig—far from it. I had lived with, and upon, the activities and antics of prize-fighters and anarchists for as much as six months in New York. But things were different now and my eyes had been opened. It was indeed in my judgment lamentable that in the midst of a world crisis, in fact in the midst of several world crises, I was to be withdrawn from the coign of vantage which I had by hard work achieved, to wander around in prize-fighting circles, apparently handcuffed to John L. Sullivan!

Of course I immediately wrote a letter of reproof to the news editor. Strangely enough he took the letter in good part, and it secured several modifications of his first drastic instructions. Nevertheless, I talked a great deal about handing in my resignation, and I even thought a little about doing it.

For a budding, or at least an aspirant, de Blowitz, I did not do so badly in my new and most unwelcome role. At all events, pleasant words came from New York, and in appreciation of my condescension the news editor let me send a man to represent the paper at the Jem Smith-Kilrain fight. "After all, Kilrain is not a national hero, and a world figure, like Sullivan," admitted the editor, "but stick to John."

And soon I was ready to admit that this close companionship with the world champion was not without amusing moments. "Gentleman John" * was a born showman, and when on his dignity no belted earl could touch him. The Liverpool docks were black with people when his ship hove in sight, and "Tay Pay" O'Connor, the Irish Member from the Irish district of Liverpool, greeted him with a round of speeches that warmed the cockles of every Irish heart. John had a sense of humor, dangerous gift; and sometimes he could not hold it in check. This was especially the case when he observed the primitive mode of living to which our English cousins were subjected, and he made at least one bad break. A day or two after his arrival in London we were all bidden to a breakfast by some City Guild or organization, and for the convenience of the city folk it was held in the Cannon Street Hotel. This famous hostelry was noted throughout the United Kingdom for a remarkable innovation known as the "rising room." Of course, in several of the more modern West End hotels, notably at the Metropole and the Victoria, there were in use quite efficient modern elevators, but the city folk had never seen them and their idea of the supreme chic and the last word in modernity was the "rising room." John behaved

* Several gentlemen more versed in Boxiana than I can claim to be, who have been good enough to look over these pages to correct probable errors, think I am mistaken in referring to Sullivan as "Gentleman John," but my memory on this point is very distinct, and I must maintain my position. It seems to me that their attitude only demonstrates how short-lived are the remembrance and fame of the greatest of men. Mr. Sullivan took the title of world champion as a matter of course, but upon the courtesy title of "Gentleman John" he set great store. My conclusion is that when James Corbett finally knocked out Sullivan some years later, in 1892, he took the championship, the diamond belt, and the great purse which were his by right of successful battle, but that he usurped the courtesy title and became "Gentleman Jim." By all accounts he deserved it, but I maintain it was John Sullivan who won it first, and how he wore it will appear in this veracious chronicle of some of the incidents of his memorable life.

rather badly, certainly he cast all reserve to the winds, when the "room," which functioned by water power, began to rise at a speed approaching five feet a minute. Its chains clanked horribly, and when the mechanism began to sputter and to cough, John took off his high hat and passed it around among the fifteen or twenty passengers who, with anything but carefree countenances, were squashed together in the "rising room." "Let's buy 'em a little more water," he roared, and started the collection with a half-crown. Well, we had some difficulty in explaining that this was only one of John's little jokes. Our hosts did not see it, but of course the English are proverbially obtuse in joking matters.

As I am reporting the mistakes of others quite fully, I must not in all fairness conceal the bad break I myself made a few days later. We were all assembled in the office of *The Sporting Life*, where the articles for the fight between Smith and Kilrain were to be signed. John went, of course, to lend dignity to the affair, and such was the outpouring of people to see the champions, though really only John counted, that all traffic had to be suspended in Fleet Street for several hours. Jem Smith was a thick-set powerful Cockney, with sandy hair and an amiable smile. Quite gracefully he submitted to being interviewed by an American reporter looking like a theological student, who was taking down on a pad, very seriously, every word that fell from the lips of the great men.

"Are you married, Mr. Smith?" he inquired.

"Yes, I've been spliced a long time. I have five children, maybe more soon. My old woman is due to pup this week." Now I cabled this statement exactly as it was made. Everybody admitted that the words were spoken, even those who later questioned the good taste of cabling them at all. When the resulting controversy arose, and indeed ever since, I have always maintained that when you mix with people of unfamiliar classes, for the benefit of those who have not the opportunities of the reporter, you should write them down as they do speak and not in Addisonian periods, or in long loping sentences suggestive of Macaulay. Jem Smith, bless his good-natured heart, did not object to my truthful relation, but some of the other English "pugs," who were doubtless swayed by an incorrect version of what I really wrote, objected most strenuously and the result was a split in our camp and a personal handicap to me, the cause of no little worry and anxiety in the days of my servitude to the prize ring and the pugilists.

This unfortunate misunderstanding came to a crisis at a great sparring match in St. James's Hall, at which John was of course the principal attraction though he did not deign to spar. Charley Mitchell came up to me and expressed his frank opinion of my honored editor and of myself in unmeasured and most unseemly terms, and I condescended to reply in kind. Then Mitchell struck me and, possibly emboldened by the fact that he was at least half seas over and by no means up to his normal fighting form, I struck back. Brisbane loyally intervened as "the mugs and the pugs" who were with Mitchell surrounded me. Soon a small-sized riot was in progress. Police and pugs all pitched in with the strange purpose of pitching us out. Brisbane, gallant fellow, standing right by me, and hitting out right and left, was a tower of strength; and then for a moment, really only for a split second, I thought I had still another friend in the hostile crowd and this one I had hitherto clearly misjudged. Above the tumult and the uproar I heard Pony Moore, father-in-law and principal backer of Mitchell, shouting, "Don't 'it 'im, Charley! Don't 'it 'im!" And then a word of explanation— "You might sprain yer thumb agin."

The upshot of the matter was that Brisbane and I were thrown out of the Hall, none too gently. As the row became furious, we had rather counted on the powerful assistance of Major ——, the manager of Buffalo Bill, who had just arrived in London. He was a strapping big fellow, with a stentorian voice, trained in the open spaces, and with a great bowie-knife scar across his forehead. But during the uproar not a peep came from him. Unfortunately, some of the American papers took up the incident and belabored Mitchell for his attack on "half-starved American reporters." This was particularly misleading, as the Lucullan banquets that Brisbane gave in his Park Lane apartment were the talk of London. However, I was able to snub St. James's Hall, where I had been treated so scurvily, several years later. On my return from what some called an adventurous journey through Morocco, I was awarded the medal of a strange association known as the Balloon Society (I must confess it was only the silver medal) and on being asked to describe my experiences from the rostrum in the famous St. James's Hall, I declined.

Perhaps with the passing of the weeks my cables began to pall upon our readers, or at least upon my editor. Certainly I could not keep up with Brisbane in his ever-fresh and almost inspired accounts of Sullivan's bulging muscles, of how he knocked out poor Toff Wall at the Pelican Club, with one hand behind his back, of how John L. looked in the evening when he broke his training and sat in the royal box at the Criterion with a tilted "seegar" in his mouth, of how all the world was on its toes now that he was matched to fight Charley Mitchell for the championship of the world and the dazzling diamond belt, or how he looked in his literary mood when he pored over his scrap-book of world press clippings about himself, which was now well on in the forty-second volume. Desiring perhaps to expose me no longer to a competition from which I must increasingly suffer, the paper sent me off to Stockholm, and while I was convinced in advance that my secret mission there would prove a wild goose chase I rejoiced at the change of air and the very different surroundings.

On my way back from Scandinavia, I of course stopped off for a few hours in Paris. That was the *bonne bouche* of the whole trip, and I felt that I deserved it. Here, however, a cable from New York caught up with me, expressing misgivings as to the immediate developments of the prize-fighting situation in England, and urging me to get into close quarters with John again as soon as possible.

"Brisbane and *The Sun* are making a great hit with a daily special column devoted to the champion. Our readers are hungry for every bit of news about the champion. Go to it."

I recognized that something had to be done and I felt rather keenly that it could not be accomplished by my single unaided efforts, and on the moment I had a happy thought; how happy it was I only appreciated twenty-four hours later. I sent the editor of *Sporting Life* a wire, asking him to dine with me at Anderton's Hotel in Fleet Street the following evening, and I crossed the Channel in a wretched night boat, but this hardship gave me a few more enjoyable hours in Paris. I had been drawn to this editor by several ties.

He was a man of magnificent thews and sinews, a son of Yorkshire, and while he looked like a bruiser himself he despised pugs and loved horses, especially thoroughbreds, just as I did. He had under him a number of reporters who were very much in the know, and as he was distinctly a man of importance in the sporting world, members of the Pelican Club were only too glad to keep him informed of anything that transpired, and of not a little that did not come off.

On the morning that I sent my invitation, the London papers were filled with stilted but nonetheless amusing accounts of a fracas that had taken place the night before at a stated meeting of the Fabian Society, in Anderton's Hotel, and it was probably on this account that I selected this place for the dinner and the pow-wow on which I set such store. It was in this fight that Bernard Shaw and Philip Snowden received their first baptism of the publicity in which they were to bask to the end of their days.

The sturdy editor and I had a substantial dinner and a long and at first a perfectly friendly discussion about the get of Godolphin's Arabian. How I regretted all this palaver afterwards when time became the very essence of the situation! As had been too often our practice, the sporting editor and I got into a hot discussion as to the reliability of the English stud-book, and finally into something like a quarrel over a subject which only race-horse men can understand. It was, as I remember the snarl, as to whether Sir Archey, the great Virginia thoroughbred, the Adam of all American race horses, was descended from Darley's Arabian or from Godolphin's Barb. Of course we got nowhere, and then, fortunately, how fortunately for me, the sporting editor changed the subject, and took my breath away by saying, "I noticed that you were not at the Guards' lunch today. I suppose you passed it up. It would have bored you as it did me. Brisbane was on hand, of course."

"I never heard of it," I admitted simply. "I suppose they did not know I was back from Stockholm."

"Quite so," assented the great editor, and then he related, with very little urging on my part, the details, the very picturesque and startling details, of the historic meeting. "Ostensibly," he continued, "it had been arranged to pit Jem Smith against a green one, I can't remember his name, for four rounds with hard gloves, but of course the real purpose was to bring about a meeting between John L. and Albert Edward. Excuse me, I mean no disloyalty, but when I find him in such company I do not like to mention that Albert Edward is also the Prince of Wales."

What a phonographic memory that sporting editor had! "All the bloods were there," he ran on. "There was Randolph Churchill and Sir William Gordon Cummings (that was before his fall). Every man of note in London seemed to be in the gym at the Guards' Barracks at Knightsbridge. From the walls there looked down upon us the portraits of the great guardsmen who had gone before, and everybody was talking about prize fights, from the Homeric days of Epeus down to Heenan and Tom Sayers.

"The Prince stood before an open wood fire, and to him there Sir Francis Knollys escorted John. I rubbed my eyes, I hardly knew him. Your John was all dressed in black, and looked like a Sunday-school teacher, or a Non-Conformist preacher. 'That's Gentleman John,' they chorused as the great man was escorted through the admiring throng. They shook hands heartily, and the Prince was most gracious. I had edged up right by his elbow and I heard H.R.H. say, 'I feel as if I had known you for years, Mr. Sullivan.'

" 'I have often heard of you, too,' answered John, 'and am mighty pleased to meet you. Do you ever put up the dukes now?'

" 'No, I never spar now, not with gloves or even with bare knuckles, for that matter,' answered the Prince, and everyone laughed. Well they might. And then the Prince went on.

" 'My boy down at York with the Lancers (this was the Duke of Clarence who died before his father) punches the bag every morning and my George who is a middy on the *Dreadnought* is a regular slugger. You see, Sullivan, I like to bring my boys up in the way I should have gone.'

"Everybody laughed again, and of course it was funny," added the editor. "But rather disgusting, don't you think? I like 'pugs' and princes, and above all, guardsmen, but when they are all mixed up together it's a bit thick," and the editor ran his hand through his hair in perplexity.

"Have you written your story?" I inquired anxiously.

"Lord, no, I shan't publish a word about it. Not such a fool as that.

"When the Prince withdrew, we all gathered around John, and I must say he had not been taken off his feet. I suppose nothing could do that but a solar plexus blow from a pile-driver. But he was enthusiastic, and talked at a great rate about our future King, whom we all admired but so few of us had met. 'He is a nice sociable fellow, with splendid manners,' said John, 'and when you think of all he has had to fight against in the way of family and education, I'll say he's a splendid all-around sport. You would like to meet him any time and you would introduce him to your family.' "

As I was sitting down when the sporting editor reeled off all these marvelous details of the amazing meeting of two worlds I cannot claim that I took the blow to my prestige, which he inflicted, standing up, but at least I did not lie down and that was something in view of the fact that the biggest news event of the decade had taken place hours ago, and I was not there! Telegraphic photography had not been invented at this time, but without its aid at this tragic moment I could see the dour wry face with which at this very moment my news editor was looking across the Atlantic toward the silent Bonsal who had been left and on what a story! And worse than that I visualized the uproar in Printing House Square with *The Sun* flooding the streets with Brisbane's story of the meeting between the Prince and the Pugilist. Of course he who was wholly responsible for the disaster was the man who had sent me to Stockholm on a wild goose chase, but while innocent to the tenth degree I knew I would be compromised in the eyes of the world and of the office. No, I could not hope to escape unscathed but I would not be shot to pieces. I would go down, if down I must go, with my colors flying.

In a jiffy I had the great stolid editor with the hitherto unsuspected gift of a phonographic memory as our representative at the royal meeting in the barracks of the Guards, and when I clinched the bargain by passing a "fiver" across the table he expressed his willingness to represent me on the same terms at any sporting functions which I did not care to attend.

Trembling with excitement and anxiety, I now felt free to leave my providential guest at the table doing justice to the liqueurs for which Anderton's was famous, and hastened off to the cable office in the Royal Exchange.

First I sent a concise bulletin and outlined the scheme of the many thousand words that would follow and then—flesh and blood could stand the uncertainty no longer—I inquired in a special message at urgent rates, "Have the evening papers touched it?" In a very short time, however long it seemed to me, the answer came, "Evening papers not a line." I am not sure but that here I broke out into a song. While the yarn was still in transmission there came another cabled message from the office and it betrayed an unusual thoughtfulness. After all, that news editor was not such a bad fellow. "Do not cramp yourself to five thousand," he cabled. "Send all you can, and push it. If there is slightest danger of missing first edition send conclusion commercial rates." Well, he liked it all right but of course he would not say so, only he had betrayed himself and his approbation as news editors so rarely do.

As I recall, while the long-suffering cable officials were at little or no pains to conceal their opinion of the expensive slush with which we burdened their wires, this was the only occasion on which they registered anything like a protest. When about two thousand words of my epoch-making narrative had gone, the manager staggered down the little winding stairs, came over to my desk and looked me over anxiously. His face revealed the fear that I had suddenly gone mad, and evidently the propriety of advising the New York office of my sad condition had occurred to him.

"Are you quite sure the paper will pay for all these words?" "Quite," I answered and drove on with my pen. "How much more do you propose sending?" he inquired. "About three thousand words," I answered shortly. "Then I'll have to send for an extra transmitter," he complained. "I hope you will be quick about it," was my answer.

As he staggered up the stairs the good soul gave me out of the kindness of his heart one more chance for a return to sanity. "That makes—about the Prince and Sullivan—five thousand words altogether and there's Lord Derby's great speech on the agricultural depression. How much of that?" "I am not touching it," I answered and, apparently bewildered and near collapse, the excellent fellow completed his climb of the spiral stairway and disappeared into his executive cubby-hole.

Returning to the West End about two in the morning I rather expected to run across Brisbane at the cabman's shelter just where the old Temple Bar used to stand. At these hours, which we were so often compelled to keep because of late cables, we frequently met and cautiously discussed the positions we had taken on world developments, while enjoying the very excellent ham and eggs and coffee which the shelter supplied at a moderate price, especially moderate in view of the fact that in these days, before the era of night clubs, they were the only eating places open at such unseasonable hours.

I did not run across Brisbane that night nor indeed for many days, and by that time the British Empire from end to end was resounding with my account of the meeting between the Prince and the Pugilist, or rather, as a matter of fact, with the comment and the echoes which the story had provoked. The explanation of what had occurred is a wholly unmoral story and I only feel justified in telling it because I am sure my readers will regard it as merely a freak exception that proves the general soundness of our traditional standards of conduct. In our city rooms we were always told that the "early bird catches the worm," and in France Calmette of the *Figaro*, who was everywhere at once, used to insist *"Les absents ont toujours tort."* With us, of course, this great truth had been translated to read "It's Johnny on the spot who gets the story."

Now in this instance, as often before, Brisbane was the early bird and he was Johnny on the spot, while I was lost in the dim distance, but as the historic scene drew to a close Sir Francis Knollys had stepped up to him, as he was parting with John, and said:

"This is a hands-across-the-seas meeting, and we are here, not as Englishmen and Americans, but as devotees of the noble science of self-defense. But the presence here of H.R.H. today would not be pleasing to a fanatical, though a very small minority of his subjects, and so he has expressed the hope that nothing be said about it in the papers."

"Of course not," answered John. "We met as gentlemen and there will not come a peep from me, or from Brisbane either." And Brisbane, noble fellow, assented, though he afterward admitted that a cold chill came over his heart. He had fondly hoped this would be his greatest story, and in all probability it would have been but for the pledge, also binding him, that John, the big fellow, had given without thought of the irreparable damage he was inflicting on the chronicles of our day and generation.

In those happy days there was little or no come-back or control to the cables we sent to the bright new world across the Atlantic. The only duly accredited correspondent of the London press over there resided in Philadelphia, and he confined his activities to mailed prophecies in regard to the cotton crop and full accounts of Mr. G. W. Childs' croquet parties. Indeed, when I recall the impunity which we enjoyed, I am surprised at the moderation we generally displayed. And so it was quite natural, and in any event it was the fact, that two long weeks had elapsed before the people of England had the slightest inkling of the great historic event that had taken place in London right under their noses, and the way the news did come demonstrated that my guardian angel was still keeping watch over my fortunes.

One afternoon I picked up *The Pall Mall Gazette* and there on the first page, under the heading "The Prince and the Pugilist," was my yarn reproduced word for word, but credited to *The Chicago Tribune!* It was some time before I learned the mechanism of what seemed at first a direct interposition of Providence. This great Chicago newspaper at the time did not have an office in London, while we were established in a most conspicuous one on Cockspur Street, with great glass windows and a blatant sign facing directly on Trafalgar Square, where so many unemployed and mischief-makers gathered every morning and every night. It was another two weeks before my news editor in New York learned of this angelic interposition on my behalf and most certainly he did not learn it through me. I was more than willing that, in the circumstances, our Chicago contemporary should have both the credit and the discredit—for there was plenty of that showered on the article, too; but not so the news editor, though I was at great pains to explain to him in cabled language, necessarily veiled, how inadvisable it was for us, and particularly for me, to advance our undoubted claim to authorship. When he learned through the exchange editor that all the papers in the United Kingdom and many throughout the British Empire had also credited the article to *The Tribune*, he became absolutely frantic. He immediately cabled that this was grand larceny on an international scale, and instructed me to get in touch with W. T. Stead, the great editor of *The Pall Mall*, to deliver a firm remonstrance and demand a restatement of the facts.

Here was indeed a dilemma. I was more than satisfied with the present situation. In those days we did not sign cables, and so my personal interest did not come into play. All the newspapermen—and all others were, of course, negligible—knew that I had written the story from the copious data furnished me by the sporting editor. They also knew, as I did, that while at the time we were without an organized syndicate, the story had been sold to some sixty papers in the United States, including *The Chicago Tribune*, for considerable sums. Unfortunately for the paper, but most fortunately for me, in this hasty wire transaction, nothing had been said as to the credit due the paper or its London representative. It was doubtless taken for granted that the right thing would be done. It would, of course, have been advantageous to me, on the other side of the Atlantic, if it had been done, but I could not ignore the fact that I was personally in London, and that *The Morning Post* and *The Westminster Gazette* and many other loyal sheets were saying unpleasant things about the article, and the words "fantastic, dastardly," and even "scurrilous" were not omitted.

I cabled New York with the emphatic request to let the matter slide. My argument was that quite a bunch of money had been gathered in by the sale of the article, and that as its publication was by no means generally approved in England, it would be wise "to take the cash and let the credit go," even if it went to *The Chicago Tribune*. Back, however, came stern orders to see Mr. Stead and, as soon as possible, to deliver the cabled remonstrance. The meeting was quickly arranged by Henry Norman, I think, then of *The Pall Mall* staff, in whose footsteps in the Far East I was soon to follow, and he also advised Stead that I personally was not strongly in favor of my paper's position.

I had seen Mr. Stead several times before, both in America and in London, but never in such a merry mood as the one in which I found him now. Always he had been frightfully serious, fighting for the Lord and some good, grave cause. But now his eyes twinkled, and it was only with difficulty that he kept the straight face becoming an Olympian editor.

"You have done the decent and self-respecting people of Britain a great, a very great favor, in describing so faithfully—what has occurred," he began. "You are deserving of great praise, and I would be the last to deny it to you, but we editors, as you know, must be careful, we must walk circumspectly, and have things down in black and white. Of course, I do not doubt for a moment but what you wrote the excellent article which our exchange editor picked up and lifted from the front page of *The Chicago Tribune*, where it was published under the caption 'By cable to *The Tribune* from London.' Now if Mr. Bennett—no, certainly not, the news editor— will write me that you are the author and that permission was given *The Tribune* merely to republish it, why I will make amends in the handsomest way I can—and gladly."

This message went forward promptly to New York with my personal expression of opinion attached, that, in case Stead's offer was accepted, I had better be transferred to another post, away from London, as far away, indeed, as possible. I never heard anything further on the subject. Possibly my personal appeal moved the editor, probably he was convinced that Mr. Bennett would not abandon his hard and fast rule of refusing personal credit to any of his men or even of allowing their names to be printed in the paper. But most probably the good news editor was now being harassed by some other matter of greater moment, and let my cable slide into the wastepaper basket. While my incognito was never unveiled in the public prints, I was, I think, too closely involved in the prairie fire of controversy which now swept through the British press and the Non-Conformist churches, to allow me to pose even for a moment as an unprejudiced observer. As to what happened, at least an inkling is given in an editorial of *The New*

York Tribune (January 8, 1888), under the caption "Sullivan and the Prince." It reads:

"The pulpits of His Royal Highness's own realm have taken the matter up and Non-Conformist preachers hold up the heir to the Empire on which the sun never sets to public contumely for associating with prize-fighters. His royal mother is said to have administered a severe chastisement to her hopeful offspring by penny post. Times have changed indeed when a royal personage cannot seek any low society he chooses without being ridiculed by the papers and pummeled from the pulpits.

"It is, however, specifically denied that Sullivan promised to see that the Prince was 'treated right' if he came to Boston. We trust Sullivan's simple nature will not be wounded by the present attitude of the Prince. He has been celebrated as a Greek in marble. A Boston poet has declared he had perfected 'the vague inchoate thing' known as the round blow and 'completed its expression in art.' "

There now followed many long weeks of anxious watchful waiting, of midday and midnight drives from London down to the Windsor Forest to ascertain if, as rumored in Chicago, Sullivan had strained a tendon in his left leg or dislocated his right thumb, and later to investigate the report that John had gone off on a "bat" and that his trainer had thrown up the sponge! At last I squelched that disgraceful invention with an urgent message from the training quarters sent at triple rates, and then all America from Sandy Hook to the Golden Gate drew a long deep breath of relief.

But except in great vital moments such as these I now kept in the background. Why should I fash myself with such a guardian angel working overtime in my behalf? Besides, a great authority on the fighting game had now arrived from Boston and as he shared with me all the responsibility I had hitherto shouldered alone, every now and then I could take a few hours off and shoot over a cable about the European powder mine, or the Cockpit of the Balkans. These were winged words in those days, however halting they may sound today, and I—well, I chose to think that I had invented them.

With all the articles and arrangements for the world championship fight with Charley Mitchell signed and sealed in London one might have thought, and we did indeed expect, that the fight would be pulled off almost immediately—and in France. Nothing, we Americans contended, could be gained by delay and, of course, the danger of police interference increased with every hour. Tentatively it had been agreed that the ring should be staked out on an island in the Seine near Vernon, but this was soon abandoned for the two-fold reason, or pretext, I am not sure which, that the island was flooded by the prevailing high water and that police boats had been seen near there.

But, once in France, Pony Moore vetoed all plans and explained that Mitchell had been seasick during the Channel crossing, and as a result was greatly weakened. About the seasickness there had been no camouflage. It had been quite open and disgustingly above-board. But of course we of the American contingent chose to regard it as a more or less specious pretext. Many of us indeed at this time thought that Mitchell would never enter the ring and that he and his backers were playing for further delay and possible police inter-ference. And that the police did not interfere can only be explained by the undoubted fact that they did not want to. The vagrant horde of uncouth sporting men, wandering around for days in northern France and swooping down upon the clean little villages of Picardy like a swarm of devouring locusts, yelling and quarreling in a lan-guage which no Frenchman and very few Englishmen could under-stand, was a patent undeniable fact. Of course the police did not know where it was planned to bring off the fight, and this they did not discover until too late for interference, for the best of rea-sons, because the managers of the affair did not know themselves. In the long series of dreary rainy days it seemed impossible to reach a decision on this question or to the—for us—equally vital one of how many spectators were to be admitted to the fight.

Brisbane and I, before we left London, had celebrated a gentle-man's agreement. We were to be helpful allies until the ringside was reached and the fight began; then each man was to go it alone. We were confident that Sullivan would not desert us, but in the last hectic moments he might forget us, so we had concluded it was wise to maintain valuable contacts in the English camp. In carrying out this plan I had been paired for several days with the Birmingham Chicken. He really was Birmingham Chicken II, as his father had been the first to bear and to fight under that honored name. Chicken Junior, or the Younger, had been a famous middleweight champion in his day, too, but on a memorable occasion Jem Smith, when he first emerged from St. Luke's Parish in the East End of London, had put him to sleep. When at home the Chicken kept a "pub"; abroad when I came to consort with him he drank only three-starred brandy, though he called it a "sissy" drink and was always descanting upon the glories that had now departed from his line and the strong waters he and his forbears had drunk in the good old days.

I would have preferred the close companionship of almost anyone to that of the Birmingham Chicken. He had not changed his clothes since leaving England, and except for brandy no liquid had come in contact with his body for the same period. After I had been his roommate for several nights, I tried to change off, but the Fates were against me. The Chicken was very "strong" with Pony Moore. He would never be left behind at the critical moment. This last night was the most terrible of all, for suddenly the joy of living departed from the Chicken and he decided to kill himself. Only my restraining arm prevented him from throwing himself out the window or burning his face "off" in the fire. Day had come before the paroxysm subsided and he went to sleep.

An hour later Brisbane, Patterson, the favorite rubber, and I accompanied the champion to the famous Amiens Cathedral and John was entranced. But he was not a man to remain for long marooned in an historic backwater. Coming right up to the moment, he said, "I think we'll fight today. I told my men to let Pony Moore have everything he asked for, but not another day of delay."

"I hope you have planned the fight, John," said Brisbane. "Mitchell can box, you know."

"Yes, I know, I'll let the lad box for a round or two, then I'll put him to sleep. Then I'll pull off Pony Moore's painted whiskers, and then in a couple of hours we'll all be back in Paree. You boys will be sittin' in my box at the Follies Begum or what you call it, and we'll be pelting the birdies with looueys."

When we came back from the Cathedral, everything was stirring and everybody was agog. Something decisive was apparently on foot. The great men had at last ironed out all the difficulties and if the weather held up and a fairly dry place could be found (it had been raining almost constantly for a week), the fight was to come off that afternoon. In carrying out a plot which had been hatched on the other side of the Atlantic and which cost the paper a pretty penny, in fact many thousands of dollars, I rushed down to the telegraph office and sent off a cipher message to the manager of the French Cable Company in Brest. He was to clear the cable from three-thirty. Any commercial messages of any kind were simply to be spiked and await their turn. The news for which the world had waited so long could not be delayed much longer, and it was to have the right-of-way. And indeed for four long hours the cables were silent and untold millions waited before the blank bulletin boards all over the United States. But who could have thought that Charley Mitchell could stand up to John, or even evade his strong arm for more than five minutes?

While I was away on this vital errand, a great many things had happened. On my return the one that struck me most painfully was the fact that those who had hung around had pre-empted all the cabs that were in town, and there were none left over for latecomers. Brisbane had one, of course, and with the chivalrous friendship which he always maintained even in those trying days that developed so many paltry meannesses in others, said, "I have a place for you, Bonsal."

But I really couldn't do it. I could not stomach that, hardened newspaper man as I was. Here I had just perfected an arrangement, to be sure contrived on the other side of the water, which would cover poor Brisbane with confusion. He was about to be beaten out of his boots, and the generous fellow was actually offering me a leg-up! I recalled almost tearfully the Christmas dinner we had enjoyed together when, as cub reporters, we sat in at Sandy Spencer's and ate crullers and drank our coffee. No, I could not now accept a lift from Brisbane. That would put me outside the pale. So I gave him a mysterious wink and said, "Thanks, old man, but I'll toddle along with these fellows," and I pointed to the Birmingham Chicken and to Billy Porter, the Manhattan bank robber.

"Toddling along" was no empty figure of speech, but fortunately the road that we pursued went uphill and down dale so continuously that we had little difficulty in keeping up with the caravan of cabs that now strung out before us, going exactly where no one knew, but to the ringside it was hoped. As we passed the baronial hall of one of the Rothschilds, there appeared a groom upon a very dashing thoroughbred, and leading another colt by a long halter, a half-broken "hot-blood," as they say in France. Because of the sleepless night I had spent and the nervous energy I had expended in preventing the Chicken from throwing himself into the fireplace, I was extremely tired and now unfortunately for me the moment for clear-headed action and sustained effort had come. I wished that I was fresher, for I knew that after spending so much money in monopolizing and pre-empting all the cables of one of the companies, my paper would demand magnificent results. The groom was a merry gray-eyed lad, and I didn't have to start our conversation. "For the love of Saint Patrick," he began, "what are all you fellows doing streaking along the Creil road in the mud?"

"Well, I'll tell you, we are going to the greatest prize-fight that has ever been staged: John L. and Mitchell."

"Murther, I would like to see that."

"I can arrange it, but you'll have to let me mount the led horse."

"I'll risk it," he answered. "You're sure you can get me in?"

Soon I was riding bareback behind the carriages that contained Pony Moore and the rest of the principals and managers of the long-delayed affair. There was no fear now of missing the great event, but my mount was only half-broken, and the halter gave me but poor control. I could afford to take no chances, and I had a Machiavellian thought. I began to throw myself around on the horse's back. I chose to sit him, to use old Bill Byrd the trainer's favorite description of a poor rider, "like a bag of sour apples." The groom looked at me fearfully. "I won't fall off," I said reassuringly.

"I ain't afeard of that," answered the honest fellow. "But I'm afeard you'll hurt his back and then—murther! what wouldn't McGinnis the trainer do to me!"

"Well, if you feel that way, I'll swap," and in a moment I had his well-broken nag between my knees and was seated in a comfortable saddle. This was my good day.

In the drizzling rain the ring was quickly and, as it turned out, not very wisely chosen. It was far from level and sloped down to a stream, and even before the fight began there were already several deep mudholes and quagmires in it. However, as everyone was now at last for haste, no criticism was made, and soon the space was staked off and the champions were in their corners. John, stripped to the waist, wore star-spangled tights with several Irish harps embroidered upon them. And now, for the first time perhaps, I realized what Mitchell and his crafty father-in-law, Pony Moore, had doubtless known from the first. I realized what a very big place a twenty-four foot ring is and how difficult it might prove to corner in it an evasive and swift-footed adversary, especially if his leg-work is better than yours, and this superiority of the little fellow was quickly revealed and was emphasized with each succeeding round.

I have been at some pains to secure a copy of the costly, if not golden, words with which I described what now took place. Costly I say advisedly, because my paper had to pay double "urgent" rates for the waiting time as well as the extra rate for the hours of actual transmission. But this historic document has disappeared from the *Herald's* "morgue," where such things are, or were, treasured for a season, and my researches in the files of at least three public libraries resulted in learning that this important page had been frankly torn out by library thieves. I was taking to my afflicted soul what comfort there was in the thought that these men who committed a felony to secure the narrative for their personal archives must have thought highly of my account, and I was foolish enough to make a suggestion along this line to the gentleman who was in charge of the last depleted file-room I visited. "I wouldn't say that," he adjured me. "No notable event is safe, but mostly they rob us of the marriage and death notices." So that was that.

So I must, and likewise my readers, be content with what I can recall at this distant day of the dreary affair. I did not like the looks of John as he stepped into the ring. In fact his appearance had worried me for several weeks. The champion was not as young as he had been; he had lived high, and it seemed to me he had been trained down too fine. Several times, indeed, he had admitted that he really never had had an idea of what training was until they began working him out and working him in at the famous training quarters near Windsor. As he stepped into the ring I realized, as never before, that John's face was white and drawn and that his under-pinnings seemed slender, not up to the gigantic torso they had to support. But all misgivings vanished when the signal was given, and with a roar John went after the slim, audacious, ruddy-faced English boy.

"Come on, Charley, knock me down again," were our champion's words. This challenge recalled the fact that several years before in Madison Square Garden, by a lucky left-hander, aided by another circumstance which I shall not even touch upon, Mitchell had knocked our champion down. Mitchell had not forgotten it; in fact, in frequent newspaper interviews, rather unwisely, he had plumed himself upon being the only man who up to that time had knocked the champion down. Of course, John had another story, that Mitchell's blow had nothing to do with his fall. "I simply got my legs crossed," was Sullivan's version of the incident; but it rankled.

Despite this invitation, Mitchell did not come on. Very wisely, he kept away, sparring beautifully, and John's blows were falling short. And as they fell short, the champion burst out into leonine roars of disappointment. Mitchell was smiling and wore an air of confidence which surely he could not have felt. Quick on his feet, he always kept on the higher ground of the sloping ring, and these tactics equalized the advantage that otherwise Sullivan would have had because of his greater height.

Around the ringside were clustered some sixty men, all that survived of the three hundred who had started from London or joined up with the gang at Calais. They were a wildly partisan bunch, about equally divided in their allegiance. Hardened as I had become from my close association with them, I still blush as I recall the suggestions they made and the advice they gave the fighters. Certainly nothing was left unsaid to make the affair as brutal and as disgusting as possible. To be sure, the fighters seemed to like it and they replied in kind with prophecies and promises which they no doubt expected to realize.

By the fourth round John had got into his stride; to the uproarious delight of the American contingent he got by with a left-hander on Mitchell's chin which lifted him about six inches off the ground. The youngster fell back with his eyes closed, but the rain-drenched ground was as soft now as a feather bed and almost before the count began he was on his feet again but with a puzzled look in his dazed eyes. Now he fought more warily even than before. Whenever he got a chance he clinched and when he clinched he would always spike John's feet, that were soon red with blood, blood which Mitchell's "Sorry, John" did not wipe away. Twice he was warned for this misconduct and once for an undeniable blow below the belt. Certainly the boy was not fighting fair, but then did David fight fair when he met the giant Goliath? I had come to the fight in the hope of seeing Mitchell promptly spanked, but now and again I could not refuse him, though I grudged it, a certain sort of admiration. In the seventh, eighth, and ninth rounds, in quick succession, John sent Mitchell to grass and once it looked as though the Englishman would take the count. But he didn't, and was soon on his nimble feet again. Then the rain turned into a mixture of snow and hail, and Mitchell maneuvered so cleverly that these unfriendly and blinding elements were always beating into John's face, and soon the ring was about six inches deep in mud and muck and snow and ice. And then suddenly things stopped coming John's way. Often missing, he was taking a lot out of himself by unproductive lunges. Often he was tricked into a wrong lead by his dancing antagonist and almost invariably from now on when John did land with a tremendous wallop there was nothing there but thin air.

By the tenth round, I had lost much of the confident spirit with which I came to the ringside. True, with the exception of the bleeding lip Sullivan's face was unmarked, but it was gray and at times the champion seemed winded and his blows were ever falling shorter, his reach seemed to be at least six inches less than it was when the fight began. On the other hand, Mitchell's face was practically unrecognizable, his eyes were half closed, one ear had swollen to the size of a sausage, but his breathing was regular and free, and his marvelous quick-step almost as jaunty and cocksure as it had been at the beginning. As the Birmingham Chicken explained, "Charley's leaving John's mug alone, but he is playing a tattoo on his slats."

In the fourteenth round or thereabouts, the fighting that had been fast and furious slowed up; both men were apparently deep in thought, meditating a change of tactics. From the twentieth to the thirtieth round, while my competent technical associate was busy keeping a tally of the blows given and those that failed to reach their destination, I would have been quite idle had I confined myself to my allotted task. It looked as though as a descriptive writer I had drawn a blank, and then suddenly human interest did develop, surging right out of this mud-soaked, snow-covered ring, in which the barbaric scene was enacted. From the very beginning the fighters had responded with equal brutality to the bestial exhortations of their friends and backers.

"Knock Charley's head off," they would yell, or "Flatten out some more his pug nose," the Americans would shout, and John would generally reply, "Watch me do it." Mitchell's friends would roar, "That's right, Charley, slug him in the slats, that's where you'll get the big boy," and Mitchell would answer, "Here goes."

And then there occurred a complete transformation. From out of the bleeding mouth of one of the victims of the show there came the halting words, I think they were from Mitchell, "I'll bet they wouldn't talk that way if they were in our shoes."

"You can bet your life they wouldn't," answered John, and then suddenly after having acted like wild beasts for several hours, something like a human relation was established between the fighters, though they continued to hit each other as hard as they could.

It seemed to me that the dreary and disgusting exhibition went on for weeks. As a matter of fact, it lasted exactly three hours and eleven minutes. After the thirtieth round there was not a suggestion of science or yet of sportsmanship in the encounter. Sullivan seemed to be fighting in a dream. Now and again a shiver came over him that you could almost hear. Was it the icy wind or the prospect of defeat that made his blood run cold? I do not know, but the possibility of defeat was now apparent to every eye and could not have been concealed from John. How did it end? Well, many stories have been told, and there is much gossip about secret arrangements between the seconds, but I only know what I saw. Both men were stopped, only hobbling lamely after each other and grinning horribly. Then suddenly I saw Baldock, Mitchell's second, rush into the ring and shout, "Shake hands. It is a draw—make it a draw." Mitchell threw his arms about the big fellow's neck and began to sob convulsively. I don't know if there was an arrangement or how and by whom it was arranged, but if it was an arranged decision it was strictly in accordance with the facts. It was a draw because Sullivan had too much pluck to admit defeat and Mitchell was by no means strong enough to win. Mitchell, of course, soon looked radiant, as radiant as a man can look whose face has been beaten into a perfect semblance of a raw beefsteak. And well he might look radiant, for the draw was a victory for him.

We Americans all crowded around John and spoke consoling words, but he did not hear them. He seemed as deaf as an adder. And perhaps it was better so, for in our corner there was one traitor, the stout red-haired Irish boy whom John had picked up in Liverpool and who had traveled with him everywhere for months, acting most faithfully and obsequiously the role of a perambulating or portable chair. Sad to relate he turned yellow now, and instead of falling on all fours as was his custom and whispering to our tottering champion, "Have a seat, John," he broke out into a frightful stream of profanity and then, "Champion of the wurld you'd be," he shouted and bursting out into ribald laughter he added, "There be boys in Oireland could break him in two with but a slap of the bare hand—and me getting sway-back these long months for the loikes of him!" Patterson, the rubber, beat him up and expelled this Judas from the faithful group.

On the larger scene there arose a great uproar now and some free-for-all fights between the rum- and water-soaked spectators. It was all about the bets that had been so recklessly made during the days of delay and tedious waiting. But this did not concern me. The only thing I saw was a certain bulletin board in far-away New York that had been blank of the long-awaited news for so many hours. We were mounted and edging away from the ringside toward the wood road when suddenly the Irish groom whispered in the patois he had picked up, *"Sergots!"* There was no doubt about it; over the hill less than a hundred yards away some fifty blue-coated gendarmes were coming toward us fast in extended skirmish order. We changed our course and were cantering down the narrow road in the reverse direction when suddenly we ran into another gang of gendarmes. There was no way to avoid them, apparently the whole countryside was swarming with police. Some of those to whom we were now very unwillingly drawing near carried old-fashioned sabres and the officer in front brandished a pistol. It might well have been a lethal weapon but certainly it was not of modern make. He shouted *"Halte-là"* and my friend and guide answered in wonderful Irish stable-boy French. His glib explanation that we were only exercising "Mooser Ler Baroon's horses" got by and, as the officer shouted to us *"Passez alors,"* we certainly stood not on the order of our going. Once around the bend in the road we put our mounts on their mettle and in ten minutes our mad pace had brought us to the station at Creil and we drew up our now excited colts under the church tower which I was not to see, or not to notice again, until twenty-six years later when I saw it spread out flat on the *Place*, destroyed by a German shell. After our departure, principals, seconds and spectators alike were surrounded by the police and for some hours were lodged in Senlis jail. Cash bail was furnished and after a date had been set for a hearing all went on to Paris. Here in the café at the Gare du Nord, as though he had not had enough fighting for one day, Sullivan got into a row and had to furnish some more bail. The next day the crowd disintegrated and crossed the Channel to England in small groups. The cash bail was forfeited cheerfully and so apparently the desired ends of justice were attained.

From Creil I had only had time to send a flash to the paper before the express from Brussels came rumbling along. In Paris, an hour later, I sat many hours on a three-legged stool in the telegraph office at the Bourse, telling the story for which the world in breathless suspense had waited so long. Then a hasty midnight supper and I was in bed enjoying the first carefree sleep that had been my lot in a fortnight. For always I and the other historians of the memorable event had been haunted by the fear that for some reason, or for no reason at all, under cover of darkness the managers of the fight would give us the slip.

But soon I suffered a rude awakening. There before me stood trembling with anxiety and with beads of cold perspiration on his brow the telegrapher from the Bourse with whom I had transacted my business. In those days the French government took no chances and made us pay in cash the tolls on our dispatches at least as far as the cable station. In the transfer of a bundle of Bank of France bills and the return of change the poor fellow asserted he had robbed himself of exactly one thousand francs, "my salary for four months," he added pathetically. I examined my purse, found that his claim was probably correct, adjusted the difference and, greatly relieved, threw myself on my bed again. I had had a great scare. On sight of the telegrapher I had feared he had come to announce that the cable was down and all communication with America interrupted. Again I was aroused and a blue telegram was thrust in. Kind words from the news editor. The story had scored a great beat. The cable company had done wonders, something approaching instantaneous transmission. And then "What has become of X? His story died away at the thirtieth round. We had to fake the rest from your human interest story."

What had become of X? I had not the remotest idea. I recalled seeing him about the fortieth round—a man who could not believe what his eyes beheld but, after all, that could wait. X would turn up, and I turned to sleep again chuckling at the thought of what a time those desk men must have had evolving a technical round by round yarn from my human interest narrative. "Serves them right," I concluded savagely. "It is very seldom those duffers get the short end of it."

Then another uproar at my door which I should have "forbidden" once the moderately complimentary telegram was received (why had they dragged in the cable company?). I opened and there was another blue telegram. I tore it open and saw it was from the news editor. Could that fellow not let me have a little sleep? I read "Emperor William dead. Expect you cover funeral Berlin. All crowned heads of Europe will be there. Cable arrival—take first train."

The light of a dull March morning was coming in my windows as, in a dream, walking in my long postponed sleep, I packed my bags, hastened downstairs to the courtyard and by the greatest good luck and by a scant minute caught the eight o'clock train for Cologne. There was no sleeper and no dining car. All day weary-eyed and hungry I looked out upon the rain-swept fields of northern France. What a busy week it had been! The end of two eras had strangely synchronized. John was no longer the world champion but simply a pugilist who had been stopped, and now the nonagenarian Emperor was gone and a career that stretched from Waterloo to Sedan was closed. Bismarck the man of blood and iron would disappear. Von Moltke would probably retire to his farm in Silesia—no more would the obsequious Berliners in rain or shine, by hail or snow, gather in hundreds in Unter den Linden and await so patiently the moment when the white-faced War Lord would graciously smile down from the palace window at his loyal lieges.

4. VALE IMPERATOR SENEX AND JOHN L. SULLIVAN

THE IMPERIAL pageant took place in arctic weather. Owing to the thick blanket of snow, unusual stillness hung over the scene. It was the strangest of phenomena, a noiseless crowd. All the vehicles were on runners, and the sleighbells were muffled. Never have I experienced a bleaker day, but this did not prevent the thousands from standing in line for hours, chilled to the marrow but hopeful of having a last look at the familiar figure, of saying Hail and Farewell to the dead Emperor, who, if not great in himself, had presided over so many great events in German history. All wore the dark blue cornflowers, the emblem of the House of Hohenzollern, and many there were who, though poor and far from properly clad against the severities of the weather, carried armfuls of the House flower which they would leave by the side of the coffin with their heads bowed and eyes veiled in tears.

The catafalque on which the open coffin rested was covered with a pall of purple velvet edged with ermine. It was flanked by gigantic candelabra of silver and by tabourets and silken cushions on which were placed the decorations and the worldly insignia which the dead monarch had relinquished so reluctantly. In the place of honor reposed the crown, the scepter and the orb, which the kings of Prussia proudly exhibited long before they could even pretend to world power. Banked up in front of the catafalque were wonderful floral tributes from many crowned heads and other rulers of the world. Of these it seemed to me a wreath sent by the Empress of Austria was the most beautiful, and certainly it was given the most conspicuous place. The guards of honor were picked giants in shining armor. On one side were officers of the Berlin garrison; on

the other officers of the crack regiment, the Garde du Corps. The
dead Emperor, with his head doubtless raised on a cushion, looked
out upon the scene with sightless eyes from his lidless coffin. He was
wearing the uniform of Old Fritz's favorite regiment, the First
Foot guards, and a martial cloak was wrapped around him. As in
prayer, his arms were folded over his chest, and the great Iron
Cross was over his heart. His expression, in the dim subdued light,
was gentle and smiling.

All day long great charcoal fires were burning on Unter den
Linden, all the way from the palace to the Brandenburg Gate.
This distance was strewn with evergreens and pine branches, and
overhead were arches of green suspended upon pillars covered with
black cloth. Around the fires the people gathered to thaw out and to
read by this light the proclamation of the new Emperor-King,
whom they hailed, and not mistakenly, as Frederick the Peaceloving. Now and again Prince William, later to become the War
Lord of sad memory, would appear at the palace window and present his youngest child to the people, who bowed their heads, and
now and then cheered in a subdued, decorous manner. What a
pageant it was! William the Great lay on his bier. Frederick the
Peaceloving was dying, but the dynasty carried on. That was to be
eternal.

The last day of William the Victorious, before his broken body
was returned to mother earth, dawned dark and forbidding. The
skies were leaden and the March winds boisterous and penetrating.
Prince William, so soon to replace both father and grandfather on
the throne, arrived at the cathedral in great state shortly before
noon. At rigid attention with head erect he took up his stand in the
great nave behind the Imperial standard. Strangely enough, as it
seemed to me and to many others, while they were doubtless active
behind the scene, neither Prince Bismarck nor Field-Marshal Von
Moltke took a prominent part in the public ceremonies. While,
outside, the people in their thousands were surging about the hideous edifice, inside, the cathedral was not overcrowded.

The Lutheran service was short and impressive in its simplicity
and it was accompanied throughout by the soft strains of low, plain-
tive music. Prince Radziwill and Counts Perponcher and Lehn-

dorf, in life the Emperor's most trusted aides, stood by the side of the coffin with drawn swords. Outside the minute guns roared, while clustered about the catafalque were, as the court calendar afterwards related, twenty-six crowned heads or heirs apparent to thrones which at the time seemed so stable. When the choir finished singing *I Know that My Redeemer Liveth* and the military bands were striking up the first notes of Chopin's *Marche Funèbre*, I made my escape and ten minutes later was ensconced in the window from where I could certainly enjoy the best view of the great pageant.

To the music of Beethoven's noble march, the *Death of a Hero*, the stately slow-moving procession reached the Brandenburg Gate, and here the innumerable royalties, who were quite fatigued with the heavy march in full regalia, were invited to mount in court carriages placed on runners, for the *Sieges-Allee* was impassable for pedestrians or wheeled vehicles. How serene seemed the prospect of the royalties who proudly carried the pall of the dead monarch, who, after having suffered so many blows of fortune, so many *Schicksals-Schläge*, had ended his days in peace and upon a proud and spacious eminence. But, had we been given the gift of reading the future, we would have seen Rudolph of Austria meeting a mysterious death in the hunting lodge at Meyerling; the little Tsarevitch massacred with all his family in the dark cellar at Ekaterinburg; and George of Greece shot down like a dog in the streets of Salonica. Mercifully, however, the future was veiled.

It is doubtless passing strange that of all the tributes to the great man the only one I can now recall was in the form of a valedictory from my old landlady, who in view of our former acquaintance in my student days had rented me one of her windows at about twice the prevailing price. The praise of pastors in court pulpits, of war lords young and old, of ministers of state and ambassadors of great powers is clean forgotten, and only her words abide. The explanation of this *lapsus* I leave to my readers. Was it because her words at least were sincere and unstudied, or was it because I am a frivolous chronicler wholly unequal to a task worthy of Froissart?

I must tell you that Frau Unsorge was a hard-headed and hard-fisted old woman, else she had not survived the exacting life she had lived for thirty years. Her contacts had been exclusively with what she called *möblirte-zimmer-Herren* (men who live in furnished rooms), vagrant and migratory students from all over the world who came to Berlin to listen to Professor Treitschke's version of German history, or young lieutenants from the provincial garrisons who came to the capital to hear the great war lords expound the art of war in the high Kriegsschule, just around the corner. However, as the solemn pageant passed, Frau Unsorge suddenly crumpled up, real tears flowed down her raddled cheeks and through her apron she bellowed: "And now he goes too! *Der liebe gute alte Kaiser. Er hat so gern Hummern und Champagner gehabt*"—Our dear good old Kaiser! How he loved champagne and lobsters!

To some the last Imperial funeral celebrated with medieval pomp and circumstance was a never-to-be-forgotten pageant. But to the Ambassador Extraordinary of the dismembered French Republic it was a trying experience beset with many unwelcome and apparently insoluble problems. The duty of representing his country on this memorable occasion, representation which *les hautes convenances* and the protocol demanded, fell to General Billot. He was a gallant old soldier who in the days of his youth had served with credit throughout the Franco-Prussian war. His battalion by desperate fighting had broken through the iron band that encircled the French army at Sedan. Later he held an important command in the army of the Loire which safeguarded French military honor, although it could not save the despoiled provinces or the war indemnity to Prussia.

While the special envoy was lodged at the Embassy in the Pariser Platz, most of his suite lived at my hotel and in my corridor. I ran across the General several times, a handsome soldierly-looking man of sixty but with a face so sad that it attracted attention—even at a funeral. Soon the indiscretions of his young officers, several of whom were old friends, acquainted me with the details of the many-horned dilemma with which their chief was confronted.

"It would not be difficult," they explained, "for the General to follow the bier with measured tread and downcast eyes, for the dead monarch was certainly a gallant soldier and as such deserving of respect. But the visit of condolence to the young prince which the protocol demands—now that the Emperor Frederick lies upon his death-bed—how is that to be managed? How can a French soldier express sorrow upon the death of our conqueror at Sedan—the man who was crowned German Emperor at Versailles while the ruins of St. Cloud still smoked? Will you tell us that?" I certainly could not and did not even attempt it.

"Of course," the voluble youngsters ran on, "had the Mission not been sent it would have been a gross breach of etiquette. *Mais oui! Mais oui!* It is not to be denied—but now Rochefort says in *L'Intransigeant*, if the General expresses but one little word of sympathy, when he makes his inevitable call at the Palace, he will summon the men and women of Belleville to build barricades as of yore and destroy this dastardly government. And even Hébrard in *Le Temps* is lukewarm toward our Mission and fails to understand our dilemma."

Certainly General Billot had a bad cold, the penalty of exposure to the many funeral ceremonies—and in the end, like the born diplomat he proved himself to be, he utilized it to best advantage. Several hours after the dreaded audience, the young members of the dolorous Mission were opening champagne, decorously but joyously nonetheless in our corridor.

"I do not have to ask you how it went off," I said.

"No, it was magnificent," came the chorus of answers. "When it came our General's turn he stood before the Prince, pointed to his throat and then with all the good will in the world opened his mouth—but from his bronchial tubes there came only a wheeze and a rumble. And I must say the Prince was charming. He came forward and put his hand on our General's shoulder. 'I am sorry indeed that this should have happened in Berlin,' he said, 'but if the truth must be told we always have *infames Wetter* (disgusting weather) here in March. But I hope to welcome you here some day under more favorable circumstances.'

"Now what can Rochefort make out of that? *Mais rien de rien!*"

.   .   .

In Europe, of course, John was finished, but not so in America. While some fell away from the great champion, there were many who would not desert our favorite son, even in the days of his partial eclipse. As a general thing the *contretemps* in France was ignored. Great preparations were made to celebrate the return of Sullivan to the land where he learned to fight. Among the announced speakers was Roscoe Conkling, but his speech was never delivered. The great blizzard of March, 1888, that followed so closely upon the fight in France and so harassed the distribution of the many editions dealing with the details of the great event, knocked out the forensic champion and Sullivan's close friend, and his voice was heard no more among men. But a rough draft of the speech which he had prepared for delivery at the banquet of welcome already planned was circulated among a few intimates, and of this I feel justified in quoting a few heartfelt words.

"Our guest has subdued the haughtiest King and the champions of two continents, carrying our beloved Star Spangled Banner in triumph through every conflict. Unspoiled by his glittering glory, he now returns modestly accepting us plain citizens as his equals and his friends."

I never had the good fortune to see our national idol on the stage which he adorned for so many years, nor yet as a scientific farmer in his beloved Massachusetts, but I did see him playing in one of his least successful transformations. When I returned from Europe after a long absence in the Balkans, Brisbane said: "John has opened a saloon on Sixth Avenue and Forty-second Street. We must call on him right away: it will please him to see you."

I had my doubts, but it was a pleasure to go anywhere with Brisbane and soon we were there. At other hours John L. may have done a land-office business, but at this moment the great saloon was rather deserted. Even after Brisbane had patted him on the back, felt his muscles, that were not so bulging as they had been in France, and I had said the words that I thought were appropriate, the great man did not seem delighted to see me. Even under the patronage of his close friend and admirer I cannot say that I was warmly welcomed. "You see he's on the water-wagon, and that makes him grumpy," explained Brisbane, and, as though reading our thoughts, John began:

"Yes, I was a 'boozer' for twenty-five years, and it was John Barleycorn who knocked me out as a fighter. The only way you can beat old John is to climb out of the ring. Charley Mitchell? It's to laugh. That bozo can't fight. He's a sprinter all right and he spiked my feet until my shoes were filled with blood. But it wasn't he, but John Barleycorn, the snow, and the sleet that stopped me—Brr!"

Even when the great man had got this temperance speech off his chest, and had offered us liquid refreshment, he did not seem happy. Evidently there was still something on his mind and suddenly, with a wink at Brisbane, he put his arm on my shoulder and drew me aside.

"I owe you an apology and I'm going to make it right now."

"Why, John, you have always treated me white."

"No, I haven't. I've done you dirt, but I didn't mean it. You see, Bonsal is a hard name to remember; it's not like Brisbane."

"No," I admitted meekly, "it's not."

"And so when I came to talk to that bozo who was writing my oughter-bography, damned if I didn't forget it."

Here John ran behind the bar and produced a well-thumbed volume.

"And when I came to that day in France I said 'there was with me good old Brisbane and a nice young fellow from *The Herald*.'"

There was something almost pleading in the great man's attitude and voice now, and I hope that for once I rose to the occasion. He repeated, "I hope you'll forgive me. It's a hard name to remember."

"Of course it is," I said soothingly. "But see what you have done for me, John. You have given me deathless, if anonymous fame, and eternal youth. I was there—'a nice young fellow.'"

"It's mighty good of you to take it that way," said John, and the clouds vanished from his mighty brow. He patted me on the back and soon we were seated around the table in the private room, swapping yarns and drinking beer, while to fill up the gaps in our conversation, which did lag somehow, Brisbane would feel John's Herculean arm muscles and, though they seemed a little flabby, to me, would pronounce them all right.

"Of course," said John, "it's only my stomach that has gone back on me. I can't eat as I did."

Then suddenly the door to the private room was thrown open and a villainous-looking little old man in shirtsleeves and draped in a long soiled apron shouted, "Come out here in front, and show yourself. You don't think people come here for the suds, do you?"

I was aghast. John did not have a gentle way with underlings, with those who did not remember the mighty respect that was his due. I recalled almost murderous scenes at Chippy Norton's training quarters, and still another at a café in Paris—where proper deference to the champion of the world had not been paid. But this was a changed John.

"The old cuss is right," he said.

"Of course he is right," chimed in Brisbane, and submissively we all three walked out into the public room. Quite a number of people were dropping in now, singly and in troops. They would give their orders at the bar and then sidle over to our table.

"How are you stacking up, John?" more than one had the audacity to say. And John would answer, gruffly, "Fair to middlin'," and go on with the subject in hand.

But when John saw a group of admirers with their feet on the rail, who with modest hero-worship were content to gaze at the great man from afar, he was truly magnificent. He would stride towards them in his big-hearted way and shout, "Pleased to meet you, gentlemen; put it there. Have a good time; this is Liberty Hall." Then he would return to us, leaving the men at the rail in the highest heavens of delight.

All this time the villainous-looking old man in his shirtsleeves hovered around, always getting in front of John, and, as it seemed to us, absurd as was the thought, the champion quailed before his insolent glance. Brisbane said, "That's a good one, John, you ought to raise that fellow's salary. Of course you must sit out in front." John smiled sardonically and the old man, with a dirty dishrag in his hand, kept buzzing about us like an unfriendly hornet. He would slap his dishcloth down on the table, clean up the foam that had fallen from the beakers, but he did it so roughly that he spilled more foam than he removed. John never said a word but when the old man retired for a moment to a corner, from which he continued to glare at us with concentrated hatred, John said, with an explanatory wave of the hand:

"That fellow's me father. You'll hardly believe it. You'll think John's stringing you, but I ain't. It's gospel truth. That man's me father, so help me. He's only five feet three, and sort of bent in the middle, but for all that they tell me that before he became a booze-hound 'Mike' Sullivan was one of the heftiest hod-carriers in Boston. Of course I take after me mother. She was five feet ten and she tipped the scales at two hundred on her wedding day. She was a Roscommon woman, I owe everything to her, and she could make that little runt behave himself. But I can't. I take after her in every way—in every other way," repeated John.

The great man now changed the subject, for the old fellow swooped down again on our table, banged the glasses and again glared with frank hatred at the son who had achieved immortality. Soon John was discussing Jack Johnson, the black Galveston roustabout who wanted to fight him for a purse of ten thousand dollars, which in those days looked bigger than a million in the era of Tex Rickard the inflationist and of Dempsey and Tunney.

"I'll never soil my hands fighting a nigger. They tell me in my business you have to meet all kinds of people, but I won't soil my hands nor my gloves neither fighting a nigger for ten thousand or even twenty thousand."

When our time was up, we really hated to leave great big-hearted foolish John at the mercy of that venomous little fellow who was still hovering around. But as Brisbane said wisely as we walked away, "I'd do anything for John, but you can't help a fellow in his family quarrels. They have to be fought out strictly *en famille*."

5. WHEN GENTLEMEN FELL OUT

In the month of May (in the spring of 1888) when Paris looked its loveliest, and when all who were gathered there from all over the world were intoxicated by the fragrance of the acacias, three of us, favored by the god of chance, came together, as is so often the fortune of young people and so rarely the lot of old folk.

I would not have you believe that our coming together was an altogether ordinary affair. It was preceded by some remarkable antecedent circumstances, and that is why it was immediately decided to celebrate the auspicious occasion with a banquet up on the cool balcony of the famous café under the umbrageous trees.

Of these antecedent circumstances, in my judgment at least, the most notable was the fact that, only two weeks before, I had successfully interviewed the Pope in Rome on the subject of the Knights of Labor, who at the time were attracting much attention at home. It is true that His Holiness had not talked much, and certainly had said little on the delicate subject of labor organization, but still he had talked and my editor was pleased.

Hal Dulany had killed, in the Pyrenees, a mountain goat or some other rare animal very difficult to come up with, which he had pursued unsuccessfully for several seasons. And, after a stubborn resistance and repeated refusals, Armisted had been admitted as a pupil in M. Julien's atelier. No doubt he would emerge a Sargent or a Dannat, and so at least one-third of the honors of the banquet belonged to him. Armisted of the Roanoke Randolphs was possessed of their many talents which would at times crop out in the most surprising manner and he rather plumed himself upon his inability to cope with the problems of daily life. He had driven a hack in New York and he had worked as a lineman in the construction of a South American railway for some years, during which he had disdained to pick up any Spanish because he regarded it as poor Latin gone to seed. His Virginia cousin Hal was making it possible for him to study art in Paris now, and our high hopes for his future were not entirely without foundation.

The banquet started as a stag affair but was later enlarged by the presence of two American ladies who had come over from London with a letter from "Admiral Bill" known throughout the Seven Seas as the "swell of the ocean," who was at the time our naval attaché in England.

Perhaps it was unwise of Hal to have insisted upon a table on the balcony. It entailed the passing of a banknote of some size to the maître d'hôtel, and, as we were soon to learn, the habitual clients of this elevated and coveted place formed a closed corporation, and were inclined to raise their eyebrows when outsiders intruded. They certainly raised them as we appeared and while we were making a great pother trying to arrange our party of five so that each one of the three men should have on his right a fair charmer, which, as it turned out, was geometrically impossible.

However, in the end we were all pleasantly seated, and after the *écrevisses* were served and our appetites somewhat stayed, we looked about us. At the adjoining table were six Frenchmen, distinguished-looking men with ribbons in their buttonholes, and calling the waiters familiarly by their first names. I thought one of them objected to the costume of the lady from Kalamazoo who sat on my left. Was the costume daring? Well, perhaps it was then, but today if anyone appeared in this guise she would be set down as a dowager and as a dowdy one at that. After a few unsuccessful sallies, and a parade or two, I saw that I had no contacts with our unexpected guests who had come to us under naval patronage, and further that it was extremely unlikely that I should establish any, so despite the general chatter I fell into what the French call a *douce rêverie*. As the charming Angèle Laurent—or was it the equally charming Mathilde Lambert?—sang

"Viens, je te promets mille delices
Je te payerai des primeurs
En mangeant des écrevisses
Au Café des Ambassadeurs,"

I recognized that I was unpaired and in thought at least I summoned a gentle soft-voiced *partenaire* to sit by my side.

The crawfish song died away and as the *vol-au-vent* appeared, the garden suddenly rang with martial music. All rose and clapped their hands and then sat down again with a great clatter, for Paulus, the song bird of the Revolution that was a-borning, remained behind the curtain. At this moment Paris was tremendously agitated over the Boulanger movement. No one knew its exact purpose and as the *brav' Général's* program was extremely vague, it could be and in fact was made to fit into any number of revolutionary plans. Many indeed were satisfied that, whether as President or Emperor, once in the saddle the *brav' Général* would introduce fair dealing at home and peace and order on the German frontier. Then as the garden rang with salvos of applause and the balcony shook under the impact of approving feet, I came back from my revery and there at last on the stage was Paulus the Great, a squat plump little man with a pudgy white face and flashing black eyes. After imposing silence with a Napoleonic gesture, in a cracked and quavering voice he called passionately upon all present to close up their ranks, to rally around the flag, to present a solid phalanx against the invader who was coming over the border. "Let not the dastard's foot pollute our sacred soil," he shouted, disdaining all melody, and the audience went wild. The wave of emotion was so overwhelming that perfect strangers and even political enemies shook hands, and some hugged each other in fraternal embrace.

Entranced, I was watching Frenchmen of all parties closing up their ranks, forgetting all past differences and presenting a solid front to the ancient enemy who lowered across the Rhine, when I heard a tremendous crash and saw that Hal was belaboring one of the Frenchmen, who sat at the next table, over the head with his chair, and that the Frenchman was attempting to retaliate in kind, but not very successfully. The mêlée became general; everybody pitched in. It was all most confusing, but I do recall, and gratefully, that at this moment the lady from Kalamazoo said to the other lady, who hailed from Broad Ripple, "This is where we skip," and they skipped and I never saw them again.

In a moment all the tables were upset, and smashed plates and carafes strewed the floor. The Frenchmen were cornered and so, at first, in a position better to receive the chair blows than to reply in kind. Hoping, doubtless, to quell the riot, Paulus continued his patriotic song; indeed, he emphasized it. The waiters and many of the guests, interpreting his words as a call to close up the French ranks and throw out the invaders, joined in the riot and chairs came flying toward us from every quarter. We were driven by overwhelming numbers to the head of the steep narrow stairway which led down from the balcony to the garden. Once here, Armisted, who had hitherto dominated the fray as a falcon would a dove-cot, seeing that the fragment of his chair, all that remained to him, was of little value against his innumerable assailants, threw it away and changed his tactics. His coat was gone now, and his arms bare, but with a smile upon his face, the kind of smile that in our childhood was associated with the Indian chief subjected to torture and bravely determined that his captors should not know how he suffered, Armisted resolutely clutched the handsome balustrade, and he held on to it despite the blows that were rained upon him with table legs—he held on until one section after another of the balustrade gave way.

I was so fascinated by Armisted's defensive and also very destructive tactics, that I am wholly unaware of how I myself came down the stairs from the balcony; but when I examined my bruises the next day, they indicated it had been a rough trip.

Once out in the garden, and on firm ground, we were still more exposed to attack. Here our innumerable assailants could approach us from every side. Things were going very badly indeed when we saw an open door into which we rushed, hoping it would lead to some refuge, or at least to a better defensive position. It was merely a garden house, however, filled with watering pots and cans, without an outlet, and immediately the door by which we had entered was slammed and bolted behind us. We were certainly in a *cul de sac*. However, we had a breathing spell, and to me, at least, our situation seemed changed for the better.

This impression did not last long, however. Peering through a little window I soon saw police agents swarming all about the place, and a moment later there came a loud knock and a sonorous summons to open "in the name of the Law."

"Open yourself," I answered, and then the bolt was drawn and a Commissaire of Police appeared in the doorway, pulling back his light coat to expose his scarf of authority. He was flanked by two clerks who carried writing materials.

"I have heard the charge," he said, "and now, I simply want you to answer my questions." We answered them quite readily, and the Commissaire was about to place us under arrest, when outside the little window there arose quite a commotion, and a loud discussion ensued. I heard our names, or at least our nationality and racing proclivities stressed, and straining both my eyes and ears I saw a fairly familiar face in the midst of all these unfriendly strangers, and I heard this man say:

"They are *des gens comme ils faut*—they are gentlemen."

"*C'est impossible*," protested one of our antagonists.

The man with the familiar face, whom I now placed as an habitué of Longchamp and of the Chatham Bar, affirmed, "Unbelievable? Nevertheless it is true." And then our unknown benefactor spoke a word for himself as well as for us.

"Why, only last week I saw them all at the garden party in the *palais de Pauline*." This was the colloquial way affected by some smart people of describing the British Embassy, because in the Napoleonic era it had been occupied by Napoleon's beautiful sister.

"I have seen them at Baron Alphonse's and often in the 'big five' at the Café Anglais with the Duc de Feltre and Baron Roger."

"Can it be possible!" exclaimed the ancient clients with unfeigned astonishment.

Our providential friend was certainly mistaken, at least as to his dates, but I was not in a mood to split hairs, and as a matter of fact I was not drawn into the conversation at all, I simply over-heard it.

Our late antagonists, the gentlemen of the adjacent table, now held a whispered conference, and then two of them left the group and came into the garden house. They bowed stiffly to the Com-missaire and said:

"There has been a regrettable misunderstanding. These gen-tlemen are—gentlemen, and the affair will be settled in a *conven-able* manner." They presented their cards to the Commissaire, and these evidently impressed him deeply. He rose, and bowing graciously to the Frenchmen, but rather coldly to us, withdrew.

One of the French gentlemen with whom we had come in such unpleasant contact, but who was now acting in such a handsome manner, presented me with his card. I gave mine in return, and when he assured me that he would get in communication with me on the following day we both bowed stiffly, in fact I could bow in no other way, and then we separated.

As we walked away under the trees toward the Champs Élysées, we came across the maître d'hôtel, gazing pensively at the demolished balustrade and the innumerable spokes and rails of it which strewed the ground of what had been the battlefield. He had a great lump on his forehead which doubtless added to his puzzlement, and he muttered: *"Ils sont des gens comme ils faut! Alors, je ne comprends rien—mais rien de tout!"*

As we left, we were joined by the stranger with the familiar face, who had so effectively re-established our social status.

"I am delighted," he said, "that everything could be arranged so *convenablement*. I had feared for a moment you would have been compelled to go to the *poste*, to face perhaps the *police correctionnel*, and that would have happened had the misunder-standing persisted." And then he added in a lower voice, "How-ever, I must tell you that M. Deschamps is a famous swordsman. He is the champion of Martignac's *salle d'armes* with both the épée and the saber."

With our coffee next morning there came a very courteous note from two gentlemen, who though unknown to us by name were not difficult to place. "It's a cartel—a challenge," said Armisted who was very familiar with the dueling lore of Lever in his novels, Charles O'Malley, Jack Hinton, and Tom Burke of "Ours." "Splendid," he added, drawing a deep breath. Here at last was a dream that had come true! The writers of the note asked that we receive them that afternoon at four o'clock, if our engagements permitted. They made it very clear that they had an important communication to make to us, the friends of Mr. Hal Dulany on the part of their friend, M. Deschamps. And a few minutes later, M. Vignaud,* the perennial secretary of our legation in Paris, appeared.

"What are you fellows up to?" he said, evidently bursting with curiosity. "An inquiry came to the minister this morning from the dueling committee of the Jockey Club. They wanted to know all about the *honorabilité* of a certain American, M. Dulany and his associates. You would have been pleased at the minister's reply. He said you were all Bayards, *sans peur et sans reproche.* If there is a duel in the wind, you had better let him in on it. What he doesn't know about the Code is not worth knowing. Fifty years ago or thereabouts, he winged his man during the Seminole War in the ditch around Fort Marion at Saint Augustine. According to his account, the Indians did not give the young officers all the fighting required to cool off their hot blood, so they were forced to fight among themselves."

We answered Vignaud somewhat evasively, but assured him that if any difficulties developed we would certainly consult the legation. As a matter of fact, the news of this inquiry made us quite angry and indignant, but we soon subsided. After all, we were forced to recognize that the Frenchmen were entitled to a more substantial endorsement of our *honorabilité* than the mere word of our chance acquaintance, whose name we did not remember.

Several hours before the scheduled meeting, we sent Hal for

* Vignaud was a Creole gentleman from Louisiana who first came to Paris as secretary to John Slidell, the Confederate Envoy to France, seeking the recognition that Napoleon the Third came so near giving him. Now for twenty years he had served as the secretary of the U.S. Legation, a striking symbol of our reunited country.

a ride in the Bois, and Armisted and I, harassed by many perplexing problems, set out for a walk. We went up the boulevard and along the Champs Élysées, and here we stumbled upon a *canonnerie* that was also an arms shop, and were soon engaged in an examination of the weapons displayed and in conversation with the gray-haired old man who presided over them. Armisted thought we had made a lucky find; he had persuaded himself that the controversy as to the choice of weapons we knew to be impending would be more than half won if we had a pair of dueling pistols near at hand. Certainly the old man had a tremendous assortment of weapons. There were hair triggers and hard triggers. In my laudable purpose of avoiding bloodshed, I chose a pair of hard triggers that were revealed to us from a fragrant sandalwood case with mauve satin lining, but I was amazed when told that the price was twenty-two hundred francs.

"But," the old man added, "I will, of course, throw in ten rounds of ammunition; that is generally sufficient."

Armisted, always fertile in ideas, suggested, "Tell the old man we have not the slightest intention of becoming professionals, that if we get out of this scrape we hope never to have another encounter, and that we want to hire the weapons." Whereupon I offered two hundred francs for the use of the pistols for a week and fifty francs a day for any demurrage after that.

"Ah, messieurs, you are honorable men, I dare swear, but *évidement vous ne savez pas l'usage.* After a *rencontre* of the nature which you gentlemen contemplate, it is the custom, the invariable custom, that each of the principals retains the weapon he has used on the field of honor as a souvenir of the memorable occasion."

"Well, that's the most encouraging thing I have heard today," remarked Armisted, "for, of course, a corpse would not have the slightest need of a pistol or any other reminder of his worldly career."

Then in amazing French and yet getting his meaning across quite clearly, Armisted made a few inquiries. "Does it not happen that at times one of the principals gets winged or even permanently disabled?"

"It happens so seldom that we dismiss this possibility from our calculations. It is indeed negligible," insisted the aged *armurier*. "Of course, accidents have happened and may happen again, but rarely, or never, with experienced men."

These seemed to be the kind of pistols we wanted, and making a substantial deposit, we immediately entered upon an agreement on fair terms, to keep them or to return them as we saw fit.

Having secured the weapons, our next duty was to engage a skillful surgeon who could repair the damage they might inflict, and first off, we were so fortunate as to secure the services of Warren Bey, an ex-Confederate who after the Civil War had gone to Egypt, where he became the court physician and the medical adviser of that great spendthrift, Khedive Ismail. Warren Bey was now nearly seventy years of age and had returned to Paris, where he was spending the evening of his life in something that approached Oriental splendor. When I asked him on what terms he would assist Dulany on the field of honor he answered, "It will be on the score of friendship. I will be acquitting a debt which I have long owed to his father, the Colonel of the Forty-sixth Virginia."

Later, however, under the protracted negotiations, and the excitement of preparing to start at crack of dawn every morning for the dueling ground, this charming old gentleman became ill and he was compelled to propose a young and, as he said, a very competent surgeon as his substitute.

"But if Hal is wounded, I will come to you on the wings of speed," he said. Young P. . . ., a competent surgeon, proved to be, to say the least, a horse of a very different color. He was a Scot and had no sentimental regard for the Confederacy or for the offspring of its survivors. He insisted upon a large retaining fee and, wise man as it proved, a per diem allowance for any possible delay, which he seemed to have foreseen. But this was not all. He then placed before us a document which we had to sign before a notary to the effect that in case his connection with the duel should compel him to absent himself from Paris his income would be assured for the period. As Armisted said, truly, this was no time to economize, so we underwrote the document and the guarantee, though the young Scot certainly valued his services at a high figure.

From the very first I was determined that if the wretched affair could not be settled, it must be fought out with pistols. With rapiers, the *épée de combat*, Hal would have little or no chance, particularly if his opponent turned out to be the formidable swordsman our chance acquaintance reported that he was. The thought that I might have to stand by and see my friend spitted and scarified was extremely unpleasant. But there was plainly visible on the horizon a still more unpleasant possibility, and knowing how impetuous Hall was, I could not but recognize this as almost a probability. The papers of the day were filled with accounts of a very one-sided duel that had recently taken place near Lyons between a famous swordsman, an inveterate duelist, and an unfortunate man who had rarely, if ever, held an *épée* in his hand. The moment the antagonists came face to face, the moment they were released from *en garde*, instead of indulging in the usual preliminary parades the untrained man rushed at his antagonist and ran him through the body, perhaps a little low. Immediately a great hullabaloo arose; for weeks the life of the famous swordsman, who had picked the wrong greenhorn, hung by a thread, and now the unfortunate novice, charged with manslaughter in having inflicted a *coup déloyal*, was awaiting trial.

As it will become increasingly apparent with every step we take, I may as well here admit how extremely unfortunate for Hal it was that he was not supported in this affair by more experienced seconds. Armisted was undoubtedly a fighter, but generally with his fists, and his ideas concerning the duel, always vague, when translated into what he was pleased to call French, baffled all comprehension. It is true I had acted as *témoin* to Jean Moréas, the celebrated Franco-Grecian poet, when he fought his famous duel with Darzens, whose Biblical play "L'Amante du Christ" was the occasion of several riots at the Théâtre Antoine and a great uproar in the literary world. And as the new affair got under way, I plumed myself upon this background of experience, but as a matter of fact the only duty that had devolved upon me on this occasion, and that in the circumstances had proved onerous, was to pay for the carriages which carried us out and brought us back from the field of honor at Villebon.

The seconds of M. Deschamps appeared that afternoon at four o'clock with the punctilio of princes. After formal but most courteous salutations and some criticism of the weather, we got down to the business in hand. Count Louis de Turenne assumed the role of spokesman for his principal and our antagonist, M. Deschamps, and a very competent one he proved to be, although every now and then his flow of thought was halted by interruptions from M. Hallez Claparède. This gentleman, while he generally agreed with his associate, quite frequently liked to put the matter in another way, or at least in his own words. Divested of preliminaries and circumlocutions, it came to this: Turenne explained that they had come on behalf of their aggrieved friend M. Deschamps, to present through us to M. Hal a fully justified demand for an ample and yet by no means an unbecoming apology for the wholly unprovoked assault he had made upon the body of their principal. With such an apology forthcoming, while to be sure as yet they were not authorized to give an engagement to this effect, they were quite confident, loyal gentleman that he was, that M. Deschamps would express himself not only as satisfied but indeed as gratified.

These pleasant words were most welcome; certainly our French friends were not running amok. Bloodshed might be avoided after all. And then came a few words from M. Hallez Claparède in explanation of the by no means stern demands that had been made. He said, "We have not the slightest desire to push to extremes an *affaire* for which perhaps no one could be directly blamed. After all it was a *café chantant* affair, one of those vexatious incidents of great city life with which no one cares to be associated, either in the eyes of the public or the press, nor would anyone be justified in pressing such an affair to undue extremes."

For our side, I was spokesman and Armisted only occasionally contributed emphasis and color to our point of view. I declined even to entertain the thought of an apology, or to deliver the demand for it to my principal, and, carrying the war into the enemy's country and paraphrasing the words of our courteous opponents, I demanded an apology from their principal, or failing that, a meeting on the field of honor—with pistols. After M. Deschamps' seconds had recovered from the state of extreme astonishment into which my words threw them, they at last began to discuss my claim that *our* principal was the offended party and consequently entitled to the choice of weapons. Our argument was that while doubt was permissible as to who had delivered the first blow, there could be no manner of doubt that the first gesture of disdain, the first unseemly facial contortion, the first contemptuous glance had come from our opponents, and upon this we based our demand for a complete and sweeping but (not to be outdone in generosity) a by no means abject apology.

If they were not really amazed by my attitude, the French gentlemen certainly simulated this feeling in a manner that was worthy of the best traditions of the House of Molière. There was a tremendous hubbub for about twenty minutes, and only then Turenne admitted that in making the claim that I advanced I was merely exercising one of my undoubted rights, and that, of course, the claim would have to go forward to the dueling committee for adjudication. Fortunately, this would not mean a great delay, as I was advised that this important committee sat practically *en permanence* at the Jockey Club, or could be assembled there at almost any moment. Nevertheless, even after this agreement was reached, it took us some time to draw up the memoranda to be submitted to the Court of Honor, and still longer to induce the parties of the first part, as it were, to countersign the statement of the parties of the second part, and of course had these *procès verbaux* carried with them an endorsement of our clashing claims, that would have been impossible. After much argument and hairsplitting, it was clearly set forth that we testified to the fact that the French gentlemen actually made their absurd statement in regard to assaults and blows *de boxeur*, and they admitted that we had gone to great length in resenting facial contortions which we thought spelled contempt and sharp elbow nudges which we regarded as tantamount to blows.

When these ex parte statements were finally drawn up and countersigned, the candles in the great silver candelabra which shed a subdued light upon the scene had burned low, and our distinguished visitors, by frequent consultation of their timepieces, had begun to show a distinct appreciation of the fact that the most important moment in the day for them, and for most Frenchmen, the dinner hour, was fast approaching. I would not exaggerate the hardships that we had to undergo in the course of these negotiations, and so I may add that while you are reading a veracious and wholly unadorned narrative of one of the most serious duels that ever went unfought in France, we never permitted the vital negotiations to infringe on the dinner hour, and indeed only once was dinner delayed.

Perhaps I have not been quite fair in setting forth the views of our courteous French friends, but it is unintentional and I shall now try to make amends. They were always extremely affable and in limpid, lucid French, they never failed to make their point of view quite clear or to demonstrate, to their satisfaction at least, the absurdity of mine.

"*Voyons, monsieur,*" explained Turenne, "perhaps we are not right and of a certainty your opinion is respectable and shall be respected by us. At the same time, you will, I am sure, allow me to make quite plain what, under the code, is the universal practice respected by men of honor in France and indeed in many other European countries. If M. Deschamps were traveling in La Virginie or in Texas and a personal difficulty of this nature should arise, he would, of course, have to submit himself to the dueling practice of the country and, however repugnant it might be to him, he would meet M. Dulany with bowie-knives if desired; now, however, we are in Paris and here our code is supreme." And then, of course, M. Hallez Claparède, who, it seemed to me, was a little more bloodthirsty than M. de Turenne, chipped in with just a shade of malice in his voice.

"*Voyons,*" he said, "as you know, *tout le monde* comes to Paris, and occasionally *tout le monde* fights. Imagine the confusion that would ensue were each man allowed to choose his native weapon and to fight as perhaps he may have been accustomed to do on his native heath. Doubtless in these circumstances the Italian would choose the stiletto, the Turk the scimitar, the Malay his kriss, the Argentinian perhaps his lasso, the Australian his 'Kanga-roo.' To avoid these complications, for international meetings the wisest and the most discreet men among us have contrived a humane and chivalrous code and I can assure you that only com-bats that are fought under the protection of this code are permitted. Upon these our courts righteously close an eye, but others—they might mean summary arrest, imprisonment, in case of accident, and most certainly exile from Paris." This last possibility was evidently most terrifying to M. Hallez Claparède.

On the following afternoon we came together at the same hour, but this time in the dueling room of the Jockey Club. My thought and all my attention were so concentrated on the difficult matter in hand that I have not the faintest remembrance of what this historic salon looked like, except that it was simply furnished and that one side of the inner wall was lined with bookcases. On the shelves were wonderfully bound tomes of ancient dueling lore which, however, I had little opportunity to examine. In handsome leather cases were also preserved the protocols and the *procès verbaux* of more modern affairs, and it was these that we were frequently called upon to consult. From these it appeared that at the moment a certain Marquis du Lau was the arbiter of last resort in matters that baffled the dueling court. To me he seemed a legendary character, of about the date of Brantôme, and cer-tainly I had not the remotest idea that I was shortly to meet him in the flesh.

Probably another reason why I recall but few if any details of this meeting is that it registered my complete Waterloo. The authorities against my contention that we had the choice of weap-ons were simply overwhelming. I was compelled to see that no amount of facial contortions, that no elbow nudging, however un-seemly, could have justified a swinging blow, much less the toss-ing of a chair into the mêlée. Consequently, the conclusion was inevitable: the Frenchmen as the offended party had the choice of arms; we could only apologize or fight with the weapons of their choosing. As an apology was out of the question, and the whole afternoon had been consumed in debate, we were com-pelled to wait until the next meeting for the announcement of the choice of weapons, and the regulations under which the duel was to be fought.

Satisfied and indeed softened by the way in which they had destroyed my contention that Hal was the offended party, our French friends when we came together again proposed a very gentlemanly duel. Had it been carried out, there can be no question but that all involved would have been in condition to enjoy the sacramental breakfast with which such affairs were usually concluded.

"Dueling swords, the ordinary *épée de combat*, with fencing gloves, or with walking gloves, as desired. Bouts to last three minutes and the rest periods, thirty seconds," wrote Turenne. "But I would not seem to be laying down the law to you," he added. "Since you have courteously abandoned the unnecessarily severe *duel à pistolet*, I think we would acquiesce in any suggestions you might make."

"Let me hear yours first," I said.

"Well, my idea is, in accordance with the best dueling practice, that the *corps-à-corps* (close quarters) be forbidden, and that the combat terminate when the first blood flows."

This was the opening for which I had waited.

"Since you demand it, and the dueling code, for which I have the greatest respect, justifies it, I am willing that my principal should give yours an opportunity to secure the satisfaction to which he thinks he is entitled, although this imposes upon M. Dulany the necessity of fighting with a weapon with which he is totally unfamiliar. Yet I have only one fear as to the result of the encounter, and that is the ridicule which is so frequently showered upon a duel à la mode, a journalistic duel. To this danger I cannot expose my friend, and therefore I must insist upon close quarters being permitted, and that the combat continue until the surgeons on the ground formally confirm that, because of wounds, one of the combatants has been placed in a position of distinct inferiority."

Turenne lifted his hands in horror, and I felt that for once at least I had scored. "That is a fight to a finish! *Enfin*, a death struggle," he protested. We argued the matter for at least three hours, but as far as I can recall, neither side added to the arguments that had been advanced in the first five minutes. Turenne dwelt at great length on his fear that in case of an accident, and as he admitted sorrowfully, accidents do happen on the dueling ground, the courts would take a harsh view of seconds who allowed such savage terms to be enforced, in a combat which after all was not fought to wipe out a mortal offense or an unpardonable injury.

"In case of accident," said Turenne, "we might have to go to prison."

"Worse! Much worse! We might even have to absent ourselves from Paris—from France—for months," added Hallez Claparède with emphasis.

But Armisted and I were adamant. We had no fear of anything but the ridicule meted out to a frivolous duel. There was only one concession that we were inclined to make. If they would abandon swords, we would fight our man with pistols even at thirty paces. But Hallez Claparède grunted that such a procedure was very dangerous to the seconds, who had to stand somewhere near their principals, and so were not entirely removed from the line of fire.

In the face of this deadlock, the Frenchmen now withdrew to the window embrasure for a conference, and only returned to the table where the unfinished draft of the *procès verbal* still awaited the substantial paragraph some minutes later.

"We are quite willing to assist at a duel which would afford our principal the satisfaction to which we think he is entitled," were Turenne's concluding words, "but we cannot and shall not expose him to a *massacre à l'Américaine.*"

"We are quite willing that our friend should fight, but we cannot expose him to the ridicule of a frivolous duel," was our reply. And so the deadlock persisted.

Turenne did not like the way I put it, and at first I did not like the phraseology of his paragraph, but we both stood by our guns and our very divergent views were at last incorporated in the protocol which I at least thought would bring our long-drawn-out negotiations to a conclusion and terminate the affair.

Parting from our courteous antagonists with many expressions of esteem and high regard, we hastened to the hotel with our precious *procès verbal* duly signed. At first glance Hal was immensely pleased with its contents and said many kind things about our prowess in dueling matters, which, as he admitted, he had not expected. "You boys certainly had your wits about you. Of course I did not want to fight a journalistic duel and once I got going I most certainly did not want to stop when the first blood was drawn," he soliloquized.

"Yes, it might have been a mere scratch, and then how the Virginia papers would have held us all up to ridicule," suggested Armisted, and I agreed, not foreseeing how unfortunately this suggestion of possible newspaper publicity might develop.

But from that moment the contented expression left Hal's face, and while I did not know from what direction it was coming, I knew that trouble was brewing for all of us. For half an hour, with long nervous strides, Hal paced up and down the apartment lighting and then throwing away cigarette after cigarette. Finally he began:

"I don't say that you fellows haven't acted splendidly in view of all the circumstances—that are known to you, but there is one circumstance you were not aware of—you, Bonsal, were in Russia at the time, and Armisted was in Venezuela. Capel got wildly excited over what I said about the running of a Hungarian horse at the Croix de Berny, and—well, before I knew what he was doing, and before I think he knew himself, he slapped me in the face. I pitched in, but we were soon separated, and then Capel began his lamentations. He protested that I was his best friend, and that if I would only provide the fire he would burn off the hand with which he had slapped me. He even began to sob, and I said: 'Well, Capel, apologize and we'll forget it.'"

"'I apologize on bended knee,' he protested. I wouldn't let him do that, and soon the silly business ended with a round of drinks. At least I thought it had ended, but it hadn't. Some weeks later there came a nasty clipping from *The Richmond Whig*, in which I read that after taking a slap in the face and receiving merely a verbal apology, I had had a round of drinks with my antagonist. 'Shades of the dead Dulanys! To what a pass the sons of Fairfax and Fauquier have come!' was the comment of the editor. And his conclusion was: 'In the olden days when men were men a smash on the face could only be wiped out with blood.'

"Now what will these people say about the present situation? There were ladies in my company. They had been made, I think, the butt of discourteous remarks, and I know that someone broke a chair over my head, and yet when I am brought face to face with my antagonist, I say: 'Well, I'll fight you this way. But I won't fight you that way.' Now I want you fellows to go back and tell those gentlemen that I'll fight any way they want. After all, when in Rome, you have to do as the Romans do, and if you fight in Paris, you have to fight in the Parisian way. Can't you hear what *The Whig* would say if we leave it as it is? They would say, 'Young Hal is mighty choosy in the way he fights,' and they would probably add 'Poor Colonel Dulany.' You fellows have had the best intentions but you have put me in wrong, and I call upon you to go back to those gentlemen and say that on careful consideration you withdraw all objections to their proposal and that I will be happy to fight one or all of them, any old way."

I told Hal that this would be a difficult message to deliver, though at the time I did not fully appreciate how difficult it would be. I saw, however, that we were certainly breaking new dueling ground, and in this I was about 500 per cent right. Hal was most sympathetic, and said frankly that if he had two other friends in Paris in whom he placed the same confidence he did in us he would call upon them, but there was no one else whom he could call upon, so he must ask us to retrace our steps and do what he was quite confident was necessary to safeguard his honor from ribald remarks as well as from justified criticism.

We had no little difficulty in renewing contact with our hitherto amiable antagonists. Apparently they had gone to the country after the long-debated protocol was signed. Fully forty-eight hours had elapsed before once again they gave us an appointment, and once again we were face to face with them in the solemn dueling room of the Jockey Club.

When we confronted them, the noble Frenchmen were courteous, but somewhat stiff. It took me quite some time to explain the purpose of our visit. And one after another they kept repeating what I tried to say, with ever-increasing accents of incredulity. "It is most informal," they repeated. "Do I understand you to say that you gentlemen wish us to reopen a *res adjudicata* that has already been filed away in the archives?" When I admitted that this was our purpose, M. de Turenne cocked his eye at the ceiling and remarked that he could not recall a precedent to guide him with respect to our proposal. "I can," explained Hallez Claparède. "It happened after the Restoration, and then the procedure was as follows. The seconds, who asked that the *procès verbal* which they had signed should be torn up, had to go out and meet the seconds whom they had put to this inconvenience, and after all this had been arranged the former principals met and the affair was satisfactorily concluded."

"Nevertheless, it is all very confusing, and most certainly it will have to be referred to the Court of Honor of the Jockey Club," said Turenne.

"Most certainly," commented Hallez Claparède, "and to avoid all possibility of misunderstanding we must reduce to writing the problem that is to be put up to the Court." Then he began to interrogate us and to take down our replies in writing. "You wish us to cancel and destroy the *procès verbal* on which we have honored you with our signatures and you have honored us with your signatures?" I admitted that this was so. "In reply I beg to assure you that, subject always to the control of the Court, I believe that Monsieur Armisted will have to meet M. Turenne and I shall have the honor of crossing swords with you. When these preliminaries, indispensable I think, are out of the way, a meeting, of course, can be arranged between the former principals of the affair." We all signed this, again we honored each other with our respective signatures, and the courteous Frenchmen bowed us out with the assurance that in their judgment the dueling court would reach a decision on the perplexing questions now raised in about twenty-four hours.

We were well aware that an unpleasant moment and a difficult explanation awaited our arrival at the hotel, and so quite naturally we returned there with heavy hearts and leaden feet. I realize now that when Hal confronted us and asked for our report on this most recent conference, it would have been wise to have blurted out the naked truth at once. But there are situations so complex that no rules of action can be laid down in advance. Every man has to learn them by personal experience but I must confess that Hal was quite as indignant with what he was pleased to term the deceitful way in which we tried to withhold the truth from him as he was with the "utter incompetence" we had displayed in defending his interests. In the first outburst of indignation his words were so brutal that even after all these years I cannot recall them without pain. Upon one point he was quite clear and lucid however. No! he would not stand by us as we had stood by him. He would not serve as our second. He would not even bestir himself to go out and find seconds, even when I explained that according to the rules of the code we would need quite a bunch of them now—at least four. Here he begged to differ from me with a politeness that was even more unpleasant than the brutal words which I have omitted.

"Forget all that," he said shortly. "You will not need any seconds. I am certain you will both die in a brawl, in a pot-house brawl, and none of your smooth-spoken French friends will be involved in it." What could he mean by these mysterious words that seemed to veil but scantily a mortal menace? It was not long before we learned.

But in the meanwhile we were confronted with a Gordian knot that had to be disentangled or cut through in twenty-four hours, and where were we to find seconds to support us on the field of honor? We had but just arrived, and if we had friends in Paris, we did not know where to find them. We pled with Hal to be reasonable; we assured him that if and when the Court of Honor should decide that Armisted must go out with Turenne, and I with Hallez Claparède, it would be a mere formality. "It is the Parisian custom and we must abide by it," and I added triumphantly, "and that is exactly what you said yourself only the day before yesterday—'in Paris we must do as the Parisians do.'"

"I said that the day before yesterday," admitted Hal, "but I tell you today that if you fight those fellows before I meet Deschamps I'll shoot you down one after another, on sight.

"You mentioned *The Whig*," he continued, turning to Armisted. "What do you think that rag would say if I let you fellows shield me? Yes, by Jiminy, it was my party all right, and it must be my duel." Now as a matter of fact, on closer examination of the *cul de sac* we were being driven into, I also was losing my temper. "It was your party all right," I retorted bitterly.

This was the darkest hour of the whole affair and it seemed interminable, but it was the prelude of dawn. How the light finally came I'm not quite sure, but I really think it was our old friend and physician, Warren Bey, who turned it on. Ever since he had been released from service as our medical man on the dueling ground, and had substituted the younger man, he would drop in upon us from time to time to make inquiries as to how things were going, and as we had no secrets from him I probably very clearly, and undoubtedly very bitterly, explained the unfortunate impasse at which we had arrived.

But be this as it may, and the point is still a little obscure, it is certain that late one evening I received a letter from Robert McLane, our minister to France, an old friend of my father and a most charming personality. When we met, which was seldom, he said that I neglected him, and I really did but with a laudable purpose. I was, I recognized, professionally, a danger to embassies, and I would have been greatly chagrined if I had caused trouble to the most charming of ministers or even drawn him into the searching light of publicity which, as a diplomat of the older school, he abhorred.

His message ran, "Will you honor me with your visit early in the morning? You cannot come too early for me," and nothing loath, I was in the legation on the rue Galilée by eight-thirty, and there he was, spick and span. One might have imagined that he had been up and about his business for hours, and he probably had been.

The minister plied me with searching questions. He wanted to know what had happened, and what was going on, and he encouraged me greatly by his approving *"bien, bien"* of my attitude in all the many turnings of this circuitous controversy. Finally I said, "Mr. Minister, I think I have pursued the proper course, but only when I overlook where it has landed us. Armisted and I are apparently to be carved up by the Frenchmen or shot down by our irate principal. It seems to me Hobson's choice."

"Nonsense," asserted the minister. "Fortunately, we have to do with gentlemen of the highest character and the purest race, and so things can be—and must be—arranged."

"But, if at all, it must be arranged quickly," I asserted. "We are expecting at any moment now a note from the Frenchmen announcing the terms of the double encounter and in this case we shall probably have to meet them early tomorrow morning—unless Hal shoots us before we start."

But the minister wagged his head very wisely. "Of course I do not know," he went on, "but I rather think that the dueling court will strike a snag as they examine all the papers of this most complicated affair. If I am not mistaken, they will ask for more time and permission to consult with the Marquis du Lau, the greatest authority."

As all my thought was then concentrated upon the matter in hand, I paid but little attention to the minister's subsequent remarks about what we may call the *historique* of the duel, but today I recall them almost with awe. "You have been quite right," he repeated a number of times, "in seeking to avoid a meeting by all honorable means. That, of course, was General Washington's idea also."

"But—did you ever speak with General Washington on the subject of the duel?" I blurted out in frank amazement.

"No," laughed the minister. "But when I came to France to be educated under the supervision of my father's friend, the Marquis de Lafayette, he showed me several times a letter from Washington which he naturally treasured. It referred to the meeting with Lord Carlisle which the young Frenchman had sought when Carlisle, who was trying to negotiate a separate peace with the Americans, had called to Washington's attention in an official letter the 'universally acknowledged perfidy of the French Nation.' Lafayette was quite confident that his 'father' Washington would approve of his attitude and support him on the field. 'I flatter myself General Washington will not disapprove of this proposition,' he wrote, but he was mistaken, and the answer was disappointing to the young hothead. In a kindly spirit Washington replied, and I think I can recall almost his very words, 'The generous spirit of chivalry, exploded by the rest of the world, finds a refuge, my dear friend, in the sensibility of your nation only. But I would not have your life exposed to danger when it should be reserved for some great occasion.'

"Now, that is just the way in which I feel about young Dulany. This clash in a café must not have serious consequences. It would be humiliating for all concerned," concluded the minister.

Of course I still had not the remotest idea how the affair could be arranged, but there was comfort in the thought that now all proceedings would be on a higher plane and that even General Washington and the Marquis de Lafayette would be drawn into consultation.

What a seer our minister proved to be! Late that afternoon there came a charming note from Turenne. Our problem had been found more complicated than had been anticipated. The dueling court was at loose ends, and had asked M. du Lau for his judgment. He had answered that he would be most happy to serve if his distinguished friend the American minister would consent to share with him the grave responsibility for so important a decision. Politely he asked, did we have any objection or criticism to make as to this unexpected turn of affairs? In my answering note I assured him that we did not have the slightest. Later in the evening came another communication signed by Turenne. He informed us that M. le Marquis in collaboration with M. le Ministre had consented to review our affair. We were all expected to present ourselves at the legation at ten o'clock on the following morning and to bring all papers and documents with us.

Hal with hawk-like vigilance intercepted us as we left the hotel for our rendezvous at the legation. He was as stern and as menacing as indeed he had always been since the unpleasant complications arose. We did not get by him until I had pledged my word of honor as a Virginia gentleman, but one generation removed to

Maryland, that I would not under any circumstances face the Frenchman in battle until I had given him a fair opportunity to take a pot shot at me with his Colt.

Of course this meeting at the legation was a very formal affair. We went to it with our now developed sense of the fitness of things, high-hatted, frock-coated, bespatted. It was a dark gloomy morning with now and then a shower, and the salon at the legation was lit only by beeswax candles. Behind a massive desk sat the minister, and by his side a small hatchet-faced Frenchman to whom we were introduced with great formality. He was the Marquis du Lau, and while we were little experienced in such matters we knew that his name was as authoritative in the dueling world as, say, that of Pierpont Morgan in finance. We were shown to chairs at the left of the desk, and a moment later our antagonists appeared and, after saluting us with formal dignity, they were directed to chairs on the right, the seats of honor because they were now the guests of America. Vignaud, the seasoned secretary of the legation, kept coming and going, now bringing to the desk bundles of papers, and now in low sibilant whispers conversing with the distinguished old gentlemen who sat behind it.

After much shuffling of the papers before him and several premonitory coughs, M. le Marquis* opened the stern session with a graceful exordium which ran much as follows:

"Gentlemen," and his language was the stately French of the eighteenth century and certainly smacked more of Tours than of Paris. "Gentlemen, the complicated affair of honor which you with extreme amiability have submitted to the re-examination of the distinguished representative of the United States and to me, duly authorized and authenticated for this occasion by the Dueling Committee of the Jockey Club, while it has been the occasion

* While the arbiter of the duel and its undisputed authority, the Marquis du Lau had other interests and even more far-reaching activities. From the *Journal* of Ludovic Halévy it appears that on the subject of Anglo-French relations he was for twenty years the confidential adviser of the Prince of Wales. Indeed from his letters which André Maurois publishes in *Édouard VII et Son Temps* (Paris, 1933) the marquis would appear to have been one of the earliest promoters of the Entente Cordiale which shaped European and indeed world history.

of great anxiety, for we immediately recognized that nice questions of honor and incidentally valuable lives were at stake, has, when regarded from another point of view, as a counterbalance, afforded us great pleasure and immense satisfaction.

"It is not necessary for me to elaborate the details of the affair with which you are all familiar. I will content myself by saying that they demonstrate once again that the instincts of chivalrous gentlemen, whether they come from Touraine or from far-away Virginia, are identical. It is, of course, true, undeniable, that these sentiments may, and sometimes do, seek and find different forms or vehicles of expression, but the underlying inspiration is, and remains, always the same. It is one of sincere and therefore spontaneous nobility."

M. le Marquis looked at M. le Ministre, who now opened his eyes and murmured "Quite so."

"What has gratified us particularly, in our careful scrutiny of a complicated affair, has been the complete unanimity as to the facts of the incident that has been arrived at by courteous, mutually respecting, opponents."

I could hardly believe my ears as they transmitted these words, but there was no mistake; there was M. le Ministre bowing his venerable head in emphatic assent. These men were truly wasted on us. Here at last were diplomats, competent to iron out the Eastern question and lucidly interpret the most obscure paragraphs of the Treaty of Berlin.

But after this majestic preface it was extremely easy for M. le Marquis to skate over many yards of thin ice. He now talked rapidly, as though he did not wish the purport of his words to be subjected to close scrutiny, or to be judicially weighed.

"By common consent, we have passed over the incident which provoked the affair on which we now have the honor to sit in judgment, but in doing so we make the formal statement that not the slightest blame should be or can be attached to either principals or seconds." Here Armisted bowed low. "Clearly it is our modern mode of life, the crowded condition of our restaurants during the *grande semaine,* the weakness of fallible human nature when subjected to these severe tests and unavoidable contacts, that are to blame. Fully understanding these inevitable conditions of our daily life as we do, we have decided to throw a veil of charity over the trivial originating incident. Surely no one was guiltless and surely no one was to blame. *C'est la vie!*"

"How true! It is life," repeated our minister.

"After weighing all the evidence, and exploring all the surrounding circumstances, we came to the conclusion that there was hardly any justification for an encounter which would place in jeopardy the lives of gallant gentlemen and disturb the peace of mind of those near and dear to them. We then approached the negotiations which ensued."

Here I confess I was on tenterhooks. How was the great authority to regard my amateurish efforts?

"Now what do they reveal? About this there can be no possible question, the conclusion springs to the eye, one glance at these remarkable papers would silence the most censorious, the most severely critical. All involved in the trivial incident have behaved with such chivalrous consideration, with such *parfaite galanterie*, that an encounter under these circumstances would really be an indictment of the Code which has shaped and fashioned the lives, and at times the death, of gentlemen for generations."

I opened wide my eyes. There was Mr. McLane assenting vigorously to the pronouncement. Armisted did not quite understand, but as always he was ready for anything, and he bowed his head intelligently; Turenne looked dazed, but only from Hallez Claparède was there the slightest indication of possible opposition. Perhaps scenting this complication, M. le Marquis continued rapidly.

"This judgment which we have arrived at only after the most careful and conscientious study, we have been at some pains to epitomize and condense in this document, which, if it meets with your approval, will put an end, a very honorable end in our opinion, to a regrettable affair." And after reading the sonorous words of his conclusion, now condensed into a formal protocol, M. le Marquis looked about him inquiringly, almost challengingly it seemed to me. First, of course, toward the Frenchmen on his right. "Is it acceptable to you," he asked Turenne, "as a representative of your distinguished principal and on your own behalf, in your affair with M. Armisted?"

"It is," said Turenne quietly.

But Hallez Claparède showed some hesitation. It was evident he longed to pink me, perhaps even to scarify me, in retaliation for all the long-drawn-out discussions and debates to which I had subjected him in the dueling room of the Jockey Club. Then at last, reluctantly, he said, "Yes, undoubtedly, who could take exception to the decision handed down by the highest authority? But would the gentlemen, the Honorable Minister, the Honorable Marquis, would they do us the honor of countersigning the protocol, authenticating it with their authoritative names?"

M. le Marquis now had a whispered conference with the minister, and then out loud he said, "It was our purpose to ask your permission to do this very thing, and so to associate ourselves fully in this honorable conclusion of an unfortunate affair."

"Then I accept," said Hallez Claparède, still a little grumpily.

I gave a sigh of relief. I thought this was all, but soon I was to learn that in spite of my intense application for the last fortnight, I was still a neophyte in dueling matters. The marquis now asked that the copies of the first *procès verbal*, in which our earlier negotiations had been set forth, should be turned over to him. Turenne immediately handed in his copy and I produced mine.

"In our judgment," said the marquis, "it is proper that these records, while highly honorable to all concerned, now that they have been displaced by a final protocol, should be destroyed."

The moment he had it in hand, the marquis stuck Turenne's copy in the candle-light, and it went up in smoke and flame. Now there was no record save in my memory of his indignantly expressed unwillingness to take part in a *massacre à l'Américaine*. The marquis then took my copy, containing my firm refusal to expose my principal to the ridicule of a journalistic duel, of which I had been so passionately proud, even after Hal threw us over, and made me abandon my position. As it too went up in smoke, however, I recalled the saying of our stern judges who now, though somewhat relaxed in port and mien, still sat in judgment upon us, "It is life."

With considerable formality and ceremony we signed the new

protocol, which terminated the affair, and then, as agreed, the marquis and our minister countersigned it.

"I am very happy," said the minister, as he flipped away the sand with which our signatures had been blotted. "I shall file it away for safe keeping in the archives of the legation." The marquis strode towards the minister and embraced him.

"What a happy thought," he said. "There it will live for all time as an eloquent reminder of the chivalrous encounter between the gentlemen from Virginia and the gentlemen of France, in which all behaved with such *parfaite galanterie.*"

M. Hallez Claparède now gave signs, I would not say of impatience, but certainly of restlessness. He was a very busy man, socially, artistically and in the dueling world, and, of course, it was hardly fair that we should monopolize all his time, but even yet our affair was not at an end. A door opened and in it appeared M. Vignaud, who said quietly, "They have been here for some minutes now." And then behind him appeared the butler, who announced that luncheon was served. With a bland smile the minister held back the marquis and urged us forward. Vignaud leading the way, we passed through several salons, and there—well, I could hardly believe my eyes, there in the little ante-chamber or salon preceding the breakfast room, I saw Hal and M. Deschamps, and soon my ears were as discredited as my eyes, for they were engaged in a courteous but nonetheless firm discussion as to the chances of the Irish mare in the Grand Steeple to be run on the following day at Auteuil. With them was a stalwart young man whom Vignaud hastened to present to me as M. Deschamps the younger, and he, as I later learned, was the famous swordsman of the family, whose reputation in the dueling world had given me anxiety—and not Hal's antagonist.

The minister and the marquis now overtook us, and a tremendous discussion arose as to who should first pass into the dining-room. Whether it was according to protocol or not I do not know, but as a matter of fact we won out and compelled the minister and the astute marquis to precede us. I recall that M. Deschamps the younger was urging me very volubly to read the new Russian writers. He stated that the memoirs of Marie Bashkirtseff had for

the first time initiated him into the realities of life and that Tur-
genieff's *Virgin Soil* was a revelation of the era that was dawning. I tried to keep up my end, of course, but nevertheless I was
frankly pleased when this literary excursion was over and I found
myself at table placed beside my antagonist of so many debates
and prolonged discussions—Hallez Claparède.

I must admit that while he did his best to seem pleased, my determined opponent was obviously bored. I ate, I fear, almost ravenously. I was indeed practically breaking a fast of several days, but
my table neighbor and quondam adversary only toyed with the
very excellent food that was placed before him. When I urged him
to do justice to the minister's table, he protested he had no appetite, and then confidentially he admitted that this was always the
case when he sat in at a dueling breakfast which had not been preceded by a duel, a thing of which he frankly disapproved.

"But," and now his eyes that had been so heavy and dull brightened as he spoke, "I would have had an excellent appetite. We
would all have enjoyed our food much better had we taken our
morning drive to the Hermitage at Villebon. You know," he sighed,
"for *nous autres, gens d'épée,* there is no appetizer in the world that
can compare to the clash of steel on a frosty morning." Poor Hallez
Claparède! But as for me, I ate well and was indeed quite pleased
with the dénouement. When the luncheon was over and we had at
last parted with our quondam adversaries, now our good friends
who showered upon us many expressions of high esteem, Hal escorted his seconds, who, through no wish of their own, for a moment had usurped the position of principals in the affair, down to
a famous jeweler's in the rue de la Paix and presented us each with
a souvenir of the occasion. Mine was a gold rapier scarf pin en-
crusted with diamonds which was to serve me as a reminder of my
dueling days for all time.

Back at the hotel we dismissed the *voiture de remise* which had
on so many cold mornings awaited our departure for Villebon, and
we also reduced expenses by turning back to the shooting gallery
the dueling pistols which, as they never had been fired, certainly
no one wanted to retain as a reminder of an encounter that never
came off. And here at the hotel a very uncouth telegram was await-

ing me from the news editor. Not a bit of news had come from me, he remonstrated, for two weeks now. This was true, but it was also true that, as far as I could see, during this period nothing had happened in Paris but the Dulany-Deschamps-Randolph-Turenne-Bonsal-Claparède duels and their fantastic complications. And as they hadn't come off—and even if they had, I would have been precluded from writing for the press anything in regard to an affair of honor in which I was involved—I sent this same news editor a pretty stiff answer. He had the last word in the matter as news editors generally do, but that is another story.

6. THE DUCHESS AND HER STAG HOUNDS

WHEN THE invitation came to assist at a stag hunt at Bonnelles on a specified date, or on any other hunt day that might suit my convenience, I was delighted, but also perplexed. The invitation meant doubtless that a mount would be provided, but then I did not want a *cheval d'invité*. The honor of the Maryland Hunt had been lodged in my unworthy hands, for the nonce, and I was determined that at least my horse would be equal to the occasion. Fortunately, I had many days in which to look about me and certainly nothing was more pleasing to me than looking over hunters and trying them out, as well as you can try out a hunter on the tan bark of a riding school.

It should be pointed out to those who are too young to recall this era that, at this time, Paris was mad about horses and also, of course, that this madness had not a little to do with the amazing growth of the Boulanger movement which, taking all obstacles in its stride, was sweeping over the country by leaps and bounds. The brave General sat his horse well, the mettlesome black charger made a gallant appearance, and the revolution was apparently nearing success in an easy well-gaited canter. If motor cars had been invented, had monoxide gas pervaded the atmosphere, as it does today, the movement would have died a-borning, or so I think. Of course, it may be, as the cables constantly report, that a mechanized revolution is brewing now. But certainly the horses have gone and much that was picturesque has gone with them.

In those days romance was in the saddle, I cannot reproduce the scene. If you care to know how we looked you must examine the drawings of "Crafty" who with the pencil of genius illustrated

horsy Paris. But at least I can tell you in those days when spring
came the trees were bright with luxuriant foliage and the Bois
and the parks were fragrant with flowers. These bright days are
gone, doubtless never to return. I may witness, certainly with
disapproval, the mechanized revolution, but I will not deign to
chronicle it. Man's useful but most detestable invention has poi-
soned the atmosphere everywhere, but nowhere has it proved more
destructive of beauty than on the banks of the Seine. There a few,
a very few, hours after the miracle of spring a blight comes over
the budding scene. The flowers wilt and the leaves are seared.
They either drop off or for a few woebegone weeks drag on a
miserable yellow existence.

Of course, the great attraction for the people of Paris at this
time were the drags and four-in-hands of James Gordon Bennett
or Hal Dulany or Ridgeway Knight or Fred Monroe as they
speeded up the Champs Élysées, freighted with princesses or arch-
duchesses, or at times with the songbirds and dancers of the the-
aters and music halls. In this day, which for a fleeting moment I
would recall, the famous equipages of the Third Empire had well-
nigh disappeared. The ladies of the fashionable faubourg would
no longer take the air in stately carriages harnessed *à la Daumont*
—which meant a four-in-hand with two outriders, or *à la demi-
Daumont* which meant a pair of spanking horses, one ridden.
When on the Avenue du Bois these lively reminders of the past
rattled by with clanking harness, it was generally the stately
Madame Otero, the danseuse, or Carmencita with laughing eyes
or some other soubrette who was out for a promenade and at the
same time doing a little advertising. Ladies, however, the queens
of society, rolled out to the Bois in low-slung Victorias behind a
pair of bays or chestnuts with an English coachman and a footman
on the box.

Those who were driven out in the afternoon would rendezvous
at the Pré-Catalan or at some more retired nook over towards
Bagatelle. But the mornings belonged to the cavaliers and the
Amazons. They would generally mount at or near the Arc and
after the gallop their meeting place was the Café des Cascades
with its music and freshness of falling water. It seemed that this

gay life would never die. Of course, we would grow old and stiff-jointed and be compelled to take what the court calendars called "gentle carriage exercise," but then, the young and the nimble would jump into our saddles. Others would rush across the meadows and be gay. Sad as it was, that could not be helped, and as the Greek wrote, "Naught that must be is terrible to mortals." We had not the remotest idea that Time was putting a period mark to the day of the mounted man, that equitation would yield to aviation, that flying over the green fields would give way to flying through the fleecy clouds.

And yet there was plainly visible the warning of the end of an era on the wall, or rather in the skies. I can see it now although we ignored it then. I recall a gay breakfast at the Cascades and how we waxed indignant at discovering not a little sand in our omelettes. In answer to our complaint the maitre d'hôtel moaned, "There is a mad Brazilian up there in the air in a strange contraption, *ma foi!* He says he is the 'Columbus of the air.' One of his tricks is to dump a bucket of sand on the breeze and that sifts into our *omelettes aux fines herbes.*"

Naturally we were angry and foolishly enough we indulged in a Canute-like gesture. We wrote a letter of bitter complaint to the *Figaro* and asked that it be brought to the personal attention of our good friend M. Francis Magnard. The madman was Santos Dumont and his contraption was the embryo of the airship of to-day. The sand in our omelette was a dark portent, but we did not heed it and gaily on we rode. Our little day was good and we enjoyed it to the last fleeting moment.

As the long-awaited day approached for the first hunt of the season, I called upon Hensman, the riding master of the Rue de la Pompe whom I had long known, to secure me a suitable mount.

Hensman entered into the business with enthusiasm. He had hunted all over Ireland and in most of the English shires, and was keen to assist at a French stag hunt of which he had heard so much but in which he had never had a chance to participate. He soon produced a likely looking Irish mare and he proposed that he should come along with my *relai*, a second horse for me to mount in case anything happened to the mare. The *relai* was a powerful black gelding that looked as though it "could run all day." "And I hear," asserted Hensman, "that when the Duchess gets going she sometimes follows the chase until the hounds bay at the moon."

These arrangements suited me admirably, and the stable boys convoyed the horses down into the country several days before the great event. We passed the night at Fontainebleau and at crack of dawn we drove over to the Château of Bonnelles.

At the rendezvous, I had a disappointment. General Boulanger, the man of the hour, did not appear. The vivacious and charming Duchess was voluble in her excuses. She explained that while the General loved nothing half so much as a gallop through the forest, except perhaps the smell of gunpowder, his campaign committee with natural caution had forbidden him to take the risk. Their decision was brought by Arthur Meyer, the extremely important editor of the *Gaulois,* and the recognized intermediary between the monarchists and the Boulanger groups. The *cheval d'invité* which had been reserved for me was placed at the great editor's disposal but, although he came to the meet fitted out in a riding costume from the Bon Marché, he preferred to follow the chase as best he could with two stout ladies in a Victoria.

The rendezvous was in a charming forest glade several miles from the Château. While, of course, the sporting Duchess was master of the hunt and out of her abundant revenues met all the heavy expenses that it entailed, she shifted all the details, "the bothers" as she put it, over to the broad shoulders of the Duke of Tremoïlle. He was a bluff, ruddy-faced country gentleman, very much of the old school who, as soon as the hounds were seen approaching, went into a huddle with the innumerable *veneurs* and *piqueurs* in conjunction with whom he was expected to plan the run, subject of course to the caprice of the forest stag who was as yet invisible.

While these plans and plots were being discussed with great solemnity, and at some length, I had a chance to look about me and take in the unfamiliar scene. Some of the men sported pink, but dark blue coats predominated. About a third of the riders were women, some in high shiny beaver hats but many in the more

becoming and comfortable *tricornes* which the Duchess also wore.
The feature of the tableau which, however, intrigued me most was
the presence of five or six mounted men in what seemed to me
a medieval garb of chestnut-colored velvet. Silent and grim, and
very much aloof from the busy scene, they sat their horses each
with a tremendous curved horn, a horn indeed you might say with
many convolutions, resting on their saddle bows.

In answer to my unspoken inquiry, the Duchess explained,
"That, dear visitor, you will not see in any other land, *la trompe
de chasse;* the hunting horn of this character, at least, has only survived in France and *les sonneurs* they are our perfect traditional-
ists. Their *fanfares* or flourishes go back to the Middle Ages and
one of my men can prove descent from that great 'winder of the
horn,' the Marquis de Dampierre who was Master of the Hunt
under Louis XV. When we are under way, I will have them give
some of their classic *fanfares* for your especial benefit." Our conversation was interrupted by a signal, from someone I could not
see, to the Duke who passed it on to the mounted musicians. From
the curved horns there came rollicking sounds and while I could
not see him as yet the energetic effect of the music made it quite
clear that the stag had left his lair and that we were summoned
to follow on. I followed the hounds and the Master at a distance
which I considered decorous, as did most of the *piqueurs*, right
into the forest. I was not slow in finding out that this was a tacti-
cal mistake. The forest was dotted with obstacles which could not
be jumped. Here, there, and everywhere were quagmires through
which, snorting with disgust, the Irish mare would slide or floun-
der, and then we would be confronted with broad shallow ditches
you could neither jump nor take in your stride and when you descended into them you were lucky if you emerged from the mire
again.

The wiser course, observed by the majority, which I later joined,
was to follow the cry along the wood roads (although some of
them were covered with slippery turf while others were simply a
succession of mud holes) by which, along geometrical lines, the
forest was bisected. The stag did not follow these lines, however,
and so not seldom we lost all contact with the chase, only to be

recalled by trumpet notes from the curved horns. When we came to a fork or junction in the wood roads, it was difficult to lay our course with the precision of Euclid. Opinions would differ as to the best road to follow and the mud-spattered groups would divide, but only for a short time. The roads that parted soon came together again and so did the cavalcades, with riders bumped off and horses thrown on their haunches, as a consequence of the resulting collisions.

At one of these mix-ups at the crossroads, Hensman appeared on my *relai.* The black gelding was yellow with mud and I must say that even the seasoned huntsman had lost his aplomb. He was flushed and nervous as he extricated himself from the mêlée resulting from two cavalcades coming together, head-on, at the junction.

"I was first off afraid for my horses," he admitted, "but now it's about my own neck I'm anxious," he added.

I must say the loose-rein riding of the French followers of the stag hounds was a revelation, and the care the horses showed in not getting their feet entangled in the dragging bridles was praiseworthy and something of an eye-opener to me. Of course, after seeing one or two *concours hippiques* in Paris, I had abandoned the idea that many Americans and all Englishmen have that no Frenchman can ride, much less sit his horse through a hunt. The riding of some of the French cavalry officers I had seen equaled, if it did not surpass, anything in the way of horsemanship I had witnessed anywhere, but the men and women who followed the Bonnelles hunt were not in this class, at least not on this day. I had to reserve my admiration for the horses and the way they avoided the dragging reins. There were only two spills as a result of this carelessness, and the results while painful were not serious.

In one of the lulls in the *chasse,* and there were many when the scent was lost, I enjoyed a chat with one of the mounted trumpeters who with their *fanfares* and flourishes directed, and indeed to the initiated, explained the activities of the day. I, though ignorant of their signals, could enjoy their trumpetings, and by not pushing myself forward avoided the pitfalls into which so many fell. There was a musical signal for every incident of the hunt, "The view halloo!", and the "Follow on!", "Lost!" How sad that signal was, but O! the joy of the *débucher*—"We have dislodged him again and he is running free."

I was struck, as often before and since, by how many things go on in France that the visitor but rarely sees. I had been in the country on and off for many years but had never come in closer contact with the "winders of the horn" than, say, the guards on Mr. Bennett's coach or Howlett's drag, and these men were flatly repudiated by my musicians of the curved horns. "We have," said the chief trumpeter of the Duchess, "more than a hundred societies in our federation and every year we come together for a prize competition in the gardens of the Tuileries. *La France, Monsieur,* is not what it was—*mais nous—nous gardons les traditions.*" It was probably on this account that in the following year the government of the Republic suppressed the musical tournament at which the mounted musicians of the sporting Duchess had promised to play on their curved horns for my especial edification *La Messe de Saint Hubert.*

The stag had been lost to view for some minutes and I hoped that he had made his escape, but this was not to be. What a difference there is between the pursuit of the crafty fox and the antlered deer! Suddenly the stag darted out of a thicket to where water was mirrored, but it was practically a mirage, a little pond of rain water, not a noble stream that would have promised safety. A wild halloo now arose and the curved horns of the mounted musicians brought riders from every quarter; even some of the stout ladies who followed in carriages, by what they acclaimed as great good luck, were in at the end.

For a minute or two the noble animal at bay, face to face with the yelping pack, gave a good account of himself. Several of the hounds had been tossed on his antlers and retired whimpering from the fray when the Duke intervened to save his pack from further injury and, as I thought, humiliation. One of the valets presented a carbine but the Duke, waving him aside, dismounted and strode out into the shallow pond with a great hunting knife bared. Knowing this was the end, the noble animal disdained to contend with man power. He lifted his head, gave one look about him at the forest scene, and then as the Duke stabbed him in the exposed throat, sank upon his knees, lowered his proud head and the hunt was over.

More knives now flashed in the air and the snarling hounds were regaled with tidbits. When *les honneurs du pied* were accorded me, I did not, I could not, refuse but I did squirm at the touch of the warm flesh. The Duchess understood and her eyes flashed approval. "I feel that way, too," she whispered. "When this season is over, I shall ask you to my boar hunt in the mountains. There I can tell you, gallant as he is, when one of *mes sangliers* is cornered, the Duke would not dare approach him cutlass in hand." But for me, at least, that hunt never came off. The government that had been so weak and ineffective was at last striking back at the Boulangists. And soon the High Court to investigate their alleged treasonable practices was instituted, and in Paris a man hunt was on.

Valets were on hand with champagne as the merry party disbanded. Everybody was charming and so gracious that even the amazed and decidedly insular Hensman had no further criticism to make as to the way the French hunted the deer. Indeed, we all promised to come soon again and have another brave gallop through the forest. Politics throughout the day were, of course, taboo, but frequent suggestions were made, not by any means closely veiled, that great political changes were impending. All were clearly convinced that soon a brave soldier and a gallant horseman would hold court at Fontainebleau and that, as with the Polish kings of old, all the courtiers would take their places in the royal circle—mounted!

7. A MAN ON HORSEBACK

SHORTLY AFTER my return from Berlin (in 1888) I was instructed to devote my whole attention to the Boulanger movement. Long ignored by the foreign press it had suddenly become of "cable" importance. True, nearly a year before, I had been presented to the "Le brav' Général" by my colleague and his warm friend Georges Laguerre. I had been struck by what the Press called the "*séduction personelle*" of this new figure in the political arena, but as my paper seemed to be little impressed with the possibilities of the movement, I did not follow up the lead. It afterwards developed that the Commodore had clashed with Count Dillon, the manager and closest adviser of the General, on at least one occasion. Dillon was a reckless speculator with a finger in every scheme that was launched upon the Bourse. Some episode of the cable war had left my chief with the impression that Dillon was a "four-flusher," and perhaps he was right, but as the sequel proved, men of his category often cause a great stir in the world before they are squelched.

So I came into the circle that was charmed by the brav' Général later than did a fortunate few. I did not witness his famous ride into Paris from the Longchamp review of the troops, nor was I present when escorted by all Paris he drove to the Gare de Lyon on his way to his post of exile at Clermont-Ferrand. No, I did not see the General on that great day when, as the Boulangist papers had it, "he refused to accept the Crown." But soon, thanks to the fact that the *Herald*, as an American paper published then in three world capitals, enjoyed an exceptional position, I was established in high favor at headquarters and could see the General whenever I wanted to. But I must confess the nearer view of

106

the wonder man furnished no explanation of the exalted position he then occupied in the hearts of his country men.

Of course, the General had an excellent war record. He had fought and bled in all the campaigns of his generation. As a mere boy he had led a company of Algerian tirailleurs in the Italian campaign of '59. He had taken part in the Indo-China battles and had distinguished himself at the hard fought encounter with the Prussians in 1870 at Champigny. From his command of a division in Tunis he had been called to the War Ministry in January 1886, but no plausible explanation for his selection could be offered. As a subaltern he had done his whole duty, but as a leader his fame could not be compared with that of Négrier and half a dozen other general officers who were left to vegetate in obscurity. It seemed to be the black charger upon which he pranced into popularity, and the chanson of Paulus,

"En revenant de la Revue
Je venais acclamer
Le brav' général Boulanger."

that suddenly converted the hero of distant wars into a national idol and caused him to be recognized as the man most likely to bring about the renaissance of France and re-establish her ancient glories.

In these days I had many talks formal and informal with the man of the interesting hour, both in his simple apartment in the Hôtel du Louvre and later on when he had moved to the luxurious house in the Rue Dumont d'Urville. On several occasions I rode with him and Count Dillon in the Bois. I described the General on horseback, at the races and in the seat of honor on the drag of one of his opulent friends. I pictured his chivalrous attitude toward ladies of all categories, and the winning grace with which he received committees from all over France who came imploring him to raise his standard frankly and save France from the yawning abyss.

I was pleased with this sequence of kaleidoscopic scenes in which the General's career was revealed, and cabled to New York day by day at great expense. What was more important, the Commodore was pleased, so when a critical dissenting voice came from across the Atlantic I was in a strong position. It came from Ed Flynn, an irascible Irishman who had been managing editor of the *Herald* for twenty years and who prided himself on the fact that he had not put pen to paper since wearing long pants! His plaint ran as follows: "Young Bonsal sends us daily generalities more or less glittering at a cost of thousands of dollars. He describes at length the General's seat in the saddle and the way he holds the reins when driving—but he does not give us an inkling about where he is riding. Now the American people want to know where he is bound. Then he describes political activities and a political organization extending all over France, but does the young man tell us where the money comes from? He does not!"

"Pay no attention to that fellow," said the Commodore after reading to me what he called "this diatribe." "If Ed Flynn had his way nothing would get into the paper but fires in the drygoods district and hold-ups on the Bowery. And, of course, he knows nothing about the niceties of statesmanlike procedure and he expects Boulanger to detail his program to the boys as though he were running for the Board of Aldermen from the 'gas-house' district."

I, of course, smiled pityingly and, tacitly at least, admitted what a handicap to us all this Flynn was. However, I do not relate the incident because I think he was wrong or because I had my little moment of triumph, but because in my judgment it offers a recipe, as it were, for the running of a successful newspaper for which so many are seeking, often at the cost of millions. Only a few months before I had heard Flynn, satisfied that the broad Atlantic stormed and raged between him and the terrible Boss, say, "That man Bennett is mad. He ought to be locked up. Why, if I let him have his way there would be nothing in the paper but long cabled letters from Morocco or Madagascar. To hell with those outlandish places and into the waste basket with those silly yarns from nowhere any decent person has ever heard about!"

This not always civil warfare between the absent owner and the man on the spot who thought the Astor House was the center of

the universe, Harlem far away and New Jersey a colonial possession, was waged with varying fortune for many years and, as
neither the absentee nor the man on the spot entirely prevailed,
the result was a stalemate in policy and a well-balanced newspaper
which enjoyed and deserved a great circulation and brought in
an income of approximately a million a year to its extravagant
owner.

But, while of course hot under the collar, I had the good sense
to profit by this rude censure. When next I saw the General, I told
him the American people wanted to get down to brass tacks, that
they were demanding to know a few facts, who was behind him,
whither he was bound, where the money came from, and what
obligations had been assumed in return for political and financial
support. The General flushed—this was a new experience for him
—but, at least, he gave me several straight answers and at last an
outline of a program that was widely printed.

"The money comes from my savings and about equally from
good people who live in great houses or in hovels all over France.
The most numerous contributors, I am proud to say, are men and
women who were born *sous le chaume* (in poor thatched cottages).
The total is not a great figure and it does not have to be, all our
workers being volunteers. When a man says 'I want to help clean
out the Augean stables' I do not ask him what his political antecedents are. I do not ask him if he has been an Orleanist, a Bonapartist, or what not. I do not reproach him for what political mistakes he may have made. There is no fear of ostracism because of
past offenses. But present day good-will I insist upon. I say to all,
'If you are ready to drop the petty differences of the past, and
how miserably petty they have been! then you are welcome. Let's
get together and save our beloved France from the waves of corruption that threaten her. When we have installed a government
of honest and patriotic men, it will be time enough to decide the
form that this government should take in the future. If you agree
with me on what is vital—the *bagatelles* we can discuss later.' "

My ears pricked up, as can be imagined when the General added,
"And they say that I have made no promises. They are wrong. I
have made a distinct pledge. I have told the various leaders of

groups who have approached me, 'I do not want your vote or your contributions as an Orleanist or as a Bonapartist, or as a "White," but if you will work to restore the national grandeur of France and to maintain the integrity of our frontiers I want both.' "

"And what was the pledge, mon Général?"

"There is no secret about this. I have told these people that if they place me in a position of power, no one of them will be punished for their former political mistakes. Mon Dieu! Who has not made them? Many think I make them every day. If I attain a position of authority there shall be given immediately complete amnesty for all political offenses and all political exiles will be invited to return. How long they will be permitted to remain will depend upon their conduct."

I, of course, thought the General's pronouncement admirable and would doubtless have thought so even if it had reached the public through a different channel. I considered his policy of conciliation wise and proper, but at the same time it was clear to me that when he came into power there would be differences of opinion and even a sharp struggle between the groups that were superficially, at least, united behind him for the moment. Most of the Republican groups expected him to play the early role of Cromwell. He was to be the Protector of democratic institutions long in the discard, while on one point at least the Orleanists and the Bonapartists were united. On the day of the downfall of the existing government, which many thought very near, they assigned to Boulanger the function of General Monk. He was, as trustee, to take over the impoverished and discredited state and then, as the Orleanists thought, place the rightful king upon the throne or, as the Bonapartists were confident, proclaim as emperor the head of the house that received the divine ointment and benediction on the battlefield of Austerlitz.

A few weeks after I became attached to the Boulanger movement, a wealthy American from Chicago and his charming wife, Nelly, friends of long standing, arrived in Paris. Billy, the husband, speculated in wheat, plunged on horses, and every now and then took a flyer in politics, and naturally enough he soon became interested in the General.

"The French are cautious and canny financially," commented Billy, one afternoon as we took our *apéritif* at a boulevard café, "but in politics they are ready for anything in the way of change —not even the sky's the limit. What I'm telling you is not from history books but from experience of a personal and convincing character. The first time I came to Paris eighteen years ago, in September, on the evening of the third to be exact, I went to bed under the Napoleonic Empire and on the next day I was living under the Third Republic."

He then asked me to present him to the General and this was quickly arranged. I had never seen the handsome soldier in better form. Never were his manners more winning, his beard more golden, his eyes more violet-hued; and Billy was captivated. On our drive back to the hotel he said, "That man is a great actor. He may go far." Then came the inquiry so natural to the business man who is not a stranger to politics, "And where does the money come from?"

"No one knows in detail. There is not much of it and it comes from many quarters. To begin with, the General is venturing his own small savings. Dillon admits he has contributed a hundred thousand francs, Déroulède has raised some money from the League of Patriots, and Madame d'Uzès is footing the heavy bills either on her own account or for Monseigneur, as she calls the Comte de Paris."

Once in his apartment Billy spoke more freely. "Change is in the air and in France, and anything may happen. We are sailing on Saturday and I have left over at the *Crédit Lyonnais* forty thousand francs that Nelly knows nothing about. Through you I am going to contribute that amount to the Boulanger campaign fund. When I return next year, if Ernest I, Emperor of the French, is in the saddle it might prove an excellent investment, and anyway I would get quite a thrill out of it."

Two days later, very early in the morning, while taking a fencing lesson from my Joinville Sergeant, there came a loud knocking at the door of my little *rez-de-chaussée* apartment in the Rue Cambon. Though disguised by plastron and mask I opened, and in rushed Count Dillon. He was breathless—and it must have been with excitement as he had had no steps to climb—and his rather bulging eyes were popping out of their sockets.

"Cher ami!" he shouted. "Cher ami! How can I thank you for that magnificent contrib—" Here I interrupted the voluble Count with a warning gesture. I had no idea what the politics of my Sergeant might be but in any event it was wise to play safe.

"Yes, I thought such a contribution, the American point of view as written by a man experienced in our politics, would prove interesting and that perhaps Laguerre would want to publish it —but, of course, I wanted you to look it over first."

Dillon immediately twigged the situation. "I find it not only interesting, but most helpful, and, of course, Laguerre will publish it." We talked about horses until the Sergeant left and only then Dillon returned to the incident which had inspired his unexpected visit. He impressed upon me the undoubted fact that from now on the General and he himself would be glad to see my friends at any time. "Just bring them along," he repeated, and then a word of explanation. "Cher ami! I hold, as I am sure you do, that only good can result from an exchange of thought and ideas between patriotic Republicans. Even though the great Atlantic flows between, there is, I am sure, a community of purpose that nothing can destroy."

I did not abuse the privilege so generously accorded me, and as far as I can recall I only presented to the General two more of my fellow countrymen. These meetings took place without anything happening worthy of note, and so far as I know no money was passed. Probably "Billy" of Chicago had set too high a record. The franc was a franc at that time and forty thousand of them meant eight thousand dollars, and in those picayune days that was a sizable campaign contribution.

I had had no reason to complain of my treatment hitherto by the general staff of the movement or at the hands of the brav' Général himself. They fully appreciated the propaganda value of the facilities which my paper afforded and they liked my generous appreciation of the news value of their candidate. But after this incident, and the contribution from Chicago, my status underwent a notable change. I do not exaggerate when I say that I

had now become the *enfant gâté* of the movement, at least so
far as the foreign press was concerned. On sight the General always welcomed me with both hands, and on at least two public
occasions he gave me the military accolade. However ignorant he
may have been as to the source of much of the money that was
now flowing into the campaign treasury in a fairly steady stream,
he evidently knew all about the American windfall and hoped
that the wind would blow steadily from that gold-bringing direction. Indications of my new importance came in the shape of invi-
tations to dine with M. Dugué de la Fauconnerie whose house in
the Rue Fortuny was the social center of the movement, and with
Madame d'Uzès, the premier peeress of France, who represented
the Boulevard St. Germain and the old *noblesse* in the campaign.
The dinners at the hôtel of the Duchesse d'Uzès were impressive.
Not seldom sixty or seventy covers with glittering service were
laid, and a footman in livery stood behind every chair, or so it
seemed to at least one of the guests. The gay Duchess always presided, and always with the Boulanger flower in her corsage. She
was ever bright and sparkling as became a woman who did not
have to drink champagne because that wine coursed in her veins,
and her sporting proclivities were emphasized by the fact that on
great occasions the coming of the courses was announced by trumpet notes. On at least one occasion the General was there and I
sat at the same table with him, though, of course, as befitting my
position I saw below the salt. That evening he delivered himself
of one of his very few impromptu utterances. "By the aid of Revision," he announced, "I seek to establish a Republic more tol-
erant, more honest and more democratic." There was, of course,
some applause and a little cheering, but it had a hollow ring for
we were in the very hotbed of those who worshiped kings.

The Duchess, charming woman! left nothing undone to brighten
these banquets, but it was uphill work. She was generally flanked
by the Duke de Broglie or the Duke of Vallambrosa, grave and
austere dignitaries of past régimes, and if anyone had been inclined to indiscretion there were always flocks of butlers and valets
hovering around. The cult that the hostess had for Boulanger was
very real and very sincere, there could be no doubt of that; but

on her horizon there were other remarkable men to whom she paid a full measure of devotion. Undoubtedly first among these men of the second line in her estimation was Rodin (wise man! though often bidden he never came to these banquets). When I blushingly admitted that at that time I was unacquainted with his work she became quite excited, and for a breathless moment politics were forgotten.

"Mon cher Peau Rouge," she cried. "He is our modern Pygmalion. You must see what he does to chunks of marble—they pulsate with life; they enjoy, and they suffer, *enfin* at his touch—they live." At the time I was too busy with the puppets of very human clay that were paraded before my eyes, and it was not until later that I saw Rodin's work. Then all these living actors and questionable shapes had passed from the scene, leaving hardly a trace behind, and only his great imperishable figures remained to reveal once again to those who are not blind that "Beauty is Truth, Truth Beauty."

At this moment the Duchess was the fairy godmother of the Boulanger movement. Once her heart was enlisted, without the least hesitation, she sold securities and mortgaged ancestral estates and poured the Pactolean flood into the campaign coffers which none the less were almost always empty. To restrain or in any event to supervise the uses to which the contributions were put, at the instance of the Duchess' great and good friend, the Comte de Paris, a committee was formed on which the Duke de Broglie and the Duke de la Rochefoucauld served with others to keep her generosity in bounds, for it was clear nothing could altogether restrain her lavish hand.

Several times after the banquets had come to an end and during the receptions that followed I had the opportunity to talk to the Duke de Broglie. Rightly or wrongly he was reputed to be the man who had sought through Marshal MacMahon to put an end to the Third Republic. While he subsidized not a few Royalist organs in France, he was noticeably wary of the American press. He would talk revolution, it was true, but nothing topical; it was the American Revolution he had in mind. Naturally he was very proud of an ancestor who had seen "Washington plain" although

he had reached America too late to share in the glories of York-
town. This eighteenth-century de Broglie had sat at the feet of
Washington in the camp at Newburg and came back to France
imbued with the ideas of liberty and fraternity that flourished
there. He accepted the French Revolution and commanded a division of Republican troops against the "Brunswickers." But his
name was too heavy a handicap in the sight of the new people and,
as his descendant put it tersely, "after losing his head in the political turmoil he was guillotined."

The Duke was a hard man to draw on the subject of the current revolution, but after I had read with interest and profit the
accounts which he had had privately printed of his ancestor's adventures in America, he departed from his reserve sufficiently to
let me know what was in his mind, and that was that the support
of Boulanger by the Comte de Paris, then in England, was an
exceedingly ticklish matter.

"General Boulanger with vigor and persistence," he explained,
"has adopted our traditional policy. For years the Comte de Paris
has insisted in all his manifestoes that the salvation of our country
demands the dissolution of the chambers (reduced to impotency
by corrupt politicians), and the revision of the Constitution, which
should restore our unhappy country to its former position. Under
these circumstances the *marche parallèle* could not be avoided and
will be continued by our groups but—" Here the Duke coughed
and when that was over he changed the subject. It was evident
that in his judgment the parallel march was approaching a fork
in the road, and the time was near when he at least would insist
upon bearing away to the right.

Undeniably the smaller dinners and the larger receptions at the
house of M. de la Fauconnerie in the Rue Fortuny were more
amusing and, what was also quite important, furnished more food
for thought and copy. They were mixed to a degree. In fact the
gatherings were often described even by those who frequented
them as a "*Macédoine de tout Paris.*" All who came were convinced that France was on the eve of a glorious revolution. There
were no footmen or valets about, and while the police were doubtless secretly represented no one seemed to give them a thought

and the most startling plans were unfolded and incautious words fell from every lip. Here I often met and talked with Maurice Barrès. He was an ardent but at times a critical adherent of the brav' Général. He gave me the impression that he, too, wondered why the General, who had really done so little, had become the man of the hour. And sometimes talking to himself but aloud, as seems to have been his habit, he would say illuminating things and one that I recall was "Boulangism—what is it? I say the collective disgust of all Frenchmen, who have unimpaired nostrils, at the *ordures* amid which we are compelled to live and breathe." At times Barrès did not conceal his belief that the General was slow on the trigger. Thinking aloud as to events in the recent past he said, "What opportunities he has missed! When all France was aflame with indignation at the way the Prussians treated Schnae-belé, he should have called upon us for a *levée en masse*. He should have led us to the recapture of Metz and Strasbourg," words which I repeat because they give an idea of the wild advice the General had so frequently to close his ears to.

Events moved very swiftly in the spring of 1888. M. Floquet with a following composed of moderate Republicans and so-called "Conservative" Radicals had become President of the Council of Ministers and, with what composure and votes he could muster, was facing the rising tide that demanded change and threatened disorder. Many people were saying that the polemic over the Constitution would lead to bloodshed.

Although, in his political platform, M. Floquet had pledged himself to a revision of the Constitution, he refused to accept suggestions made along this line by General Boulanger, who had agitated for revision ever since his entrance upon public life. The discussion that followed in the Chamber led to recrimination, and soon most unflattering epithets were being exchanged between the man of the "Black Horse" and the shrewd little lawyer who, according to his enemies, had entered politics "through the sacristy" * though what they had in mind when saying this I cannot recall.

On this occasion, for once in his life at least, M. Clemenceau

* Doubtless the fact that he had been educated in a Jesuit College. S.B.

was a peace talker. In after years he often told me that, having secured, for the first time since the fall of the Empire, a man whom he considered a real middle-of-the-road Republican to head the government, he was exceedingly reluctant to have him carved up like a turkey by the swashbuckling soldier, and that is what he feared.

In his campaign for peace, M. Clemenceau failed. According to the court that sat upon the question, the epithets that had been exchanged between Floquet and the General were of an unforgettable and unforgivable nature. They would have to be wiped out with a little blood, at least, unless apologies were forthcoming, and this, in the circumstances, with all France and the Boulevard sheets looking on, was unthinkable.

Many of the foreign correspondents in Paris, including myself, were present in the garden of Count Dillon where on July 13, 1888, the much-discussed duel finally took place. Paris was wild with excitement, and all the world was interested, for by this time *le brav' Général* had become a world figure, and a most disturbing one. I should here frankly admit that practically the whole corps of foreign correspondents in France had departed from the neutral attitude in political affairs they should have maintained, and in reviewing the situation now I can find some justification for this attitude. The government of President Grévy had fallen in disrepute. He and his associates were treated, at home at least, with deserved contempt. Details of the Caffarel and the Wilson scandals were on every lip, and Sadi-Carnot, the new President, was still unknown. In contrast to this the Boulanger movement seemed to many to promise a healthier and a more honest régime.

Be this as it may, we were for the most part at the time of the duel outspoken partisans of the General and of the vague program he advocated. It should not be thought for a moment, however, that we had any feeling of ill-will toward poor M. Floquet. Indeed, quite the contrary. We spent considerable time and thought in devising methods by which we hoped he could be extricated from his perilous situation with honor unblemished and physically unhurt. Some of the older correspondents could recall with sympathy the day, twenty years before, when M. Floquet for one dazzling moment had appeared on the political stage in a romantic role. It was in 1867, and Alexander II was making the first of those Imperial Russian visits to France which have always marked turning points in French history. As became a traditionalist and an autocrat, Tsar Alexander, with his host Napoleon III, made a respectful pilgrimage to the Chapelle Expiatoire, erected on the very ground where during the days of the Terror some of the guillotined royalties of France had been interred with their sheets of quicklime. All Paris in its best attire was afoot and shouting gaily and thoughtlessly, "Long live the Emperor! Long live Russia!" when suddenly, as the Imperial cortège passed his house, M. Floquet opened the window and shouted, "But I say, Long live Poland, Sir!" This was, of course, the Poland of the Revolution of 1863, to which the soldiers of the Tsar so recently had given a bloody quietus.

Upon this romantic episode the whole political career of M. Floquet was built up. But many years had passed since those stirring days, and while Floquet had become a leader in the Chamber and at the Bar, he had also become a roly-poly figure of a man, white-faced and meek of eye; as you beheld him you could hardly believe that this was the same idealist who in a moment of enthusiasm had dared to beard both the emperors as they drove their triumphal way through Paris to the shrine of monarchy.

On the morning of the duel, an historic moment if there ever was one, we were all assembled in the spacious garden at Neuilly, and the Countess Dillon, wife of the *brav' Général's* most confidential adviser (indeed many called Dillon his "inventor"), assisted by a group of charming young ladies in muslin dresses, dispensed cooling drinks. Between us and the rear garden, where the duel was to take place, there intervened groups of plants and shrubs, so though we were very near the field of honor we could not be accused of peeping at it.

We chatted cheerfully, and made the usual jokes about the dueling breakfast and who would be present and who would be nursing his wounds when it was served. But some of us, indeed many of us, were deeply concerned as to how the outcome of the combat would affect the General's fortunes. Not a few thought that General Boulanger at the moment was in grave danger, not of his life but of losing his reputation as an officer and a gallant gentleman. As I recall it, it was Campbell Clark of *The London Telegraph*, the dean of the Paris correspondents at the time, who first voiced our fears. He further announced that, in his judgment, so great was the danger that he had felt justified in telling Count Dillon that what was most at stake was General Boulanger's reputation as a *beau sabreur*.

"He must be considerate and merciful," insisted Clark. "I told Dillon that the French people were chivalrous and that our General must be careful to let the fat and almost blind lawyer come out of the encounter with but the slightest scratch, only deep enough to permit the termination of the affair."

"Oh, I hope, too, there will be little bloodshed, and that everybody will be able to sit down to breakfast, and soon," said the charming Countess. "My chef is on pins and needles; he wants to know when he should be ready to serve."

Suddenly one sharp-eyed observer in the front garden whispered that figures were moving up and down behind the screen of shrubbery, and then there fell upon our expectant ears the unmistakable clash of steel. But it only lasted a second, and then a harsh voice ended it with *"Halte! Arrêtez!"*

We, of course, commiserated with "poor M. Floquet," and thinking that now all danger was past, that probably the Prime Minister had received a scratch on his index finger causing a flow of blood sufficient to place him in a "state of inferiority," as the Code provided, we gave a more complete attention to what the Countess was saying about breakfast. And then, suddenly, to our utter amazement, through a circuitous path in the shrubbery two figures appeared. Yes, there could be no mistake, there was M. Floquet, without collar and coat, with his chest bare, walking towards us, the very picture of unconcern on the arm of M. Clemenceau, who was laughing in what seemed to us a most unseemly manner. The unseemliness of his behavior was also apparent to the seasoned duelist, but try as he might he could not suppress his mirth. Wonderful M. Floquet! He walked past us quietly, gravely saluting the ladies with a low bow. We were absolutely speechless and indeed remained so until M. Clemenceau, having turned the Prime Minister over to friends who were awaiting him in his carriage out on the avenue, returned to explain the situation and relieve our anxiety. Now that the Prime Minister was out of sight, M. Clemenceau became quite boisterous in his mirth.

"I am afraid your *brav' Général* is seriously wounded," he began, "but I must say he insisted upon it. This is how it happened. I said to Floquet, 'Cher ami, you are blind as a bat, you are at a tremendous disadvantage; as I see it, all you can do is to extend your sword-arm and he may—' and that is exactly what happened. Boulanger rushed on him like an enraged bull, and spitted himself on Floquet's rapier." Here all conversation was interrupted by a procession coming through the shrubbery. All lifted their hats, and even Clemenceau became serious, as two stretcher men carried the *brav' Général* by us with two grave-looking doctors following closely. The golden beard of the Paladin of the army was crimson with blood now.

How deep was the discontent in France and how strong was the hold that Boulanger had at this time upon the affection of the people was quickly demonstrated by the fact that the result of this ridiculous duel had little or no effect upon the General's political fortunes. For once ridicule, the most potent weapon in politics, failed, and as a dominant figure in the situation Boulanger became more powerful with every succeeding election.

I have gone into the details of this incident because it illustrates a side of the man's character which has generally been overlooked, and at the same time it gives me an opportunity to reveal how this breathless career of Boulanger appeared to M. Clemenceau on one of the few occasions that he exhibited the least inclination to look back upon it.

"The papers were saying," remarked M. Clemenceau on this later day of plain speaking, "that I had invented Boulanger and Boulangism. What they said was not entirely without foundation and I see that this view of the matter has lodged in some of the volumes that deal with recent history. When I came to the conclusion that Boulanger was a menace to the Republic, I felt that I should help get him out of the way since I had, as part sponsor at least, introduced him to the political scene. I suppose it is true that I tried to pick a quarrel with your brave General but he was wary and he avoided it, as he had the right to do, and then the lot to fight him came to M. Floquet and he fought very gallantly in view of his physical handicaps. Of course I never behaved on the dueling ground in the unfeeling way you seem to think I did, but if it amuses you—it is all right. There is far too little amusement in this drab world. But I will make frank confession. When the absurd outcome of the encounter did not kill General Boulanger politically, at least not immediately, I was puzzled and for a moment I thought I had been mistaken and that the people saw qualities in the man that were hidden to me. But in this instance I was right and those who pinned their faith to him were mistaken."

Almost from the very beginning of his political career the devotion of the General to Madame de Bonnemains had been an engrossing topic of gossip. As there was but slight if any attempt to conceal the General's visits to the little house in the rue de Berri, or his frequent absences from Paris in this lady's company, everybody knew about the liaison and discussed it volubly. There was little criticism of the General. In Paris at least, whatever the legal and family complications may be, all the world loves an ardent lover and it must be admitted that Madame Boulanger was a singularly austere and unattractive person and it was widely known that the tie that bound her to the popular soldier had for many years been merely nominal.

And in July the interest in this affair of the heart equaled if it did not eclipse the political aspects of the movement. The rumors of an impending divorce had been hushed in deference to the many Catholic adherents of the General, and the subject would in all probability have been dropped had not Madame Boulanger by her failure to observe *les convenances* at a critical moment outraged the feelings of *tout Paris*. Immediately after the duel, from which the General emerged so seriously wounded, Count Dillon hastened to Madame Boulanger and after informing her of the General's condition invited her to take her place by his bedside.

"I have nothing to do there," she answered dryly, "but I will send a good doctor."

Perplexed and not a little disgusted, Dillon then hastened to Madame de Bonnemains and she, throwing discretion to the winds, "without even putting on her bonnet," as the Boulevard sheets had it, hastened to her wounded hero. Public opinion in Paris blamed the wife and applauded the mistress and it was in these circumstances that the General, discounting the effect it would have upon his followers of the Right, sent lawyers to Rome and renewed his application for a divorce. But the Vatican turned a deaf ear to their appeal and the General was then compelled to have recourse to civil proceedings.

"Madame does not want to perform the duties of a wife," asserted the General. But Madame answered glibly, "Give me your arm, Monsieur, and let us return home," and that was the end of the civil proceedings and for the time being at least of all steps leading to a divorce.

Despite the duel and the impending divorce the General continued along his triumphant path to power. The *Vie Parisienne* suggested with fine irony that Madame d'Uzès should secure the Place de la République for her receptions and indicated that only the Parc Monceau was large enough to accommodate the new friends of M. de la Fauconnerie. The zest of these amusing and tumultuous gatherings was, of course, intensified by the favorable election returns pouring in, representing as they did in the eyes of the now frank conspirators so many milestones in the progress of the revolution.

In at least half a dozen departments scattered over France and representing every class of voters with ever-increasing majorities the General had won. The victory in the Charente took place in June and that in the Dordogne followed. True, the General was beaten in the Ardèche because (this at least was the official version) the simple peasants could not understand the orders that came to them from the Orleanist headquarters. While I kept it to myself I was of the opinion that, as this vote followed closely on the duel with Floquet, the not so simple peasants did not see how a soldier who had been disabled by a sexagenarian *pékin* could be expected to lead them with success against the Prussian hosts. The celebrations, both in the St. Germain quarter and in the Rue

Fortuny, passed all conventional bounds when the news came of the triple victory in the Somme, the Charente, and le Nord, all on one never-to-be-forgotten day. Now, at least, there was unanimity in the council chamber. By this series of astonishing victories the Revision policy and even more the *politique plebiscitaire* were justified before all men. Many thought that all was over but the shouting—certainly there was plenty of that. It was not thought premature for the deserving to begin to pick their jobs.

8. BOULANGER DISMOUNTED

As so often in the affairs of men, the Fates now intervened and presented a problem difficult for mere mortals to solve. M. Hude, the obscure deputy for Paris, died suddenly, and under the then existing law, a special election was ordered and all the voters of the Department of the Seine, about half a million men, were called on to choose his successor. The conservatives of his following, certainly all with Orleanist or Bonapartist leanings, were opposed to the General's entering the contest. His successes for the most part had been scored in the sparsely settled and conservative rural districts, or in the revolutionary industrial centers. These had no doubt been emphatic and the voters were impressed, but why hasten? Why tackle radical, socialistic, and even communistic Paris before you had to? Before the full force of the provincial victories was appreciated? For once even Rochefort was not enthusiastic for a forward policy.

His far from optimistic pronouncement infuriated those who, headed by Dillon, were opposed to the General running at all. The only thing that would justify him in facing the voters of Paris before they were fully prepared for the new gospel was the certainty of an avalanche of votes in his favor. "If we should pull through with a small majority," these doubters asserted, "that would spell defeat and the end of the movement." For once the General took control, and as the sequel proved, he showed excellent political judgment. Several times I heard him explaining the course he intended to pursue to those who opposed it, and finally he won them over, but had the result been different there were many who had on the tips of their tongues the refrain, "I told you so."

His defense of his course was admirable and I recall almost his very words. "I have presented my name and asked the suffrages of people who live in far away departments which I have never seen," he said, "and now when a vacancy occurs and an election is called in my home department, where I have lived for years, do you think I can dodge the issue? Would not all France say this man is afraid of the votes of his neighbors, the men who should know him best? Well come what will, I will contest the election."

The government of the day was not caught napping. They presented for the vacant seat a certain M. Jacques, a millionaire distiller and a staunch Republican. He was old, and an uninspired speaker, but he was willing to spend half his millions to secure a seat in the Palais Bourbon before he died; in cynical materialistic Paris and the environs, the government thought he would "go over big" and prick the absurd Boulanger balloon.

It cannot be said that M. Jacques welched on his sponsors. He certainly spent one hundred francs for every sou the Boulangists were in a position to disburse. And of course the distilling interest worked overtime and illegally in his cause. For days before the election every *débit de vins*, every drinking shop, and the saloons of the *marchands de vins* were so many centers and rallying places for the adherents of Jacques, and in most of them drinks and food and money, too, were dispensed freely and liberally.

But all to no purpose. Many who ate and drank and made merry on Jacques' money voted for Boulanger and when the polls closed they marched in their thousands through the streets of Paris shouting, *"Pauvre Jacques! Il est mort."* And as a matter of fact by eight o'clock, it was evident that politically, at least, M. Jacques was dead and by ten o'clock on the evening of the historic 27th of January, it was apparent that Boulanger was coming in. It was no longer a wave, he was coming in on the crest of a tidal flood.

On this historic evening, the adherents of M. Jacques made their headquarters at La Rue's, then, as now, a famous restaurant on the corner of the rue Royale and the Place de la Madeleine. When last I entered there, poor M. Briand was enjoying an abundant luncheon and pontificating about world peace at the very table where M. Jacques received the returns which ended his dream of entering the Chamber of Deputies. The Boulangists assembled at Durand's, just across the street, an equally famous resort of gourmets which, however, years ago succumbed to the competition of cheaper eating places.

As darkness fell, all Paris was afoot. There seemed to be literally millions of men, women, and children surging back and forth along the boulevards from the Place de la Madeleine to the Porte St. Denis. The narrow strip of asphalt between the rival headquarters was the scene of many clashes between the factions, and indeed fighting took place at other points. Several times, within my limited horizon, I saw that the Republican Guard was called in to support the police and clear the way for traffic. Excitement was mounting and a general outbreak of mob violence was expected, when suddenly an avalanche of returns came in from Belleville and other workingmen's quarters which made it quite certain that *le brav' Général* had been elected and indicated the wholly unexpected majority of a hundred thousand.

The lights were out in La Rue's on the moment and M. Jacques went home, but thousands upon thousands of voters kept rushing up and down the boulevards, many of them intoxicated with the liquor which the defeated candidate had so generously distributed. As they marched, they sang or rather shouted the slogans with which they capped their victory, and several of them still run in my memory.

"Malheur! O! quel malheur
De s'appeler Jacques!"

This finally blended into a funeral chant which ran:

"Hélas! Pauvre Jacques! Il est m-o-o-o-rt!"

In the expectation of stirring events, I had dined that evening at Durand's. The general staff of the movement *au grand complet* was present, and as the returns became more and more favorable, all differences as to policy vanished and on many sides I heard the opinion expressed that the moment had arrived for a *coup d'état*.

Time and again little Naquet sprang on a table and bellowed out inflammatory sentences. One that had popular acclaim was, "Not only is Jacques dead but also the Government! Let's bury them together!"

Soon the restaurant was invaded by thousands who came to congratulate the victor on the very field of battle. The General stood at the head of the stairway and his admirers, old and new, filed past him. It was a marvelous opportunity for him to show his power of *séduction personelle,* and judging by results the General exercised it to the limit. Some, as they passed by, were too much a prey to their emotions to say anything, but others whispered, "Mount your black horse, *Mon Général,* and lead us on! We will place you where you belong!" To all of which Boulanger answered with playful gestures of mock reproach, but he was pleased all the same, as who would not have been with Paris at his feet!

About half-past-eleven all the members of what might be called the steering committee of the movement withdrew into one of the upstairs dining-rooms. After a short confab several of them came out in search of the General, but for some minutes they could not find him. Finally one of the English correspondents related that for purpose unknown he had lent the General his "Macfarlan," as the Parisians call a tweed ulster, and in this disguise had seen him slipping out a side door. Soon the General reappeared, however, and explained that he had had a delightful incognito walk down the boulevard to the office of the *Gaulois* where the Duchess d'Uzès was hearing the returns, and there he had, right in the flush of triumph, thanked her for the sinews of war which she had furnished so generously.

The general staff grabbed Boulanger and all disappeared in the improvised council chamber and four or five strong-armed men were placed on guard outside the door. In the streets the monotonous refrain about the death of *"pauvre Jacques"* had died away, but thousands were shouting, "The Government is dead! Let's cart it away." Others were making the welkin ring with the cry, *"En avant, Mon Général,* Paris will follow wherever you lead!" Outside by the iron grille of the Madeleine church a commissary of police stood with two score of the most villainous-looking plain-clothes men that I have ever beheld. Now and again when the obstreperous paraders hustled him he would pull back his coat and expose his scarf of office and, what was more unusual, a brace of pistols stuck in his belt. This was Clément, an officer frequently selected for unusual work and wholly devoted to the régime in power. It was rumored and afterwards verified that he had with him a warrant for the arrest of the General in case he should by some overt act or indiscreet speech justify its use, but I very much doubt that had he served it he could have held his man.

True the *place* behind the Madeleine was filled with mounted detachments of the Republican Guard, and as far as one could see up the Boulevard Malesherbes it was blocked with platoons of police. Troops too, according to reports, though I did not see them, were cached in all the courtyards of the adjacent houses, but the loyalty of these men was in my judgment questionable. Many of the agents were certainly fraternizing with the mob and not a few were drinking with the Boulangists (*Pauvre Jacques* still doubtless paying the piper!), and of the mounted men not a few had the red carnations, the General's flower, in the headgear of their horses.

In this critical moment in the history of the movement and perhaps indeed of France, while the course of the next few minutes was being debated behind closed doors, many striking remarks were made and some of these have passed into the permanent chronicle of the day. According to all accounts, in the council Naquet, Rochefort, and Laguerre urged the General to send for the "black horse," to don his uniform and lead his devoted adherents on to the Élysée Palace. Undoubtedly the General replied, "I am against a revolution, especially when it is unnecessary. We are coming into our own by legal methods. Why take illegal steps and cause bloodshed?" The words of this discussion came to me second-hand but what I heard with my own ears, confirming this decision, follows. It was a few minutes after midnight when the council dissolved and, again disguised in tourist ulster and a great broad-brimmed hat pulled down over his violet eyes, the General was whisked away by a side exit. As the lieutenants and advisers now trooped down the stairway into the great *salle* of the restaurant, it was not difficult to divine the decision that had been reached or the fact that there were some who were displeased with it. The men who wanted the General to carry out the "mandate of the people of Paris" and seize the reins of government had been defeated. Those who wanted the General to bide his time and continue to float with the favoring tide looked pleased. As they appeared, I came close to Rochefort, the man of the barricades, and Thiebaud, generally regarded as the Bonapartist member of the Committee. Rochefort looked angry and Thiebaud depressed. I had often noted, as was natural, that these men were none too friendly but now, jostled together in the crowd, they became quite affable.

"*Cher ami*," I heard Thiebaud say to the fighting editor, "I think that for some minutes now our friend's star has been on the wane." Rochefort nodded his head wearily and then Thiebaud went on: "*Cher ami,* what is the hour? It is important that I should mark the time and I have left my watch." Rochefort pulled out from his waistcoat pocket a handsome open-face timepiece. Reading it Thiebaud said, "Twenty minutes after midnight." Smiling sardonically, Rochefort added as he turned away, "But it is at least an hour too late."

The uproar and the jollification lasted until daybreak, but after this I had no hesitancy in taking a cab to the Bourse and sending a rush cable to the effect that there would be no further Boulanger news that night. Had I not been over-cautious, I might have added, "and for many days to come." *

* Other and more important correspondence than mine was leaving Paris at this moment. In his life of King Edward VII, Maurois quotes from a letter that was sent off to the then Prince of Wales by General de Gallifet, his constant correspondent, who dates it, "In the first year of the Boulangerie." The unfortunate Prince in these feverish days was not allowed for obvious reasons to visit Paris officially, but he did slip over every now and then and was seen on at least one occasion climbing the Eiffel Tower with Lady Warwick, then known as the "Babbling Brook."

"The Boulangist party" writes Gallifet, "is composed of 160,000 socialists, communists, convicts who have escaped, and souteneurs and street sweepers whose pay the General has promised to raise." Then in the next paragraph: "Today the Conservatives, whether Royalists, or Bonapartists, are alarmed by the victory of their *protégé*. They have started something they cannot stop. They have builded

There was a lull in the campaign after the decisive victory in Paris. The General relapsed into masterly inactivity, as some thought, while not a few maintained he was neglecting his chance to strike while the iron was hot. For days the General disappeared from view and it was soon known to almost every man, woman, and child in the gay capital that the victor at the polls was spending his first real honeymoon with Madame de Bonnemains at the famous inn of *la Belle Meuniere* in Royat. Of course, the General was surrounded by spies at this time and equally, of course, not a few false friends had crept into his entourage. Some of these were known and were utilized for the dissemination of misleading reports and yet not a few were successful in concealing their real activities. On the other hand, in the various ministries, and particularly in the office of M. Constans, the most forceful member of the cabinet which Rochefort was denouncing in his paper as the "German Ministry—selected in Berlin," the General had agents who were devoted to him.

It was one of these men who, wittingly or unwittingly, furnished the information upon which the General based his unhappy decision to leave Paris. By all accounts on the last day of March this man brought to headquarters the facsimile of an order for his arrest which was to be served at daybreak on the morning of April 2nd. There are many melodramatic and not a few fantastic versions of this incident, and as to their truth we now know little more than we did then, which was that the French government was of two minds as to the advisability of active steps and of taking the bull by the horns once and for all. All this was gossip in the air and a wide field for conjecture was open. However, some facts were available that foreshadowed drastic action. The trial of Paul Déroulède and his fellow members of the League of Patriots had commenced and the law instituting a High Court was before the

---

stronger than they planned. *Pauvres Gens!*—The two most beautiful duchesses in France, Mesdames de la Trémoille and d'Uzès dined last evening at the Café Durand to be the first to congratulate Boulanger. They were in the company of all the barber-assistants in Paris and this experience was shared with them by Messieurs de Breteuil, Hallez-Claparède, Sagan, and others." The General is wrong about the dinner-party which took place in the editorial rooms of the *Gaulois* but the letter reveals quite a different point of view from mine. S.B.

President for approval. The Procureur General in office had declined to bring these cases up for trial and he had been forced out, and M. Beaurepaire, a more complaisant official, had taken his place. Startling rumors of impending events were rife and it was probable that shortly again the movement would become front page news.

While, as far as I could see, the General was walking very circumspectly and all his political activities, in public at least, were well within the law, the cafés on the boulevards were suddenly flooded with rumors that acts committed in the recent past had been unearthed by the *mouchards* of the indefatigable M. Constans and that the arrest of the idol of Paris would not be much longer delayed. It was true we all knew that during a recent secret trip to London the General had chatted with the Comte de Paris. But what was the harm in that? It was explained by his partisans that when Frenchmen meet on foreign soil they should drop all political differences. And what was more natural when two soldiers met, who had both been dismissed from the army, despite their gallant services, than that they should exchange words of sympathy and regret over their broken careers?

But unfortunately information had reached the desperate government of the day, of a much more serious imprudence, all the details of which were later verified. While still on active service and in command of the army corps in the Clermont-Ferrand area the General had slipped over the Swiss border in disguise and spent an afternoon with Prince Napoleon, the Bonapartist pretender, who was constantly attacking the French Republic in his manifestoes. Later, when he too was living in exile, the General explained that he had yielded at this time to a desire to see the kinsman of the Great Captain but that national politics were not discussed. "The Prince showed me the sword which the First Consul carried at Marengo and told me that it would be mine when I restored Alsace-Lorraine to France—that was all."

It was not strange that M. Constans should take a very different view of the incident. He was reported to have said that the indiscretion of the Duc d'Enghien was trivial in comparison, a mere bagatelle, for which, however, he paid with his life. It was also not strange that by many these words were interpreted as meaning that the government was preparing to drag the General before a drum-head court-martial and shoot him at dawn in the dry moat of the historic Vincennes fortress. It is certain in any event that they exerted a disastrous influence upon the course of the Boulanger movement.

To run down these rumors, to secure some definite information if I could, early on the morning of April 2, 1889, despite the driving rain and the intermittent hail and sleet, I drove out to see the General. Joseph, the little mulatto groom who always knew more as to what was going on than he should have, told me that the General was not in, and then excited my suspicion by adding that he did not know when he was expected back. Joseph, like most little grooms, remembered past favors and had a lively anticipation of *largesse* to come, and so it was not long before he took me in a corner and whispered that the Master had gone away for a few days and, in all probability, could be found at the Hotel Mengelle in Brussels.

So the *brav' Général* had run away! The rumors to this effect which we had denied with such emphasis three weeks before, now, at least, were true. As I drove back to the boulevards I felt that this was the end of the Boulanger movement, but in any event decided to be in at the finish. Shortly before noon I reached the Gare du Nord and boarded the express for Brussels. I carried with me a bundle of the midday papers and also Blakely Hall, the roving correspondent of the *Sun*. I had come across him in the courtyard of the Grand Hôtel where I had gone to study the time-tables. He was in a melancholy mood, protesting that he had cabled Laffan for permission to return to New York, as in this benighted country he could find nothing to write about. Acting on the impulse of the moment I said, "If you come with me you will have plenty." And he followed me blindly and it was only an hour later when we were clear of Paris that I told him what had happened.

It was dusk when we reached the old-fashioned hotel in Brussels and the clerk in the bureau assured me that General Boulanger had not arrived nor was he expected. Our prospect was not very alluring and Hall snarled out something to the effect that tips from little colored boys were not invariably reliable. For some time we sat out in the damp courtyard sipping vermouth and wondering what the next move should be. The hotel seemed nearly empty, but in a suite which opened out on the courtyard the lights were blazing and voices pitched in high key reached us. I went to the office and asked for connection with the long distance telephone to Paris which had only been opened a few weeks before, and was told that it was in use and probably would be for some time. I took my seat outside the booth, but the occupant certainly tried my patience. He was not skilled in the then new art and the doors were far from soundproof. At last, however, he emerged and I thought to recognize the man as one of the Boulanger henchmen, but I did not know him. Instead of taking his place in the booth I followed him upstairs, entered a drawing-room right behind him, and there found myself face to face with General Boulanger!

Whatever his real feelings may have been, the General greeted me in a friendly manner and then sank back apparently exhausted in an armchair. He was hot and tired and his hair, usually so docile, was in great disorder. He said he had been telephoning to Paris a manifesto to the people of France explaining his action, and he begged me not to mention his arrival in Brussels until the formal announcement was made at his Paris headquarters. This I agreed to and it was only several hours later when our Paris bureau got word to me that the General's flight was published in the last edition of the *Temps* that I filed my dispatch.

About ten o'clock the General sent for me. He was now alone in the same drawing-room where I had discovered him, but the door to the adjacent room was ajar and in there people were stirring about and conversing in low tones. For once the General had lost his aplomb which generally stood him in good stead. His talk was discursive, but it was soon apparent that he wanted to fathom my reaction to his sudden change of base. He emphasized the fact that he had only left Paris on the advice of his most trusted advisers, and while I think he was sincere the impression he sought to convey was certainly misleading. The truth of this complicated matter I was only to learn some days later, but as here it falls into its proper sequence, I shall tell it now.

Nearly a month before, or to be exact on March 12th, convinced that he was about to be arrested under a charge of high treason, the General called in Laisant, Laguerre, Naquet, and several more of his closest advisers and told them that he was leaving Paris in a few hours. They, from all accounts, went to great lengths in combating this resolution, but when the General remained unshaken, for the good of the party and out of personal loyalty, they sat down and put in writing warm approval of the course which verbally they had been opposing for hours.

Several of these loyal letters the General placed in my hands and while I noted that they were dated some three weeks back, as I was at the time ignorant of the first clandestine flight from Paris, this seemed to me only to prove that the departure had been under consideration for some time. As a matter of fact, the General on this occasion had been in Brussels with his lady for twenty-four hours, but listening to the pleading of Rochefort and Count Dillon had then returned and both the flight and the return had been so cleverly managed that none of the foreign correspondents had the slightest hesitancy in declaring that the rumor of his flight was a contemptible campaign lie.

After we had threshed this out, to the General's satisfaction at least, he gave me an opportunity to express my opinion as to the situation with which he was now confronted, but I was not eager to enter upon a discussion and as I was sure, however heavily I might sugar-coat them, my views would be unpalatable, I said nothing.

He then gave me an epitome of the manifesto which he had so laboriously telephoned to Paris for distribution to the papers. "In it I have informed all Frenchmen of the reasons which have forced me to withdraw myself from the reach of the desperate men who are now in control of the Government. I have informed them that I shall return to France before the elections, indeed just as soon as our people are fully aroused to the tyranny under which we are living. I left Paris because I had learned that a warrant had been issued for my arrest and that in a few hours I would be dragged to Mazas prison. From there, if I was ever to emerge, I was to be brought before an illegal tribunal to be tried and undoubtedly convicted of crimes that I never committed. For the time being, the Deputy of Paris was not safe in the capital. All the laws of traditional immunity from arrest having been violated, I am forced to accept the hospitality of a friendly people, for a few days at least."

There was much that was sound in the General's contention. Even I, who thought from the first that he should have faced the music, and accepted as cheerfully as possible the risks inseparable from the career of the political adventurer, never denied this. M. Constans, the new Minister of the Interior, was a desperate fellow. In fact, it was his reputation for what we were pleased to term "frightfulness" in those milk-and-water days that had recommended him for the job. Many were convinced that once he was placed in Mazas prison the General would never be seen alive again. According to persistent rumor a certain stubborn king in Cambodia who stood as an obstacle in the path of M. Constans, when he was Governor-General in Indo-China, died quite suddenly and, as many thought, mysteriously. There was a tremendous outcry but, after all, there was nothing to do but to give the poor man a magnificent funeral and to this Constans contributed most generously. Of course, there would be an indignant protest from the voters if the recently-elected Deputy for Paris was arrested on flimsy charges, but if the Deputy died, and deputies are like other mortals, all that could be done would be to give him a state funeral. This line of thought was suddenly interrupted by a direct question from the General whose repeated hints had failed to draw me.

"Now what will be the comment of the foreign press? How will the step I have been forced to take be judged in England and America?"

There was no escape now. I admitted that the dangers of the General's position in Paris had not—could not be exaggerated. I conceded that Constans was quite capable of energetic measures, but— It was hard to go on and yet the General insisted. "On the other hand, you are technically guilty of desertion in the face of the enemy. You have left your troops on the firing line." Of course, I softened this blunt statement of fact as much as possible, but even so the words were ugly and the General winced, as well he might.

"Then you, too, would advise me to return to Paris?" he inquired. Evidently this suggestion had already reached him.

"On the first train," I answered. "If your trip here cannot be concealed, then you should say important business brought you to Brussels. If you move quickly, you can be back in your home early tomorrow morning and then the *Cocarde* could say that the whole thing was merely a *poisson d'Avril,* an April Fool's day jest." At this moment the door that had stood ajar was pushed wide open and Madame de Bonnemains slipped in and, without paying any attention to the General or me, took up her post in a window recess.

A rather awkward pause then ensued. The General lit a cigarette and strode up and down the room. Soon Madame de Bonnemains emerged from the window recess and placed her hand caressingly on his shoulder. He smiled brightly. "You know our frank friend from America," he added, and she bowed although, as a matter of fact, I had never been presented and indeed this was my first near view of the unfortunate woman who was being called with increasing frequency "the *femme fatale* of the man on horseback." Later, it became apparent she helped to dismount him and at this critical moment she certainly opposed with all the arts at her command his return to Paris, but unlike most other chroniclers of the movement I think she had absolutely nothing to do with inspiring the unfortunate flight. She simply came along as was only natural in the circumstances.

On this nearer view Madame de Bonnemains was by no means as prepossessing in appearance as when seen at the races or when driving around the lake in the Bois behind her pair of spanking chestnuts. She was quite a little taller than the General, her figure was not good and her movements were rather ungainly. Her eyes were red with weeping and her face was lined with weariness. Her lips were trembling with anxiety. Evidently during the clandestine trip from Paris, in fear of possible arrest every minute, the poor woman's nerves had given way. It was, of course, an unfair moment to make an appraisal of the lady's charms, but she was certainly lacking in all the traditional graces of the Parisienne. Doubtless, as so often is the case with the *femme fatale,* her power of seduction was mental rather than physical.

I now rose to go, but with a somewhat nervous laugh the General detained me. "Thanks—a thousand thanks—for your frankness—but I shall now repay you in your own coin. What you say is, of course, the opinion of the Paris press that has always, and not without reason, opposed my mission. May I say you have been in Paris some time and perhaps have been impressed by the attitude of that press? And, *mon Dieu!* How natural that is. Again I thank you for your friendship, but what I would like to know is how the foreign press will judge the step I have taken. But I suppose I shall have to wait a day or two."

An idea came to me almost before the General had finished. "There is," I said, "downstairs an American correspondent of many years' service on a great New York paper. He is far more influential than I am and because of his longer service he is much more competent to speak for the American press than I am. In his whole life he has only been one week in Paris and he has never read a French newspaper—well, because he does not know a word of French—and I can vouch for the fact that he has never come in contact with a Parisian journalist—"

"Why, that's our man," interrupted the General, and I went after Hall. When I returned a few minutes later Count Dillon, who had brought the fugitives back from their first runaway, was with the luckless pair. He had just arrived from Paris and while, as always, he sought to exude confidence, it was plain that he was greatly worried over the latest development on which it was clear he had not been consulted.

Dillon approved of our plan of putting Hall on the witness-stand, as it were, and in a few minutes the General had stated his points very clearly and I followed with my argument as briefly as I could. I translated the General's statement to Hall and every now and then Count Dillon put in a word (he had a perfect command of English from his Irish ancestors) which indicated, or so it seemed to me, anything but absolute approval of the General's course.

When all the evidence was in, without a moment's hesitation Hall began, "I assume you have asked me to express my opinion with a maximum regard for truth and a complete disregard of courtesy." When this reached him, the General bit his lip but nodded assent. Hall went on, "Of course there is much force in the General's contention. It would have been unfortunate for the cause if he and his most energetic and useful lieutenants had been clapped into prison, but these are I think professional risks which patriots cannot escape when they seek to overthrow a crew of usurpers."

Here Hall evidently wished to stop, but the General urged him to continue. While he hesitated, Dillon sought to stave off the unfavorable verdict which clearly impended.

"Will not the foreign press say, in approving the move to Brussels, that the General who alone knows the plan of the campaign must not be permitted to expose his life on the firing line?"

"I think not," answered Hall emphatically. "At least, not in America. In America they will say that the General has abandoned his men in the face of the enemy—under fire. Of course, it is unjust and unfair but that is the way of the world. The General should return immediately to his headquarters. Once there, his people should protect him." Evidently Madame de Bonnemains understood English, and before Dillon began to translate these words burst into tears, and was sobbing convulsively when the General led her out of the room. Before the door closed we could hear the voice of the frantic woman saying again and again, "Pay no attention to them, Ernest. They do not love you as I do," which was, of course, perfectly true.

When he returned, the General was calm and collected, but obviously depressed. Again he thanked us both for our frankness and expressed the hope that we were mistaken. As he escorted us downstairs, Dillon explained how the General had been suddenly confronted with a very difficult decision. "But I am sure he has acted wisely. Now that France knows what desperate and unscrupulous measures are being considered, our citizens will rise in their might and insist upon fair play. Then it may be expedient for the General to return to Paris and place himself under the protection of an awakened and aroused people." Turning particularly to me, Dillon continued, "Do you not recall what our enemies said after that silly duel? The movement was dead. It would be smothered in laughter and ridicule." "I do," I answered. "No, the movement will move on," he added, "because it has its roots in the heart of a great people."

Hall thought differently. Saying that he took no interest in post-mortems, he left by an early morning train for Paris while I stayed on for nearly a week, watching the battle that ensued between the leaders and the lieutenants of the various groups as to the course it was wise to pursue.

For days the adherents of the "man on horseback," whom I now considered definitely dismounted, gathered in Brussels to cheer their leader, and almost without exception to advance arguments which they hoped would induce him to return to Paris. They came singly, two by two, and then in larger groups—Naquet, Laguerre, Barrès, too, I think, all the lieutenants of the movement except Rochefort. In his paper the militant journalist maintained a dignified silence, but personally he let it be known that he had washed his hands of the General. As to the movement, that was another matter. Rochefort had been instrumental in bringing the General back to Paris after his first breakaway, but the second?— No, he was through.

The still faithful leaders sat around in disconsolate groups in the cheerless courtyard of the hotel. They brightened, of course, and exuded optimism when a representative of the press appeared. At these times Naquet was almost invariably the spokesman. When he thought he was unobserved, the strange little man with the swarthy skin, long dishevelled hair, the bent shoulders that gave him the appearance of a hunchback, was bowed down with grief and disappointment, but when the occasion demanded it, he spruced up wonderfully and nothing but the most undiluted optimism fell from his lips: "When the people of France awaken to a full appreciation of the crime which was planned, our General will be invited back to Paris by universal acclaim. It was his duty to safeguard his life from that murderous crew who for a moment have usurped power which they are using with criminal purpose."

M. Naquet was slated to be Minister of Foreign Affairs under the Boulanger government. I recall a statement he made at the time when, as spokesman, he was outlining the policies of the group: "I would arrange for a general disarmament of the powers and then the blessing of universal peace will descend upon Europe —and upon the Americas too," he added as an afterthought.

I applauded the goal of the Senator's policy, but I could not follow the course by which he proposed to reach the happy conclusion. Some of the steps which he proposed taking seemed clashing and contradictory to me. This was quite natural, I suppose, then, as now, when every day we are told that no American can understand European politics. I am afraid this was true then, and is true now, and this want of understanding has cost us dear.

But at times the Boulangists would make the courtyard of the hotel ring with their campaign songs. Not seldom they became vocal merely to keep up their spirits, but more often it was to welcome a delegation from Paris or speed the departure of some distinguished visitor. Generally the war chorus was led by the inimitable Paul Déroulède, with his handsome but rather foolish face.

It had a fine swing to it, their marching song, and it seemed to inspire the singers with renewed confidence in their cause and their leader—at least while they were singing. And as I remember, it ran something like this—

> *Il reviendra*
> *Quand le tambour battra.*
> *Quand l'étranger m'nac'ra*
> *Notre frontière.*
> *Il sera là,*
> *Et chacun le suivra.*
> *Pour cortège il aura*
> *La France entière!*

which in doggerel reads—

> He will come back
> When the drums beat.
> When the stranger
> Menaces our frontier.
> He will be there,
> And all will follow.
> Behind him will stand
> All France.

To me, these demonstrations were not convincing of the high hopes of the singers, and on the last evening of my stay in Brussels, a police officer appeared and announced that, while he knew nothing about French politics, or when the General would return, of one thing he was quite certain, and that was that if the uproar continued, the General would be expelled from Belgian territory.

The following morning I returned to Paris and reported to the Commodore. "Boulanger is *ausgespielt*," was his terse summing up of the situation, making use of one of his favorite expressions which was also the only German word he knew—and the next day he sent me to Russia.

I was back in Paris on a short vacation from the Balkans a year later. For the most cogent of reasons—my limited resources—I ate at the Taverne Anglaise in the rue Boissy d'Anglas not fifty steps distant from Durand's where, fifteen months before, General Boulanger had tasted the intoxicating wines of success and balked at the decision which might have led to triumph.

Besides the economic there was still another reason why I, at this moment, affected the lowlier *taverne*. Just across the narrow street beautiful Lily Langtry had an apartment and from time to time, generally about noon, she would dash into this hostelry to have a late breakfast or an early lunch, and when this happened she brought into the dingy place the fragrance of fresh spring flowers and the sweetness of newmown hay.

But this day she did not come and perhaps I was inclined to be critical when Jules brought me my eggs. They were not what they should have been, they were certainly not above suspicion and, sniffing them as he took them away, Jules admitted the justice of my protest. *"Ma foi,"* he said, *"Monsieur* is right. These eggs are *bien Boulangistes."* I was thunderstruck. A few months before the name of the "man on horseback"—the man of destiny, was a talisman to conjure with. A million of his fellow citizens had voted to place unlimited power in his hands and eight million more impatiently awaited the opportunity to do so. Everyone in France with but few exceptions wore his flower, the red carnation, and now his name was used to designate a category of eggs which all self-respecting restaurants and clients spurn!

This was the last of my personal Boulanger experiences. I never saw the General again, but history adds a footnote to his story. Twelve months later, deserted by his fairweather friends and now almost ignored by the press, General Boulanger, in Brussels, blew out his brains on the grave of Madame de Bonnemains who had died after a lingering illness a few weeks before.

In my judgment of the movement and its leader, I differ from many writers. I think Boulanger was an honest man and sought the security and the well-being of his country. Many millions passed through his hands and he died without a sou. He was admittedly a gallant soldier and yet he exposed himself to the charge of cowardice, because by so doing he thought to safeguard the movement over which he had been called to preside by the suffrages of the great majority of his fellow citizens who had had an opportunity to vote on the question.

I have read many of the "revelations" that have been published in Paris of recent years as to what happened behind the scenes and as to who pulled the wires of which the General was but the mechanical puppet; but they have in no way changed my opinion of this unfortunate man. He was, of course, unequal to the task he was called upon to perform, but he tried to do his duty as he saw it and as hundreds of thousands of his countrymen pointed it out to him. I readily admit, however, that men of this luckless category often contrive to do much harm.

I never saw again the sporting Duchess, Madame d'Uzès, "the

angel" of the Boulanger movement, though she lived to be nearly ninety and was always active in what she considered good causes. But during the Peace Conference in Paris, I came in contact with one of her closest friends and so learned how it had fared with the gallant lady during the many intervening years. "Of course the collapse of the Boulanger movement was a great blow to Anne —and left her embarrassed financially. She hung on to the stag hounds, naturally, but for a long time she could keep only four footmen. But, poor dear! she never complained and hated to be commiserated with. Once I heard her answer an aged friend, who was also a kinsman. 'You should have thought twice before you threw away that pot of money, three million francs!' he insisted. 'As you say it was a lot of money—but not too much I think to pay for a *beau rêve,*' was her answer."

9. THE STORY OF A GREAT BEAT

I HOPE to disarm the censorious by frankly admitting that the incident I am about to relate, long since forgotten, or only remembered by the members of an ever-narrowing circle, was not a great journalistic feat at all. It did not change the map of Europe, it did not even dislodge the Prime Minister involved, although many thought it would and not a few that it should. But James Gordon Bennett, my honored and greatly feared chief, thought it was a "great" beat and I certainly was the last one to gainsay him. The achievement had a tremendously favorable influence upon my fortunes at a moment when they were frankly precarious. The matter has been on my conscience these many years and today I gladly admit how passive was the role I played in what was accepted as an extraordinary achievement. My lucky star was in the ascendant, and that is all there was to it.

There were, I have no doubt, thousands and tens of thousands of the readers of the *New York Herald,* in those days a world power, as it was published daily in London and Paris as well as in New York, who did not even deign to read the article, but Mr. Bennett did, and this fact tided me over a critical period when some of my colleagues, many of them more deserving, were left high and dry on the lee shore of unemployment in strange lands. Not a few of my brilliant successors in the field of foreign service will, at least at first off, assume that in dwelling upon my interview with the Austrian Prime Minister I am making a tremendous pother over nothing and trying to endow a molehill with the majestic proportions of a mountain, but I hope on second thought they will absolve me of attempting anything so silly.

Of course I realize the situation as it is today when our foreign observers are pestered with the incessant attentions of prime ministers, and I also know how many of them are forced to rent private chambers because they are so constantly harassed in their official bureaus by the visits of ministers of foreign affairs and other high officials. But in the era I recall and seek to portray, things were different. Indeed they were very different. What relations there were between mighty officials and the occasional peripatetic or stable newsgatherer were, despite the blowing of the mighty de Blowitz, extremely tenuous and often clandestine.

A few months before the mysterious feat upon which I am at this late date endeavoring to shed a little light, when the Emperor Francis Joseph was informed that his son the unfortunate Crown Prince Rudolph, to whom he had forgiven, according to report, all the sins enumerated in the Decalogue, and a few others, had visited the Concordia Club and there hobnobbed with press men, the Emperor announced sternly "That is the unforgivable offense," and according to all reports he never relented one jot of his displeasure even when the unfortunate heir to the throne he was never to ascend, pleaded, and indeed proved, that he went to the club for the purpose of securing press notices, not of himself but for his patriotic volume *Austria-Hungary in Word and Picture* which was just off the press. So I hope you will believe me when I conclude by saying that in that day, whether by divine right or merely by the exercise of police powers, a "divinity did hedge about kings" and also their mighty men, and that they lived far aloof from meaner folk, particularly far aloof from writers for the press.*

* Very shortly afterwards this period closed, and we of the Fourth Estate came into our own, and perhaps even a little more. Two years later I spent three intoxicating (in more senses than one!!) days at Friedrichsruh with Prince Bismarck as his guest. But perhaps my greatest triumph came some years later, in 1915, when I was in Berlin and Wilhelmstrasse was reaching out for friends. I arrived at the Foreign Office quite late for an appointment with Baron Mumm von Schwarzenstein, the former Ambassador to Japan and Washington who was in charge. I excused my lateness by saying, and it was quite true, that I had been unable to secure a cab and had been compelled to come on foot. At this time, while it was not generally known, to conserve benzine the public cabs had been reduced to one hundred for Greater Berlin. Of course it was not desired that this economic measure with its many implications should be cabled to the Western world. And

I was playing the fool one evening in Vienna, (nothing unusual about that I must admit) but on this particular evening I was playing the fool in very distinguished company. It was, in fact, *Narren-abend* when everybody plays the fool. I had gone to the masked ball at the Kunstler-Haus with my old teacher Erich Schmidt, who was to become in later years Rector Magnificus of the University of Berlin. At this juncture he was lecturing in Vienna on Goethe and as I was, at least up to this time, the only American who had ever attended his courses, he was literally consumed by a desire to make me a *Goetheaner*. In moments of enthusiasm, and he suffered from them frequently, Professor Schmidt pictured me as his apostle in America, preaching the gospel of Goethe from the Hudson to the Columbia. He admitted that I was still weak on the subject, but he amiably recalled that some years before he had given me a high rating for my thesis entitled "From Walther von der Vogelweide to Klopstock."

We had a very good time, and when we unmasked, many of the roisterers greeted me amiably, showing that I was not unknown as a result of my eight weeks' stay in the Kaiserstadt. Of course I had been industrious, I had gone to the races every day they were run on the Freudenau and I had missed but few of the dances at Ronachers. My Polish friends, and there were many present at the ball, addressed me as "Stash" in French or German, while the sportsmen and race-horse men of the Jockey Club talked to me in an English that smacked of Newmarket. And then all at once a woman who was still masked—she was posing as Diana the chaste huntress—hailed me with the unmistakable accent of a foreigner who had lived a considerable time in the cosmopolitan quarters of New York. "Hello, New York Herald, " she said, "have you any news from old 'Subito'?"

There was an empty table nearby and there we sat and discoursed

---

so for the ten days I remained in Berlin, until I went to the Eastern front, one of these hundred cabs was stationed at my hotel all day and far into the night. To all others it was *besetzt;* it only awaited my coming and the best of it was I only had to pay for the running time and not a *heller* for the hours it stayed there awaiting my pleasure! I have always regarded this incident as the most significant illustration of the changed attitude of the German government toward the foreign press even when inadequately represented as it was by me.

about "Subito" at some length. She was evidently a foreigner of Slavic extraction and she spoke New Yorkese to perfection. She did not know "Subito" as well as I did, although she admitted frankly that during a dark six weeks of her transatlantic career she had taken all her meals at his place on Eighth Street. Good old Subito! what a bond of camaraderie his name was, and how we laughed at his menus in retrospect, though I confess to be confronted by them was no laughing matter. It is perhaps fair to say that nobody ever ate at Subito's unless starvation was staring him in the face. His restaurant was not to be mentioned in the same breath with the mysterious Solari's just around the corner on University Place, or with Madame Marinelli's, a lady from Siena who dispensed excellent food and sound Chianti on Fourth Avenue near Twelfth Street. The great attraction about Subito's was that, while the food was bad, the prices were fixed and low and you were allowed to eat all you could stomach of his food for twenty-five cents. And further, Subito was the most trusting man I ever met. With him your signature, anybody's signature, went.

For at least half an hour the masked lady and I ate over again the dinners in faraway New York of which we had so frequently partaken at adjacent tables. And remember, these were not stodgy, table d'hôte dinners at which you had to eat what was placed before you; it was not that way at all. You had your choice of several soups, at least three entrées, and two roasts; there was no limitation of any kind except on the bread supply, which clients were inclined to attack ravenously towards the end of the repast. The lady had forgotten the why and wherefore of Subito's, and why we had given the little quick-moving, reddish-haired Italian from Piedmont this name. It was simply because if you did not like the food that was listed and asked for terrapin or for a haunch of venison, a buffalo tongue or a shoulder of bear, the little fellow would shout *"Subito!"* ("Immediately"), and would shortly reappear with something that bore at least a faint resemblance to what was asked for.

We had a number of good laughs about Subito, and while my fellow citizen by adoption was one of the last to unmask, she certainly had nothing to hide or be ashamed of. She had great brown eyes, a pale Slavic face, masses of black hair, charming dimples and an inclination to smile indulgently. I recognized her, though for the life of me I could not recall her name, but this embarrassment was soon relieved. As she unmasked, Lady Diana said, "New York Herald, please forget my real name, my New York name, I mean, and if you don't mind, call me Lady Hamilton."

I assured her that this would be easy, that it was a most suitable name and that it was a thousand pities that Romney was not alive and here to paint her too. She said that Haydukevich was at the moment engaged in painting her portrait, but that he made her look like a horse. The same gentleman was a famous horse painter and I promised to boot him for his inefficiency when next I came across him at the races.

But Lady Hamilton's thoughts went back very willingly to the little cellar restaurant on Eighth Street. She teased me about Carlotta, the dancing girl from Milan to whom I would send bouquets of flowers, although this recklessness on my part compelled me to eat for weeks on end at Subito's, and as I have said that was no joke. And also about Loie Fuller, who could dance even then but who had a consuming passion to act tragic roles such as Camille and Adrienne, snatches of which she would try out on the sawdust floor; and she also recalled the stately Miss Williams, with whom Loie lived on Fifteenth Street just off Union Square, where we often adjourned and smoked and cast each other's horoscopes until the dawn of a new day penetrated into the dark and narrow street.

We were having a splendid time indeed when suddenly Lady Hamilton became serious and inquired, "New York Herald, what are you doing for the paper?" This was not a welcome turn to our conversation, but I gave an honest answer, a full and faithful account of my laborious days. How I read, and that was no joke, the *Neue Freie Presse,* the *Tageblatt,* and the *Fremdenblatt* with all their editions, and how I subscribed to Nevelinski's sheet with its political correspondence from the Balkans, and how I sat, in the few moments of the day that were left over, with the polyglot correspondents of southeastern Europe who day and night foregathered in the Café Central and talked and talked.

"New York Herald, that's old stuff, anybody can do that. Now, you ought to interview the Prime Minister."

"Gracious lady," I whispered, "do not say that out loud. It might reach James Gordon Bennett. You know he has wonderful ears. I don't mind your saying it—but if he once got that idea in his head—well!"

"It would certainly please Tiger Jim," she said. And I knew now, if I had had any doubts before, that Lady Hamilton had listened to the talk at the *Herald* table at Subito's.

"I am going to think about it hard," continued the unmasked Diana. "It would be a great feather in your cap."

"It certainly would."

"Well, I'm going to see about it."

A little later, when we had drifted apart, I had a good laugh about Lady Hamilton's proposal, for it had really come to that. She was a downright thinker and a forthright talker with just this little bit of humbug. It was too amusing! Interview Count Taafe, Minister-President of Austria, Prime Minister of the Holy Roman Empire, a courtesy title to which they had no legal right since the days of Napoleon but to which he and his predecessors had clung tenaciously.

However next day in the saddling paddock at the races, Lady Hamilton bustled up, dismissed her Polish cavalier, and whispered to me, "I am working on our plan, it may be arranged soon or it may take a little time, but arrange it I will. You leave it to me."

"I certainly will," I promised.

But the miracle came off. Three days later I was looking out of the window of my entresol over Madame Forsati's flower shop on the Kärntner Ring, wondering what in the world I should cable next to the insatiable and far too frequent editions of the *Herald*, when, suddenly, there was quite an uproar at my door, and the frightened maid ushered in a gorgeously uniformed flunkey with an impressive looking envelope covered with seals which he insisted that I should sign for *eigenhändig*—with my own hand—in a formidable looking book. I signed and gave the fellow five florins. I tried to be calm and so I was, at least outwardly, until he was gone. This was the first official communication I had received since my arrival in Vienna. Poor Magda, the maid, had gloomy forebodings: "Jesus-Maria," she said, "I hope the Herr Graf has not gotten into trouble. Have you been striking a *Beamten-person?*" I broke the seals, saw that the communication was from the Präsidium or the cabinet of the Prime Minister, and my unbelieving and uncomprehending eyes read as follows:

"His Excellency, Count Taafe, Minister-President, etc., etc., begs me to say that if Herr von Bonsal, correspondent of the New York Herald, would trouble himself ("sich bemühen") to call at eleven o'clock on the morning of Thursday, it would give the Prime Minister great pleasure to welcome him to Vienna."

With the knowledge that I alone had of the great event that was impending, I kept my own counsel, that is, up to midnight before the day when Western journalism and the Prime Minister of Francis Joseph were to have their first encounter. Then I ran into a charming old gentleman, whose name was Shanhowski or something like that, and he was the correspondent of the *Tzas* or *Times* of Cracow. He had been very helpful and friendly to me, so I told him what was in the air, and he begged me to let him have the first look at my copy if anything was said about Poland or the Polish group in the Reichsrath. I assured him I would let him have a carbon of the whole thing, but that he must credit it to the *New York Herald*, which he promised to do, and did.

When the fateful Thursday morning arrived, I did not dress in topper and frock coat, preparations that were in those days indispensable preliminaries for a visit to the Ball-Platz. I had heard that the Prime Minister was careless in his attire, some said even slouchy, and I thought it wise not to oppress him with my magnificence. When the hour arrived, I engaged my favorite *Zwei-Spanner* on the Kärntner-Ring. "Jahnni" was terribly disappointed when I did not give the word to go to the races or the Prater, but when I said "Präsidium of the Minister-President, Herrengasse," he brightened and called me "Herr Graf" while hitherto I had been addressed by him as Herr Baron, which merely connoted the possession of wealth. The Herrengasse, where you enter the bureau of the Prime Minister, is a narrow affair, and the moment after "Jahnni" halted his fiery Hungarian horses with a great clatter, we were shooed into the tranquil courtyard by a gigantic creature in a three-cornered hat, a long yellow ulster covered with decorations, and carrying a great staff which reminded me of the formidable batons of the drum-majors at home. I was immediately ushered upstairs to the *chef de cabinet*, who seemed embarrassed, as though he were doing something he had certain doubts about; and then a moment later I found myself face to face with the great man, who certainly did not look his part. He came towards me with a slouching stride, and as he motioned me to a seat I noticed his fine black eyes, his straight black hair, and the innumerable wrinkles on his high forehead, the marks of many an anxious moment, the scars of many a political battle. Right out of the box, he asked me if I was Irish, explaining that he heard that they were very numerous and influential in America. I admitted that I was not, and then the Prime Minister went on, "I am an Irishman, but my people have been here for nine generations."

He was pleased when I assured him that, thanks to the *Almanach de Gotha*, I knew that he was still Baron of Ballymote in the peerage of Ireland. He then asked me if my name was not French, and I said no, and in a spirit of mischief I explained that the sound of names is often deceptive. "For instance, with us," I explained, "according to our nursery rhyme 'Taffy is a Welshman.'" With commendable tact, however, I suppressed the following lines which in my nursery, at least, ran:

> "Taffy was a thief,
> He came to my house
> And stole a piece of beef."

The Prime Minister knew no English, and as he did not volunteer French, our conversation went on in German, and his German was pure Viennese. I liked it, but when I reported a particular Viennese expression he used to my friend and mentor, Erich Schmidt, a few days later, he was filled with horror, and said *"Der Kerl!* Minister-President of the East Realm and he makes three grammatical mistakes in one German sentence! No, I beg pardon, it was not German. It was hog-wash." But whatever else they may have been, his words were all grist to my mill.

After we had gossiped along for a moment or two, and he had explained that he had never heard of any Welsh Taafes, the Prime Minister insisted that his people, though absentees for three hun-

dred years, retained many of the characteristics of those who are born
on the "Ould Sod." "That is," he explained, "we are all fond of the
grog and of horseflesh, and not at all averse to getting into debt."
He thought my chair was uncomfortable, and drew up another, and
as he did so I noticed that he was wearing a shockingly shabby pepper-
and-salt suit of clothes, and that his trousers were very baggy. And
then, to my dismay, the Prime Minister began to talk Africa which
at the moment was very much in the news. He wondered whether
Tippoo Tib was a great rascal or merely the stage villain of the day.
Of course I had to let the great man have his head, and we talked
for some minutes about the Dark Continent of which he was even
more ignorant than I. He envied me the fact that I had shaken hands
with Stanley, and when I told him that the great correspondent had
even guided my toddling feet he asked any number of questions. It
dawned upon me that the mighty minister was turning the tables and
that I was being interviewed. This would never do, so politely but
firmly I brought him back to southeastern Europe which after all
was his and my concern of the moment. And then, and only then, it
was that we reached the discussion of the present state and the prospects of the Dual Monarchy for which I had come.

Our interview was far from plain sailing. The Prime Minister
was evidently averse to illuminating the topics of the day. Frankly,
indeed, he asserted his inability to do so, and continually he would
turn back to the earlier pages of his personal history.

"You see," he complained, "I was never cut out for a politician,
much less for a statesman." And with this he lifted his arms on high,
emphasizing his repugnance to the thought with a *Gott bewahre.*

"I was meant to be a farmer, only cruel fate has made me a bureau-
crat. Still I have a farm and I raise pigs."

"The gentlemen who pay the taxes?" I inquired.

"Not always," answered Count Taafe sadly. "Not when you are
an absentee and do your farming by correspondence. My career began in this way. It chanced that my mother and the Archduchess
Sophie, the mother of my August Master, were educated in the same
convent school, and out of this many things have come, among others
the fact that I was named after her little boy at a time when, as you
know, he seemed to have but little chance of ascending the throne.

Then came the '*wirr-warr* of 48,' I think Treitschke calls it that. Metternich the mighty had to take refuge in England and the Archduchess who, as you know, was a very clever woman, substituted her young son Francis Joseph for Kaiser Ferdinand who had not risen to the occasion.

"I had been for many years the young Emperor's *spiel-kamerad*. The Archduchess had given us an acre of land out at Schönbrunn, and there we raised vegetables together, and played hide-and-seek among the bushes. When later my playfellow became my August Master, he insisted that I should take the State examinations and so enter the official class. I was doubtful about the outcome of this, and not without reason, but Franz—" Taafe was smiling now, most affectionately and ignoring all titles—"said he would help me over that stile, and he did.

"In a very few years I was Statt-halter in the Tyrol, and that was very pleasant. The people were most *gemütlich* and never gave any trouble to anybody, and Franz would come every year to hunt the chamois and shoot the *capercailzie* and so we were *spiel-kameraden* once again. But now things were going from bad to worse in affairs of state. Far from settling century-old controversies, the Ausgleich with Hungary in 1868 had started an uproar that soon had all the peoples of the Dual Monarchy, not at swords' points, it is true, but immersed in language problems that we had forgotten existed. The people of the Tower of Babel were unanimous in comparison with the councils of the Austrian peoples. Even the Czechs now recalled that once upon a time, centuries before, they had had a language of their own, and they resurrected it. They did not stop at that; some clever rogues among them invented a literature, classic songs, epic poems and ballads galore, but in this they went too far even for a folk intoxicated by racial pride and prejudice. It was not long before one of these people, an obscure school teacher whose name I do not recall, came out in the open and proved that all these epic poems were apocryphal and that the manuscripts upon which they were based were modern and rather clumsy forgeries! *

* This obscure teacher whose name the Prime Minister could not recall was probably Professor Masaryk, who at the end of the Great War founded the Czecho-Slovak state and became its first President!

"But the craze for the ancient language and the venerable traditions persisted and even my old friend and neighbor Gregr (the father of the Young Czech movement) came to see me and began to orate in that disinterred language. I said '*Mein lieber*, I can do better than that,' and I went after him in the two or three phrases from the Erse which the Taafes brought with them from Ireland (the only thing they did bring, by the way, except their good humor), and had handed down from father to son. So the good Gregr was forced to talk German for the business in hand, but only this once he assured me would he so demean himself, and as a matter of fact he never came again.

"For ten years now my policy has been one of *versöhnung*, of reconciliation. I seek to moderate our racial antagonisms. It has been a long and often weary task but who can deny that it has worked well? My purpose and my practice has been to bring the hostile racial groups together. I try to seat them around my conference table. The result has not always been completely successful but no murders have taken place (rows yes! and plenty!) since the outlook is improving and indeed I think it is promising. Mine is a *utilitäts-politik*, a policy which I hope will be worth while for all of us. I hope to see the more boisterous and selfish of the national groups dissolved, and indeed I believe the day is near when no one of them will pursue an opposition policy merely for the barren pleasure of being in the opposition. Of one thing I am quite certain, the adherents of my utility policy, the number of those who are working for the common good, who are tired of bashing their heads against the hard wall of stubborn facts, is increasing.

"*Anhänglichkeit* to Francis Joseph is my battle cry, and loyalty to and belief in the purpose of our patient Kaiser is the keystone of my program and my policy. You can tell as well as I can, and perhaps better, if this policy and program is proving successful. Of course the danger of war hangs over us as always, and that is a menace to any program of internal peace, but in my judgment the outlook for peace was never brighter. I am hopeful, though I cannot say that I am confident, we have gotten past the era of barbarous wars and yet alas! we cannot—we should not—forget that *Krieg kommt*

wenn am wenigsten erwartet (that war comes when least expected);
—at least so it has been in the past.

"I became Minister-President in 1879, ten years ago, and what have I done?—nothing very much, nothing very good, and I hope, nothing very bad. The comic papers say I am an acrobat, and double-jointed—that if I came face to face with a political principle I would not know what it is. I do not think that is fair. I have at least one political principle, that is, *Kaisertreue* (loyalty to the Emperor), faith in and devotion to my August Master. I have, I think, been very frank and aboveboard in speaking to and in acting for all the diversified people in our conglomerate Empire. I have commiserated with them each and every one, and I think I have shown an understanding of their joint and also their especial problems. I have said very frankly that it was a great misfortune for us all to have been thrown together as we have been by the fortunes of wars and by dynastic marriages. Many historians have said, and truly, that Austria-Hungary was not an empire but a geographical expression, and someone said, perhaps it was Kaunitz or perhaps it was Metternich, that if the Empire had not been welded together by the force of circumstances, it would have had to be invented. I always kept an open mind on these vital matters. All the leaders must admit that I have listened to them patiently for unending hours. I have asked them 'Have you anything better to offer' and in the end they had to admit they had nothing better. We must hang together, disagreeable as that undoubtedly is, or be swallowed up by our more homogeneous neighbors, and few want that.

"I have always maintained that our political and racial situation was anomalous, and conceded that it was unfortunate for all concerned. I have frankly admitted that in these circumstances it was impossible to develop and enforce a system of government that would be equally acceptable to all our ethnic factors, to the Syrians, the Slovenes, the Czechs, the Tyrolese, the Ruthenians, the Italians and above all, to the Germans; and then there were the Jews! Herr von Schönerer,* who as you know, holds forth every evening just

* Curiously enough Adolf Hitler's obscure father was an ardent disciple of Herr Von Schönerer, the outstanding illiberal Liberal of his day and to his son,

around the corner in the Michaeler Platz café to his National-Germanen! used to come to see me with his proposition, which he said would bring happiness to all. 'Let's kill five hundred Jews and then the rest will run away; then we would have their business and all be rich and comfortable.'

" 'But, *mein lieber*' I replied 'they wouldn't run away. They have looked the whole world over and they know that there are no people in the world as financially incompetent as we are, so they remain and batten on us.'

"And the Germans, the *Uralte-Germanen*, they say, 'Just look at Hungary across the Leitha. There the Magyars are not in a majority, mixed up with them are millions of Roumanians, Croats and Slovaks and a host of other savages, but they do not give them any recognition and so why should we have to knuckle down and share the government with all our wild tribes?'

"Well, I answer, we should and must because we are a civilized people and the Hungarians—" Here again the Prime Minister raised his arms with his expressive gesture and whispered again his *Gott bewahre*—"I grant you they raise good horses and make excellent hussars, but they are savages, at least half Turk and only about five per cent of them know how to read or write. Well, in the face of all these difficulties, I have generally been able to retain in the Diets and in the Reichsrath a working majority for a sensible middle course. I have given each nationality what they wanted in so far as the others would permit me to do so, and when the 'wild ones' have gotten out of hand, why my August Master has never hesitated to dismiss these unreasonable assemblies. Fortunately, the Germans are easily divided and I have generally gotten by with the doctrine of *Kaisertreue*, and it may go on for some years more.

"I claim that I am not a mere opportunist. I am increasing everywhere, as quickly as our finances permit, the educational facilities and opportunities of the people. Of course, I will not favor Slovene or Czech schools with Imperial funds. Why should I? Only

---

who seeks to destroy what remains of public law in Central Europe, he bequeathed his anti-Semitic, Pan-German and perhaps his pro-Hohenzollern creed. Never was it more true than in this instance that, "The evil that men do lives after them; The good is oft interred with their bones."

our enemies wish to have the Tower of Babel continued and extended. How can a man make his way in this hard world if these are
the only languages he speaks? We are a polyglot people and speak
many tongues, but I never knew a man who had completely mas-
tered and was absolutely at home in more than one language. Slowly,
it is true, but without a backward step, I am lowering the property
qualifications and extending the franchise. From America we are
getting unexpected help in this matter. Many of the former emi-
grants from the Austrian lands return from your country, with ideas,
with money, and best of all, with some experience in self-govern-
ment. And those who do not return send money to their less enter-
prising kinsmen, and that is helping us immensely. Today America
is very popular in every village, and many families bless her because
of the butter they are having on their bread. I admit it was not always so. For years my August Master thought that the government
in Washington could have saved his dear brother Max from execution at the hands of the Mexican rebels, but all that was cleared up
long ago."

At this time the members of the Polish group in the Reichsrath
from Galicia were riding the Prime Minister very hard. They were
becoming very arrogant, insisting upon being the tail that should
wag the dog. "What is to be done about that?" I inquired.

"Things might be different," said the Prime Minister, "if I lowered the franchise there as I have done in Upper and Lower
Austria—" He looked out of the window and reflected for a moment
and then added, "If I am not mistaken, there are a lot of people in
Galicia who are not Poles and apparently do not love them."

These words, I thought, were the key to the mystery of the interview; at least it is the only one I have ever had. This was perhaps
the word of warning he had wanted to let drop. We had chatted
now for more than an hour when, as the Count did not dismiss me, I
dismissed myself. I tried to make arrangements for someone in his
confidence to look over my transcript of the interview, but he would
not consent to it.

"I have confidence in your discretion. You will not let anything
slip in that could be distorted by my enemies or by the enemies of
Austria, and after all, all that I have said is a few words of welcome

to the first American correspondent who in my day has come to Vienna." And very graciously he added, "You are heartily *willkommen,* and when I can do anything for you, let Baron M. . . . know."

I only bothered him on one occasion. It was for permission to see the Emperor wash the feet of the selected beggars on Maundy Thursday, and the invitation was immediately forthcoming. I took the best of care of the translated Irishman who had given me his confidence with what amounted to amazing recklessness. Curiously enough Count Taafe went down to defeat on presenting the measure which he outlined to me as a possible club over the arrogant heads of his, at the time, Polish allies. Four years later in October, 1893, he introduced his Reform Bill which extended the franchise to anyone who could read or write in his mother tongue and had been domiciled six months in the voting district. The opposition was immediately very noisy and unfortunately it did not die away. Many groups agreed that the new legislation would take power away from the well-to-do and give it to the indigent, and so it did.

The Poles saw that it meant the end of their supremacy, that Galicia would go Ruthenian, and it was their vote that killed the measure and ended the Taafe era. The Count, tired and more than willing to go, sent in his resignation and went back to his beloved pigs before the adverse vote was taken. He was succeeded by Prince Alfred Windischgrätz who, for all his promises of hitting out from the shoulder and nailing his colors to the mast, in a few days was compelled by the various blocs to form a coalition ministry. Supported principally by the Clericals and the supple Poles he carried on for about eighteen months and then fell. As an acrobat he was not in a class with Count Taafe. Perhaps I am mistaken, but as a matter of fact in looking over the notes of my talk with this long-forgotten statesman, I seem to recognize why Treitschke called Austria-Hungary "a devitalized state" and why, now that it is fallen apart, all the wise men in the world (much less the Hapsburgs!) cannot splice it together again.

While this circumstance had but little influence upon my career, which to me, of course, was a most important feature of the situation, I should not omit to say that the Taafe interview created an uproar in the Austro-Hungarian press. The statements that it contained and the fact that it was given at all to a transatlantic interloper, were severely condemned, the opposition was up in arms and many of the Prime Minister's adherents were displeased. Had Taafe not been a gentleman, as well as an Irish peer and a Count of the Roman Empire, this tradition-breaking interview might have proved disastrous to me. For reasons of policy it would have been wise for the Prime Minister to say at least that my report was filled with inaccuracies, and that, of course, would have fulfilled the *fromme wünche* of so many of my colleagues in Vienna who were being hauled over the coals by their respective editors.

But as I have said, fortunately Count Taafe was an honorable man. He sat tight and said nothing. To many hopeful scribes his silence seemed to give approval to the whispering campaign which was soon under way, questioning the authenticity of the interview. I breathed more freely when the *Fremden-Blatt,* in confidential relations with the Foreign Office, republished the interview, but I held my breath when on the following day the *Vaterland* put the interview on the first page with headlines, the most flaming I had ever seen in Vienna, and which read, "History and Plans of Count Taafe as told by His Excellency to the Correspondent of the *New York Herald.* A remarkable interview which as *yet* has not been denied."

I was urged by many to secure in some way an official approval of the interview, but I am happy to say that I did nothing. It seemed to me that the matter was entirely in the hands of the Prime Minister. He had been reckless and I had been reckless. If an official denial were forthcoming I could not disprove it. There was nothing on paper except the invitation to call. As to what had been said, it would be the word of the Prime Minister against that of an obscure correspondent. I lived anxious days and the *Vaterland* and several other papers added to my anxiety by insisting in almost every issue that, of course, the interview which was so surprising in its tone as well as such a complete departure from tradition had not been officially confirmed. It was in one issue at least surmised that the imaginative effort of the American correspondent would shortly be denied, and it was even suggested that the sooner this was done the better it would be for the impaired dignity of the government.

This crushing statement, Taafe being the gentleman he was, proved my salvation. The Prime Minister issued a communiqué which reached me first by wire from my good friend the editor of the *Tzas* of Cracow to whom I had given the *primeur* of the interview as far as the Austro-Hungarian press was concerned. It was very generally published in all the papers of Central Europe and of course in the *Herald* was triple-leaded. It ran, "I have not a word to say in regard to my interview in the *New York Herald* except to praise my interviewer's intelligent comprehension of my ideas and the phonographic accuracy with which my words are given. I shall stand by everything I said and also by my interviewer because, though he had a splendid opportunity to launch canards and indulge in exaggerated statements, he confined himself strictly to a painstaking and accurate statement of what passed between us."

For reasons which I was only later to fathom and which were even then admittedly out of all proportion to the importance of the achievement itself, Bennett was most enthusiastic over the interview. In a somewhat excited and staccato telegram from Beaulieu, he even called me his "young Murat." "Eight weeks in Vienna and you interview the Prime Minister!"

Then came a letter from the business manager urging me, *mirabile dictu,* to send on my expense account promptly. "This *coup* must have cost you a pretty penny," he wrote. "And we had better have the items passed by the Commodore while he can deny you nothing, while the hot fit is on."

I had never had an opening like that and I have never had one since. In the circumstances I behaved with moderation. I gave a dinner at Sacher's to Lady Hamilton of some thirty covers, and in arranging it I gave the famous Frau Sacher *carte blanche* and she certainly availed herself of it. We had a private dining room that was embowered in flowers brought up by special courier from Bozen. Lady Hamilton made a speech and a Polish prince whose name I forget thanked me with tears in his eyes for bringing into the clear light of day the real sentiments of the Prime Minister. Later, when the fun was coming fast and perhaps a little furious, a perfectly strange man, wonderfully attired, wandered into the room. It was quite evident that he was a *bischen angeheitert,* but amiably so. On his head he wore the *federbusch* of a staff officer of high rank, but as he had laid off his tunic and appeared in his undershirt it was impossible to determine his rank or the arm in which he served. Below the waist he was fully attired, booted and spurred.

"N'abend meine Herrschaften" he bleated to the assembled company, and then to me he extended his hand, "Servus—your servant."

Tilly and Willy Sandrock of the Burg-Theater, before whom he came to a halt, were suddenly strangely subdued and embarrassed. They seemed about to rise and make a court curtsy when Frau Sacher rushed into the room and, grabbing the interloper by his bare arm, began to lead him away.

"Verzeihens," she whispered. *"Es ist nur Der Otto* (it is only Otto) and he has just lost his way, that's all. He's giving a supper tonight to some of the dancing girls from the Theater an der Wien and has just lost his way."

I had not recognized the Archduke in this strange attire, or rather want of it, though I had often seen him at Baden and at the races, but there was no mistake about it now. The amiable intruder was the Archduke Otto, the second son of Francis Joseph's much-married brother Carl Ludwig, and the father of the little boy who, upon the death of his uncle the old Emperor in 1916, was to become the Emperor Charles. He was by all odds the handsomest of the Archdukes of the House of Hapsburg-Lorraine, and in saying this I am doing but scant justice to his personal appearance. By this time I had seen as many as thirty of them, and they all had horse faces, but "their Otto" was tall, with a graceful figure and wonderful eyes. Soon Frau Sacher came back with the apologies of the Archduke, which she said he was too embarrassed to deliver in person.

"Er thut sich furchtbar langweilen, he bores himself—but terribly, it is unbelievable," she explained. "His wife, the Josefa, a good woman, but she bores him most of all. A good fellow," sighed Frau Sacher in conclusion, "a *schwarzer teufel,* but so bored. *Hörens*— can you believe it? only last week he said to me 'Frau Anna, how I wish I had been born in the Alser-Grund and not in the Hof-burg. Then I could drive a zwei-spanner, make money and go to dances in the Sausage-Prater.' "

Poor devil! dissipation and boredom brought him to an early grave; his son the Emperor Charles did not inherit his wonderful good looks, but his bad luck—yes—

I was perfectly open and aboveboard in the matter of this expense account, as I hope I have always been. I sent on Frau Sacher's whopping big bill for the dinner "in honor of those who had helped me in the matter of the famous interview," and it was paid without a murmur.

Some may still survive who will recall that one of the Commodore's most striking idiosyncrasies was a way of quoting winged words which, rightly or wrongly, he attributed to Abraham Lincoln. At times he would cable them from the particular end of the earth where he was sojourning, to be inserted on the editorial page. Some thought his cult of Lincoln affected; I thought it sincere. The man himself, of course, was a curious anomaly. While his accent was far from academic, the Commodore spoke French even more fluently than he did English, and this was natural enough as he had spent the better part of his life both as boy and man in French-speaking countries. I knew of the Lincoln cult, and so I was not surprised to receive, in a few days, a letter which ran much as follows:—

"You may recall how a week after the fall of Vicksburg, when there was some gossip in Washington about the prodigious quantity of whiskey Grant was reported to consume daily, that Lincoln wrote him a letter, not to blame but simply to inquire the particular brand or blend he affected, so that he might send it on to the other generals? With a similar purpose I am writing you. What is your tipple, and, of course, any other details of how the great beat was secured, so that I may pass them on to your colleagues."

Now I was a fairly honest youngster and I did suffer at the thought that I was receiving praise far beyond my deserts. I even wrote a letter containing a frank confession. In it I told the Commodore that a young Polish-American girl I had chanced to meet in a cellar-restaurant on Eighth Street in New York had gotten the idea in her head and had arranged all the details of the interview with the Austrian Prime Minister. Here I stopped as well I might. That apparently was the simple truth but how absurd and unconvincing!

How could I give a convincing account of the way the great

achievement was brought about, when as a matter of fact I did not know myself? I never sent that letter, and I was not slow in recalling incidents which confirmed me in my dark incommunicative course. I soon persuaded myself that if the laurels and the praise that were being given me now were perhaps not wholly deserved, yet after all they were only evening up the score a bit. How callous and unappreciative the Commodore had been on many an occasion! There was that trip in the first submarine in New York Harbor which General Sherman, who followed with interest the experiment, said was the most foolhardy thing he had ever witnessed and of which Julian Ralph wrote in *Scribner's Magazine* that it was the most daring. Then the balloon venture with Larry L. . . ., who turned out not to be a balloonist at all, but simply a lunatic. Fortunately, after some misadventures, we came down softly in the refuse pond of the gas works at Bergen Point. Did I get a word of praise from the Commodore? I certainly did not. You might imagine I had in each case performed a routine assignment in a manner that required no notice of any description.

So I simply wrote the Commodore that I drank light beer and a little red wine that was grown on the slopes of the Kahlenberg— that, of course, the representative of the *New York Herald* in Vienna was in a very strong position because we had no delicate pending questions with Austria, that we were neutral on all the problems that divided southeastern Europe, and that the publicity we were able to give prominent men was unusual because the paper was published with incredibly large editions in all three of the great world cities, London, Paris and New York. As to the physical condition and the professional standing of Brinsley Richards of the *London Times*, Lavino of the *Daily Telegraph* or Felix Dubois of the *Figaro*, I said, in answer to the Commodore's sarcastic inquiry, that they were bearing up as well as could be expected and that, while they had received severe telegrams of blame from their respective editors, as yet no one of them had been dismissed. I added, and I think I was justified in so doing, that Richards deserved to be dismissed because he had printed my interview practically verbatim in his paper with the announcement that it was taken from the *Tzas* of Cracow, leaving out all reference to me or to the *Herald*, the original source.

I wound up with a generous word for my disconsolate colleagues, and also with a hint that I did not care to remain for all time in Vienna. I said didactically, "The newcomer has many advantages. In the performance of their duties as they have understood them in the course of the years they have remained here, these men, my competitors, have made powerful enemies. It is quite possible," I added, "that if I remain here for a year or two and continue to tell the truth, I might not be able to interview the Prime Minister. Of course, I was careful and diplomatic in making my approaches to the Prime Minister, but the credit is due in a large measure to the non-partisan position of the paper—the prestige of the *Herald* as an open forum."

I hoped this was the end of the matter. I disliked the position into which I was being forced, but as a matter of fact these inquiries were but the opening wedge on the why and wherefore of the Taafe interview, of the painstaking investigation and persistent cross-examinations to which I was subjected for weeks. I tried to narcotize my guilty conscience by throwing myself into my work as never before. Programs of what we should do to electrify Europe and make America sit up flowed from my pen almost daily. Once I thought I had definitely changed the subject. "Would it not be a good idea for me to go and interview the Senussi Mahdi in Tripoli? He is making great headway," I assured the Commodore, "soon he will have a Mohammedan block of five hundred million behind him." In this he seemed interested, but the idea faded out, and the Commodore, to my dismay, began to harp again on the old string. Then there came a wire asking me to join him in Gastein in the Tyrol for a few days, if I thought I could leave Vienna in comparative safety.

The moment he saw me the Commodore brought me to book; he evidently sniffed a mystery in the Taafe business and he was a little vexed that I would not let him in on it, and once again he insisted upon threshing over all the details of the interview. And now I tried another line. "I came at an opportune moment," I asserted. "The Polish bloc was driving the Prime Minister very hard. Without their support in the Reichsrath, he could not maintain his nicely balanced control of the situation. But the Poles were growing arrogant, and by their demands for patronage might soon upset the balance. Doubtless the Prime Minister thought," I explained, "it was high time to let them know what might happen to them and to their personal fortunes if they did so. Did you notice," I inquired, "the somewhat obscure reference he made to lowering and extending the franchise in Galicia? That was a note of subtle warning. If he did that, the Ruthenians might outvote the Poles and then—goodbye to the old feudal days on the manor farms. He used me and we used him, and we both won out," I added.

"It may be so," admitted Bennett. "But you must explain all this to my friends the Fürstenbergs. They cannot understand it at all. They say that our interview means the end of the Holy Roman Empire in the West."

The Fürstenbergs were at this period in his career the most intimate and certainly the most charming of the Commodore's circle of cosmopolitan friends. He, Prince Max Egon von und zu Fürstenberg, was a mediatized ruler with large estates at Donauschingen and almost everywhere else. But the treasure of the family was his charming sister, the Lady Wanda, as we called her, though this was not her given name. We gave it to her because of a fancied resemblance to one of Ouida's stately Austrian heroines. They were real friends and not merely spongers and profiteers, as were so many of the prominent figures in Bennett's circle. They cruised with him on his yacht, but they turned their estates over to the Commodore for his famous shooting parties. They were very smart socially, and while their political principles were dated in the seventeenth century, their apparel was up to the hour. The Prince was fitted out by Poole of London and the Princess by Drecoll of Vienna, and so attired the Commodore was always pleased and proud to have them on his drag when the big events were run at Auteuil or Longchamp.

It soon developed that when the interview appeared, the Prince and Princess had written Mr. Bennett a joint letter in which they expressed the opinion that by a few strokes of his pen his agent had destroyed the last vestige of prestige that remained to the Prime Minister. It was soon apparent, even to me, that but for the repeated complaints of the Fürstenbergs my exploit would have been forgotten in a few hours.

To my deep disgust, as we now drove up to his hunting lodge in the hills, it developed that my chief had forgotten all about my splendid Senussi suggestion and was determined to elucidate the sickening Taafe affair if possible.

"The Fürstenbergs say," he said, "that in ventilating his political views in the press, the Austrian Prime Minister has fallen to the level of Gladstone. They maintain, however, the thing could never have happened but for the fact that Taafe is an Irish interloper. You see his family has only been seated in the East realm for a few generations," explained my chief. It was all very boring, but, of course, the more the Fürstenbergs lamented the Premier's departure from silence and fall from grace, the more Bennett was pleased, and above all else the more he was pleased with Bonsal.

For his amusement, and I think in the hope that I would at last clear up the mystery he chose to attach to the interview, the Commodore brought me in contact with the Prince and the charming Princess in the course of several breakfasts and excursions which he arranged in their honor. I came with no little trepidation to these *land-partieen*, especially after he told me with mistaken kindness that his friends had fallen into the habit of speaking of the interview as an explosive bomb that had shaken the millennial edifice of the Hapsburgs to its very foundations!

Fortunately the Fürstenbergs were well-bred people, and while they made it quite plain that neither they nor their kind would ever forgive the unfortunate Taafe, they had not a word of reproach or even of blame for me. Perhaps I flattered myself unduly but I did think at the time that the Princess Wanda welcomed my presence with eager curiosity—as one would today an arrival from Mars or a traveler from Altruria. I must admit the Prince was of sterner stuff. He by no means regarded me as a visitor from the upper regions, and I once heard him explaining my position to Count Hans Wilczek as that of a young Lucifer of the American press. "The one," he explained, "who with his Ithuriel spear bore Taafe down from his proud position and deposited him in the mud of democracy with all the other statesmen of western Europe." However, even the Prince absolved me from all personal blame, placing the responsibility of what he regarded as a blunder that was worse than a crime squarely upon the shoulders of the intruder Taafe.

What might be called the mechanism of the interview which had such a far-reaching influence on my fortunes is still mysterious. I, myself, never fully understood how it came off, or why, and this may condone the reticence, bordering on duplicity, which I have hitherto always maintained on the subject. But one or two facts I must emphasize if only to still the voice of scandal. It is certain that Lady Hamilton did not personally know the Prime Minister, and consequently could not have brought her undeniable charm into play. I owe this statement to the shade of Countess "Fanni" Taafe. Lady Hamilton was not one of the women of whom the Countess had some right to be jealous. But it is equally certain that at this time my acquaintance from Eighth Street had much influence over a Polish nobleman who was one of the Prime Minister's lieutenants and close advisers, and it was probably through him that Lady Hamilton's wild suggestion came to its fruitage. In after years this remarkable woman changed her name, quite legally this time, and carved out for herself in Poland both fame and fortune. Sorry indeed I was to learn that during the Soviet invasion of 1920, in defending her home against marauders, my charming friend and benefactress, to whom I owed more than I can say, had been murdered.

While I cannot flatter myself that it was because of the interview which he considered so degrading to his country, it is a fact that a few months later Prince Egon withdrew entirely from the Austro-Hungarian world and became quite a power in the German Empire although he always tried to remain behind the curtain. He was bitterly attacked in his memoirs by Philip Eulenberg, whose place he took in the Emperor's immediate entourage, and Prince Bülow after his fall wrote, "Prince Max may have intrigued against me," and he writes further that the distinguished emigrant from Austria had acquired great influence over the German Emperor. If he did, I can at least be certain that it was exerted in a reactionary direction.

Suddenly, presto! change!! We were all called by wire to Paris, instructed to bring our heavy luggage. I was delighted; of course I was to go after the Senussi Mahdi! But the presence of the other fellows?—that was puzzling. There we all were looking out upon the slowly falling raindrops on the Champs Élysées—his correspondents from Berlin and Vienna, from St. Petersburg, Constantinople and Rome, and the Commodore was smiling benevolently upon us.

I had seen Mr. Bennett at close quarters many times before, but on each of these momentous occasions I had been so transfixed with awe that I had not ventured anything like a scrutinizing look at him. I came away from these confrontations with the impression that he looked like a tall and lonely timber wolf, and that he had bored right through me with steely suspicious eyes. Today his eyes were friendly and his weatherbeaten face that revealed his fondness for the sea and told of the many adventurous cruises he had made in storm-swept waters was wreathed in a gracious smile. He motioned us to be seated and said he was glad to see us, and it seemed to be so. Certainly not one of the five young men he had called to Paris from their distant posts thought for a moment to question his sincerity.

"You men have done wonders," he said. "In all my long experience I have never been better served. But the conclusion has been forced upon me that the people do not care for a foreign service of the high order that you have maintained. I cannot support it alone, unaided, much as I would like to. Yesterday I was advised that the one-hundred and seventy-sixth suit for libel had been filed against our London edition. It was by a man who sells cheeses, admittedly, but he has brought an action against the paper and I am advised we shall be mulcted in heavy damages because he was mentioned in our columns as a cheese-monger. Of course the foolish fellow who let that get by has been fired, but this is the last straw that has broken the camel's back. I have ordered the London edition to suspend after the issue of Saturday next."

The thought of the libel suit had darkened the Commodore's face for several moments, but soon he was beaming on us pleasantly again. "I hope you see and recognize how I must bow to the inevitable, how we must all bow to it."

"Of course, of course," we chorused.

"You men should have the consciousness of difficult work well done and I love to think that the experiences you have gathered and the outstanding work you have been able to accomplish has not passed unnoticed in the newspaper world, and will stand you in good stead. You all have my warmest thanks, my very sincere good wishes. And while your work, I am sure, will speak louder for you than anything I can say or write, my letters of appreciation will reach every one of you tomorrow."

With a hasty but hearty handshake, we parted, and then filed out. The proceedings had been so pleasant that only as we stood together on the sidewalk before going upon our separate ways did we realize that, collectively and severally, we had all been "fired." But who cared? certainly none of that group did. When you are under twenty-five, and in Paris, and have at least one of those beautifully engraved *billets* of the Bank of France for a thousand francs in your pocket, who should worry at being fired? As a matter of fact, for the moment at least, only one of us cared a hoot. A splendid evening was opening before us, and tomorrow was another day.

For the man who grumbled and was inclined to rebel there were, it is true, extenuating circumstances. To begin with (and to end with for that matter!) he was no longer young. He must have been nearly thirty and in our eyes he often seemed to be in his dotage especially when, as he often did, he would orate on the subject that was ever in his mind. It was, put briefly, which C. . . . rarely did, that every self-respecting man should so arrange his life that at sixty he would be financially independent. C. . . . had been attached to the Washington bureau for some years and then by some caprice of the Commodore he had been sent to Rome. There he was famous for shaving infrequently and for wearing what we called a "Prince Albert" morning, noon and night, and some said that the wrinkles indicated it was also his sleeping robe. C. . . . called this garment his body coat; some observers called it his "soul" coat but they were ill-natured. For a time now with a cynical expression on his timeworn face C. . . . listened patiently to all our cackle about how "gentlemanly Tiger Jim had been." "He certainly wore velvet gloves over his claws," asserted the cheerful man from St. Petersburg. But as he prepared to withdraw definitely from the thoughtless group C. . . . said, "You fellows make me ill; you remind me of a politician in Washington who was always glorifying James G. Blaine and belittling Benjamin Harrison, until one day someone who knew the circumstances interrupted him with, 'You seem to forget that Benjamin Harrison made you minister to Greece and Blaine—well he gave you the glad hand—empty!'

" 'Well, that's so,' admitted the office seeker, 'but I would rather have James G. Blaine kick me downstairs than have Ben Harrison boost me to the Court of St. James.' "

And as a matter of fact that is the way all of us youngsters felt about Mr. Bennett. He had a way with him and we all liked "Tiger Jim" even when he handled us without the velvet gloves, and that was not infrequently the case.

We had, or at least I had, a very pleasant evening.

> *En mangeant des écrevisses*
> *Au café des Ambassadeurs.*

And there was a still later session at the Café Américain (long since disappeared), with some of the great correspondents residing in Paris.

There Mlle. Francine sang in her inimitable manner the song of the day, or rather of the night, in a way that convinced every man jack in sight that he was the fortunate Nicolas and it ran something like this:

> *Jadis à Pontoise*
> *Y avait un beau gars*
> *Que toutes les filles de l'Oise*
> *Trouvaient plein d'appas.*

With the refrain in which we all joined uproariously,

> *Le voilà Nicolas, ah! ah! ah!*
> *Le voilà Nicolas, ah! ah! ah!*

But while we talked to the young ladies, and indeed opened wine for Mlle. Francine, we were serious young people and not to be drawn away, at least not for long, from the vital problems with which we were all professionally confronted. We agreed that there were clouds over the Balkans, but as a matter of fact there always were. Upon us dull care had not once obtruded itself, but that was not to be long delayed. On reaching my little hotel, L'Amirauté, in the Rue Daunou, there on the ancient brass candlestick outside the *loge* reposed a letter. Well, I could tell a mile off, or nearly so, who it was from. The paper was robin's-egg blue and the address was written with a dark blue pencil that must have been as blunt as a walking stick. It contained few words indeed, but written large they sprawled all over the page. To my surprise they read, for I had merely expected a formal letter of endorsement: "If convenient, please call on me at seven o'clock tomorrow. Bennett."

I walked upstairs in a daze. I had thought that chapter closed, and now perhaps it was to be reopened. "Seven o'clock tomorrow." I looked at my watch—it was after three. "That is today," I reasoned. But what did he mean—A. M. or P. M.? How careless he was! Not the first time, to be sure, I had noticed this trait in my correspondence with the Commodore. When I reached my bedroom, well up under the roof, I turned right around and toddled down all the sloping, uneven stairs again and, to the manifest disgust of the concierge, sallied out. "A. M. or P. M.?" If it was A. M. it was certainly inadvisable for me to go to bed. It was best for me to go to the Hammam or Turkish bath just around the corner on the Rue des Mathurins and there, as so often before when early starts were made and early trains had to be met, await the coming of more seasonable hours.

Well, I had a good sweat and a nice cool swim, my head was very clear now and I enjoyed a good laugh at my expense. Of course the mere idea of Bennett receiving me at seven o'clock in the morning was a joke, and at the thought of it I alarmed my rubber by laughing out loud. Nicely wrapped in toweling, I was about to go to sleep when a shadow passed the door of my cubby-hole. It seemed to be the shadow of Bennett, his tall slouching form, his long stride, the swinging arms, the "swing of the sowers" which he and Gourgaud, the Duke of Gramont and Ridgeway Knight, his particular pals of the moment, affected. I scurried around and got another glimpse of the man who looked like Bennett, as much like Bennett as any man could look with his head and manly form enveloped in towels.

I was wide awake now and determined to remain so. Perhaps I

was not the only *Herald* man who depended on the Turkish bath for the keeping of early engagements. After all, I concluded, if I called at seven A. M., I could only be turned away and then I would drop in again in the evening. A few minutes before seven I drove up the Champs Élysées in a night-hawking *sapin*. The driveway door was ajar, and I started up the stairs towards the inner door out of which we had been bowed with so much grace and civility a few hours before. Here I stumbled upon the concierge or one of his understrappers, scrubbing away at the marble steps, and though we were only at the entresol, he evidently regarded me as a second-story thief. "And what might I want and what could he do for me?" he asked querulously. And then, in no pleasant tones, he ordered me not to tread where the steps were still wet. Not liking the fellow's manner, I stepped around him and touched the bell. "I have an appointment with Mr. Bennett," I said sternly.

The scrubber dropped his brush and it went rattling down to the floor below. He raised his voice and was mad all through now. "You should know, and you will know very soon, that Monsieur Gordon-Bennett does not receive at these hours." And the door opened and there stood Bennett himself. He gave a very stern glance at the scrubber and ushered me in. He looked fresh as paint, like a man just out of a Turkish bath. He led the way into the great room with the long Italian windows facing on the Champs Élysées, and then motioning me to take a seat, he fixed his eyes upon me for half a minute. I was young, but twenty-three; I had not learnt to dissemble. I suppose my face did register surprise that here I was, fifteen hours after being discharged, face to face with Bennett, practically at the crack of dawn, and he fit as a fiddle and as fresh as paint.

"You seem surprised," he began in a surly voice. "I suppose you thought, as everyone else does, that you would find me boiling drunk at seven in the morning."

"Not at all," I protested, "not at all." Somewhat mollified, he gave me a fat Serbian cigarette, lit one himself, and:

"Have you made any hard and fast plans since—our talk yesterday afternoon?"

"None," I answered truthfully.

"That's good," he brightened. "Well, I have made plans for you —that is, if you are footloose."

I assured him that I was superlatively footloose, and then the Commodore went on. "I have not lost interest in European conditions, but I think our system of stable correspondents and a constant flow of cables and letters from the capitals has not worked out very well, so I am going to try another scheme, and if you are willing I shall begin with you. I would like you to leave tonight on the Orient Express, and take charge of the Balkans. If you pass by the cashier's window, you will find I have instructed him to let you have what money you need. Charley Christianson (this was a young Scandinavian, long a cabin boy on the *Namouna*, who had now become Bennett's factotum) will secure your tickets and reservations and leave them at your hotel."

"Instructions?" I asked.

"Well, I shall expect you to take charge of the Balkans and be on hand whenever and wherever anything happens. I advise you to go now directly to Sofia. Wire me to the secret code address when you arrive. There is a promising rumpus going on, as you know, in Macedonia, and in Bulgaria Prince Ferdinand may be kidnaped, as was his predecessor, any moment. When things quiet down, of course you can come back to Vienna where your good friend Taafe will take care of you and when you go on to Constantinople I will send you a letter to Tashin Pasha, he is the Sultan's right-hand-man, and can be useful. Of course you have complete liberty of movement. You can swing back and forth as you please between Vienna and the Bosphorus, that is your beat. But if and when Hell breaks loose in that territory—well, I shall expect you to be on the spot."

I assured him I would do my best and that I was duly flattered by his confidence, and I was being dismissed when the Commodore had another thought. "Do you correspond with Billy Reick?" he inquired.

"No," I answered. "He is my very good friend, so we never write."

Reick was Bennett's head man in New York, his managing editor in fact, though very wisely he never assumed the honorific title.

"Well, don't write Reick or any of the other men. Envelop

your mission in mystery. Only turn up when the fireworks begin."

I had a good laugh going down the stairs, where the former scrubber now in gorgeous livery followed me with profuse apologies. I had heard of Mr. Bennett's extraordinary jealousy of the New York office, and how he loved to mystify and even deceive those who worked there. Even in the years when he had agents scattered pretty generally throughout the world, he would never let New York have a complete list. What he enjoyed more than anything else, perhaps, was to have the searchlight of world interest focus, let us say for a moment, upon Madagascar and get a despairing cry from New York about the impossibility of securing news from that distant point and then be able to reply, "I knew of course what was coming; I have had my man in Tamatave waiting these three months. You will have five thousand words about it— at least for the late edition."

Often, but not always, the Commodore exhibited a wonderful prescience in these matters and a foreknowledge of things that were to come. And when he had rescued Reick from real or feigned despair, he would preen his feathers and pat himself on the back in the most amusing and boyish manner. But sometimes the big events that he had anticipated did not come off, and then his agent in some faraway, somnolent place drifted into the discard of the forgotten men. Henry M. Stanley, the greatest of the Commodore's correspondents, once told me a story, that at the time struck me as amusing, of a *Herald* man, a colleague of his, who was forgotten in Persia, and being without funds to return home, joined a caravan of Mecca pilgrims who fed him well because he acted the part of a holy, howling dervish to perfection. Later on I was to be forgotten too in many strange lands, but for the moment I basked in the great man's favor and it was very pleasant.

As I passed through Vienna on my way to the fabulous Balkans I stopped off for a few hours and gave another banquet to which my friends had been summoned by wire. Lady Hamilton was there and Ilka Palmay and "Rudi" Kinsky and Countess O'Sullivan, the name by which Charlotte Wolters, the great tragedienne, was disguised in private life. She called down blessings from heaven upon her *edles Indianer Kind*. Fräulein Abel from the Opera came too,

she of the goddess-like walk, and Fräulein Cerale did a few pirou-
ettes between courses. On this occasion "Der Otto" did not intrude.
Because of an incident I shall not dwell upon, he had been placed
under arrest in a Tyrolean castle where no one was allowed to visit
him, not even Frau Anna or the Archduchess Josefa. This time I
paid the score out of my personal funds and felt very *nobel*, "grand"
in the Viennese meaning of the word.

10. IN THE BALKANS

WHEN THEY were committed to my charge in the summary manner I have indicated, I knew very little about the Balkans* and, despite the flood of news that has been poured forth from that region in the last thirty years, some of my readers may still be in the same plight. Of course I knew the catchwords, and during my stay in Vienna I had forwarded much information from these distressed lands, but it was, I fear, mostly based on the flashes of the agency which we called, and not without reason, the *Agence Volcanique*, though that was not its name. But, of course, I did not have the remotest idea of what the Balkans and the Balkan peoples, with whom I was to be confronted, looked like. I was soon to learn by harsh personal contact, and in the course of the next two years I crossed and recrossed the length and breadth of the peninsula half a dozen times, and I was to become more familiar with its outstanding features, geographical as well as political, than with those of my native land.

While, of course, geographers are by no means in perfect agreement, these are the generally accepted metes and bounds of the peninsula. Its northern boundary extends from the Kilia mouth of the Danube (where it enters the Black Sea) to the Adriatic near Fiume. On the east it is bounded by the Black Sea, the Sea of Marmora and the Aegean, on the south by the Mediterranean, the Ionian Sea and the Adriatic; and the whole looks rather like an inverted pyramid, with the great river courses, the Danube, the Save, and the Kalpa, romping through it. Apart from the valleys

---

* *Balkan* is the Turkish word for mountain, so the name only dates from the Ottoman Conquest. In the Roman period the mountains were known as the Haemus range.

of the Danube and the Maritza, the region is very mountainous, and this fact is important. I wish I could recall the name of the geographer, also a philosopher, who stated that the character of the inhabitants depends upon the rugosity of the land they occupy. Mountain peoples, he insists, have a rugose or belligerent character. This man understood and in a sentence explained the Balkan peoples.

The great chain of the Rhodope Mountains traverses the center of the peninsula, shooting out spurs both towards the Aegean and the Black Seas. Further west rise the lofty Shar Dagh and the mountains of Montenegro and Albania. Owing to this distribution of the mountain chain, the rivers flow generally in a southeasterly direction, but the Maritza and the Vardar turn to the south and enter the Aegean.

The summers are exceedingly hot and the winters, although short, are intensely cold. Little wonder that the Latin poets, including Ovid who was exiled to Thrace, complained of the northeast winds that blow so frequently. But October and November, before the great winds begin to blow, are wonderful months indeed.

The population at this time (1889) was about twenty-one million, mixed as to race, confusing and antagonistic as to customs, and irreconcilably divided by religious dissensions. The Turks numbered barely two million, and they were decreasing, while the Slavonic population was increasing rapidly. Among the ethnic fragments were the Vlachs or Tzintzars, or Arumani as they call themselves, who according to tradition were left behind when the Romans abandoned Dacia. The Albanians, generally thought to be a remnant of the primitive Illyrian population, were and are still seated along the Adriatic littoral from the southern frontier of Montenegro to the northern boundary of Greece; for obvious political reasons these peoples were greatly encouraged in their racial aspirations by the Turks. The Greeks, who according to the wise pundits of the Berlin Congress (1878) controlled the whole country, I found in the minority almost everywhere. Seafaring men and traders as a general thing, they clung to the coast or to the towns and commercial centers. The Jews, while they composed at least half of the population of Salonica, were very sparsely scattered throughout the country districts, and the gypsies in small groups were to be found practically everywhere.

I shall not endeavor to go into details as to the many Slavic tribes; as will appear later, this is an impossible task, but there were certainly ten million of them divided into many discordant groups. The Armenians also were quite numerous in the commercial centers, but they were shortly to be greatly reduced by the massacres of 1896. Including about half the Albanians and the converted Pomaks, of whom more later, the Moslem population must have numbered about three million. Since at this time, as now, all religious and political questions were intimately connected, I shall only endeavor to assort them as it becomes necessary later on. The church feuds of the Greek Patriarch and of the Bulgar Exarch were quite as disturbing to the peace of the peninsula as were those of the temporal Powers. The Armenians, unfortunately, had two patriarchs, representing an unhappy schism, and the Roman Catholic Church had many followers in Dalmatia and Croatia, and among the Gheg tribes of Albania, and in the Greek Islands off the coast. To make confusion worse confounded, in Macedonia and in several other districts were to be found not a few members of the Uniate Church, accepting dogma from Rome but with Greek Orthodox rites.

As to language, the peninsula was a veritable Tower of Babel. The Bulgarian, as a written language, was just emerging from the monastic retreats where it had taken refuge and been preserved during the Dark Ages. Turkish and Greek were, of course, the only languages officially recognized. The Albanian speech, handed down possibly from the ancient Illyrians, was just discovered and is still the most fascinating study of philologists, to whom we shall leave it.

Before the coming of the Slavonic tribes in the fourth century, the Roman Empire was in more or less complete control of all the lands south of the Danube. Driven back by the onset of these migratory tribes, the Thracians and the Albanians took refuge in the mountains, while the Greeks were pushed to the seacoast and the near-lying islands. The Bulgars only came in numbers towards the end of the seventh century, and under the great Tsar Simeon they ruled from the Adriatic to the Black Sea, and to this period hark back the dreams of a Greater Bulgaria that have been the cause of so much bloodshed in our day. After Ivan Assen II (1230), the Bulgarian Empire declined, and then came the period of Serbian dominance under Stefan Dushan, who extended his power over the greater part of the peninsula. But shortly after his death in 1391 his empire, too, disintegrated. His day of power and of glory is, of course, the foundation of the Greater Serbia idea.

Then came the conquering Ottoman Turks under Mahomet II, 1460 or thereabouts. Their empire increased in power and extent under Suleiman the Magnificent (as a particular favor, I was once shown his wonderful war tent in Stamboul), but after the defeat before Vienna, their power also declined (1683). Characteristic of the decaying power of the Turks was the formation of practically independent pashaliks within the realm. Later, in 1829, Greece became independent; Serbia, nominally a tributary principality, in 1830. But the great changes in the political complexion of the peninsula came as the result of the Russo-Turkish war in 1878 and the arrangements that were made at San Stefano and modified by the Congress of Berlin. Bosnia and Herzegovina came under the wing of the Dual Monarchy, Roumania was recognized as a kingdom in 1881, Serbia in 1882, and Bulgaria, as a principality with the Sultan a nominal suzerain.

Practically this was the Balkan situation as I entered upon it. Of course even an eye as unskilled as mine can see many gaps in this picture, but it should convey an idea of the racial, political and religious antagonisms which made of the Balkans the cockpit of Europe, from which the World War at long last emerged. It should, however, be noted that even in these discordant days a voice for conciliation was heard. Under Ristich, the Serbian statesman, as early as 1877, attempts were made to confederate the Balkan peoples, but then, as later, they failed, and in view of the increased animosities that now prevail and divide this unhappy region of the world, anything like reconciliation would seem impossible in the near future.

On reaching Sofia, I found the "City of Wisdom," the head center and the source of canards which amused or affrighted the world, and depressed or exhilarated the stock and grain markets.

The heat was intolerable, about 110° Fahrenheit in the shade, but the atmosphere of the political world was still more torrid. Stransky and Salabashoff had resigned from the ministry rather than sign the death warrant of Panitza; but Stambouloff had prevailed with the Prince, and the hero of the Serbian War was shot, tethered to a tree like a traitor, on the windy plain without the city. Prince Ferdinand had gone to Carlsbad, Stambouloff was known vaguely to be somewhere on the shores of the Black Sea, the remaining ministers were recruiting their health at the various thermal springs scattered through the Balkans, and Bulgaria apparently was ruling itself.

The town was thronged with the correspondents of world newspapers, and a confusion of tongues reigned in the cafés. The ex-ministers—and their name was legion—worked through the early morning at the great Bulgarian dictionary, which was the only means of livelihood for politicians out of office, slept through the noonday heat, and in the evening assembled in the Café Panachoff to read the *Times* and *Le Temps* by the aid of pocket dictionaries, and concluded the evening with checkers and tric-trac, the while as uncommunicative as schools of fish. Army officers, looking very fresh and cool in their white duck uniforms, sat about in the public garden, sipping successively glasses of grenadine, slivo vitz, raki, and mastique, and telling in undertones how grandly Kosta Panitza had led the Macedonian "brigade of bandits" to the storming of Pirot, which they captured at the point of the yataghan. In the cool of the evening the newspaper "specials" could be seen giving their Barb ponies gentle "breathers" on the plain beneath snow-crested Mount Witosh, preparing for the hour when the news that the world was awaiting would come, that Stambouloff was assassinated, that Ferdinand had abdicated, that the independence of the principality had been declared, or that the Russians were crossing the Danube— awaiting the great news that would send them out like a flight of hawks through the night on a mad race for the wire which encircles the world, and which could only be entrusted safely with a dispatch at Pirot, a hundred miles away, across the Serbian frontier.

Every morning there came a surprise which sent the "special" to his stables, and every evening some bitter disappointment which sent him to bed or to the baccarat tables. Strange signs and symbols appeared on the political horizon, but the great event hung fire. The little stunted willow where Panitza had been shot began to play an important if objective role in politics. One morning it displayed a banner with a touching tribute to the worth of the patriot or traitor who had died so bravely in its shadow. There followed on the next day another banner bearing a threat and a menace to the life of the Prince. The official and diplomatic world was aghast to see waving from the willow this black ominous banner with the regicidal device, *Tirani zai tooka ste luidi grabot ne Fernanda.* ("Tyrant! know here will be the grave of Ferdinand.") Then it was decided to cut down the tree which bore such anti-dynastic fruit, but when the soldiers reached the plain with axes, the willow had disappeared.

The arrival of a Georgian prince and an ex-chamberlain of the Great White Tsar furnished an amusing interlude in the succession of more serious scares. With singularly tenacious filial piety, the Prince had come, he claimed, to visit the tombs of his ancestors who were sleeping in a cairn near Sofia. Their resting-place had been neglected by his forefathers for more than a thousand years, yet he had come to put it in some repair, and to plant a few rose bushes. But the Prefect of Police packed him off to the frontier, sandwiched between gendarmes, without as much as a short delay for breakfast.

News came through strange channels in Bulgaria. As we slept in the hotel, proclamations with mourning bands would flutter in through the transom in the most mysterious manner, and not rarely the "special" would find neatly tucked away in his boots outside the door the prophecy of a coming pronunciamento. In opera, at least, the Barber of Seville was a remarkable gossip and agent of rumor; in real life his colleague of Sofia was an inveterate disseminator of news. He was at once the stumbling block and the mainstay of the "special." His news was rarely "ready for the wire," but at the same time his information could not be dispensed with. A sign in a dozen tongues in Mustapha's shop told that a "silent shave," without conversation, cost ten piastres; but the gossipy shave—which Mustapha advised—with a cigarette and *les dessous* of the latest political move, what Mustapha heard from Yildiz Kiosk, from Belgrade, Moscow, or the Minister-President, the creamy Turkish coffee, with which the canard was washed down, and the salaam with which the rather inhuman treatment of your chin was gracefully rounded off, cost thirty piastres, and was cheap at the price.

Once at midnight I left Sofia, to cross the Balkans and find M. Stambouloff in the vague somewhere in which, according to the Foreign Office, he was awaiting the course of events, and especially the upshot of the interview between the Tsar and the German Emperor, which was soon to take place at Peterhof. I had purchased half a dozen scraggy and sorry-looking ponies that, however, were reputed to climb mountains like goats, and procured a guide who knew the Balkans well.

By daybreak we reached the mountains and later the Petrus *han*, or inn, famous for its bad food and wide sweeping view. Though I came with letters-patent from the Foreign Office, which Mihail, my guide, displayed with great pride to everybody we met—and would naturally have been taken for a friend of Stambouloff's government, the sturdy proprietor of the *han* replied to my question, as to what sentiment of the people toward Russia really was, as follows:

"*Gospodin Amerikanitz* (Mr. American), we have not forgotten our brave brothers who took away the heathen fez, and gave us the Christian kalpak to wear. When we pray, we pray for the soul of the Tsar Liberator. *Gospodin Amerikanitz*, we love and revere Russia." During my subsequent journeyings through Bulgaria, I never heard anything which made me change my belief that the voice of the sturdy little keeper of the Petrus *han* was the voice of the great silent majority of Bulgarians. As we trotted along the road which, until we reached Klissourah, was the historic highway between Belgrade and Stamboul, I noticed that the few huts that we saw were generally a mile away from the road, and that the doors were so low one must enter crawling on hands and knees. Mihail explained, with a grin of gratification, that this state of things was only a memory and a reminder of the unhappy days of Turkish domination, that the hovels were hidden away as much as possible from sight of the road in order that the peasants might escape the requisition for *mouna*, or provisions, of the passing Pasha, and that the doors were cut so low that the Effendi might not enter the houses and carry off whatever chanced to please his looting fancy.

I did not know whether Mihail was a good guide, but his Bulgarian was limpid, and every now and then through the remnants of the Russian that Stepniak had imparted to me the previous year in London I grasped his meaning. In his earlier days Prince Alexander had sent him to Vienna to learn the veterinary art. In this he had not progressed very far but he had acquired a few words, key words they proved to be, of Viennese, and these helped to clear up several difficult situations later on. Everything looked all right as we left Sofia, but in the morning I was surprised and not a little exasperated to find that the tails of my ponies, the only good points they had, were gone. They had disappeared during the night, and as with daylight the horseflies renewed their cruel activities, all the poor animals could do was to swish at them with their pitifully shortened stumps.

I never was more angry in my life, and not at all pacified by Mihail's statement, which seemed so completely satisfactory to him, that he was engaged to be married and that his bride was awaiting him at our next halt! I am afraid I treated Mihail very roughly, and his protest after the fracas to the effect that I was entirely ignorant of Bulgarian customs was undoubtedly true. Finally he was successful in conveying to me the idea that when a man in Bulgaria became engaged the proper way to proclaim his good fortune to the world was to cut off the tails of his horses and present them to the lady of his choice to be entwined with her own coarse long hair. My statement that, after all, the ponies belonged to me did not carry conviction, and for the next three days the unfortunate animals suffered terribly from the onslaught of ravenous bluebottle flies, against which they had been robbed of their natural means of defense. Of course I made him tie the tails back, but they were switched off and at last, as on so many subsequent occasions, I had to submit and conform to the custom of the country.

On the evening of the second day we reached Klissourah, and Mihail dashed off after his sweetheart, brandishing in the air what remained of his booty of pony hair. The ostler of the *han*, after having conveyed in pantomine the information that I was at liberty to utilize his head as a footstool if it should so please me, greeted the ponies with an effusive kiss, and inquired if they had been "good boys." My pony replied with an affirmative whinny, whereupon the delighted ostler grasped him firmly by the ears, and pulled with all his might, until the joints of the ears cracked. This operation is popularly supposed in the Balkans to bring surcease to a pony's headache resulting from his pounding along the rough roads, and certainly they are very fond of it, and insist upon its being gone through with at every post station.

That evening the notables of Klissourah assembled on the green beside the *han*. It was a holiday. The pretty but dull-looking girls danced the *hora*, a Grecian dance, which has, however, become acclimated throughout the Balkan countries. It is rather a rhythmic march, a *quatre temps*, than a dance. The arms of the dancers, who are drawn up in a single or double line, cross and rest around the neighbor's waist. Between the dances a minstrel, who was popularly supposed to have lived several centuries, twanged away on the one-stringed monotonous *gusle* the epics of the country celebrating the champions of Bulgarian liberty, from the days of Tsar Simeon down to the Battenberg Prince who, as the epic ran in about the thousandth stanza, "stooped to tie the latchet of his Bulgarski brogans on the battlefield of Slivnitza, so little did he fear the Serbskis."

In the course of the evening I was initiated by the village gossips into the mysteries of Mihail's love affair which, as it reveals a novel custom, never departed from in the Balkans of that day, seems worthy to be told. He was in love with Raïka, a girl who was not pretty, but endowed with great capacity for work. She had made many journeys with gangs of working people from Klissourah into Roumania, and was supposed to have amassed a dot amounting to nearly twenty pounds Turkish, which she had buried away in the ground. She loved Mihail, and what his sentiments were the barefaced robbery of my ponies' tails plainly revealed. Still, the ceremony could not come off, because Raïka had an elder sister who did not as yet have the right to wear a head-covering which only comes to the Bulgarian girl with matrimony, and no well-brought-up girl would marry, her elder sister being still a spinster. I was presented to the elder sister, and was surprised to find her very beautiful; her hair was long and black as the raven's wing; her eyes soft, melting, and she was altogether charming. I immediately advised Mihail not to delay the ceremony any longer, but to conform to the custom of the country and marry the simply adorable elder sister. This he absolutely refused to do, saying that Magda was very idle, had not accumulated a dot, but spent her time dancing and listening to the weird morbid music of the Tsiganes, as they played in the quarter of the village allotted to them. So Mihail is doubtless a bachelor still. Romantic love does not flourish in the Balkans, as I found out later on.

The next day, diverging from the Belgrade road, we bore off to the east, along bridlepaths and sheep tracks, toward the Danube. The heat was terrific, and the sad fate of the Roumski traveler, who in these high mountain lands, with the rarefied atmosphere and the intolerable heat, generally loses his front teeth, owing to the relaxing of the gums, haunted me. I remember very little of these last two days, except that we seemed to be swimming in boiling oil, and that dreams of great tankards of rich, brown Bavarian beer came to torture me. Of one thing I was quite certain, that when next I crossed these mountains it would be in winter. What was freezing to death in comparison to roasting alive? . . . I became rational in the evening of the second day, as the frantic ponies dashed into the waters of the Danube, icy with the floods from the Tyrolean and Styrian Alps, and after a swim I made my apologies to Mihail for much harsh treatment. He was not rancorous, but carefully tapped my teeth, and thought they would not fall out, though very loose.

I came up with the mysterious Prime Minister, who seemed to be hiding, even from his own people, at Sistova, where in 1878, in their advance upon Turkey, the Russians had crossed the Danube. He was a short thick-set man of sturdy build, with a dark olive complexion, and most uncouth in his manners. But his whole appearance breathed vitality. He was a doer, and not a word-monger. From under his heavy beetle brows there looked out with suspicion upon his surroundings as penetrating a pair of eyes as I have ever beheld. I spent many instructive mornings with him, and he spoke with what at first appeared to be engaging frankness on every subject under the sun. He admitted that he was ruling the country backed by a small but active minority of his people against the will of a majority which would have been overpowering had it not been, as he observed with contempt, "so lethargic."

He frankly admitted that under his rule every article of the Constitution had become a dead letter, but he justified this by stating that the Constitution had been bestowed upon the Bulgarians by the Tsar for the purpose of sowing discord and general political dissatisfaction among his countrymen, until finally, like a ripe peach, the principality would fall into the lap of Mother Russia and be incorporated as a crown land in the Muscovite Empire. Like many other Balkan statesmen, Stambouloff had served a stage in journalism. Representing a Sofia paper, he had followed the Russian army for a few weeks during the war and had witnessed many interesting incidents in front of Plevna and during the delay at Shipka pass. Here he had received an indelible impression of the corruption in the non-combatant services of the Russian army, the incompetence of many officers in high command, and the pathetic ignorance of the rank and file.

"Two years before the war began," he explained time and again, "I thought that Russia could whip a world in arms. After what I saw in the bogs of the valley and on the bloodstained heights of Shipka, I came to the conclusion that, without the Roumanian contingent and the Macedonian volunteers, the Great White Tsar would have been stopped at Plevna. The conclusion was forced upon me that Bulgaria would have to stand on her own feet, and that is why I am now trying to walk alone." In confidence he admitted that he had no illusions either as to the value or the motive, nor yet the permanence, of the friendship which the Austrians and the English were displaying. "They are seeking their own selfish political ends. I do not blame them; I am doing the same thing; but I shall thwart their purpose, in mine I shall succeed."

I confess I was a little surprised when the semi-barbarian Stambouloff went on to speak of his sovereign, Prince Ferdinand, the grandson of Louis-Philippe, descended from a long line of mighty kings, in much the same tone that a millionaire merchant might refer to one of his clerks who was diligent in small things, and for the moment useful, but who could be easily replaced. There was not a suggestion of personal loyalty to the young Prince who, at

his urgent request, and after many others had refused, had em-
barked on the Bulgarian adventure. The only thing he seemed to
dwell upon with satisfaction was the fact that, thanks to the generosity of Princess Clementine, his devoted mother, Ferdinand was
spending a great deal of money in the principality, and he congratulated himself and his people on the fact that, come what might,
much of this would remain.

We spent our mornings talking politics, and during the heat of
the day, which was still very great, we enjoyed siestas. In the early
evening we would go for a swim in the Danube. Soldiers would row
us out into midstream and then, favored by the current, we would
swim down the river, often as far as Giurgevo on the Roumanian
shore, always followed by a police galley and under the protection
of a score of rifles. The Prime Minister swam like a seal. It was his
only form of exercise. In winter, he told me, he hibernated and
never took a step he could avoid or a bath.

It was perhaps natural, in view of his antecedents and upbringing,
that Stefan Stambouloff was such an uncouth individual. In his
seventeenth year he ran away from a seminary in Odessa, where
he was being educated for the priesthood, and since then it was his
boast that he had never opened a book. Embarking at this early age
upon a life of adventure, he had become the lucky survivor, not the
hero many asserted, of plots and counterplots against the Turkish
suzerain as well as the Christian overlords. He was at this time one
of the very few that were left of the band of adventurers and patriots, for both categories were as usual represented in the movement,
who in 1875 started the uprising against the Crescent which provoked the atrocities committed by the highland Pomaks and the
bashi-bazouks, brought about the Russo-Turkish war and in the end
resulted in the freedom of Christian Bulgaria from Ottoman rule.

This band of brothers, as Stambouloff called them, to whom Kat-
koff and the Moscow Pan-Slavs furnished the sinews of war, was
greatly reduced in numbers now. Some, the best of them I fear, fell
as volunteers in the Russian army. A few, it is true, still survived,
though broken in health and spirit by the *bastinado*, a Turkish form
of punishment which Stambouloff had not abolished. Some of these,
like Petko Karaveloff and Peter Stanchoff, had been rewarded by

long imprisonment in the Black Mosque. Others had been executed for treason (to Stambouloff) and without trial, like Kosta Panitza, though in his breast there were lodged many bullets received in fighting for the Fatherland.

Stambouloff was only thirty-seven when I met him, and he complained quite bitterly of his loneliness. "All who began with me have fallen," he said in a voice which did not ring quite true. And when I returned to Sofia and looked up the meager records that were available, I was not surprised to read the name of Stambouloff on the death warrants of many of his comrades of the early days. Certainly, if a smiling countenance and an unwrinkled brow is a reliable criterion, the dictator enjoyed at this time the blessing of a quiet conscience. Certainly he had an iron constitution and a digestion—well, I am completely at a loss for an analogy. I saw him devour repasts that would have staggered an ox and put a ravenous wolf on a diet for weeks. His sturdy health and enduring strength were, I have no doubt, the natural result of the years of hardship and exposure he had spent with the shepherds in the bleak fastnesses of the Balkans, always on the move with the Turkish *zaptieh* ever at his heels, with but a sheepskin between him and the weather, a sheepskin that was his cloak by day and his couch by night.

If I ever reached a full understanding of Bulgarian aspirations, or of the extraordinary man who at the time, and for five years longer, presided over the destinies of this long submerged and voiceless people, I have to thank a visit I paid two months later to the ancient crowning city of the Bulgarian Tsars, to Tirnovo on the Yantra. Again Stambouloff had disappeared from the face of the earth and a cabled instruction from the Commodore sent me from the relative comfort of Sofia in search of him once more.

After some fruitless wanderings and many uncomfortable days and nights, I came up with the vagrant Prime Minister secluded in the house of one of his closest political associates within a stone's throw of the Church of the Forty Holy Martyrs, the Westminster Abbey and a sacred place of pilgrimage for all Bulgarians, whether born in the principality or outside its boundaries, in Thrace or Macedonia. But for this ancient shrine, the town of Tirnovo of this day might aptly be described as a pig-wallow and a very common pig-wallow at that. But in this church over which so many hordes of conquerors have passed are still to be seen the inscriptions which for many, with the force of Holy Writ, lay down the metes and bounds of the ancient empire upon which so many base their dream of a Greater Bulgaria in the future.

After we had discussed the topics of the day, the Bulgarian Prime Minister came with me to the shrine and, with the aid of local anti- quarians, we read the testament carved on stone of the great Auto- crat which the Bulgarians still regard as the covenant of their far- reaching claims and aspirations. It runs:

"In the year 1230, I, John Asen II, Tsar and Autocrat of the Bul- garians, the son of the old Asen, obedient to God in Christ, have built this most worthy church from its foundations and completely decked it with paintings in honor of the Forty Holy Martyrs by whose help in the twelfth year of my reign, when the church had just been painted, I set out to the war in Roumania and smote the Greek army and took captive the Tsar Theodore Comnenus with all his nobles.

"And all lands have I conquered from Adrianople to Durazzo— the Greek, the Albanian and the Serbian lands. Only the towns around Constantinople and that city itself did the Franks hold; but these too bowed themselves beneath the hand of my sovereignty, for they had no other Tsar but me. And I prolonged their days according to my will as God had so ordained. For without Him no word prevails and no work is accomplished. To Him be Honor and Glory forever. Amen."

"What a truly great man he was," commented Stambouloff, and his dark and rather dull features brightened with the glow of patri- otic enthusiasm. "Today I am working to the end that some Bul- garian, some son of our soil, may come into his patrimony and rule over all our brothers just as did the Tsar John—eternal glory be to his name."

Little wonder then that in the years to come Prince Ferdinand, at once a Bourbon and a Coburg, feared Stambouloff. In the eyes of the Bulgarian leader this princeling with his Franco-German back- ground was but a stop-gap, filling for a season the throne that be- longed to a son of the blood-drenched soil. (And why not to Stefan

Stambouloff?) Men being what they are when driven by ambition, is there any wonder that Prince Ferdinand some years later accepted the brutal assassination of his ambitious lieutenant with Christian fortitude and resignation or even, as some thought, with levity?

When the news was flashed around the world of Stambouloff's murder in 1895, I did not rejoice, but I certainly shed no tears. He had lived by the sword and he died by the knife. At the moment I was passing through Paris on my way to the Far East from Spain, where for three years the Pyrenees had shielded me from most of the Balkan rumors, and there, at the corner of the Café de la Paix nearest to the Place, as I strolled along I saw a woman and at the same moment she saw me; the woman whom I had set down in my mind, when the first news of the assassination reached me, as the murderess of Stambouloff, not indeed with her own hands, but surely it was she who had nerved the arm that struck him down and then cut him to pieces. Her smile broke into laughter as she caught sight of me, not with joy at our chance meeting, I cannot claim it was that, but because of what she called "the good news," "the comfortable news" from the Balkans, which she immediately began to retail with many bloody details that had been overlooked in the press dispatches.

"Ah! Stefan Stefanovitch, you must return to our country and dance the *ryllo* on his grave, as I will when things quiet down." I protested that my return to the Balkans in the immediate future was unlikely, that I was bound for Japan, and that in any event I did not propose to dance on his grave.

"You are a good friend, but a poor hater, Stefan Stefanovitch. Think how the *sapages* dogged your footsteps and how Petkoff, the dictator's jackal, in his newspaper called upon the patriots to put you out of the way. The people can show their true feelings now, and when you return they will bless—they will adore you."

There is high authority for saying that revenge is sweet, but in this instance, as I can testify, it was also beautifying and rejuvenating. The woman who now sat at this corner of the universe preening her feathers was absolutely transfigured; and those who passed by beheld an unmistakably happy and contented human being. For some five years, in and out of Bulgaria, she had preached and plotted destruction to the little dictator, and undoubtedly she had been behind several of the attempts that had been made on his life; but always there had been a slip and Stambouloff had escaped, his lieutenants had fallen, but he had survived. With every failure a mark of disappointment and of suffering had been added to her deeply-lined face, but now all these wrinkles and furrows had been smoothed away. Joyous contentment sparkled from her eyes, the worn, bedraggled woman had grown quite beautiful and her constant smile was fascinating. Perhaps I should conceal this bloody recipe from the knowledge of beauty parlors, lest the quota of murders be greatly increased!

I delayed my return to Bulgaria too long. Nine years had elapsed before once again I put in my appearance in Sofia; and many things had been forgotten, among them even the dynamic woman whom I had last seen in the hour of her greatest happiness sipping a liqueur in a corner seat at the Café de la Paix. She too was dead, quite as dead as Stambouloff, her unmourned victim. By persistent inquiries I at last learned that she also had fallen by the sword—in one of those guerilla skirmishes in Macedonia, where neither age nor sex, nor anything else, was respected by the blood-crazed combatants.

The following lines which I wrote the Commodore at the time of my first visit, and which rather carelessly he published, will help to explain the situation in Sofia, at least as I saw it, on my return from the Danube excursion.

"The seeker after truth here at the very outset is confronted with the fact that while the men and women who play important roles in the Bulgarian capital are very few—say at a generous estimate half a hundred—they are divided into half a dozen cliques and of these it is impossible to know more than one at one and the same time.

"Here you cannot avail yourself of the foreigner's pleasant privilege in most European capitals of being on polite and even friendly terms with members of all parties at once. You, too, for the nonce must be a partisan. If you bow to Radoslavoff in the Tergoska Street you cannot shake hands with Petko Karaveloff when you meet him in that arid waste which is known officially as the Public Garden. If you salute Madame Panitza you cannot take tea with Madame Karaveloff which would be a pity, and if you are even suspected of having the most incidental contact or conversation with a Zankovist, your career at the palace is closed.

"So the seeker after the truth has no choice. He must dissemble. Only after having loudly proclaimed his loyalty and learning all the ins and outs of palace politics can he allow himself to be converted seriatim by the leaders of the hostile groups until finally he descends to the camp of the Zankovists who are supposed to receive the sinews of war and their guidance from St. Petersburg.

"Then the seeker should desist or better still leave Bulgaria, or the *Swoboda* (the government gazette) will denounce him as a Russian spy and stout-limbed *sapages*, political heelers who carry long sticks and use them ruthlessly, will dog his footsteps and then come forward to swear that he endeavored by means of the traditional ruble notes to shake their allegiance to the throne. And then the *Narodny Prava* will publish his photograph under the caption 'another traitor unmasked' and demand his expulsion from the sacred soil. But if he dissembles there will be interesting and even amusing moments in his sojourn and most certainly he will be rewarded by an invitation to lunch at the palace and there, from the silver service, a reminder and a legacy of Prince Ferdinand's ill-starred predecessor, the Hessian lions will frown at him."

This publication was far from helpful to me personally but it did outline the things that were to happen with a correctness which some of my other peeps into the future fell short of. Certainly the *sapages* dogged my footsteps, the doors of the Black Mosque often seemed about to open for me, decrees of expulsion were drawn up— but I must not anticipate. Before it became apparent that I had become set in the ways of error all the parties sought my favor and even the forlorn Prince in his palace assured me that there was always a place for me at his table.

I should and will admit that the dictator whom I now began to dislike cordially not seldom was subjected to experiences which serve to explain, if they by no means justify, the way in which he discarded the restraints and even the amenities of political life, at least as they are recognized in the civilized countries. His footsteps were constantly dogged by assassins and, though years were to elapse before they hacked him to pieces in the streets of Sofia, it is certain that attempts upon his life were most frequent. Indeed only a few weeks after our visit to the Tirnova shrine the Minister of the Interior who bore a striking resemblance to the Prime Minister was shot down and killed as he came out of Stambouloff's office. As an indication of the savagery prevailing at the time I may say that it was generally stated in the capital that this man owed his portfolio to this resemblance which was indeed remarkable, and soon signs appeared on many of the government offices with the announcement, "I want a man who looks like me to share my responsibilities—and the bullets that are aimed at me. Stefan Stambouloff."

In mid-summer, from the standpoint of the "special," a most unholy calm spread over the stormy Balkans; even the commercial skirmishes subsided and hardly a sibilant word came from the conspirators who wished to restore Prince Alexander or in any event to remove Prince Ferdinand, and something like a truce was apparently (but only apparently!) arranged between the component parts of that ethnic salad which was and is Macedonia. But there was to be no peace—suddenly the slumbering religious antagonisms entered upon an acute phase and these require a few words of explanation.

For many years the pleas of the Slav peoples of Macedonia that they be given the benefit of clergy had been on file at the Sublime Porte. Now and again they were brought to the attention of the Sultan himself by a good-natured ambassador from western Europe, but they made no headway. Ever since the fateful battle of Kossovo, which established the supremacy of the Turk, the war-waging Christian bishops had been expelled from their sees although from time to time humbler clergy in a clandestine manner had been permitted to shepherd the unfortunate Christian *rayahs*. Even these interlopers were persecuted after 1860 when it was thought, and not without some justification, that their activities were political rather than spiritual.

Then by a master stroke the Sultan split the Christian churches in twain. From the days of the Byzantine Empire the Christians had been under the control of the Greek Patriarch in Constantinople and so it happened that until the middle of the last century, and even down to the Congress of Berlin, the Serbians, the Bulgarians and even the roaming Roumanians of the Peninsula were regarded as Greeks and were so called from the Church to which they were in subjection. But as the spirit of nationalism was awakened in the Balkans, and as the poor *rayahs* learned of the corruption of the Holy Synod and saw how all the ecclesiastical plums were given to Greeks, men often far from worthy, an effort was made to separate the congregations according to race. With characteristic alacrity the Porte saw the opportunity of sowing discord among the Christians and in 1870 by a special firman the Sultan established the exarchate, which was given religious control of all the professing Christians of the Bulgar tongue. The outraged Greek Patriarch of the day denounced the new church as outside the pale and radically schismatic, although its members professed the same doctrines and held to the same dogmas—but there was the difference of the languages in which they prayed and, of course, their political objectives were as far apart as the poles.

And so in 1890 the Sultan threw another apple of discord into the midst of the warring churches. It was announced that, in pursuance of their immemorial practice of religious toleration, the members of the Divan who sat at the Sublime Porte had issued *berats* to two Bulgarian bishops, nominated by the Exarch, who would soon be installed in the Macedonian sees of Usküb and Ochrida. It would be of little interest to inquire at this late day what the motives were behind this concession. At best it would only shed light upon a state of affairs which has gone forever, but certainly the idea of encouraging Stambouloff in his anti-Russian policy, which could not fail to strengthen the hold of the Turks over the Christian provinces, entered into the calculations of the astute men in Stamboul.

It may be explained that the Turkish word *berat*, at the time so confusing to the world press, has no relation at all to the Italian word *berretta*, a cap which I believe is conferred by the Holy Father in Rome upon certain of his bishops with whom he is well pleased. The *berat* is simply an ecclesiastical exequatur, passport or permission to carry the comfort of the word and the blessings of the sacraments to a benighted people who, in this instance at least, and for many generations, had been deprived of the benefit of an official clergy. At the last moment, for some reason that never was quite clear, the *berat* for the Bishop of Ochrida was held up, but as it was announced that the other *berat*-bearer was leaving Constantinople in a few days for his dangerous post I determined if possible to be there when he arrived. In those days we had no diplomatic or even consular representative in Bulgaria, and the Turkish agency there refused to recognize my Washington passport. However, Stambouloff and Sir Nicholas O'Connor, the British diplomatic agent in Sofia at the time, were good enough to concoct between them what might be called an Anglo-Bulgarian passport for an American citizen. However lacking in legal status, it was a formidable looking document and on several occasions it served me and my purpose well.

I took the night train north and on the following morning at Nish, once the capital of Servia, I transferred to a train bound for Salonica on the line which Baron Hirsch constructed and which had only been opened to the sea a few weeks before. My passport sustained a careful examination at the frontier station of Zebeftche and soon I found myself in Macedonia or in Old Serbia, in Greater Bulgaria, or in the *vilayet* of Kossovo—for here geographical terms depend upon the ethnic origin of the speaker. It was an uneventful journey through a gray gaunt country until, in a district of free Albanians, as we came out of the Karadjik tunnel, our train was greeted by a well-sustained volley of musketry fire. All the windows were shattered and the passengers in my car, a Greek merchant and two Jewish peddlers, struggled with me, whom they evidently regarded as an interloper, as to who should lie nearest to the floor.

"The bullets were intended for His Beatitude, the Bishop Theodosios," explained the Maltese conductor of the train. "But what numbskulls they are! Of course he will be on the up-train." Be this as it may, as the smoke cleared away, the not very sharp shooters emerged from behind the rocks and exchanged cordial salutes with our engine driver and his fireman. "They are on very friendly terms," explained the conductor drily, "they exchange presents— the crew gives cartridges and gets Macedonian tobacco, and every

now and then obliges by running over a donkey who has seen better days but has to be paid for by the company in piasters." Well,
it was quite an unusual railway in many ways.

Three days later I rubbed my eyes which for some moments I
thought were victimized by some Biblical mirage. The hills and
crags about Usküb were alive with people. Crouching behind boul-
ders or squatting in the innumerable cemeteries that surrounded the
shrunken town, that was once the imperial city of Justinian, were
gathered the forlorn children who, descended from the martyrs,
had survived the generations of persecution. Here with their sick,
their crippled, and even with their recent dead I was told, the
Christians of the highlands had gathered and were waiting in the
shadows which the tall tombs of bygone pashas cast, like arrows
over the arid plain, the coming of the holy man who was to mend
their fortunes and perchance make whole their crippled bodies.
All wore the somber dust-colored garments they have worn since
the day of the destruction of the churches, when the empire of Stefan Dushan was dismembered—"while the good Lord was sleeping" as the Macedonian peasants say.

Even in the town the narrow winding streets were thronged with
the most venturesome of the mountain folk, but the large Turkish
garrison was conspicuous by its absence. Of this surprising circumstance two explanations were current. Some said Edhem Pasha,
second in command, had led most of the troops to the Montenegrin
frontier where trouble was brewing. Others, and these, the timid and
fearful, were the most numerous, whispered that the garrison had
been sent out of the way so that there would be no restraining force
in case the Albanian *arnauts* who had also assembled in the town
should decide to oppose the decree of the great Padishah and make
short shrift of the Bishop and his flock who, as they thought, were
preparing to defile the holy places by their presence.

One morning shortly after daybreak the long awaited cortège
appeared, coming from the railway station. It was headed by a tall
cross-bearer immediately followed by the Bishop in gorgeous epis-
copal garb but riding upon an humble ass. Thousands upon thousands followed, mostly, it seemed to me, the lame, the halting and
the blind, as the Bishop led the way to the desecrated and ruined

shrine of St. Dimitri where in the darkness of the forgotten ages his predecessor had been stoned to death. Soon the great multitude outpaced the procession and, as the Bishop approached the sacred edifice, a path had to be made for him and his almoner, his chaplains and his theologians. His path was blocked by the sick and the dying who kissed the hem of his garment as he passed. For hours the holy man blessed all who were in the reach of the benediction that he gave with outstretched arms, and upon those who were near him he laid his trembling hands from time to time. In praise of a God, who had at last relented, psalms were sung, and when the darkness came that followed on the long day the people still crowded around their shepherd with hope and confidence in their eyes. All defilement had been washed away from the long deserted church, every stone of the walls that had been thrown down in fury by the Moslem had been blessed and in some measure replaced. Thousands pressed their wan cheeks against the cracked foundations of the long abandoned church and tenderly caressed every standing pillar. To them it was not a picturesque ruin but the Ark of the Covenant of their Lord and Savior, which after so many bitter years of probation they had been found worthy to have and to hold again.

I too was weak from fasting and all the emotions of the day when, the ceremonies of reconsecration being over and as the multitudes were returning to their campfires on the hillside, before supper I stumbled into the Turkish bath over which my friend the barber Omar presided.

"And what do you think of it all?" I asked.

For a moment the good Omar was silent and then, "What do I think? Well I think it is a great misfortune for me that a man has come to town with an income of forty pounds Turkish and that he wears a beard!"

On the following day the thousands of Macedonian Christians who still lingered about the ancient shrine awakened with an indefinable feeling of disappointment and anxiety. To begin with, the advent of the good Bishop had not been signalized by the signs and wonders that, long predicted, had, of course, been confidently expected. For four centuries every plague upon their race, every blight upon their lives and crops had been dismissed by these people of the Macedonian hills and valleys with the confident assurance, "Ah! when we have in our midst again an anointed of the Lord our slavery will end, our misfortunes vanish and on that blessed day the black magic of the magicians and the Moslem wizardry will not prevail against our prayers." And then mad Ivan the town crier strode through the camps, and it was anything but cheerful tidings that he croaked out in his raven voice.

"Myriads of blackbirds are alighting on the field of Kossovo," was the burden of his warning message. "Not so many have been seen there since the evil day when the sky was darkened and King Lazar and the champions of Christendom went down before the Horde. Woe is me! The curse survives even unto the twentieth generation!"

And, of course, the hostile bearing of some of the Turks and of all the Albanians on the preceding day served to depress and further disturb the Christians. On the other hand there was comfort in the thought that both the Vali and the Mudir of the town had been polite and even, to some extent, helpful. The good Theodosios had, as the protocol demanded, called upon them and with much ceremony drunk the three obligatory cups of coffee, and the greetings exchanged had been formal and dignified; however it was now recalled that not a word was spoken to indicate that the officials regarded his presence among the Christian flocks, so long without a shepherd, as anything but a fortuitous incident of the travel season.

About nine o'clock the fears of the anxious people were intensified by the appearance of a messenger from the Mudir accompanied by a horsed troop of irregulars before the hovel where the Bishop had spent the night.

"His Excellency sends his salaams; Your Beatitude is bidden to the Divan." Swifter than the flight of birds these ominous words traveled through the wretched camps that clustered about the shrunken city, and a low wail arose from the anxious people. Some indeed hastened to leave, to secrete themselves in the mountain recesses whence the first ray of hope and salvation that had shone upon their race for four centuries had lured them. But by far the greater number sat about, pitiful pictures of hopeless woe and dejection.

Most of them maintained a helpless silence but not a few were crooning as I passed in their midst. "Mad Ivan has spoken truly— and to our blight. Again the blackbirds are winging their flight over the dark field."

In a few minutes Bishop Theodosios, followed by his yellow-haired cross-bearer and by about a score of mountain Slavs, who were too brave or too curious to remain behind, and by myself, entered the courtyard of the *konak* where we were met with unctuous politeness by the Vali and a number of other officials. Behind the Vali, encased in a uniform strung with many decorations, sat Akmet Ayoub the last Field Marshal of the Turkish Empire, who had always shown himself as a fiend incarnate during his long reign in the *vilayet*. His great red face was blank of all expression but in his eyes were reflected the green banners which the Prophet of Mecca had unfurled. In sullen silence the Field Marshal overlooked the scene, ignoring the presence of the Bishop and the Christians who came with him. And only the Vali spoke:

"Men learned in the law, Your Beatitude," he said, "have throughout the night studied the *berat* and the papers you brought, and this study has confirmed in our minds the suspicion of a misunderstanding which was apparent to us yesterday but of which in all hospitality, in the moment of your arrival, it would not have been courteous to speak. But even now the confirmation of our suspicions has come by wire from Stamboul and we must inform you, I need not say with what regret, that the hours of your stay among us, until a more propitious season, are numbered." The last words of the Vali were emphasized by a shrill warning whistle from the railway station, and in conclusion he added, "I have the honor to announce that His Beatitude's train is even now awaiting him."

Much that was said was well beyond the reach of my meager Turkish, but I knew the language of the human heart, and when the wail from the inner courtyard was caught up by the waiting multitude outside I recognized the despairing cries as coming from a people beaten down upon their knees—and in poignant, mortal anguish.

For all answer the Bishop made a low obeisance, and followed by his supporters withdrew from the courtyard. His features expressed the humility of a saint but in his upright carriage and sturdy stride there was something militant, something that suggested to me that the thought of resistance to the stern decree was not entirely absent from his mind. In the crowded streets outside the *konak* the reserve that had been evidently imposed by orders from on high had vanished, and as the sad cortège passed, the Albanians, and even the Turks, with the Vali's consent if not by his express command, gave full vent to their hatred.

"Ey! Ey!" they shouted. "His Beatitude is not staying long with us. Can it be that he has shriven clean his flock in so short a time?" "Dog brothers you are! And dog brothers you remain," cried the Albanians, nervously fingering their crooked knives as the slovenly rag-clad Slavs, bowed down under the weight of their years of servitude, stumbled along the rough way, cringing before their arrogant conquerors. "Ey, ey," they moaned. "It is true that the plains of Kossovo are black with the birds of ill-omen." And some whispered one to another, "In the beginning there must have been grievous sin for even in this the thirtieth generation His face is turned from us. How long O Lord! How long must we wander in the wilderness?"

As one in a dream the good Bishop walked at the head of the sad procession. He seemed oblivious of the vile words and the menacing gestures of the conquerors. Now and again he would stop for a moment to smile upon and bless his own people, who crouched at his feet and for the last time sought to kiss the hem of his garment. Perhaps a realizing sense of the misfortune that had overtaken his mission, and frustrated it, only came to him as the cortège reached the Church of St. Dimitri, the ruined shrine which only yesterday he had consecrated anew, for the preservation and sanctity of which so many hundreds of martyrs had died in vain. There, as his eyes fell upon the holy ruin which he had vowed to upbuild, a tremor ran through his frame. He turned and cast a searching look upon his cringing flock. And then suddenly, as though in answer to a command which had not been spoken, a tall, stalwart young man, clothed in the shaggy fleece which the shepherds of the highlands wear even in summer, strode out from the wailing multitude.

"Your Beatitude," he shouted. "In God's name, raise here the standard of revolt. Bid us die for you and our faith rather than we should see again the shrine of St. Dimitri become the kennel of the dog brothers."

The yellow-haired cross-bearer and two others stepped to the Bishop's side and raised on high the sacred symbol, but the many were too slow, perhaps too apathetic, and the Turks too quick.

"Seize him, the speaker of treason," shouted a police captain, "seize him in the name of the Padishah." In a moment the *zaptieh* were upon their man. He was beaten, bound and gagged, and no helping hand was raised as they led him away.

An hour later the good Bishop, the vicar of Christ on earth, regarded by all as the messenger from Heaven, was gone with but a silent blessing, all he was allowed to give, to his unhappy flock.

When it was all over I went to the *han* to talk over the events of the day with Schilka, the Austrian Vice-Consul, and Spadoni, the Maltese telegraph agent. I found that the magnificent Albanian Arnaut, a picturesque, silent figure who had adorned their table for some days, was gone, but not without booty. He had availed himself of the excitement of the Bishop's reception to carry off to the mountains the most beautiful girl of the many born to the Christians of the town. Omar, the gossipy barber, had all the details, and on his way to the Turkish bath to attend a noble patron he stopped in at the *han*.

The last seen of Scander Beg, for such was the illustrious name the Arnaut bore, was his dignified retreat up the mountainside with the girl slung across his shoulder, while his stalwart slave covered the rear with glistening silver pistols in his hands and a crooked knife in his mouth. The girl, the "rose" as Omar called her, screamed and sobbed, "but not overmuch," averred the barber. "I have no doubt that she will live to be consoled. And now," concluded Omar triumphantly, for in politics this barber was not a trimmer, "she will wear the *yashmak*, and none but the eyes of her lord will feast upon the rare beauties of her face and form."

There had been reported to Omar some commotion among the Christians, based entirely upon a misunderstanding of the incident, as he explained; for when it was noised abroad that Scander Beg had sent back to the bereaved father the wedding gift, a ransom of five pounds Turkish, it was admitted by everyone that the kidnaper had behaved with perfect gallantry, like the Albanian gentleman he was.

Three of the brave but foolhardy peasants who had urged the Bishop to resist the Turks and raise the standard of the Cross were kept in close confinement in the vermin-infected prison for a week, and then staggering under their weight of chains and their days of starvation, I saw them walk to the new railway station which all Europe had said would exert such a civilizing influence upon Macedonian conditions, and there embark for Constantinople, where their judges were awaiting them.

On this the day of their departure the narrow lanelike streets of the once-Christian city were empty; none seemingly dared to wish these martyrs of liberty Godspeed upon their calvary. Two of the brave fellows were simple peasant lads, who had acted instinctively and without thought of what the consequence might be. The other was a man of very different caliber, a born agitator and one whose trail in the mountains the Turkish soldiers had been following for weeks. He was, I learned, this stalwart fighter for the Cross, a Serbian of excellent family, who had devoted his life and the considerable fortune which he had heired to the propaganda of the Pan-Slavic doctrines in Macedonia in general and to the re-establishment of the old Serbian Empire in particular. His name was Bozidar Illitch,* and the Servians should recall his services in this the day when the dreams he dreamed have at last taken on form and substance.

Some years later another bishop came to the villages along the Vardar. This time he was a Serbian. On close examination the wise men in Stamboul had ascertained that Stefan Dushan who built the cathedral church in Usküb was a Serb, and, of course, the government in Belgrade was more tractable and Prince Ferdinand in Sofia was leaving nothing undone to cultivate friendly relations with Holy Russia. In any event the appointment of a Serb would sow discord among the Slavic tribes and all other Christians of the pen-

* Undoubtedly a "war" name such as all revolutionists assumed to shield their families from ruthless retaliation.

insula, and that was a boon from Heaven for which all good Moslems pray every day in their afternoon prayer! *

I shall now relate with considerable detail an incident of my Balkan experiences, not particularly noteworthy perhaps, but because it had an influence upon shaping my course and because it reveals the obstacles we met with in presenting the news of the turbulent peninsula to the Western world. I do not think our clients, that is our readers, appreciate the difficulties of such situations as I was called upon to describe, with which my successors in this and other equally perplexing fields of reporting are today also confronted. Facts are slippery as well as stubborn things; and human nature is —well—human nature! As a prelude to my confession I must tell you how shocked I was in the early days of my apprenticeship, when one night in the Union Club in Sofia, as we stood before the bulletin board and read the news of the first Armenian massacres that took place in and around Erivan, I heard H.B., that famous correspondent who had been for twenty years purveying news to the English public, say, "I'm sorry so many Armenians were murdered—if they were murdered. But I am convinced, if the Turks acted in this way, they had good reason for it."

I was outraged at this callous remark and showed it. To me this Turcophile correspondent was always anathema, but two years later I had descended from (perhaps it would be more correct to say I had been toppled off!) my judicial pinnacle and was becoming as guilty of partisanship as H.B., but the descent brought me frankly and openly into the pro-Christian camp. Everything they did was quite right with me. Fortunate it was that the changes and chances of my profession transferred me at this juncture to another and less complicated field of investigation, and when I was returned to the Balkans I had in a measure regained my equanimity. I at least thought so.

These weighty thoughts are suggested by the memory of my

* Those who are familiar with the nationalistic rivalries and the church feuds that prevail in this unhappy country, will be surprised at the reverent enthusiasm with which the coming of the Lord's anointed was greeted by the followers of the Patriarch, and of the Exarch, and indeed by all other Christians without distinction of race or ritual. It was indeed "A truce of God." Unfortunately, it was not long before the propaganda of the churches resumed its devastating sway.

second foray into Macedonia (May 1889) and its consequences for me and the unfortunate people involved. Suddenly out of a clear sky an "atrocity scare" possessed London. Great meetings were held and the indignation of large church congregations was provoked by the burning words of divines who in Exeter Hall described with many bloodcurdling details the sufferings and the tortures to which the Christian peasantry of Macedonia were subjected. An English Cathedral Canon, who it developed had traveled down the Danube on a freight boat, was quite certain he had seen the mangled and disemboweled bodies of Macedonian peasants hanging from bean poles as he passed. This far-sighted Canon was by no means discountenanced when it was pointed out that his ship had navigated in waters at least three hundred miles distant from the Macedonian highlands.

But while this was doubtless the spark that started the conflagration, from other sources came more circumstantial stories. They came from correspondents who though for very good reasons they had not ventured out from the security of their bases in Salonica or Zemlin (now Zemun), described the villages they had beheld going up in flames and how the villagers, after seeing their women ravished, had been shot down or marched off to exile in Tripoli, a fate that was worse than death. Sharp-eyed Argus in Paris (as we often called the Commodore) ordered me to the scene of these atrocities and with me went—very reluctantly—my interpreter Tryko.

After three weeks of hard riding, during which the Turks neither assisted me nor placed obstacles in my path, I was satisfied that this atrocity yarn was the most fantastic fairy tale that ever came from the Balkans—which is saying much. It soon became apparent that many of the villages reported destroyed had never existed. Others we found quite peaceful. The inhabitants were not aware of their extinction or that their countryside had been devastated by fire and sword. Of course I saw many things that made my blood boil, and I said so. It was indeed a sad and moving picture of a weak and long oppressed people who were suffering for their faith and for their racial determination, to both of which they clung so tenaciously.

But I had to report that the indictment fell to the ground, no—not a single count could be substantiated.

I came upon one village where atrocities had indeed been committed, but they had occurred twenty years previous to my visit. They had taken place at the time when the Bashi-bazouks had been let loose in the highlands to wreak their vengeance on the villagers who, hearing that the Russians were coming to liberate them, had thought it their duty to help. These unfortunate people lost their property and their lives because they did not appreciate for one moment that, to maintain the balance of power in southeastern Europe, the concert of Christian Powers would block their emancipation that had been so nearly accomplished.

When my dispatches dealing with this episode were read in the House of Commons by the Under Secretary for Foreign Affairs, and when they were endorsed and confirmed in every detail by the report of Her Majesty's Consul-General in Salonica who was sent to the scene of the alleged atrocities, some weeks after my visit, the matter was dropped. Heartrending as was the state of affairs in the *vilayets* as described by Mr. Blount (the Consul-General) and myself, it was so much less terrible than had been reported by the sensation-mongers that the English public and the English press with a sigh of relief let the matter drop, and the note of protest dealing with general conditions in Macedonia, which might have served at least as a word of warning, and which I asked for, was never sent to the Porte.

Not even in the most hot-headed days of my Turcophobia did I say that the authorities in Constantinople had launched this atrocity scare as a *ballon d'essai* to test out the strength of righteous indignation in western Europe. Yet this may have been the case and they certainly profited by the demonstration of our weakness that followed. Within three months the atrocities which I had disproved were perpetrated, the lands that I had found peaceful and fairly smiling were devastated, and many of the villages I had found intact were ruthlessly wiped out. The news of what was taking place gradually leaked out, but it fell upon the ears of a public that had heard the cry of "Wolf" too often and grown cynical. The unhappy thought possessed me that these crimes would not have been committed but for the clean bill of health I, and others, had given the Turks a few weeks before. As a result my departure from the role of an impartial and fair-minded observer was complete, so when a year later Tashin Pasha, the "gray Eminence" of Sultan Abdul Hamid, wrote and asked the Commodore to remove me from the field of southeastern Europe on the stated ground "that I always held with the Greeks and other Schismatics and would not believe a Turkish official even when he took an oath on the Koran or swore by the beard of the Prophet," I could do no other than admit the truth of the accusation. In reverse, my attitude had become very much like that of the Turcophile H.B. When, as sometimes happened, the Christians got the upper hand and behaved in an unchristian manner I was slow to believe it, and I consoled myself with the thought that after all, at the worst, they were only engaged in evening up a bit the terrible score.

11. THE LAND OF INCORRUPTIBLE VIRGINS

RATHER AT loose ends, after the Biblical scenes I have sought to describe had been enacted, I lingered on in the now famous town on the Vardar. It was in those days a place that was hard to get to and even harder to get away from, and besides I clung to the belief that the ambassadors of Christendom in Stamboul would react energetically to the snub that the Sultan had administered to them. I thought the good Bishop would come back. I had witnessed his humiliation and naturally I wanted to be present when he was exalted and then, as usual, I fear I was actuated by mixed motives. Before his return (and clearly I would be justified in awaiting it), in the intervening days, I would have an opportunity to make a superficial scamper into Higher Albania, by the back door. If anything sensational exploded elsewhere in the Balkans during my absence I would have a defense. It was high time for me to have a look at Albania; certainly it was my duty to go there although specific instructions to that effect had not come.

It was my good friend Herr von Smucker, the Austro-Hungarian Consul-General, who, while he quite properly disclaimed all responsibility for the venture, by his good offices made it possible. When the plan was first suggested, Tryko, my Bulgarian interpreter from Sofia, a former student of Robert College, declined to accompany me. As he knew but little Turkish and no Albanian, in any event he would have been of but slight assistance. Smucker, however, had with him as *cavasses* or soldier-guards of the Consulate two brothers, handsome young Albanians, who, by some freak of fortune that was most lucky for me, had been educated in a mission school at Durazzo by the Italian Franciscan fathers and spoke Italian well. At that time I could also speak Italian fluently, although mine was certainly not the *lingua Toscana in boca Romana*.

It was decided that we should travel light and only avail ourselves of ponies as far as possible and then foot it. Our first objective and the only one we disclosed was Kossovo Polje, the "dark field of the Blackbirds" * where five hundred years before, the Christian Host had been defeated by the Turkish Horde in one of the decisive battles of history. This was in the permitted zone of travel. "When you have concluded this pilgrimage you will return here, but, of course, conforming your movements to circumstances," said von Smucker with a portentous wink.

Our early morning start was marred by an incident which I did not appreciate at its true value until later. After we had drunk the stirrup cup in excellent Tokay wine, the memory of which often tortured me in the thirsty days that were to follow, it became apparent that the *cavass* who had been selected as my guide did not want to serve me and that his brother was very loath to see him go. But with an imperious gesture the Consul silenced all remonstrances and then, consuls were consuls in those days! at least in the East, he took the *cavass* who was to remain behind, by the arm, escorted him to the consular jail and locked him up behind formidable iron bars!

In answer to my inquiry he said, "The prisoner and his brother, your guide, both belong to an important highland clan. The prisoner will serve as hostage for your good treatment and safe return. Of course I shall treat him well and when you come back unharmed he will be liberated immediately and, if you like, you can reward him for the inconvenience he will have suffered. It is the custom of the country and we must conform to it and in fact it is the only halfway safe way for you to attempt the journey."

Usküb, my point of departure, then the headquarters of the Turkish forces in the *vilayet*, and now Serbian again, is the key to Macedonia, and as it commands the Kachanlik Pass between Shar

---

* Kossovo, under the rule of the Sultan was a *vilayet* or province and comprised the *sandjak* of Usküb and the *sandjaks* or districts of Prisren and Novi Bazaar. This territory I saw something of in a later journey.

Dagh and the Kara Dagh into Kossovo, it also stands guard over the approaches to Albania from the East. Along this road and through this Pass were herded the "tribute" children, the "sons of the Eagle" who for centuries furnished the backbone of the Turkish armies and the Janissaries of the Sultans. Curiously enough in the end it was these *Yeni-asker* or "new soldiers" who brought about the overthrow of Abdul Hamid, the last independent Ottoman Sultan. It was a case where a guardian of the guards was needed and fortunately was lacking.

Even I, though little versed in military matters, as I looked about me could well understand why Usküb (Skoplje of the Slavs) has from the dawn of history been a place of strategic importance even before the Roman era when it became the capital of Dardania and the residence of a Pro-Consul. Our first night we spent at the "Sheepfold" of Kumanovo where, in 1912, the German-trained troops of the new régime in Turkey gave way before the impetuous Serbians. In this war the tables were turned completely. At Bregalnica the Serbians wiped out their disastrous defeat by the Bulgarians at Slivnitsa, and at Kumanovo the defeat of Christendom at nearby Kossovo was cancelled, or rather should have been. The victory at Kossovo made southeastern Europe Turkish for centuries, while the defeat of the Turks at Kumanovo did not send them packing to Anatolia and out of Europe altogether, as it should have done.

About noon of the second day we descended into the desolate plain of Kossovo. It sits like a great amphitheater beset on all sides by the frowning Macedonian highlands. It was a predestined battlefield and here on that never to be forgotten day in June 1389, the armies of the Cross and the Crescent met and the fate of the Balkan peninsula was decided for five hundred years. The people we met were mostly Albanians heavily armed and gorgeously attired. They seemed most arrogant and were evidently encroaching on the lands of the obsequious Slavs.

"Soon we will manure the plain with the carcasses of the Christian dogs," said one of them.

I wandered over the dreary fields but how the battle, so tragic in its consequences to Christendom, was fought I got no idea; but how and why it was lost I was to learn when evening came. We had no tents, but a Slav peasant bowed low and asked the mighty *Effendi* to share his humble hovel, but with good reason I wrapped myself in a blanket and lay outside under the stars. After he had enjoyed the cigarettes I gave him the peasant came and sat beside me and upon his monotonous *gusle* and in a broken voice told the story of how the great Tsar Lazar, who on the fateful day commanded the Christian Host, had chosen the Heavenly Kingdom and let worldly triumph go, how he and his chief men had elected for bliss eternal, leaving the poor *rayahs* to the chains and the servitudes they have borne for centuries and still were bearing.

As the ballad filtered through to me it runs,

"Flying came a gray bird, indeed a noble falcon, from the Holy City of Jerusalem. No little sparrow brings he to the Imperial tent but a letter from God's blessed Mother. Sinking upon his knees our Champion received the missive which said, 'O! Tsar Lazar! Thou of glorious line. The parting of the ways is near. Between two empires which wilt thou choose? Dost thou desire the Kingdom where God's beloved dwell or dost thou choose the empire of this World? If 'tis the worldly empire that thou lovest most, call thy mighty men to arms, bid them saddle their horses and tighten their girths. Let them gird on their sharp swords and lead them on and then the Turkish horde will be brought low. But if it is the Heavenly Kingdom that thou wouldst choose then have Christ's Bread prepared, for here on this dark plain where the blackbirds moan you and they destruction shall find. . . .'

" '. . . Dear God, what shall I answer? What decide? Upon which Kingdom shall I set my choice? The Empire of this world or the Heavenly Kingdom and the days of joy and Grace. But Dear God! How can I hesitate? The Empire of this earth is a little and a fleeting thing while Thy Kingdom endures for ever and aye.' So the great Tsar Lazar summoned his warriors and kneeling before twelve bishops of saintly mien they received the sacred host and still kneeling they met death at the hands of the infidel horde—and life eternal from God."

From the first my *cavass* was not a gay companion. He was always mumbling to himself or to me something about how precarious was the position of his dear brother whose life was forfeit unless he brought me safely back to the Vardar. But I did not really appreciate how dark was his foreboding until the third night of our wandering away from the permitted zone of Kossovo. A sullen virgin in her strange mannish attire was guarding us. The wolfish watchdogs stood by our sleeping place in ominous silence. The food that I offered the dogs had been refused with growls. It was very cold, and owing to the recent rain our campfire would not burn. I sat up and there, too, was the *cavass*, sitting on his heels and with tears streaming down his cheeks.

"Have you had a bad dream?" I inquired, as sympathetically as I could.

"It was not a dream," he answered. "I have just seen my brother. He tells me he is dead."

Then for the first time I began to appreciate the situation. My own death was an indispensable preliminary to the demise of the greatly-loved brother, and I determined to walk circumspectly, to get through smilingly if I could. I would go to great lengths in my endeavor not to bring another sorrow to the already overflowing cup of my dreary companion and guide.

The fact that from the moment we arrived footsore and weary in one of the mountain villages we were placed under the guardianship of a woman whom the *cavass* always qualified as a "virgin *incorruptible*" requires some explanation, although the only one I can offer may appear to the reader, as it did to me at the time, one that is halting and far from plausible. They were always women no longer young who had put away all thought of love or marriage. They were unveiled, although they might well have been veiled to their advantage, and they wore men's clothes. At times they carried blunderbusses of ancient make and always their belts bristled with crooked knives. They would indicate the place on the village common where we were to camp and they made it quite plain that we were to camp nowhere else. Their countenances were always dour and forbidding—so forbidding indeed that their incorruptible status was immediately accepted and neither I nor my *cavass* made the least effort to undermine it.

These women were the acknowledged mistresses of the wolfish watchdogs that abounded, and the appearance of the dogs was such

that I could readily believe as reported that their sires had inter-
married with the wolves of the mountain. Obedient to an emphatic
gesture from the sinewy hands of their mistresses these wolf-dogs
took up their posts of duty. If we moved they moved too. They
were stationed to the right and the left of us, in front and behind
us, and I must say that they displayed one virtue which I came to
appreciate. During our stay in the village which was evidently so
unwelcome to all, man as well as beast, they never approached
nearer to our anxious persons than ten feet. It was only years afterwards that I learned why we were always placed in the custody of
these women who once for all had put men out of their lives. It
was Essad Pasha, the hero of Scutari, who, as will be disclosed on
a later page, gave me the explanation of this arrangement which at
the time was so puzzling.

I made a map of our wanderings with a list of the mountain
villages and the traces of the goat tracks by which they are reached,
but I gave it to Consul Smucker in recognition of his assistance in
the foolish venture and the rough copy that I retained has now
disappeared. With the reconquest during the World War all the
names have been changed, I am assured, so even if my map had
survived the wear and tear of time it would not prove helpful
today to the wanderer in these parts.

I remember Pristina very well and the clear mountain stream
in which I bathed my blistered feet, and also the Greek inn-keeper
who was not afraid to serve us with food which after the unchang-
ing diet of goat's milk or goat's cheese was delightful. But the
little villages in which we met with such a cold reception were certainly picturesque, and each and every one of them was on a war
footing. Over and above the crazy crooked hovels in which the
villagers housed, there always arose in a commanding position a
kula or fortress stronghold. It was built of rough uncemented
stones and the walls were loopholed to command the approach from
every direction. The fort when the nature of the ground permitted
was four-sided, and at each of the corners there was a little tower
in which invariably there was a man or woman on the lookout with
rifle near at hand. The only entrance to the stronghold was an
opening about two by four and about ten feet above the ground.

Through this when the guard was changed the fighting villagers crawled. Sometimes they were aided by a ladder they drew into the fort after them, but more often they would pile a few stones one upon the other which, once inside, they pushed over with a great beam which seemed to be retained at the entrance with this purpose in view.

On a high pole before each *kula* was suspended a grinning horse's skull. Why, I never learned. My *cavass* simply said it was the custom of the country, and this was the only answer I received to many queries which I considered pertinent. Inside, as far as I could judge from the distant view, which was all that I was permitted to obtain, the men and the women of the garrison took potluck together and they certainly drank a good deal of *raki* before the meal was served. Then they would squat around a huge bowl suspended over a charcoal fire and with their fingers they would draw out what appeared to be morsels of goat's flesh. Only once I saw that the mess was equipped with one great communal wooden spoon.

In the evening, sometimes but not often, these stern and generally silent sentinels of the mountain villages would break out into weird music. The only instrument I saw in use was one that resembled the Serbian *gusle* but with two strings only from which stiff fingers coaxed pathetic mournful notes. Several times late in the evening the sentinels in the towers broke out into monotonous song. What the words were and what they portended I never made out. Invariably my *cavass* would say, "He is simply recalling his family tree—so that he may not forget it." But I cling to the interpretation of the German professor who maintains that these were the songs that the Pelasgians sang in the days when Homer was assembling his great song book.

In the villages our relations with the fair sex, as I have made quite plain, were of the most distant character, in fact they were practically non-existent save with the stern-visaged, heavily armed virgins, who invariably stood guard over our bivouac. But sometimes on the mountain goat paths we met rather beautiful girls all unveiled, although truth to tell they were generally a little too stalwart for my taste. As a rule they were carrying great sacks of charcoal from their lofty nests to be exchanged in the valleys for flour.

My journey was nearly ended before we came into even remote contact with the blood feuds for which this turbulent country is famed. Outside Prizren we were overtaken by a violent thunderstorm and decided to stop for the night at a little village which lay right across our path. If I cherished the least hope that in the circumstances some sort of shelter might be offered the drenched travelers I was soon disillusioned. Only the usual guard was furnished, and the unpleasant dogs. I was depressed by the weather conditions and the innumerable sepulchres that here abounded. They were quite as numerous as the one-sided stone hovels where the living were lodged, and certainly they did not strike a cheerful note. About our smoky fire, however, we later heard a tale of the custom of the country and what is called the "law of the mountains," which indicated that even at that day the toll of life as a result of the vendetta was very high.

This was by way of being a Christian village and on the Sabbath before our arrival, in the little square plot of ground which served the community as an open air church, the solemn mass had been said. The visiting priest from one of the coast parishes had just concluded his benediction when suddenly a shot rang out and a man fell dead. It was explained that as service ended one of the worshipers looked about him and unfortunately caught sight of a man whose family, as the saying is, owed his family a "life," and of course as in duty bound he shot him dead in his tracks. The affair might have passed off without the massacre which followed but for the fact that the man who fired the first shot, who did not live more than a few seconds to enjoy his victory, and his victim, were both united to many in the congregation by the closest blood ties, and the inevitable result was a pitched battle. The priest by all accounts behaved very gallantly, rushing here and there over the improvised battlefield, now imploring the wild men to desist and now lifting on high the Host, seeking to terrify them. Before reason prevailed, or more probably when the call of the blood was satisfied, there lay in the place of worship eleven dead, two of whom were women, and this was not approved and indeed deeply regretted—as now inevitably some of the males would have to carry the charcoal down into the valley. . . .

In the morning, at dawn, as our incorruptible virgin of the guard snuffled and the watchdogs withdrew snarling, we, in leaving the village, had to cross the grass plot where the savage scene had been enacted. Here on this consecrated-desecrated patch of ground where the villagers had gathered to beg forgiveness of their sins, prisoners of tradition, they had run amok, and in the performance of an inescapable duty had taken part in mass murders. Gingerly, in and out among the eleven grave mounds, some of them still be-spattered with blood, we slowly picked our way. But once out of sight we moved more quickly. That was a rude village; we were glad to leave it behind and for good.

After many long days, each followed by its even longer night, we got back to the valley of the Vardar—somehow. Long before we saw it we heard the roar of the mountain water as it rushed through its rocky bed toward the sea. The moment the welcome sound fell upon his ear my *cavass* was transformed. "Our lucky star has been in the ascendant," he shouted, and though footsore and weary I did not gainsay him. An acquaintance of his bobbed up out of the bush and on the moment the *cavass* abandoned his limping pony to the care of his friend and dashed off down the rocky road. Every now and then he would turn handsprings and then his *fusta* skirts would billow out in the breeze like so many balloon jibs.

Half an hour later I hobbled into the consular compound and surprised Smucker with the keys in his hand standing before the little prison, and saw the affectionate brothers embracing, as best they could, through the dungeon bars.

"Ah," said Smucker, "There you are! Now I will let him out," and a moment later the sorely tried brothers were enjoying a fraternal embrace. The kindly Consul led me to the Turkish bath which he pre-empted for the evening, one of his diplomatic privileges. For an hour I revelled in the steaming atmosphere and the hot water. Then he produced some river-cooled Pilsner, we had supper and I felt much better; indeed in a few minutes I was bragging about the trip and saying how I would not have abandoned it for many pounds Turkish.

To celebrate my return to what with some exaggeration we chose to call civilization, Smucker wanted to make a night of it, and sent for the lean dark-skinned Gypsy dancing girls, but I soon limped off to my room at the *han*. At first and indeed for long I could not sleep. At the foot of the bed stood the incorruptible virgin in man's attire with her ancient musket and her sash bristling with crooked knives, and all about me lowered the band of unapproachable wolf-dogs who would not come near and yet would not go away. Then the friendly Omar came and by the light of a lantern cut off my long locks. Confidentially he remarked that while most of the "sons of the Eagle" professed a noble faith after all, under the skin, they too were but so many "dog brothers." When at last I fell asleep I slept for eighteen hours on end.

It had been a foolish business and wholly unprofitable, how unprofitable it had been I was only to learn the following day when I began to move about and face my situation, when on my blistered feet again I went to our "treasury," under a brick in the floor. There I found that most of the money was gone, but there was an explanatory note from Tryko, my Bulgarian interpreter. He wrote that his life was in danger from the despicable Serbian propagandists and so he had gone away and had been so free as to take the funds that were necessary for his escape, "as he knew I would like him to do." He said nothing about my wonderful Albanian shirts with which he had outfitted himself for the journey and of which I was very proud and at the moment in sore need.

It would be most unfair if in closing this incident I should leave Tryko under the implication of a charge of cowardice. He was far from timorous, and on several occasions in journeys with me he had demonstrated his courage, but here in Usküb, in this hotbed of racial animosities and religious feuds, he had recognized that discretion was the better part of valor and so took his departure in the somewhat indelicate way I have described. Of course his position was far more precarious than mine. In the circumstances by which we were surrounded the interpreter is held responsible rather than the dolt to whom the information is translated. Of course I was regarded as outlandish, a freak of no particular importance, and probably idiotic, but there was no reason why the agitators and the propagandists should not cozen up to me. But if their information failed to stick, only Tryko was to blame.

Tryko was not indifferent to the situation into which he was born but the lessons he had learned at Robert College had not developed a broad philosophy. His views were those he had imbibed with his mother's milk; the Turks were dog-brothers, the Serbians were pig-brothers and the Greeks? Well, I shall not put on paper what he thought of the Greeks! On the other hand, he was confident of the future, there was no justification for desperate measures, at least not as far as he was concerned. In God's own time and according to His will some day the Exarch would be reading prayers according to the ritual of Saint Cyril and Saint Method in the Church of Holy Wisdom so long defiled by the Mohammedans. In the meantime he wanted to amass wealth, though with me it was uphill work. However, there was consolation in the thought that he was learning American newspaper methods that would prepare him to launch a great paper in the Balkans, just like the *New York Herald*, some day. His slogan was "the Balkans for the Bulgarians" —but as far as he could see there was no reason for hurry. Yet in spite of his aloofness from the current agitation, and his non-political devotion to the daughter of the Maltese station-master during my absence, the Albanians and the Serbians had combined against him and Tryko was doubtless wise to sneak away from Usküb between two suns.

At the time, outsiders, and particularly those who occupied official positions, led very precarious existences along the Vardar; notable among these was the Serbian Consul-General, a very cultivated man who in addition to his official duties was writing what he regarded as the definitive history of his heroic people. I often called upon him and he frequently pointed out to me the mistakes that the great von Ranke had made in his standard history. This official, whose name escapes me, was by no means a coward, but for twelve months now he had not left the narrow precincts of the consular compound. He had advised the Belgrade government of the attitude of the people and the course he had thought it wise to pursue, and Belgrade had approved. It was enjoined upon him to avoid all public appearances and to leave nothing undone to escape assassination. At that time Serbia wished to avoid war or any incident that might bring it about.

Well, what did this fatiguing and undoubtedly dangerous journey profit me? I fear very little; I at least had the satisfaction of doing a thing that for months I had wanted to do—and that, of course, was something. As many pointed out on my crestfallen return, the pilgrimage to High Albania was doomed to failure from the very beginning. I was under the patronage of the Austro-Hungarian consulate and under the guidance of the Consul's *cavass*. I was consequently identified with their politics and racial plans, and the idea that I was a collector of rare plants which so delighted Smucker that on setting out he thrust a trowel in my hand, hoodwinked no one. But it can be said I had no alternative. I had to go in this way or not at all, and so I went and in retrospect I enjoyed the experience. I learned to like the Albanians even though they used me despitefully. In fact I came to like them better than some of the other Balkan peoples who perhaps when judged by Western standards are more worthy of esteem.

It was interesting, even for me, a rank outsider, and far from the family circle, to listen to the sing-song pedigrees of these strange Pelasgian people. Most of them ran back to Adam but even the parvenus knew by whom they were begotten, or at least thought they did, back to the Homeric days. And these were not bought and paid for pedigrees produced by a professional genealogist. These were the names of stalwart heroes handed on through the generations, that had been learned by heart. It was the tale of a proud line that extended from the dawn of history to the present day. It was a family creed clung to from the cradle to the grave, as long as there was life in their bodies. They were, and I have no doubt still are, a serious and a silent folk, as well they might be. At this time, by conservative figures, at least seventy-five per cent of the men died violent deaths and the casualties among the women who became involved in blood feuds reached a not inconsiderable figure.

Many of the things that happened to me during this ill-advised journey were inexplicable at the time, but years later at the Paris Peace Conference Essad Pasha, who represented some of the Albanian wild tribes at the great pow-wow, made them plain to me.

"Why were the virgins, the incorruptible ones, always detailed to watch over us? Was that not a man-sized job?"

"Yes and no. You see the village Elders expected, and not without reason, that, resenting your intrusion, you might be attacked. Certainly your behavior justified suspicion. Now it would have been the duty of the guard to defend you, as well as to see that you did not escape. If a man had been killed in your defense that would have been a serious matter, but if a Virgin had fallen in the performance of her duty a cause of *jak* or vendetta would not lie. The incident could have been arranged without starting a blood feud of the kind that so often entails the loss of scores of lives."

"But why were all the doors closed in our faces? Did they fear we brought smallpox with us?"

"Not at all, the villagers acted in strict accordance with the 'law of the mountain.' Had you been admitted into a household and then been slain as an intruder by other angry villagers, the head of the house and indeed all his kinsfolk would have been compelled to declare a blood feud against the murderers and that would have been very annoying. You see our laws of hospitality are very exacting. They are our birthright and above all our obligation. Many a man has died with his boots on because he ignored them. I am sorry you were not received in a more hospitable manner. If you had had a line from me things would have been very different, but in the circumstances you were lucky." And I have no doubt we were. . . .

Three months later it fell to my lot, under instructions from the Commodore in Paris, to spend six weeks with Edhem Pasha and his so-called mobile army in the hills and valleys of Macedonia. In Usküb we heard that the expulsion of the Bishop had exasperated the Christian Slavs of the *vilayet*, and it was also asserted that Turkish patrols had been attacked, and in these circumstances the Vali had ordered Edhem, as a preventive measure, to traverse the disturbed districts with his troops and overawe the malcontents. There was no demur from the authorities when I announced my intention of joining the expedition, although, of course, the Pasha must have been well aware of the thought behind my instructions. The Pro-Macedonia Committees in Paris and London had announced that the purpose of the expedition was to destroy the Christian villages and put the unfortunate inhabitants to the sword.

When I joined Edhem he was encamped with his force on a broad open space down the valley of the Vardar about twenty-five miles below Usküb. Apparently the Pasha welcomed my coming and he made me as comfortable as he could. He had with him what he called two infantry brigades and a small detachment of cavalry, all told about five thousand men. The rifles of the infantry were of many makes, and the distribution of ammunition was a difficult problem. The mounted men all carried smart Spencer carbines and they were the best trained and the most energetic men in the little army. The infantry were the strangest assortment of soldiers that I have ever seen assembled under war banners—not even excluding from the comparison some Moorish and Chinese armies I was to march with in later years.

In getting together this heterogeneous force, the recruiting sergeants had, as the saying goes, evidently "robbed both the cradle and the grave." Even after making due allowance for the hardships they had sustained, it was apparent that many of the so-called *redifs* were well over sixty, while of the youngsters more than fifty per cent were but half-grown. As far as I could learn, none of them came from Thrace. They had all been brought from Anatolia across the Straits. At this time conscription in the Turkish army, barring a happy conjunction of most unusual circumstances, was a life sentence, and well aware that they would never see their distant homes again its victims were a very depressed lot, as indeed have been most of the drafted soldiers I have accompanied in my long career as a camp-follower. Once in the Turkish army, the only way of escape was by stopping an enemy's bullet. The Young Turks when they came into power in 1908 changed all this, and a three- to five-year term of service was ordered, but as the Old Turks remarked after the crushing defeats of 1912 this did not improve the *morale* of their forces!

I can only find praise for my treatment by Edhem Pasha, into whose family I was catapulted by circumstances over which he apparently could exercise no control. Orders had come from Constantinople to accord me every facility, and he carried them out with good temper and grace. He was quite different from any Turk I have ever known and I have always regarded him as a "sport" in the Ottoman tribe. Indeed many and curious were the stories that circulated in the bazaars as to his origin, and the one that appealed to me as the most probable ran as follows. During one of the innumerable Cretan insurrections a Turkish detachment stormed a mountain village, and after setting fire to the hovels and putting to the sword all its Christian inhabitants as was the orthodox custom, was marching away to the next devoted hamlet when the soldiers were amazed by the appearance on the scene of a smiling child crawling toward them from a still smouldering ruin. The child was too young even to walk. In one of those moments of compassion, that overtakes even the most cruel and hard-bitten, the soldiers adopted the waif, and this firebrand from the burning pile became in a way the regimental pet and mascot. When the campaign was over, the orphan was carried to Stamboul where he attracted the attention of, and was adopted into, a family of high official rank. Through their kindness and influence he received an excellent education and later was given a commission in the army. Step by step he won his way, but at the time I was thrown in with Edhem the only indication of his future power and renown was the magnificent war tent in which he lived.

In front of his gorgeous headquarters, wherever camp was pitched, two great spears were driven in the ground and from each of them was suspended a horse tail. I had an idea that this was an indication of the general's army rank, that he was then a Pasha of Two Tails although, of course, he climbed much higher and I believe sported as many as seven tails in later years. When the Ottoman Turks came out of Asia and overran southeastern Europe they came as mounted men and it would have been natural for them to have indicated military rank by the equine symbol, but I am bound to admit that, while I often made discreet inquiries, I was never given a frank explanation of the horse tails which were, however, always in evidence in any camp that I visited.

While Edhem Pasha, unless for reasons of his own he concealed it from me, had no knowledge of French or English, he could read German well, and at the time of my visit he was greatly interested in a book on tactics and strategy by Verdy du Vernois, a famous Prussian General with a very French name. Over this we often mulled in the evenings, and while my German was more fluent than his, he, the trained soldier, always got at the gist of the military problem which the writer sought to explain, more quickly and above all more understandingly than I did.

I must admit that these days with what the Turks called the Peace Restoring Army of Macedonia were very trying to my patience, to my nerves and to my sense of smell. Not that the little army of Edhem Pasha was more unfragrant than that of the Christian or the Confucian, the Shinto, the Moslem or the back-sliding Buddhistic hosts with which I have consorted in Europe, Asia and Africa. I would not give that impression, as that was far from being the case. No! the powerful smell of an army, pungent and penetrating, rises superior to race and creed and is always nauseating. All armies smell alike and what they smell like can only be described by a word that our wise censors are in perfect agreement in saying is not fit to print.

During the days of waiting, while information was being collected and news was being sifted by the Staff, none of which was worthy of being placed on our Broadway bulletin board, I used to get away from camp whenever I could and indeed I continued to do so, for the reason above-mentioned, even when the Pasha through one of his aides asked me to restrain my restless feet and stay closer to headquarters. When it was quite apparent that no important movements were contemplated, I would often take my horse to where the grass seemed fresher, less weedy, and then once out of sight of headquarters, I would wander down the river to dells and dingles where the atmosphere was sweet with flowers, where the alpine waters made music as they rushed through a narrow gorge. And there was still another attraction to what had become my favorite retreat. Here the river bank was dotted with tumuli. They were of ancient mud brick and evidently of great antiquity. In one of Charles Diehl's delightful as well as learned books I came across a reference which led me to conclude that before he started on his career of world conquest, Alexander, the greatest adventurer the world has ever seen, had campaigned along the Vardar. These mounds might well mark the resting places of some of his soldiers who fell in the first skirmishes. Here indeed appropriate sacrifices may have been made to their manes and on this very spot, with Alexander himself presiding, what M. Diehl calls the *carrousel sacré* may have been celebrated. . . .

At last the army began to move. Leaving about five hundred men at the base camp on the Vardar, and also two very ancient cannon of Venetian origin and dating well back in the eighteenth century, we sallied out into what for me at least was the unknown. An excellent and sure-footed horse was assigned to me, and also a cheerful orderly whose Turkish, if Turkish it was, did not harmonize with the wayfaring dialect I was fast picking up. Our food arrangements were casual and sketchy but we had plenty of Turkish coffee and excellent Macedonian tobacco, and so as far as creature comforts were concerned I have been much worse off in climes and with armies reputed to be more civilized. In long snake-like columns we wriggled through the passes and visited scores of mountain villages. It was apparent that, warned of our approach, most of the inhabitants and all the women had sought safe refuge elsewhere, but we were always welcomed by a delegation of old men trembling and perspiring in the furs they wore even in mid-summer and always offering, often on bended knee, a sheep or a goat for the table of the Generalissimo.

Owing to the prevalence of smallpox none of the men were quartered in the villages. At the end of the day's march the soldiers would drop exhausted in their tracks, and camp for the night in the open where they had fallen. After a short rest they would begin to move about, start small charcoal fires for the coffee they ground and cooked very carefully and also very slowly, and anything else they may have been so fortunate as to "rustle" on the road. I was with the column for three weeks and never witnessed a distribution of rations or anything that indicated the presence of a commissary. The Pasha lodged in his magnificent tent and I shared with four staff officers a nearby tent that was much less regal. Neither my food nor my quarters were anything to boast about, but they were luxurious in comparison with the fare of the soldiers. In wind and all weathers, wrapped in dirty ragged blankets, they lay through- out the night until the bugle gave the signal that another marching day had dawned.

In this way and without any adventures worthy of record we wandered about for a week in this gray treeless country, and then to my surprise we found ourselves back at the base camp. Several times the column had been fired upon as it wound its way along the goat tracks. Two men were crushed by a great boulder human hands had set in motion, but we had no other casualties and the strenuous efforts that were made to catch these bushwhackers did not, as far as I could see, lead to the shedding of blood. Edhem was of the opinion that the rumors of unrest and of a probable up- rising were greatly exaggerated, and he so reported to the Vali. But after an idle day in camp to rest the footsore and the weary, in belated recognition of the extent of the territory he was expected to overawe, the Pasha changed his tactics. He announced that half the force was to remain in the base camp while the other half, divided into patrols of one hundred and fifty men each, was to zigzag throughout those less accessible sections which the larger force had not visited.

I will not disguise the fact that I was extremely suspicious as to the motive behind this change of plan. Quite unduly, no doubt, I flattered myself that it was due to my presence with the army. It was a plan to escape my surveillance and, of course, I would leave nothing undone to defeat it. As three or four columns were sent out at the same time I could only accompany one of them, but which one?—there was the rub. Which was the column that had been told off to do the particularly dirty work that I was now con- fident was being planned?

The Pasha said I could go with the column that I preferred, and I thought to keep him on pins and needles by not indicating my choice until instructions had been given and the column I had chosen was well under way. In the course of the following weeks I participated in four expeditions, and until the last one they were as uneventful as the grand march of the main force had been. But the last one was different. We were halted at a junction of goat tracks and quite a discussion ensued as to the path we should take. Suddenly a volley came from what I had regarded as a deserted sheepfold of stone on the hillside, and three saddles were emptied. The young officer ordered an attack and it was made courageously, but three more men fell and the sheepfold was never reached. Our dead had ghastly wounds inflicted doubtless by old-fashioned rifles loaded with slugs; one of the wounded indeed had a side of his face blown off. The young officer said in answer to my unspoken inquiry, *"Komitadjis"*—"revolutionists"—and then called the attacking party back. The dead he left in their tracks but the wounded he brought off out of the line of fire and soon we were jogging back to the distant base camp which we reached with our disturbing report long after midnight.

On the following morning for at least five minutes the Pasha seemed to have lost the equanimity which I had regarded as his most marked characteristic—but he soon regained it. He was, I could see, enraged that his report assuring the pacification of the country should have been so quickly contradicted by developments. He made haste to retrieve the situation but, like the good soldier he was, he made haste slowly. Three days elapsed; all the other patrols were back, having met with no opposition, and then a detachment of one thousand men was selected from among the most able-bodied for the campaign of retaliation which was planned. In the evening the mounted men went on their way with the purpose, I think, of holding and closing all the possible avenues of escape. The following morning the infantry column was to start for the district that was now devoted to destruction, and the Pasha said he would not have the slightest objection to my joining it.

But did I want to go? I knew perfectly well what was in store for the people of the unfortunate villages and I knew that the punishment of bushwhacking which would be meted out to them would be in strict accordance with the laws of civilized warfare, so called. The village nearest the sheepfold from which the deadly volley had come would be destroyed and its inhabitants put to the sword. If I went along would I prove a restraining influence? I could hardly flatter myself that this would be the case. I had reached

no decision when the matter was taken out of my hands by a disagreeable experience, the like of which I had never suffered before.
As I lay down for the night I developed or perhaps only then became conscious that I was running a high fever, had a splitting
headache, and that my bones hurt as though they were being
crushed upon a rack of medieval torture. From what I have read
of the thousands who suffered in this way from the intensive local
malaria of the Vardar valley, as the army of Salonica pushed its
way inland from Salonica in 1918, I conclude that I too, doubtless
was laid low by a violent attack of malaria. Be this as it may I was
certainly laid low. The only medicine that remained in my traveling case was quinine and I helped myself to large doses. All next
day I lay on my cot stunned and certainly powerless to move—but
the quinine bottle lay close at hand and I ate up the pills and on
the morning of the second day after the attack began I could sit
up. I was without fever for the time being but weak and giddy. . . .

The Pasha insisted that I return to Usküb and said that, as the
campaign was over and the little army would be distributed as garrisons at strategic points, he himself returning to Constantinople,
I would miss nothing that was of importance and, with great kindness, he offered to send me to Usküb in one of the two army litters
available. As I had seen the litters engaged for some days now in
carrying smallpox patients over the hill to the pest house I asserted
that I could mount my horse and by a sturdy effort did so. While
I was saying goodbye to the Pasha the Commander of the punitive
column came in and gave what I am sure was a frank account of
how it had fared with him and his expedition. The villagers had
gone away before his arrival and as the cavalry who were to inter-
cept them on their probable flight had been unsuccessful up to that
time, he concluded they had doubtless taken refuge in caves. The
komitadjis had put up a stout defense of their stone sheepfold but
after bringing down ten of the Turkish soldiers they had all been
killed.

"All?" inquired the Pasha.

"Yes, all"—and then he added, "There were only five of them."

"And then?" asked Edhem.

"Then," continued the officer, "we built a gallows and hanged their bodies from it—in front of the church which we set on fire."

"You did well," commented the Pasha, and I went on my way.

Certainly there was not the slightest indication of window dressing on the part of the Pasha in the way in which he handled this terrible incident. . . .

We left the base camp about two o'clock. I was in charge of a young lieutenant who had studied under von der Goltz Pasha, the German military adviser of the Sultan, and spoke his language fluently. He had with him ten mounted men and before sunset we were through the dark defiles where danger might have lurked. I must confess, however, that the only danger I apprehended was that of falling off my horse. As a matter of fact when I dismounted at Usküb I fell sprawling, and was so weak I had to be carried into the Turkish *han*. As my escort trotted back toward the mountains where unenviable fates were doubtless in store for them, the young officer shouted, "*Auf Wiedersehn*" and the soldiers muttered softly, "*Ade Hadji*." My good friend Smucker, the Austrian Consul, appeared shortly and placed his great store of quinine at my disposal. In three days I began to hobble about, but some weeks elapsed before I could claim to have regained my normal good health. In my later Balkan experiences I had to visit Usküb on several occasions, but fortunately I was always able to give the lower valley of the Vardar a wide berth.

In later years I was to see Edhem Pasha frequently but, as I was at the time involved in the preparations for our own war in Cuba, I did not accompany him in his campaign in Thessaly in which, after the victories of Pharsala and Domokos, he crushed the Greek army, imposed a war indemnity of four million Turkish pounds, and was given the title of *Ghazi* or Conqueror by the grateful Sultan.

12. THE VEILED PROPHET OF
THE SAHARA (A DISTANT VIEW)

I was in Varna on the Black Sea, not then the Newport of the region it has since become, but a backwater from which in those days your best escape was as a deck passenger on a Russian tramp bound for Constantinople. I was not only physically marooned but in a mental quandary. My responsibility for revolutionary outbreaks and all other news developments in the Balkans was weighing more heavily than usual upon me. There was little difficulty in detecting the symptoms of approaching trouble, but alas! while unmistakable at this moment they were widely scattered. As a result it was most difficult to say (and yet that was my job and I had to say it every day) where the next world-peace-menacing explosion would occur. Would it detonate in that great swamp land of the Dobruja on the Danube, now in control of the intruding Roumanians, or under that pile of rocks and dynamite which is Albania frowning down on the Adriatic from its banditti-ridden crags?

Well, worse luck! the chances seemed to be about fifty-fifty. The Austrians following the will o' the wisp of the *drang nach Osten* were at their stuff in the home of Scanderbeg and— Well, I have forgotten his name but a claimant Bulgaro-phone patriot, who had his day of renown, was calling upon the web-footed inhabitants of the Dobruja to cast out the descendants of Trajan and join their fortunes with their brethren of the Principality. It was indeed a dilemma. Which horn should I grasp? Only one thing was certain, grim-visaged war might break out here, and worse luck it might break out there! The decision could no longer be delayed when a happy solution presented itself in the form of a wire from the Commodore. He ordered me to report to him personally in Paris, as soon as possible and, he added, pregnant phrase! "Bring your heavy luggage."

Nothing loath I was there in five days, as fast as the Orient Express I picked up in Sofia could carry me. And then, as on not a few previous occasions, the Commodore opened up a question with which I had often harassed him as though the subject was quite new to me and indeed that he had initiated it. In a confidential manner he imparted to me all the information in regard to the Senussi Brotherhood of the Sahara with which I had pestered him twelve months before. But I must be fair; he made many additions to my report and so added greatly to my slender store of knowledge. Perhaps I should only claim that I had spurred him on to further research by drawing on the innumerable sources of information which he enjoyed.

"I think the situation in the Balkans will remain stagnant for some months to come," he said, "and as that will not suit you, or for that matter, me, I have decided to transfer you temporarily to a more active and I hope a more profitable field of activity. I want you to visit the Senussi Mahdi, the veiled Prophet of the Sahara. I want you to get behind the veil with which his activities are cloaked. In my judgment his shrine in Djerboum may shortly become the greatest new news-center in the world. Today the Mahdi is in close touch with five hundred million Africans and probably with two hundred million Asiatics. This is a news-center that has never been tapped, and I want you to tap it. His missionary agents are swarming all over the Mohammedan world; what are they preaching? While there are many rumors as to their activities, I want you to find out exactly what they are up to; that is your job. Pick up all the Arabic you can, and I hope you will be ready to start in about six weeks. Probably I shall land you from the yacht at Bengazi on the Tripolitan coast. In the meantime devote yourself to making all possible preparations for the adventure. Be very discreet and do not go near the office; above all, do not let anyone even remotely connected with the French government know what we are planning."

This was a very characteristic move on the part of Mr. Bennett. I knew, and he knew still better, that the great American people were absolutely without any contacts with the Senussi Brotherhood, physical, commercial or intellectual, and that if he opened up this new channel of information, and obviously it would cost a pretty penny, he was one of the few of the hundreds of thousands of readers of his paper who would be interested. Financially the venture might prove a dead loss, but while Mr. Bennett valued the revenues of his paper for the things that they enabled him to enjoy, still not seldom he was prepared to incur great expense in a venture which, as he well knew in advance, could only result in satisfaction to himself.

I must say this novel assignment was greatly to my liking. I soon procured the few books available on the subject, especially the Senussi gospel which bears the promising title of *The Rising Sun*. It was written, or more probably dictated, by the First Prophet, the founder of the secret Brotherhood. It was the Third Prophet who now presided over the mysterious shrine, and it was upon his privacy I was to intrude. In this source book there is no pretense of latter-day revelations. What Mahomet preached is emphasized, and the *Koran* is accepted as indispensable and fundamental. The old doctrines cannot be improved upon, but it is asserted they must be purified of all the comment and interpolations of latter-day theologians by which they are disfigured.

The most interesting feature of the book was its strong political bias. The Sultan in Stamboul and the Bey in Tunis were denounced as subservient and cringing to the Christian rulers of the Western world. The Turks, indeed, as a race, are classed with other heretics and schismatics. Wine, as of old, is forbidden to all True Believers, also coffee and the solace of tobacco. Tea, however, can be enjoyed in moderation. The writer, whether the Mahdi himself or his scribe, makes rather short work of our boasted principle of freedom of worship, and again and again it is set forth in the book, and who can gainsay it? "Wherever the political power of the Christian is installed, there the rights of the Mohammedan True Believers are abridged."

Posing as a modern Harun Al-Rashid and practicing all the arts of mystery in his personal and professional life, Mr. Bennett always demanded the observance of the greatest secrecy from his servitors. Under his orders I had left my familiar haunts in Paris within a few hours and was lodged on the Left Bank in a little student hotel, des Étrangers, on the Rue Racine where it enters the Boul' Miche. I secured the same room, the triangular one on the fifth floor with the charming balcony jutting out over the Boulevard, which I had occupied eight years before when first my eyes had opened on the, to me, bewildering life of Paris. Then I had come attracted by the fact that the neighborhood was reminiscent of Gambetta, the trib- une, and that in many of the cafés the tables upon which he so often sprang to make his flaming speeches against Napoleon the Little, were still reverently preserved. And not to be forgotten, just around the corner was the little bookstore whose proprietor did not deny that he was the veritable Schaunard immortalized by Murger in *La Vie de Bohème*.

No one seemed to know or care about these people now—nor, as a matter of fact, did I. I came here because I recalled that in this quarter lodged many African students, especially those who fre- quented the clinics and the medical school. I had become, at least so I thought, quite a stolid young man, prepared to accept with perfect equanimity any change of climate or condition that might be ordered. You had to when you wore what Edmund Yates in his day called the *Herald's tabard*, but for all that this startling change of territory and purpose was something of a shock.

It may be recalled that when a year before I mentioned the news possibilities of the Senussi, I had no other purpose than to change the subject from the distasteful topic of the Taafe interview. True, the idea had not come to me out of the ether nor had I evolved it out of my inner consciousness. I had at that time been talking a great deal with Dr. Junker, a most charming African explorer who was in Vienna seeing his many-volumed work through the press. He had said something about the new prophet that had arisen in the land, and he urged me to read the writings of Freid- erich Gerhard Rohlfs who was the great authority on Libya and Cyrenaica and the other provinces which the Senussi Mahdi now controlled. Then I had some correspondence with Rohlfs who was as amiable as he was daring, but as my suggestion had not been approved at headquarters, I let the matter drop and turned my thoughts and my reading in other directions.

It should be clear that when the new mission was imposed, I was as ignorant of the subject and the problem I was to study as millions of Americans and Europeans, and indeed, as a matter of fact, as millions of Africans. Years later when, by varied and checkered experiences, I had become more familiar with Mr. Bennett's methods and technique, I would not have been so surprised with his selection of me for the job as I was at the moment. Whenever a new problem loomed on the horizon, or a new world question arose, it was Mr. Bennett's invariable policy to detail two men first "to investigate and report" and then to popularize and later, I fear, to vulgarize it. One of the investigators was always the man who in his judgment knew most about the new question that had appeared on the news carpet, and the other was a man who knew as little about the subject as the average reader. It wasn't a bad plan, this combination of the expert and the ignoramus, though truth to tell, the expert often complained bitterly of the space in the paper accorded the ignoramus. The result was not a balanced ration, but under the system the reader could choose between the recondite and the superficial, and little more than that can be expected for two cents. In the enterprise to which I had so unexpectedly been called no expert was available, but I certainly qualified for the less flattering role in the investigation.

In a few hours my room was cluttered up with the available volumes on North Africa and its religious sects and I had also sent out tracers for the books on the subject, very numerous these, that were out of print. Soon, in thought at least, I was transported to the Senussi country and turned a deaf ear to the uproar in the Boul' Miche below, which had not been without its attractions in former days. By the aid of strong coffee I read and read, not closing my eyes for forty-eight hours. When next I was summoned by the Commodore, he would be amazed, and I hoped delighted, by my mastery of the subject he had so unexpectedly turned over to me for "study and examination." Surely I would be able to give him what we now call the close-up and the low-down on the Veiled Prophet of the Sahara.

My reading soon disclosed a number of side journeys that were fascinating, and not a few second strings to the main plan. Of course I would enter upon the land of fable and mystery by the port of Bengazi. There the Commodore's agent would await me and put me in touch with the local *Zawia* or lodge of the Senussi brethren. Here while securing needed background, delightful excursions would be permissible. These, of course, I would not mention to my chief; they would only confuse him, his knowledge of North Africa being superficial. No, these I would reserve as consolation prizes in case the reading public in America did not go absolutely daffy over the revelations from the world of the Senussi that I would not fail to bring them.

This first correspondence I felt confident would not be dated from Bengazi. I would restore to the ancient roadstead on the Tripolitan coast the beautiful and romantic name it bore in its days of splendor. In the long ago, almost at the dawn of history, the place was named Berenice after the beautiful wife of Ptolemy III. There was music in that word, and if proof were wanted, it was furnished by both Poe and Racine who gave the sweet-sounding name to not the least attractive of their heroines. Just outside the historic port, in the sandhills, I would visit the troglodytes or cave dwellers who have been living there ever since the day long ago when, after a sojourn in their midst, Strabo the Greek geographer put them on his map. I decided I must be careful to note what Leo Africanus says about these remarkable people who throughout the centuries have been living in these comfortable caves, with Mother Earth as a generous rent-refusing landlady, keeping them warm in winter by the heat of her body, and insulating their quarters to delightful freshness in summer. There would be, I had no doubt, a lot of interesting stories awaiting me in those ancient air-conditioned caves. Human interest stories must have accumulated there; all one would have to do would be to brush off the dust of the ages and furbish them up a bit, with here and there a touch of modernity, as it were.

In the precincts of the *Zawia,* in those cloisters overlooking the turquoise waters of the Sidra Gulf, which I had every reason to expect would be shaded by umbrageous date palms, I would have my first contacts with the traveling brethren of the Order who skip from the Mediterranean to Lake Tchad with as little concern, though with a greater expenditure of time, than we require for our pleasure jaunts from the Great Lakes to the Gulf of Mexico. The *Zawia,* the shrine of these latter-day crusaders, was, of course, my first objective. From there I should follow the plainly marked trail of the Senussia until it led me to where the Prophet was enthroned. From this trail I must not deviate, not more at least than a properly certified compass permits, but the thought of a minor deviation would not down, for see here what the guide to Tripoli reported, "Very near to the port of Bengazi are to be seen the still noteworthy Gardens of the Hesperides so often sought for by the adventurous among the ancients."

To say that this bald statement took my breath away is to put it very mildly. On the moment I knew that my compass would graciously permit of the needed deviation or I would know the reason why. Fancy the dumb luck of the thing! From the dawn of history men had been sneaking and slinking away from the paths of rectitude to secure but a glimpse of these gardens and the gracious ladies charged with their upkeep, and here they lay practically across my trail—the path of "commanded duty"! Here grew, and as the guide book said nothing to the contrary, mayhap still were growing, the golden apples that Earth gave to Hera upon her marriage with Zeus, the glorious fruit that had tempted so many adventurers. True they were in those days guarded by lovely maidens, the dark and lissome daughters of Erebus endowed with a dangerous gift of entrancing song. True in the ancient legends it was related that when the fruit-loving trespassers came near, and with all suspicion dispelled by the cadence of the sirens' songs, were enticed into the magical orchard, Ladon, the ever-alert dragon, who never closed an eye, would suddenly appear and romance fled to be replaced by carnage.

But was this always the case? Might not a fortunate traveler prove the general rule by enjoying an exceptional experience? Was

it absolutely necessary to close eyes and ears as these nymphs appeared to those who dared to approach the gardens by the turquoise seas? I thought not, for Jason says when he returned from
his voyage in the Euxine Pontus with Medea that by their song
the kindly nymphs warned him of the whirlpools and the quick-
sands that would otherwise have engulfed his fragile ship. In any
event the records revealed that the intrepid traveler had at least
a sporting chance. They further furnished flat contradiction to the
accusation that the great historian Lecky had hurled at a roomful
of war correspondents at a Black Friars' dinner in London a few
months before, to the effect that we were responsible for all wars,
that we never tired of fomenting ill-feeling between the nations,
and that coming in as we did with modern times we were largely
responsible for making such an unpleasant mess of our day.

But here it was made plain by these legends (that as Sancho
Panza averred "were much too old to lie"), that economic rivalries
had existed from the earliest days and had converted the earth into
a cock-pit before the printing press or its bond slaves, the war correspondents, had been invented. I would at the next opportunity,
I assured myself, call the great historian's attention to the fact that
the struggles for the golden apples were the forerunners of our
wars for coal and iron and oil, and that apparently they had not
been fomented by the scribes who were content merely to chronicle
them.

There were moments indeed when I found the expedition as
planned embarrassing, because of its many promising prospects and
its quiver filled with tempting alternatives; but even in the first
flush of my enthusiasm over the fact that my investigation of the
new world problem, the so-recently launched religious creed, would
lead me to one of the cradles of history, I was not absolutely blind
to the fact that there were many people in the world, including
thousands of *Herald* readers, who were quite content to limit their
knowledge of what they would doubtless call mythology to a first
or at most a second reading of Hawthorne's *Tanglewood Tales*.
For these realists my resourceful pilgrimage held a great surprise
in reserve. Its path would lead me across the trail of William
Eaton, the first and as many think the most daring of our adven-

turers, who in 1805 led his American marines and a band of Greek
mercenaries across the North African desert from Cairo to Derna
in a gallant but often-misrepresented attempt to displace the bad
Bashaw of Tripoli, who had the habit of holding American seamen
for ransom, and to replace him on the throne with his "good"
brother, Hamet Caramelli.

Here on this lonely strand Eaton and his gallant marines defended our flag for many months against all comers, until Tobias
Lear and the other diplomats compromised the situation by their
mealy-mouthed intervention. Here was an episode of a long forgotten war that would stir the blood of every American. I was confident that Flynn, the phlegmatic news editor with his weakness
for fires in the drygoods district, would let me have space for this
story, especially if I dwelt on the fact that one of the O'Bannons
was second in command! In any event it was certain that I would
visit Derna and recall the thrilling days when it was American
territory.

In my second talk with the Commodore it developed that, while
the plan of unveiling the long masked Prophet of the Sahara was
a darling project of his friend, the ingenious Marquis de Morès, the
first practical suggestion which captured his attention came from
a Maltese shipchandler in Bengazi, in the then Turkish *vilayet* of
Tripoli; and his scrappy letter in which words from at least four
languages were jumbled together and clashed, was at this time the
only document that was turned over to me for my enlightenment.

This letter, while not particularly helpful, did disclose the fact,
little known then and entirely forgotten now, that while pursuing
his vagrant course around the world on his great yacht, manned
and equipped on the man-of-war scale, the Commodore was not
simply philandering, as many thought, but was engaged in estab-
lishing for the benefit of the *Herald* what he considered to be invaluable lines of world communication. In this list of his secret
agents, which he guarded jealously from the prying eyes of his
news editors, until great events "broke" in a quarter of the world
which he alone had foreseen, shipchandlers and lighthouse-keepers
predominated. The latter, owing to their isolation on the rock-
bound coasts where they were stationed, had considerable difficulty

in getting off the news that was cast up at their feet by the sea, but the shipchandlers were almost always in close cable communication with the outside world and enjoyed the Commodore's especial favor and confidence.

The Bengazi agent with whom the roving news-king had come in contact on one of his cruises off the Tripolitan coast, Mangiabuono by name, was considered by the Commodore a "live wire," and when later his cables and letters that had to be relayed from Sicily to escape the surveillance of the Turkish authorities were placed in my hands, I could readily agree with his estimate of the man. However, as they were couched in a language that was a strange mixture of French, Maltese, Arabic and Italian, it was at times extremely difficult to discover what they were all about. But lively they were!

This world-wide network of secret agents was the Commodore's especial hobby and pride, but it was regarded with disfavor by the business end of the paper. The Commodore had a little book in which were entered the cable addresses of these strange news hawks —but that was all. No record was kept of their services. "I carry all that in my head," the Commodore often proudly asserted, but when these men turned up in Paris or New York and wanted funds for their *menus plaisirs*, there was always trouble, and at times litigation. But as our chief was generally off on another cruise in the most distant of the Seven Seas, he was not personally involved in these complications.

After I had immersed myself for several days, and very pleasant days they were, in the literature and the legends of the Senussia, it occurred to me that while not irrelevant my studies were leading me nowhere. It was contact with the living that I needed, not familiarity with the archives of the dead. It became hourly more apparent that I must meet men who had been to the Senussi lands, who could talk their lingo, who could give me some idea of what the new religious crusade proposed and what was the role its adherents intended to play in world politics. Obviously my first question would be, "Do you accept the partition of Africa as arranged by the representatives of the white nations, recently assembled in conference in Berlin?" (at which it might be mentioned, incidentally, not a single black man was present!).

Above all I needed the closest contact with someone who could tell me how best to undertake the long journey to the distant shrine of the veiled prophet, and here indeed I was beset with difficulties. My first suggestion, a visit to the famous school for *les Langues Orientales Vivantes*, had been frowned upon by the Commodore, and the inquiries that I thought of making at the offices of the Tunisian Protectorate in the Palais Royal had also been disapproved; and even to me, hard-driven as I was, an advertisement in the newspapers for a Senussi pundit and teacher seemed imprudent. But what was I to do? That was the quandary in which I was mired for several days.

In quest of inspiration that would not come, I walked about quite a bit in the Quarter, and when it drizzled, which was often, I became an habitué of the bookstalls under the arcades of the Odéon. Here I observed quite a number of be-turbanned North Africans but, as their attention almost invariably seemed to be arrested by the cover illustrations of more or less naked women on books which promised salacious reading, I concluded they were not the "pure of heart," consequently not followers of the "Great Pure One," so I let them go upon their way, gabbling volubly about white women and their physical characteristics.

It was only on the third day of my quest that the miracle man appeared. He was about fifty and evidently not very strong. He wore dark glasses and in addition something like cloth blinders which, while an added protection to his eyes, must have interfered with his impaired vision. His turban came down low, almost to his eyebrows, and his muffler came up to his chin; but what I could see of his grave, thoughtful face was altogether charming. He was looking at a new edition of Fromentin's *Une Année dans le Sahel* that had just appeared, and hoping to scrape acquaintance I entered into book chat which, as I had noticed, was quite the custom among the habitués of the stalls.

"Yes, it is an honest book," was his answer to my inquiry. "It is well for us to learn how our land appears to the eyes of strangers." And then he added in excellent, if halting, French, "But only a son can describe his mother," and while I pondered these words he was gone.

I was sorry; something had told me this was my man—but of course there was no reason to despair. There were plenty of Moors and Algerians and Tunisians about, but how to meet them was not as simple as at first it had seemed. Should I accost them on the street? To say the least that course would be open to misconstruction, but precious hours were slipping by and at last I determined upon the courageous course. A blue-turbanned man was preceding me down the narrow rue Racine. With his many cloaks and *jellabs* he seemed as broad as he was long. He was lounging along just ahead of me and I determined I would jostle him and then apologize so courteously that he could not end the encounter with a curt nod, and perhaps he would go with me around the corner to the Café Voltaire for an apéritif and a talk.

And then suddenly the man upon whom I had these bold social designs disappeared, as though obeying the unspoken words of some lamp-rubbing genii of the Arabian tales. There he had been ten feet in front of me, and now he was gone, gone altogether! For a moment I was bewildered, but soon I pulled myself together. That sort of thing happened in Bagdad, of course, but not on the rue Racine. So I turned and retraced my steps and was rewarded with a very prosaic explanation of the miracle. There was a narrow slit of a door blocking what had doubtless been an alley way for foot passengers from the street. On it were inscribed a number of signs in Arabic lettering and underneath in French "Mets, Spécialitiés Tunisiennes."

I was delighted. At last I had unearthed a lair of the North Africans, but nevertheless I did not lose my head. I was very hungry and yet well aware of the danger of strange new dishes. Since I had been called upon to explore the Senussi land I would, of course, have to get accustomed to them, but gradually and at first only in homeopathic doses, as it were. On the following day after a filling repast at the Panthéon,* I would make my first excursion into the Tunisian cuisine.

About noon, after a hearty breakfast, I returned to the door of mystery. Pushing it open I found myself in a dark alley. Thirty feet or so beyond, however, the passage came out into a garden

* The well-known restaurant—not the historic monument.

house of glass, the panes of which were smudged with cobwebs and the accumulated dirt of ages. The space was filled with tables at which about a score of Africans, mostly in tribal costumes, were lapping up mushy food rather noisily. There were other visitors in French clothes and as they talked among themselves, for the most part in the *lingua franca* of the Mediterranean, I soon learned that they were debating the price of ostrich feathers and bargaining for scents and perfumes, vials of which were passed around and sniffed from time to time. I ordered *kouscous*, the dish which was most highly praised in the notices on the wall, and then a cup of aromatic tea. No one besides the beetle-browed waiter paid any particular attention to me. I seemed to be accepted as a man and a brother, probably because I had had the forethought to wear a suit of clothes fashioned for me in a wardrobe crisis by a Greek tailor in Stamboul.

It was an unsavory place quite irrespective of the food that was served up. The atmosphere was heavy with disinfectants and eye-washes and I soon learned from the words that passed that most of of the clients had dropped in after visiting the clinic where many of them were undergoing treatment for various eye troubles. Some of the men who were engaged in bartering for feathers, and offering vile scents in exchange, were Maltese peddlers, and several of them as a sideline seemed to be acting as runners for brothels, and touting for aphrodisiacs of great power. The general conversation ran to white women and to details of their sex life as compared with brown. My company was accepted in a detached way but none of those with whom I scraped acquaintance were in the least helpful. My announced purpose of visiting Tunis at an early day was taken as a matter of course, but no one offered the least assistance in my search for a reader and teacher versed in the Tunisian dialects.

But while three days went by without any progress toward the realization of my project, I had learned a great deal about the table manners of the people I was to frequent on a familiar footing, and to a certain extent I had become hardened to them. One thing, however, I did not get over, and that was my not unnatural dread of the eye diseases which abounded. After every repast in the Tunisian lair I carefully used an eyewash highly recommended by a nearby druggist. My discomfort was heightened by the fact that, at the time, the *Herald* in New York was, in its usual boisterous manner, leading a crusade to have the eyes of all arrivals at American ports carefully examined in the hope of stopping the increasing ravages of the deadly trachoma disease. The apprehension would not be lightly dismissed that though by the help of the *Herald* I might reach the Senussi shrine, by the same agency, I might be cut off from kith and kindred on my return!

If I were called upon to describe the outstanding characteristic of those who frequented the Tunisian *gargote* in a single sentence, I would say it was their habit of belching. Of course I was no stranger to the belching ritual. I had become familiar with it in the bazaars of Stamboul and Salonica and on the banks of the Vardar at Usküb, but this was certainly something else again. What I had encountered in Turkey and in Macedonia was the belch of the protocol, if I may be permitted to bring that austere formal word into such low company. When the third cup of coffee had been served to me by the servants of the Edhem Pasha in his wonderful brocaded war tent in the Macedonian highlands and he marked a period with a belch I was not so green as not to know what that meant. It did not mean simply that the Pasha of Two Tails had wind on the stomach—though, of course, the wind must have been drawn from somewhere. No—this belch of the protocol indicated that in the judgment of my host the interview was at an end and that it would not be unseemly for me to withdraw. It was up to me, or to any other visitor, at such a moment to belch in reciprocity and then depart.

But the unseemly sounds that reverberated through the length and breadth of the Tunisian *gargote* were democratic and tumultuous. They sprang from natural but untoward conditions and are neither prescribed nor described in any book on Oriental ceremonials that has come to my notice—they were, I thought, beyond the pale of etiquette. In the end the stomachic roar and uproar got on my nerves, and a serpentine shoestring slumming along in my *kouscous* just about finished me, although I could see the complacent waiter's point of view who, when I called his attention to the intruder, admitted that it could have been worse, and as for the string, he put it in his pocket with the remark that it might prove handy at an early day!

This was the last time I would go through the form of eating in the wretched place. I was no weakling and could eat my peck of dirt with the rest, but I soon persuaded myself that I was barking up the wrong tree, that these were not the noble people of the limitless Sahara and spacious Soudan with whom I was soon to consort and travel, and I was about to leave the place for good and all when, guided by my guardian angel, the man of the Odéon bookstalls appeared in the doorway, and passing many vacant tables came and sat down opposite me and began to talk books. I knew that this miracle man was awaiting me somewhere and that sooner or later my good fairy would lead him to me, but the confrontation could not have taken place at a more suitable moment, for my spirits had sunk below zero point and strange voices were interrogating me as to whether my assignment was not rather silly and boded but short shrift to a life that was held in high esteem—at least by myself.

My vis-à-vis was much more amiable than on the afternoon we had had our chat about Fromentin. Indeed he now ranged himself to my point of view and urged me to read more of Fromentin, "because, because, I assume that the narratives of the Arabian travelers are so many closed books to you." I admitted this was so but the remark gave me a very desirable opening, and soon I was prattling to an evidently interested listener about my plans and my studies. He expressed warm approval of my projected trip across northern Africa and agreed that a knowledge of the Tunisian and Mogrebbin dialects would prove most helpful. Before his dish of *kouscous* was finished we were fast friends, and the good fellow had promised to make inquiries among his countrymen as to a suitable teacher. Then with parting salaams and good wishes to the other clients, and without a single audible belch, we left the terrible atmosphere of the place behind us. The fresh air outside revived me so instantaneously that I had the courage to ask my heaven-sent acquaintance (he had already agreed to lunch with me on the following day) to drop in at the Voltaire with me for a liqueur, and after a moment's hesitation he accepted.

We were getting along swimmingly, the Hadji seemed to have been fashioned expressly to meet my needs. He had traveled all across Tripoli and was evidently familiar with the teachings of the Senussi Prophet, and I was about to initiate him into further details of my project, within the discreet limits laid down by the Commodore however, when an incident occurred which illustrates the danger of a widespread acquaintance although I do not see how a special correspondent who is hurried from one quarter of the globe to another, and must meet all sorts and conditions of people, can be insured against it. Hardly were we seated at a little table and I was just beginning my inquiries when a tall, thick-set black man dressed in a formal frock coat and with a rather remarkable Van Dyke beard came toward me with his hands cordially extended. Even before he opened his mouth I recognized the at the moment unwelcome intruder as Monsieur M. . . . who was presiding over the Haitian treasury when I had visited Port-au-Prince three years before. Volubly he explained his presence in Paris. As a reward for straightening out the finances of the Black Republic the government of Simon Sam had granted him a traveling *bourse* and he had come abroad to write a *fin de siècle* novel and was even then engaged in making the social studies that would fit him for the task.

The tête-à-tête upon which I had based great expectations was interrupted by this robust interloper, and the three-cornered conversation which perforce followed did not prosper, and yet it was an unusual occasion and one would have thought that a black and a brown and a white man coming together in this accidental way would find much of interest to discourse upon; but it most certainly did not work out that way. Soon our forced exchanges languished and indeed as Akmet Mahommed, my new acquaintance, withdrew it seemed to me, as he glanced across the table at the traveler from Haiti, that his fine sensitive lips curled just a trifle into something that denoted race arrogance. I, too, was shorter in my replies than I meant to be. Of course I had just suffered a terrible disappointment; had the financier from Voodoo land not appeared on the scene I would have learned a lot, have been measurably nearer to the Senussi shrine. But perhaps after all, I hope so at least, it was the black man's magnificent French which flowed on and on and left us with a depressing feeling of inferiority, far from pleasing to representatives of either the white or the brown race, that cast a wet blanket over the chance meeting of men of three antagonistic worlds, in great need of getting better acquainted.

This incident was certainly in the nature of a setback but, as is so often the case, the dark hour immediately preceded the dawn. At lunch the next day when, although full of fears, I ate unflinchingly my last bowl of *kouscous* in the Tunisian restaurant, Akmet Mahommed who now revealed himself as the assistant custodian of manuscripts assembled in the famous Mosque of the Olive Tree in Tunis again seated himself at my table and soon consented to become my guide in the world that was so familiar to him—where I was a complete stranger.

The talk of remuneration was jarringly unpleasant to his sensitive soul, but sooner or later we had to tackle it. Akmet would have preferred that I read English to him for an hour every day and that, he insisted, would be ample payment for his services, and on that basis we got under way though I was confident that for me it was a loss of valuable time and of little advantage to him. Later, thanks to an Arabian manuscript displayed in the window of a rue de Lille antique shop, our relations were established on a more businesslike basis.

"If you give me as much of your time as you can spare for a month," I said, "that manuscript will be yours." He flushed with pleasure and was voluble in his thanks.

"I shall take it back with me to Tunis," he said, "and place it in the Library of the Olive Tree Mosque—where it belongs and will be appreciated," and when I later turned over to him the long-coveted treasure he insisted that I place my name upon it. A name which he assured me would frequently be mentioned in grateful appreciation by the thousands of students who frequented this seat of learning.

At first my patient teacher in the Arabic maze gave me four hours of his time every day. He was insistent on beginning at the beginning, and upon grammatical construction. This was, of course, the highway to the goal of knowledge but after many grueling hours I convinced him that in view of the shortness of the time available we would have to pursue a by-way and my hope was, *inshallah!*, that it would prove a short-cut. I was in favor of Sir Richard Burton's plan. I studied my teacher's facial contortions, his lip service and his bronchial rumblings. In pantomime I made good progress but as to sound and inflection I was not so good, the gutturals especially were baffling. The strict rules as to the ordering of words in the sentence were perplexing, and then the embarrassing richness of grammatical forms and the wealth of words for a single object!

For instance, should a lion cross my path in Tripoli, and as the Hadji admitted nothing was less unlikely, how should I call attention to his presence? Of the many words which I might with propriety use at such a critical moment I can only recall a few. "The Mangler, the Tearer, the Lord of the Mountains, the Scourge of the Plains." Then there was another complication which was most difficult to prepare against. Admittedly the vernacular of the nomads was quite different from that of the sedentary tribes. The basic word might be the same but in all probability, as my teacher illustrated to my utter confusion, it would be pronounced with strikingly different vowel sounds. There was, however, comfort in the thought that the current language was spoken in many different ways and that in the land of the Senussi there was no Academy to lay down the law.

In a week I had induced my teacher to accept the limited objective. As on my journey theological subjects would dominate all discussions I concentrated on the *Koran* and the Mahdi's book of Life. Soon I could repeat *suras* of the Mohammedan scriptures appropriate to almost any occasion, and I could say the Five Prayers of the Senussi Prophet with parrotlike accuracy.

When my voice and my patience deserted me, and I could do no more, the Hadji would reward me with long periods of rest in which he would recite fairy tales and legends of the Mohammedan wars. Even though he chose the simplest words, of course, I understood but little. Still my ear became attuned to the new sounds and this was, I think, the way to mastery. But even when the sense of what was said escaped me I was not insensible to the beauty of my teacher's diction. He was a man of letters, a lover of the music of words, and like most lettered men of his race something of a poet.

Even when dealing with commonplace matters and everyday needs he made them picturesque, and almost always fell into what I believe the Arabs call *sàj* or rhymed poetic prose, short clipped sentences terminating in rhyme or assonance.

I would not have you believe, however, that even by my method the study of Arabic is all beer and skittles. There were hard cruel moments when the teacher forced me to spell, and then I would almost invariably mistake a *cad* for a *sin*. The *gaf* was, of course, impossible and how wearisome was the constant exercise in hissing sibilants! Indeed when the teacher was showing me how to bring them out I often imagined that my room was swarming with "rattlers" from the Rockies!

The son of the Otsmane was the most charming of teachers. As he came into the room his invariable salutation made with courtly gesture was "Peace be unto you—and the mercy of God." And when the lessons were over, however flagrant my shortcomings had been, he never failed to say, as he bowed himself out with dignity and grace, "May His blessing and His approval abide with you." Upon sitting down he often produced his *Koran,* and with rosary in his supple fingers he would recite the five prayers, too long to repeat here, but I must give the concluding promise.

"By observing these precepts you will gain everlasting good and great profits which can never be taken away from you."

The Commandments which he insisted upon were simple and easily understood. They were, "Observe the month of Ramadan. Give tithes and make pilgrimages to the sacred places. Avoid all things forbidden of God, such as telling lies, bearing false witness, drinking wine and killing people—unlawfully."

This last admonition with its qualification gave me an opportunity to inquire whether he regarded the killing of Colonel Flatters and all his companions while in Senussi territory as lawful or otherwise. The French official version is, of course, that while engaged in surveying in 1881 the line for the then projected railway from Algiers to Senegal this gallant officer was murdered under direct orders from the Sheikh es-Senussi. The son of the Otsmane answered without hesitation that it was difficult to shed light on desert mysteries, but by all accounts the party was set upon by Tuaregs who most certainly were not acting under orders of the great Sheikh.

"In one way or another these nomads make their living from the caravans that pass," he explained. "The railway meant the doom of this method of transportation and starvation for those who followed it. These killings were certainly unlawful," but the teacher's eyes flashed and for once his words did not ring true.

My teacher's most cherished possession, second only to his well-worn copy of the *Koran,* was his family tree inscribed on parchment and carried in a silver tube. Without skipping a single generation it ran back to the thirteenth century and a certain sheikh who was easily the star of all the savants of his day. There were moments when, as Akmet reeled off the proud names, I feared that he too indulged in the not uncommon weakness of family pride. But I did him injustice. The sonorous name of many a sire rolled from his lips and then, bowing his head in a characteristic attitude of humility, he added, "And now we come to the father of all men—the Progenitor Adam—who was made out of mud."

Very frankly Akmet described the policy, part philanthropy and part politics, by which the Senussi Sheikh had achieved practical control of the Sahara and the western Soudan. He had ordered his men to clean out old wells and dig new ones on the desert trails where needed. Humble rest houses were erected by his orders along the most desolate stretches, and here dates were often stored to succor those who arrived with their provisions exhausted. While Akmet did not stress this point he did not deny that the Sheikh and the Brotherhood in return for these good deeds secured substantial earthly profits in addition to the treasures which they were storing up in heaven. He described how almost invariably the caravans were accompanied by agents of the Sheikh, frequently important men of *mokaddam* or disciple rank. They smoothed the path of the travelers and often received a tithe or some proportionate percentage of the value of the goods they had helped to safeguard, and Akmet did not disguise the fact that the reward in money or in goods thus received was far less valuable than a by-product of these journeys which penetrated to the most distant provinces. This was the information gathered and the contacts made by these traveling agents. As a result the Senussi Sheikh was always informed at first hand as to what was happening in the most obscure and inaccessible corners of the Dark Continent, and few indeed were the tribes that failed to learn in this way of the far-reaching power of the growing Order.

But now suddenly a strange air of diffidence, indefinable but very real, came over my teacher and threatened to arrest the progress of my lessons. I, too, suffered from a certain *malaise*. I had been less than frank with this warm-hearted, generous creature. Had he found this out? and in any case what was to be done to re-establish the charming relations which from the first I had so enjoyed? I registered a high resolve that this deceit imposed by my chief should end. I would make a clean breast of our plans—but Akmet Mahommed came out with his confession first.

"What I have told you is the truth," he admitted, "but not the whole truth. I am indeed one of the custodians of the treasured writings in the Mosque of the Olive Tree but first and always I am a brother of the Senussi Order and a follower of the blessed one whom you call the Veiled Prophet. Seeing the decay of Islam all about me, with hope and despair fighting for the mastery in my heart, I traveled across the desert to his Shrine. During the journey the merciless sun and the sweeping sand storms impaired my sight as you see, but with the joy I brought back with me I count my loss but gain. I do not wear the symbol of my new faith upon my sleeve and I have not deserted the sanctuaries where I worshiped in former years because—because—these are the orders of the Prophet whom I have seen unveiled. 'Watch and pray' are his orders. 'Pray to Him in weakness and in strength.' Say 'God have mercy upon me. I am as thou hast created me. Pray and wait upon the Will of Allah.' "

I was deeply moved and could no longer dissemble. There must be a limit to my servitude to my suspicious chief. "Son of the Otsmane," I began, "though with no sinister motive I too have been far from frank, but now I shall tell you all that is in my heart. I am as your great countryman Ibn Batuta called himself centuries ago, 'a man astray—' But I also seek the Truth. I, too, would make the pilgrimage to the Shrine and what I see and what I hear there I shall faithfully report to my people."

"You would be welcome," said the teacher to my surprise, "to the pure of heart the road is broad and straight and easy, to the seeker after the Truth the Gate of Knowledge is gladly opened, but to those who are self-seeking, who have political designs—the way is barred." Then followed a sinister silence and it was only days later that I was advised of the blood-curdling fate of these faithless and foolhardy pilgrims, of the subtle poisons in the desert wells and the other extremely disagreeable forms of death that awaited the agents of unfriendly powers and the spies of alien religions.

With his tendency to rhapsody it was, of course, difficult to extract prosaic facts from the teacher, and yet that was what I was in such great need of. Often for hours he would discourse in this wise. "The Great Sheikh is of all the sages the most wise. He is the sun of the firmament in which glow the planets of divine Knowledge." And then protesting his inability to convey in mere words an adequate picture of the Prophet he would slump in his chair and moan, "But who am I that I should presume to describe the perfect Teacher? When the Falcon appears the cock dare not crow. In shame I too must remain silent." To secure bit by bit the prosaic facts I sought I had to follow my teacher on many a flight into the empyrean of Oriental imagery, such as, "when the Great Sheikh died, after he had passed the blessing of heaven on to his nephew-successor, there was by day an eclipse of the sun, by night the moon was hooded and the stars stopped in their courses. Many days passed before the world went about its business again."

Nothing convinced me so completely that I was entering on a new world as a few words as to tactics and what might be called campaign methods of the Order that my teacher let drop at this time.

"The power of our Prophet will prevail over all enemies," he asserted, "because it draws its strength from humility, not from arrogance. When the First Prophet felt the weight of years and saw that he must look about him for someone worthy to carry on the great work, he recalled the prophecy in the ancient writings by which he knew he should be guided. It announces that the Mahdi who would regain the ancient lands and free the faithful from foreign yoke would attain his majority in the month of Moharrem and in the year 1300 of the Flight, and that he would be born of parents having the blessed names of Mahomet and Fatima. So one day at the hour of afternoon prayer when all assemble at the shrine and bow toward Mecca, the young Mahomet, nephew of the most holy one, after divesting himself of his sandals, entered the holy precincts but the Mahdi picked his sandals up and placed them on his feet again. 'You are the Pure and the Holy one,' he said, 'You, though shod, in all humility can approach the Shrine'— It was in this way that the succession of the Prophet was indicated and, of course, joyfully acclaimed."

When the opportunity presented I, naturally as delicately as I could, interrogated Akmet as to the Great Sheikh's attitude toward slavery and the great slave traders like the famous Tippoo Tib who, still unrestrained, were dealing in what they called "human wool and ivory." His answers were frank but confusing. They revealed that the reaction of the Sheikh and the Brotherhood to this thorny problem was not essentially different from that of other men in other climes in other days. The Senussi compromised with their consciences as did for so many generations men of lighter complexions.

"Of course," said Akmet, "the Great Sheikh is opposed to slavery on principle. While I was with him a slave caravan arrived from Bornu—the booty of successful war. The Sheikh entertained the merchants and as there were funds in the treasury, the offerings of the faithful, he purchased all the slaves outright to the joy of the merchants who had their profit without being compelled to prosecute their journey to the regular slave market on the coast. The great Sheikh immediately formed a caravan, placed at its head one of his most trusted *mokaddam* and sent the freed men back to their homes. The *mokaddam* is in these instances chosen from among the class of men capable of founding a school and so forming a religious center from which the new gospels would reach the hitherto overlooked heathen."

Very interesting to me was my teacher's description of the many-sided *mokaddam*. His functions evidently are those of an apostle, a disciple, and not seldom those of a business agent or manager combined. It is he who interrogates the arriving pilgrims. By him the gifts are placed in the Treasury. It is he who is the custodian and the controller of the *baraka,* the benediction of the Senussi Sheikh which carries with it absolution for past shortcomings. "And it is the *mokaddam* on duty who reveals the *deker,*" said Akmet.

Here indeed was information of practical value. I had begun to suspect that there was nothing talismanic in the five prayers though they might be useful in bridging awkward moments, but the *deker* often jealously guarded is a password as well as a prayer. If you know it you are initiated. You belong, as it were. I extracted three *deker* from my kindly teacher. These were of low degree, however. They would admit me within the pale but I would still be far, very far, from the inner shrine. Still it was progress. Of the *deker* I remember two. One was to shout madly "Allah" three times with a rising inflection which I found most difficult; the other was the *deker* of perfect obedience in which the pilgrim protests, "I am as passive in the hands of the Great Sheikh as lies the dead man in the hands of the Washer."

Akmet Mahommed did not minimize the difficulties he had encountered on his pilgrimage or those even greater that probably awaited me. At Bengazi he was detained many weeks, for it was harvest time and consequently no caravans were starting for the interior. He had been fortunate in making a valuable acquaintance; a merchant of the family of El-Zouga who live near the oasis then hallowed by the presence of the Prophet. "This excellent man," explained my teacher, "stopped in the caravansary with me and until he had sold the burden of ivory and feathers that his three camels had brought to the coast, he often took his meals with me. Later, after we had begun to drink tea together, when the heat of the day was passed, I told him the sad story of the decay of Islam in the West. For my encouragement the merchant then described the growing power of the new Prophet, new though his coming had been foretold of old. He explained how the Senussi Lord controlled all the markets of the interior, how he preached fair dealing to the traders and turned the thoughts of men to God. He saves souls from the spoiler, he provides food for the needy and his servants convoy the great caravans coming from the South across the lands of thirst and through the red wilderness long infested by robbers." I listened with rapt attention—that was unfeigned, and then when he paused I said, "That man I must see. Before the Holy One I must bow down."

Then and there we came to an agreement as to the journey and we sanctified it with a fresh brew of tea and by reading together a verse of the *Koran*. "Secretly and by night we left the port, having no passports or the other papers for which the intruding Turks demand many sequins. On the 16th day of our journey we reached Zella where we camped outside the gates, as within the cholera was raging. Here happily was the end of the Turkish dominion and here began the 'black' desert over which travelers must carry their own water and even their own dates. For five days now our course led us across a wilderness which was spotted with black stones about the size of walnuts and then we came to the district of the gum trees and later, at El Jdoug, we entered on the territory of Sidi Mahomet, the anointed of the Lord, the ruler of the Western Soudan and of the tribes of the Sahara.

"From now on our way was smooth and all difficulties disappeared. As we neared Kaufea, by countless signs we knew we were approaching the Shrine. The narrow trail we had followed broadened into a stately avenue pleasantly shaded by palm trees. On the last day, after a march of ten hours, we came out upon a great square in which there were innumerable uncovered market stalls and about them were gathered merchants from Wadai and Fezzan selling or exchanging their wares with the men from the Coast.

"At the far end of the square rose the prayer house, the mother lodge of the order where so many brave words have been spoken. It was of clay and simply roofed with palm branches. Behind the lodge was an enclosure surrounded by a high mud wall. Within this barrier our sovereign lord and pontiff Sidi Mahomet had his abode. Out of the prayer house there rose no tower from which the muezzin could proclaim the hours of prayer but from time to time holy men would appear in the market space and, heeding their call, the faithful would leave their worldly pursuits and assemble for worship in the mud-walled mosque. On either side of the greater entrance to the holy place were displayed green pennants. On one was inscribed, 'God is

Great and Mahomet is His Prophet' and on the other you could read the watchword of the Senussia, 'Be watchful and patient! He too waits.'

"We came to the holy place as the sun was setting and as we looked about us for a resting place three Khouans of the Order appeared and gave us cordial welcome. After the exchange of greetings they hastened away but soon returned with a high official of the Prophet's household. After, by his direction, we had been regaled with rice and camel's flesh, the welcoming brethren inquired our business. Assuming the attitude of prayer I told them that my sole purpose in traveling so far from home and kindred was to receive the blessing of the Prophet. Armed with this I would return to whence I came, blessed among men not only in this life but in the greater life to come. My prayer was graciously received and on the next morning, the thirty-fifth that had dawned since we left the sea, I made obeisance to the Prophet and saw him unveiled."

I cannot better describe the ceremony at which the Prophet, so long veiled, was made plain, than by repeating here the very words of the poet-pilgrim himself although, as a matter of fact, several weeks elapsed before he took me into this his fuller confidence.

"When I was not more than four yards away from the Sheikh Sidi el Mahdi," he said, "I suddenly found myself penetrated and almost overcome by a feeling of the greatest awe. However, I assembled my thoughts as best I could, and began to read before him the poem I had written during my pilgrimage in celebration of the majesty of his person and character:

" 'In coming to visit the saint elect of God, the moon of Djerboud, I have hoped to merit the pardon of my sins,' I began. 'To do that I have crossed the plains and climbed the sand hills of the desert, indifferent to fatigue. I have come upon a young camel, whose feet have left a great furrow in the sand. With swiftness we have climbed even the high mountain paths.

" 'I mounted my camel at the hour when the heavens were as gray as my temples, and thanks to her tireless feet, the most distant lands have drawn near.

" 'My camel is born of two noble animals of Hedjaz, which were trained to cross the plains which stretch as far as the eye can see under the dazzling glare of the salt licks which ostriches love.

" 'She goes a swifter gait when soothed by the songs of the poet.

" 'The hot suns of the noontide have not detained me and I hastened my steps because I was going to a friend.

" 'I have watched through the night with the stars, and the sun has given me escort from its rising to its going down.

" 'I have not tasted the delights of sleep and my camel has not quenched her thirst during the heat of the day.

" 'Oh, my friends, be not anxious or sad—what can one fear when sustained by the confidence which the saint inspires—the saint whose prayers are always granted?

" 'I have traversed the land of God with the pilgrim's staff in my hand. I have crossed the deserts and endured the sorrows of the absent.

" 'All that I have borne, though I grew to manhood in a well-policed city and loved the quiet of my study.

" 'In Tunis, the green, are my parents and my companions, and in the mosque of the Olive Tree are the stars of my education.

" 'My tribe, my teachers and my friends—all my kinsmen are descended from the Pure Woman (that is, Fatima Zohra, daughter of Mahomet).

" 'I have entered into the spiritual family of Sidi Senussi, the greatest of saints. Should I ever abandon him, may God punish me.

" 'Thanks to his Brotherhood, the most distant regions of Yemen enjoy peace and Arabian G'rak has grown rich.

" 'Thanks to his secrets, the Syrian lands have grown green again and the fertility of Egypt no longer suffers droughts.

" 'The glory of thy cities and thy places of prayer make the celestial firmament seem pale. They indeed are the beacons which shine in the darkest night.

" 'In the name of God, I conjure thee, do not reject him who comes toward thee, he who with radiant face has at last arrived in the land of the noblehearted men.'

"As I read these verses," related the pilgrim, "I saw an expression of joy overspread the Prophet's face. When I had finished I advanced toward him. He rose and took from my hands the paper upon which the poem was written and he prayed for me. Then we recited the *Fatiha*, and later I was taken to the apartment which had been prepared for me."

The poet-pilgrim thought well of his salute to the Mahdi. He translated it for me, of course, and wished me to paraphrase it and learn it by heart so that when for me too came the great moment, I would not stand speechless before the mighty Sheikh. By a very practical demonstration I soon showed him this was impossible, and in the end we compromised on a salutation of forty words which would at least have been approved by the pilgrims who came after me on the long line, whatever the Sheikh might have thought of it.

After a few more days of study my teacher advanced the idea that it would be an excellent plan for me to acquire a wardrobe and so learn to be at my ease in Arab garb. Often in the dusk of the late afternoon we would sally out and visit the shops where North Africans, sojourning in Paris, replaced their worn garments. Soon I had acquired a gorgeous outfit, *jellab*, kaftan, baggy under-trousers and cruel long-pronged spurs attached to bright yellow leather riding boots. The teacher insisted that so attired I should sit throughout the study hours. It was not a bad idea. I was soon quite at home in my new raiment and acquired not a few of my teacher's tricks in tossing my *jellab* about.

Dropping in one afternoon with a message from the Commodore, de Morès reported quite favorably upon my changed appearance. "With a beard," he reported, "he will be the picture of an Arab. Indeed he is one now—until he opens his mouth."

I assured de Morès that the beard was only a matter of two or three weeks, but my pronunciation of the obligatory prayers was the subject of some discussion. Evidently my teacher and the gay cavalryman were of different schools and I let them fight it out between them. I still had some weeks to improve my inflection and harden my guttural sounds, and I was greatly comforted by the assurance the son of the Otsmane gave me to the effect that while the shrine of the desert was the exclusive meeting-place of the pure in thought, many *barābra*, strange peoples whose language was as barbaric as mine, were welcomed.

One morning the "sing-song" lessons were interrupted by the appearance of one of Mr. Bennett's sailors. He brought one of the famous notes on paper of robin's egg blue asking me to come to lunch at the Café Anglais. There would be no one present but the Marquis de Morès, and to secure greater privacy our food would be served in the Grande Seize—the private room of that number which the Chief always reserved for his parties.

Of course I was on hand and on time, and equally of course the Commodore was not. De Morès appeared and was charming. "I feel as if I knew you well," he said, "because I was with Bennett at this very table when he wrote the telegram that brought you from the Balkans." As a matter of fact I had met the Marquis several times in Paris and before that in New York where he married a charming American girl who was also an heiress. This marriage had not only resulted in great happiness for those immediately involved but had enabled the young nobleman to restore the shattered fortunes and the ruined palaces of his stately father the Duke of Vallambrosa. It had also supplied de Morès with the funds for a persistent attack on the American Beef Trust—that had not been particularly successful. The Duke was the head of an ancient and distinguished family originally from Sardinia. Most of his landed possessions had been lost at the card table, it was said, but all members of the family still retained their ancestral right of coming into the local church on horseback. Unlucky at cards, the Duke had been fortunate in love, and when he married the beautiful and talented Mlle. Cars of the House of Molière he came to Ste. Clotilde, where the marriage was celebrated, on foot.

De Morès, born of this union, was a very handsome young man of soldierly appearance, as was natural in view of the fact that he had graduated at St. Cyr and served for some years in a crack cavalry regiment. He was a man of strong likes and dislikes. He adored Mr. Bennett and his pet aversion was Theodore Roosevelt the First. I am quite sure that had he not passed some years before from the world scene of which he was one of the most romantic figures, de Morès would have had a stroke when Roosevelt reached the Presidency, even though it came about by the accidental and tragic death of President McKinley. De Morès and Roosevelt had been unfriendly neighbors in their cattle-ranching days out in the Dakotas and Wyoming, and had come very near to fighting a duel over water rights or the boundaries of their respective pasture lands.

On this occasion, fortunately, de Morès did not talk Roosevelt. The Commodore blew in and after apologies we sat down to an excellent luncheon, which I attacked with a vim natural to a man who, while he now ate elsewhere, still had poignant memories of the meals at the Tunisian *gargote*. In a few minutes it was clear that my chief and de Morès had together plotted the expedition on which I was to serve as the advanced pawn, but it was equally apparent that they were animated by very different purposes.

De Morès' interest in the African situation was inspired by patriotic motives and also by a dream of trade expansion. In the first place he wanted to divert the Soudan caravans from the Tripolitan ports on the Mediterranean, where they generally debouched to the great advantage of the Turkish treasury, to the Algerian and Tunisian markets. Then he cherished the hope that the Senussi Chief might be persuaded to make common cause with the Dongolese tribesman, the Mahdi of Khartoum, and so stop or at least harass the British advance into Central Africa. When he was under the fascinating spell of this prospect the young Frenchman would hail the Senussi Brotherhood as a great civilizing force. On the other hand it was clear that should they prove deaf to his arguments, de Morès would be in favor of destroying these presumptuous people root and branch. He saw clearly that if the Senussi could not be mobilized against perfidious Albion they would prove an obstacle to the expansion of French power in northern Africa. In time they might even oppose the "peaceful penetration" of Morocco by the French. They would arrest the spread of civilization and, of course, that could not be tolerated. Upon this point de Morès was quite insistent and most emphatic.

My chief listened with growing impatience to the voluble explanations which de Morès made, greatly to his own satisfaction at least, of the many African problems that were then engrossing the attention of the chancelleries of Europe. At last he rose and took me away with him. When we were out on the Boulevard he put his arm on my shoulder and said confidentially, "Of course all that talk of de Morès is—what would you call it in Washington—'bunk or buncombe'?"

I assured the Commodore that both words had their devotees and that either would be understood on the other side of the Atlantic.

"To you I shall only repeat what I have already told you," he continued. "We are not interested in the politics of Africa except in so far as the partition of the Dark Continent may interfere with American trade, and breed war. I merely want you to get in touch with those five hundred million people who regard the Veiled Prophet much as our Irish do the Pope. His shrine with the thousands of pilgrims coming and going daily is the greatest untapped center of information in the world today, and I want you to pre-empt it exclusively for the *Herald*. If the project turns out, as I think it will, we may have to establish a bureau out there and recruit a corps of couriers and," he added with a laugh, "a squadron of trotting camels. Mangiabuono writes you should start inland in about six weeks— that means you must leave Paris within a month. I will land you on the coast at the point he selects." I assured the Chief that my preparations were advancing steadily and that I would be ready to start when he fixed the day.

. . . Hours of interesting work, interspersed with day dreams, pass very quickly and one morning when I pricked my calendar I was surprised to find that I had been in Paris, though enveloped in a Senussi atmosphere, for seven weeks and five days, and yet at first six weeks was the limit for preparation that had been assigned to me. Could anything untoward have happened? Certainly not. The last time I had seen the Commodore he had said he was so interested in the adventure that if possible he would personally escort me to the Tripolitan coast and there wish me the best of luck as I began my journey into the unknown.

All the same I grew restless. I could not keep my attention on my parrot-like lessons and finally I gave the son of the Otsmane a holiday. Some hours later when I began to think of lunch, one of the sailors from the *Namouna* appeared, without a note this time. The Commodore had sent him to bring me as quickly as possible in his carriage to the apartment in the Champs Élysées. I could hardly restrain my joy. What could the Commodore have to say to me now but the long-awaited words "shove off"? Only the day before I had read in the *Figaro* that the yacht had arrived off Villefranche after having had her bottom scraped in the dry dock at Venice.

In the great salon where I was introduced by the sailor there was no one, but on several ash trays Russian cigarettes were smouldering, giving out their unmistakable smell. From the next room came loud voices and I thought to distinguish Russian words. As he strode into the room the Commodore was smoking a fat Giubec cigarette and after giving me one, "I have a great disappointment for you," he began, "and I am free to say I share it. I have a cable from Mangiabuono who says that the Veiled Prophet has abandoned Jaghbub and is moving his headquarters many hundred miles inland, probably to Jof, in the oasis of Kufara. De Morès confirms this bad news from what he has been able to pick up in the rue St. Dominique.* He is furious and thinks the French War Office has been very foolish. By sending large reinforcements to the border garrisons, the Generals have driven the Prophet into the interior where it will be much more difficult to keep him under observation. Now what shall we do?"

"That is for you to say," I answered. The Commodore nodded, walked over to the window, and for a time watched with interest the passing throngs surging up and down the broad avenue and then, apparently quite oblivious of my presence, he began to talk aloud, but in a low voice.

"Now we don't know where the frightened bird will alight. Kufara is nearly a thousand miles from the coast and he may not stop there. The story will cost me at the least fifty thousand dollars (this was the only time I ever heard the Commodore count the cost!). Anything like a swift dispatch from the interior to the cable office, Mangiabuono says, would cost five hundred, and then young Bonsal might be killed before he gets through a single story. I would hate that." Then the Commodore turned and welcomed me again.

"About the Prophet we shall wait and see. I shall let you know when the propitious moment arrives. In the meantime I have every reason to think that there is going to be a blow-up in the Balkans." Lowering his voice he continued, "I think Ferdinand will be kidnaped as was Alexander and perhaps he will be handled more roughly

* French War Ministry.

than was the Battenberg. Make for Sofia as quickly as you can. I shall be pleased if you catch the express tonight. Keep the carriage as long as you need it and send me a wire when you arrive—and lots of good luck," and he was gone.

I had concluded my business arrangements with the son of the Otsmane the day before, and with the illuminated manuscript under his arm he had gone out into the narrow street with an expression of almost ecstatic rapture upon his charming face. My packing and the other details of departure did not take up much time. Only for a moment did I hesitate as to what I should do with the gorgeous garments in which I had so often pictured myself riding across the desert to the Senussi shrine. Then I made a bundle of them, spurs and all, and tagged it with a little note in bad French and broken Arabic which ran:

"Please accept this souvenir of your grateful pupil. I have been called away to a distant country and I may never see you again. Do what you will with this noble garb which I can no longer hope to wear on the Pilgrimage we planned. Try not to forget the student from across the sea with whom you have been so patient and indulgent."

I ended my last message with his favorite prayer, learned with so much difficulty, but fresh in my memory even today.

"May God guide your affairs and shape your life to conform to the book, and may our prayers that His blessing and His approval abide with us be answered!"

I left the bundle for him at the little restaurant where we had so often foregathered, which I was never to see again, and two hours later I was on the Orient Express hastening back once more to the cockpit of southeastern Europe. And so ended one of the most interesting of my many journeys that were planned but never came off. Seven years later, after a stormy political career marked by many sensational duels, de Morès undertook the journey to the Senussi shrine which he had planned for me. Near Simoun in the Sahara he was attacked and murdered by Tuaregs under circumstances which have remained mysterious to this day. Both Mr. Bennett and his gallant widow were of the opinion that the desert nomads acted under orders received from the Veiled Prophet.

13. COURT LIFE IN BULGARIA

I TRAVELED to Sofia now as fast as the Express would carry me. I did not venture to leave the train in Vienna even for a minute, for fear of being left behind. I read very carefully the account of the Zankovist plot to kidnap Prince Ferdinand which Christianson had turned over to me at the station, and then carefully destroyed it. The kidnaping was to be pulled off on the following Sabbath and as I reached the Bulgarian capital on Thursday, I was in plenty of time for the fireworks. I called at the Palace and wrote my name in the book. As I came away I noticed that the Princess Clementine was looking out of the window at the dreary scene which, in those days at least, and to my eyes always, Sofia unfolded. She seemed very pensive and for a moment I was tempted to warn the poor lady who, seeking popularity with the Bulgars, was spending, or as it seemed to us, wasting, such huge sums in her son's opera bouffe principality. But it was not my secret.

I was surprised in the course of the next twenty-four hours to meet almost all of the correspondents who, like myself, were responsible for this dynamic news center. Their presence seemed to substantiate the rumor that had brought me back to the Balkans, but made it quite plain that whatever happened I should not have an exclusive story. All the correspondents were visibly embarrassed as they ran across their colleagues and competitors at the club or in the Café Panachoff, and made labored explanations of their presence. Beaman of the *Standard* had come from Constantinople where things were deadly quiet, he reported. His purpose, he avowed, was to kill a black wolf that had been seen on the slopes of Witosh. Starshenski, the sportsman of the Austrian legation, was on its tracks but he hoped to get ahead of Starshenski as he had, he added in his blustering way, so often before. Bouchier of the *London Times* came from Athens. He was exceedingly hard of hearing, and this failing had aided him to ignore a number of revolts and many more discreditable things for which he was later rewarded by having his picture on one of the Bulgarian postage stamps.

The *Times* was further represented by Sir Donald Mackenzie Wallace, who at this juncture arrived most unexpectedly from London. That was a surprise to all of us and a disagreeable one for Bouchier. Wallace was a diplomat, and he made it quite plain his visit had nothing to do with current politics. He averred he had come to seek out original documents for his long-planned history of the Bulgarian people, from Tsar Simeon to Prince Ferdinand. It was to run to seven volumes and as he was approaching sixty he felt that the time had come for him to get on with it.

On the Sabbath, the critical day, we were all bidden to luncheon at the Palace. It was a stag affair, the Princess-Mother remaining in her own apartment, a prey, doubtless, to many fears. Most of the reasons I have presented as to why my colleagues had come in a bunch as it were, and so unexpectedly, were extracted by the cross-examination to which the Prince subjected us one and all as we appeared. "And you?" he inquired, and, unblushingly, I answered that I was simply making a routine round of my beat which, as he knew, extended from Vienna to the Bosphorus. We had a pleasant luncheon and when it was over the Prince led the way out on to a balcony where, protected by glass from the rude winds of November and embowered in flowers, we had a charming view of the snow-tipped heights of Mount Witosh. Then he handed us Giubec cigarettes (and there are none better) and began his cross-questioning again. His eyes fastened upon us with a searching expression and then suddenly he burst out into an uncontrollable fit of laughter. I, as the youngest and certainly the least court-broken of the company, insisted that he share the joke with us; and then, growing serious, he said, "Of course, I believe it has happened casually, just as you say it did. But I must admit that when I heard that you had all arrived here, coming from the various points of the compass and within twenty-four hours, I said to myself, 'The vultures are gathering; soon Ferdinand of Coburg will be carrion.'" While I made a deprecating gesture, I felt guilty and tried to hide it by laughing heartily and so did most of the other men, but not so—decidedly not so—Mackenzie Wallace. After all, he belonged to quite a different category. He was a newspaper correspondent recently knighted because for years he had shaped world news so that it would be most useful and helpful to the British government. He flushed deeply and bridled. It was some weeks before the witty if unscrupulous Ferdinand made his peace with him.

I have not given anything like an intimate picture of Prince Ferdinand. My reticence is due to the fact that up to now I had seen very little of him. He was frequently taking the cure in Carlsbad or visiting his Hungarian estates, and when he did return to Bulgaria I was often away in Macedonia or in Serbia or some other trouble zone in my large and turbulent area. He rather plumed himself on the fact that he had been in America, and he had an amusing way of mixing up the empire of Brazil, which he knew, with our republic, which most certainly he did not know. He had visited Rio during the reign of Dom Pedro as the guest of his kinsman, the Comte d'Eu, who was the prince consort of the learned Pedro's daughter. At this time Prince Ferdinand was unmarried and led an exceedingly lonely life, which probably accounted for the fact that he set such store by our visits. There were only two foreigners in his household, M. de Bourbalon, a courtly Savoyard of a family that had served the Prince's forefathers for generations; and Baron Lobner, a smart cavalry officer, who in his day had "witched" Vienna with his horsemanship and was now engaged in the difficult task of teaching the Bulgarian cavalry the Austrian seat in the saddle.

The Prince was not unprepossessing in appearance. At this time his Bourbon nose, upon which so many caricatures have been hung in later years, was neither abnormal in size nor unpleasing in its effect. His eyes were light blue, a little too light and washed-out, but they did reveal the great intelligence which he possessed. In his cavalry boots he stood a little over six feet, and he had the easy graceful carriage of every Austrian cavalry officer I had ever met. His voice was unpleasant. He had a nasal twang and, in spite of his many French ancestors, vocally at least the German strain dominated. This was a great misfortune and a heavy handicap, as the Bulgarians at this time had a very healthy hatred of everything German or "Swab." The Prince was exceedingly friendly to all the correspondents; and, while he evidently preferred ornithology to political situations as a topic of conversation at the luncheon table, he was often quite amusing.

In the more private conversations which I frequently enjoyed with him, at this time and later, the Prince was at pains to explain the ill luck which had so often attended his family engaged in the kingly *métier* both in Europe and America, and he made it quite plain that he proposed to avoid the pitfalls into which they had fallen. Many a sermon he preached about Dom Pedro the Second, for so long Emperor of Brazil. "He had only himself to blame for his deposition and later his exile. The poor man was a savant," the Prince was wont to say. "He devoted himself to the history of the dead past and to speculations as to the future of science. He was surrounded by antiquarians conversant with what happened in the Middle Ages, and with star-gazers whose speculations as to what the world would look like in the twenty-second century fascinated him. But he ignored absolutely the living world. The statesmen and the editors who were shaping the destinies of his people he did not consult; indeed, he did not even know them by name, and he paid the penalty. For this he forfeited his throne and lost his crown." These criticisms were to the point, and well taken I am assured, by those who knew Brazil in the critical years. But, while he was able to avoid the pitfalls that he knew of, Prince Ferdinand fell into others; and, as a last resort in 1918, rather ingloriously, he fled the principality which had become, under his tireless fostering care, a kingdom.

The career of the Prince, afterwards king of Bulgaria, and now, after the days of *sturm und drang* are over, an aged exile in the little town of Coburg where he potters about collecting coins and birds' eggs, is rather startling to those who believe, if any such survive, in the divine right of kings. After the kidnaping of his predecessor, Prince Alexander, and his subsequent abdication, owing to the opposition of the Tsar to his return to power, the Bulgarian throne went begging, as was natural in the untoward circumstances, and the situation of the country grew daily more critical. The Regents to whom the administration was confided were having great difficulty in carrying out their duties in the face of the unfriendly attitude of the Tsar, as represented by General Kaulbars. Stambouloff ruled the Regents and he in quick succession offered the uneasy throne to Prince Waldemar of Denmark, brother of Alexandra, Princess of Wales, and of the Empress of Russia, and then to King Charles of Roumania. They, one after the other, declined the honor and then the Turks, a humorous gesture doubtless, put forward a Prince of Mingrelia, but this nomination did not prosper.

It was at this juncture that the Regents who were entirely controlled by Stambouloff sent three delegates to inspect the royal cadets of Europe in a search for an eligible ruler. One of these delegates, M. Stoileff, who afterwards became Prime Minister, told me later many amusing details of this adventure. Apparently they had been rebuffed in many quarters and, preparatory to returning to Sofia by the Orient Express the next day, were spending the evening at Ronarchers, at the time a famous night café and music hall in Vienna. Their quest had been a failure and the vacant throne still stared them in the face. The princelings who were willing to go to Bulgaria, to secure what Bismarck called in his famous talk with the Battenberg prince "an interesting souvenir for their old age," were not eligible. And those who were, did not want to go.

Everybody in the night café knew the Bulgarian trio. They had been the subject of many cartoons in the comic papers, so Stoileff was not greatly surprised when a man who was a complete stranger to him and whose name he never knew came over and sat himself down at their table. "You gentlemen are looking for a prince," he said. "Why don't you take Prince Long Nose over there? We could get along without him—splendidly." Prince Long Nose, who sat at an adjacent table, was no other than Prince Ferdinand of Coburg, then a lieutenant in a Hussar regiment. It was notorious that he had no inclination for soldiering and that he spent his time stuffing birds and collecting rare coins. He lived at the château of Ebenthal near Vienna where his widowed mother, a daughter of Louis Philippe, resided. The unknown man and the Bulgarian delegates clinked glasses and soon separated, but the suggestion stuck.

The next morning Stoileff made inquiries and learned that the Princess Clementine was exceedingly ambitious for her children, and also very wealthy. After the failure of the Comte d' Eu to realize her dream of empire in South America, the hopes and aspirations of the ambitious woman centered upon her young son. The more he thought about the matter the more Stoileff became convinced that a promising lead had been given him. He told me that he immediately wired Stambouloff and that the Regent came incognito to the Austrian capital to look the princeling over. This statement has been disputed, but I believe it is in accordance with the facts.

The people who hated and feared Stambouloff, and they were many, said that the reasons why the choice of the Regents finally rested upon Ferdinand were selfish rather than patriotic. It is certain that at this time Ferdinand had none of the popular and even endearing qualities which his unfortunate predecessor, Alexander, had possessed to a remarkable degree. Despite the French blood that flowed in his veins, Ferdinand was very German in appearance, and the Bulgarians hated all Germans, especially the blond ones and those who have, as Ferdinand had, a high, almost falsetto, voice in which nasal tones dominated. He had, of course, traveled far and wide in Europe and had enjoyed and availed himself of unusual educational advantages, but he had never been in southeastern Europe and was wholly ignorant of the languages and the customs of the people over whom he was to rule. It may not be true but, by those who knew the ambitious man best, it has always been believed that Stambouloff with his eyes open brought to the throne a young man whom he expected would remain unpopular and consequently but a puppet in his strong, masterful hands. It is true that Ferdinand always remained unpopular among his adopted people, but it is equally true that he soon showed an aptitude for Balkan diplomacy and that in many a tangled intrigue he bested his bullying Prime Minister.

Ferdinand accepted the offered throne conditionally upon his being elected by the Grand Sobranje or extraordinary legislative assembly and upon the approval of the Powers. Russia, however, ignored the selection and so from the start Ferdinand was subjected to a diplomatic boycott. Indeed, it was only in 1908, twenty-one years after his accession, that the position he had made for himself was generally recognized. In May 1894, Ferdinand summoned up the courage to dismiss Stambouloff. He had forgiven his many high crimes and his misdemeanors, but as he was an obstacle to recognition by Russia, the liberating nation the Prime Minister had fought so bitterly and so unfairly, the Prince finally kicked him out. Then Stambouloff, in an access of fury which even his friends deplored, unbosomed his secret thoughts and uncorked all the vials of wrath to a German journalist. It was a terrible story and what was untrue was unimportant. The Prince instituted legal proceedings for defamation of character and would not permit Stambouloff to visit a German spa which the state of his health made advisable. And yet the libel suit, for some reason, never came to trial. A few weeks later, in July, while returning from dinner at the Union Club, Stambouloff was set upon by three assassins. He defended himself manfully, but in the end was well-nigh cut to pieces with the curved *yataghans* the assassins carried. And three days later the ex-Premier, the maker of much that was good and much that was bad in modern Bulgaria, died.

It was, of course, most unfortunate for me that my dispatches from Sofia, and, indeed, whatever news I was able to get out of Bulgaria, should have been reproduced in the *Temps* and other Paris papers with a promptness which even I, with the high opinion I had of their worth, thought remarkable. The editor of the *Swoboda*, the Stambouloff organ, initiated a newspaper crusade against me on this charge, but he overplayed his hand and a few of the open-minded publicists rallied to my support, in conversation at least, if not in their papers. The editor of the *Swoboda* even went to the extreme of saying that I was a Russian by birth and that the exceedingly bad Russian that I spoke was an elaborate and clumsy camouflage!

While I became *persona non grata* at court later, under amusing circumstances which I shall relate, Prince Ferdinand at this time often asked me to the Palace and seemed to endure what were generally considered my "attacks" on his Prime Minister with fortitude, and at times I thought, with pleasure. Once he asked me how it happened that *Le Nord*, admittedly a Russian-subsidized organ, published in Brussels, reproduced my articles a very few hours after they had appeared in the *Herald*, and he advised me to have this stopped if I could; but the thing was, of course, impossible and I never attempted it. While, as the Stambouloff papers charged, Mr.

Bennett was on terms of intimacy with leading Russians and with members of the Imperial family, it is only fair to say that when he sent me to Bulgaria, he neither then nor later gave me the slightest intimation (much less pro-Russian instructions) as to how he viewed the situation. So I found it not difficult to explain to the Prince that, as I was apparently trying to send out the only impartial news that came from Bulgaria, it was natural that such papers as were seeking the truth should reproduce it by arrangement with my editor, or simply pirate it.

About this time the difficulties of my position were increased by an incident that most certainly was not of my contriving. On my return from a Macedonian foray I found that Petko Karaveloff, a former Prime Minister whom I knew and admired, was being held in prison although no charges were advanced against him. Stambouloff hated him because he was a man of culture and breeding and also because he was one of the few men in public life upon whom the groups hostile to the little dictator might possibly unite. In my absence, Karaveloff had been lodged in the Black Mosque, a noisome dungeon, as I was well aware, because I had visited it to interrogate my former guide, Tryko, who was being held there on charges which had nothing to do with his relations with me.

When it became apparent that Karaveloff, who was old and very feeble, would not be brought to trial, but was to be held in the filthy prison until he died, I began to move in his behalf. Madame Karaveloff told me that she had reason to believe that her unfortunate husband was subjected to the *bastinado* at least once a week. Having asked permission to visit the prison, and having been curtly refused, I published the facts that were known to me and also the rumors as to the treatment of the unfortunate statesman which, as I cabled, Stambouloff made it impossible for me either to verify or to deny.

This aroused the Vienna papers and de Burian, who during the World War served as one of the last foreign ministers of Austria-Hungary (at the time he was Consul-General in Bulgaria) became interested and insisted that I see the prisoner. As I stumbled into the filthy place I finally made out the emaciated forms of three or four hundred wretched vermin-ridden men crouching on the floor of the mosque. The only light there was came from a hole in the minaret.

When my soldier escort asked for Karaveloff the prisoners pointed to the topmost rung of the ladder that led up into the minaret and here I found the former Prime Minister reading by the feeble light, and with the aid of a dictionary, *The American Commonwealth,* the classic which, although only published a few months before, had already, and most literally, reached "darkest Bulgaria." Karaveloff admitted that he had been roughly handled, that in all probability he would soon be brought before a firing squad, but he denied he had been *bastinadoed*. Many thought this denial was inspired by fear, but I cabled what he said and two weeks later he was liberated and sent into exile.

After the death of Stambouloff this charming old man became Prime Minister again. Lord Bryce enjoyed the picture I drew of the unfortunate statesman who was given by the convicts the right to always sit on the topmost rung of the ladder, the only one where you could see to read, with the understanding that he would pass on to his comrades in misfortune the story of the bright and happy land beyond the seas. And indeed the story is told at great length in the official biography of Lord Bryce by Mr. H. A. L. Fisher.

As I have said, the *Swoboda* people overplayed such cards as they had to use against me and, as far as I was concerned, things were quieting down, although Stambouloff, as was his nature, remained relentless, when an incident occurred which in government circles at least reduced the belief in my impartiality to the vanishing point. On this unlucky day for me I was riding with some friends along the foothills of Mount Witosh when a heavily bearded, and from the newspaper accounts of the incident, an important-looking man arrived at the station on the international train, coming from "Europe" as we exiles in the Balkans were accustomed to call all those countries west of Serbia. He drove directly from the station to my hotel and expressed regret and unfortunately some surprise that I was not in. He wrote on his card on which was inscribed the name "Tatistcheff, (his given name I have forgotten) Privy Councilor to the Emperor of Russia, St. Petersburg," and in French he scribbled, "It is most important that I should see you." Being told by the porter that I would probably be back at the luncheon hour, Tatistcheff went into the café for a drink and was immediately surrounded by military police and a bevy of the plain clothes "Stick men" who were always dogging my footsteps. At first Tatistcheff demanded to be taken before the Russian Consul; but, as all relations with Russia had been cut off for a year and there was no consul present, this would have been most difficult for the police to do. With little ceremony they bundled him into a conveyance, and surrounded by half a dozen mounted men he was escorted back to the railway station. A few minutes later I reached the hotel and, hearing what had happened, I, in my turn, hastened to the station as fast as one of the three horse phaetons that then abounded in Sofia could carry me.

The station was heavily guarded by troops and at first I was refused entrance. When I finally got into the waiting room, Tatistcheff was in the midst of the guards and, while he was not manacled, one of the plainclothes men was swinging a chain and clinking what seemed to be handcuffs in a menacing manner. As he saw the effort I made to get within speaking distance, the prisoner smiled wearily and waved his hand. A few minutes later the slow train to Constantinople lumbered in. To it was attached a prison caboose with iron barred windows through which the stranger waved a sad farewell. I never saw or heard from him again, nor did I ever secure any light upon the incident. I never again heard Tatistcheff's name pronounced until, on the eve of the Great War, Emperor Nicholas in one of his last desperate efforts to avert hostilities, cabled to Emperor William, "Delay all you can; I am sending Tatistcheff to you with special instructions." This may have been the same man and it may not have been, Tatistcheff being rather a common name in Russia, and one borne by many bureaucrats of high rank as well as by court officials. One, during the Great War, became Finance Minister and another was faithful to the end and was murdered together with the Tsar and the Imperial family at Ekaterinburg.

After this unfortunate incident it became increasingly difficult for me to get my dispatches out of the country or, as a matter of fact, to receive any news from Europe. The cables were closed to me and all my letters that were openly posted were intercepted and suppressed. Not a single copy of the *Herald* reached me for weeks and even the *Temps* in the issues where my telegrams or letters were reproduced did not get past the censorship. Two of the messengers I had hired from time to time to carry my articles across the border to the nearest Serbian telegraph station were in the Black Mosque prison and I could do little to help them, except supply food, because they were held on trumped-up charges that had, ostensibly at least, nothing to do with their relations with me. In the circumstances, I did not feel justified in employing other messengers and, as we had no official representatives in Bulgaria (at the time the existence of the Principality was not recognized by the State Department and travel there was not covered by our passports), I had no justification for an appeal to Washington. O'Connor, the British diplomatic agent, did what he thought it was proper for him to do, but the first step he took was unfortunate. He had met the Commodore in London, and so he wrote him a personal letter to the effect that my life was in danger and that it was advisable to send me to another post. No one, not even Stambouloff, wanted to get me out of Bulgaria more than O'Connor, but he tackled the business in the wrong way. His perhaps kindly-meant letter provoked a curt note from the Commodore which read, "I am surprised you do not know that I never withdraw my men when under fire."

For some weeks now I maintained clandestine communications with friendly informants, who could not afford to come out into the open and be seen with a correspondent who had been placed under the official taboo, by a very simple device. The Hotel Panachoff where I lived was a public place, and as open to all as the railway station or the square before the Sobranje building. At some hour of the day or night every inhabitant of the capital of the Peasant State passed through it. So, upon going to bed, I would, following the American custom, place a pair of boots outside my door. Of course, as I admitted when rallied on the subject, I knew there were no bootblacks in Sofia but it was a practice, a habit, of which I could not break myself. In the dark hours of the night ghostly figures would hasten stealthily through the dimly lighted corridors and slip into my boots invaluable information in a disguised handwriting but with a key word to inspire me with confidence. But, alas! one morning my letter-box-boots were gone and no trace of them was ever discovered, and I abandoned the system without a moment's hesitation. In the Balkans news was valuable, of course, but boots were invaluable as they could not be replaced.

Cut off from routine communications I sometimes slipped down to Constantinople and sometimes up to Belgrade to find out what was going on and to orient myself. But this was doubly dangerous and I soon abandoned the plan. In my absence some important news event might break and also, despite the fact that the border control was exceedingly stupid, and rather easily circumvented, I might on my return from one of these jaunts be refused entrance into Bulgaria. I escaped from the dilemma in which I was then placed, and broke the blockade against me, by an expedient so simple that it seems almost incredible, and yet it worked like a charm. I went down to the station when the international trains were expected, which happened every other day. Many other exiles in Sofia had this habit and they came merely to felicitate the fortunate people who were on their way to Europe or to Turkey. When the train arrived I would slip into the mail car box a letter which was not very important, as I knew it would be immediately fished out and destroyed. Then, with a Tauchnitz or some other volume of light reading under my arm in which was concealed a letter or a cable marked, "Receiver to pay," I would walk through the train and when I came to a decidedly European-looking passenger I would greet him effusively as one would an old acquaintance. In a loud voice I would say, "I'm delighted I was able to find the volume you said you wanted," then in a lower tone I would explain the situation. With but one exception, a stodgy suspicious German who said, "Dot ist nicht der volume I wanted," all my chance acquaintances were game and all the letters or cables I sent in this haphazard way got through to Paris with little delay.

I was very friendly with the train men and they often smoothed my path. One and all, they loathed Stambouloff and, indeed, most of them detested all Bulgarians, so at times I would find that they had, even before I appeared on the scene, prepared some passenger for the role he was selected to play. The police remained on the platform and apparently were quite content to secure and suppress the letter I would mail so ostentatiously. Finally it seemed advisable to give Sofia, for a few weeks, at least, the absent treatment and, if possible, to escape from constant police surveillance which, increasingly harassing, was getting on my nerves. I also, somewhat to my surprise I confess, received from Mr. Bennett his approval of this step. So one night, with my good friend S. . . . , a Polish landowner who served as Secretary of the Austro-Hungarian Legation, although he was one of the many Poles who hated the Dual Monarchy intensely, I left the Union Club with pack horses and ponies laden with provender and ammunition, ostensibly, and even ostentatiously, bound for the pursuit of bears in the fastnesses of Mount Witosh. Three days later, having caught one of the slouchy local trains at a way station, I was in Philippopolis, greatly pleased at my translation to the rest and quiet and the charm of this romantic town.

At this distant day Philippopolis was as different from dreary and dusty Sofia as night is from day. Still a Turkish community with its uphill and down dale streets and its wonderful gardens musical with bubbling springs and living waters, it was not only charming and above all invigorating in itself, but it was also the starting point for many delightful excursions which live in my memory as the most pleasant of my Balkan experiences. The town sits astride the brawling Maritza which, despite the admonition of the song which all Bulgarians sing from the cradle to the grave ("Be quiet, Maritza!"), will not be still.* Perhaps it is the song of the great days, before the Ottoman Turks came this way, that will not be hushed; when here in Trimontium, as the town was called from the three high hillocks on which it is built, the Roman Pro-Consuls planned their forays into the lands of the barbarians.

One of these rocky crags rising above the plain and river to the height of six or seven hundred feet still bears the Turkish name of Dschambas-Tepe. This was the preferred residential quarter and along its dark and narrow streets, particularly on the north side, rose the picturesque residences of well-to-do Turks and Greeks, all painted in as many colors as Joseph's coat. Here and there one

---

* In my day there were current as many versions of this folk song as there were singing cavalcades coursing through the Balkan passes. It has now become the national anthem of the Bulgars and the official version runs "Make silver music, boisterous Stream," etc. Certain it is that we shall hear of the Maritza in the years to come. S.B.

caught a glimpse of the little summer pavilions behind the main buildings where the Turk took his ease (as far as that is possible for a true believer who must live under the Cross) in neglected gardens embowered in flowers and fragrant with the blossoms of fruit trees. Hanging over the narrow streets, where two mounted men could pass only with difficulty, were verandahs of beautifully carved woodwork. The sliding shutters were perforated with peepholes and the flashing eyes that often were pressed upon them seemed to justify any dream, however extravagant, of harem beauty.

From the south side of this mountain crag rising out of the center of the town was a wonderful view of the Rhodopian Mountains, with their peaks not seldom capped with snow. From my first sight of them this prospect fascinated me. There lived Akmet Agha and his pure-blooded Bulgarian henchmen. They, after going over to Islam at an opportune moment, figure in Balkan history as the oppressors of the Bulgarians of the plains who, while they have remained steadfast to the teachings of St. Cyril and St. Method, have, through the lawless lust of their overlords, received a considerable admixture of Turkish blood and show it.

I lodged in a little inn kept by a Greek which, though not picturesque, like the great Turkish caravansary next door with its ten massive leaden cupolas, was fairly clean. My good friend, Slaveikoff, a graduate of Robert College, the American educational foundation near Constantinople which then (as now) was doing so much for the advancement of Balkan youth, owned a summer house and fruit farm a few miles out on the Dermendere road, and here in his garden bright with flowers and aromatic with tempting fruits I dreamed many hours away. As in duty bound, I explained to the Slaveikoffs, father and son, how disastrous I had proved to my friends and even to some of my chance acquaintances in Sofia, but they asserted this did not bother them. They had, apparently quite frankly, if somewhat passively, opposed Stambouloff for many years and, for reasons which they could not understand, he had not gone after them in his usual ruthless manner; in fact, he had left them severely alone, the father to write poems which recalled the heroic days of the Bulgarian people and the son to tend his fruit trees.

With young Slaveikoff, who proved a charming companion, I

rode to Shipka Pass where for long months the Russians were stopped by the entrenched Turks, and where so many were left in their shallow graves. When you review their history throughout the bloody years from Plevna to Gallipoli, the conclusion is forced upon you that as trench soldiers the Turks are second to none. Then we went on to Kazanlik some twelve hundred feet above the scorched and sultry plains, a charming place where invigorating breezes are ever stirring through the pines. I delighted in these surroundings and I was prepared to share the enthusiasm of Field-Marshal Von Moltke when I visited him in Silesia a few months later and the silent soldier recalled his Roumelian memories in terms that were almost lyrical. I was glad to tell him that the whole countryside which he loved was still shaded by the great nut trees, and that the air was still redolent with the perfume of hundreds of rose farms. And indeed rose farms they are, rather than gardens, some of them running to fifty or sixty acres and I must add, regretfully, the rose bushes are planted in great furrows like corn or potatoes! As was the case with the Spaniards in Andalusia, after the Moors were expelled, I noticed that the Bulgarians had taken on much of the folklore of their predecessors in this happy valley. Certainly they were of the opinion that there were no roses in the world until Mahomet made his remarkable flight to heaven. When he came back from Paradise the peasants who dwell in this great flower garden say that the Prophet brought with him a few rose slips hidden under his prayer rug.

"And how do they account for the great variety of colors that abound in the fields?" I inquired. "Well, the white roses were watered," they explained to Slaveikoff, "by the sweat drops that fell from the forehead of Mahomet. The yellow roses were colored by the lather that fell from his horse." * "And the red roses?" I asked. "Well, they were colored and invigorated by the perspiration of the Archangel Gabriel who on this occasion acted as the Prophet's guide. If you do not believe this, read your *Koran*." As I looked about me and feasted my eyes upon the acres of red roses, it was clear to me

* We also heard the tradition that on this remarkable journey the Prophet rode his famous white donkey, Albornek. But, incorrigibly romantic, Slaveikoff rejected this version.

that on this arduous night journey it was the Archangel Gabriel who sweated the most.

After enjoying this ride through the vale of Kazanlik in an atmosphere fragrant with attar of rose, with my eyes fascinated by the great fields of the Damascene flower, extending before me to the horizon, a sense of duty hitherto ignored compelled me to visit the mountain villages where the Bulgarian atrocities were committed; above all, to go to Batak, where thirteen years before many thousand unarmed men and helpless women and children were murdered in cold blood. The name of the hamlet still connoted horror, even in Philippopolis, which narrowly escaped being included in the mass murders; men shivered when Batak was mentioned. Slaveikoff could not go with me, but after some difficulty I secured an agreeable guide, a small tradesman in the Roumelian town who soon, however, developed into a poet and a ballad singer, qualities which served to brighten the toilsome two days' journey to the beautiful village where one of the most ghastly scenes in the history of horrors was enacted.

My companion was a Stoyanoff, I think, although I am not sure. I can see him now as he rode ahead of me on the mountain trail, singing the story of his long-downtrodden race and putting into verse his hatred of the Moslem invader. His face and his voice I shall always remember, but his name I fear I have forgotten as I have the names of so many who have helped and guided me on many journeys in my vagrant career. Our capacity to forget is really given a wonderful illustration in these mountain villages. Who could have thought that thirty-nine years after the massacres, and twenty-four years after my visit, when the atrocities were still a living memory to some, these villagers should march shoulder to shoulder with the Turks and so help to delay the triumph of civilization in the Great War by at least a year! The only answer to this question, I suppose, is the negative one—that man is an incomprehensible animal!

I had in my pocket a transcript of MacGahan's letters, the correspondent of the *New York Herald* and the *London Daily News* who, aided by Eugene Schuyler of our legation in Constantinople and harassed by Sir Henry Elliot, the British Minister, (who under his instructions from Disraeli and Salisbury was, as they later put it, "backing the wrong horse"), had visited the villages while they still smouldered and sought out in their mountain caves the few villagers who had escaped.

On the long journey I had ample time to recall what Stanley and also Fox of the *Herald* had told me of their most distinguished contemporary, MacGahan. At twenty-six he was apparently a lawyer without clients, but he had the gift of tongues and Mr. Bennett had the good fortune to secure his services during the Franco-Prussian War. The speed and the brilliance of his dispatches, as Forbes admitted to me later, gave the "old-line" correspondents a cruel shock. In 1873 he was in revolutionary Cuba with Jim O'Kelley. He rode through Mambi land and made a gallant attempt to save the men of the *Virginius* from execution. The next two years he was campaigning in Central Asia. He was with the Russians throughout the Turcoman wars and when Skobelev saw that the young American could not be kept out of Khiva he took him into his official family. There followed ten months with Don Carlos in the mountains of Spain and when the rising collapsed he was captured and sentenced to death, for this was a war in which no quarter was given and war correspondents were not recognized. His execution was fortunately stayed by the energetic representations of our minister in Madrid, who was no other than General "Dan" Sickles, a fighter on his own account at Gettysburg who later became the one-legged First Nighter, and a very familiar figure to the theater-goers of New York in the Nineties. After this close squeak MacGahan in 1875 took part in the Arctic expedition of the *Pandora* under Captain Allen Young. Then fortunately for the Bulgarians his steps were turned to southeastern Europe. Hearing of the atrocities he, though his life was openly threatened by the Turkish authorities, rode to the scene of the mass murders and told in simple but forceful language the terrible story to an, at first, incredulous world.* MacGahan was denounced in unmeasured terms by the Turcophile press of London,

---

* As the Russians crossed the Danube and marched south to liberate Bulgaria MacGahan joined them. He was present at the battles in front of Plevna and saw the horrors of the Shipka Pass. With the conquering Russians he reached San Stefano and a few days before the treaty of peace was signed he died of typhus fever in that wretched village. In eight years what adventures! What experiences! What a loss to American journalism his untimely death! S.B.

with the mighty *Standard* leading the pack. He was reviled as a sensationalist or, at best, an ignorant young American who lent a willing ear to what the cynical Disraeli had called the "babble of the coffee houses."

I thought at the time of my visit to the scene of the atrocities that such callous indifference to the conscience of civilization and such a complete abandonment of all humane principles under the spur of a fancied political or financial advantage would be impossible in America, but ten years later I found that I was mistaken. In 1897, when "Butcher" Weyler had herded the non-combatant inhabitants of Cuba, in revolution, into the concentration camps where within four months three hundred thousand of them were doomed to death by starvation or disease, the *New York Evening Post* (which had long before fallen from the pinnacle in American journalism on which it had been placed by Whittier and Godwin) struck the same contemptible note. The planned extermination of a liberty-loving people at our very doors, its editors maintained, was none of our business and, besides, the true situation in the camps had been grossly exaggerated where it was not entirely false. It has always comforted me to think that the editors who were responsible for this attitude, and plumed themselves upon it, were both of foreign birth, and that their paper failed, as did the *London Standard,* in these disgraceful campaigns.

I read MacGahan's affecting narrative as we toiled up the steep goat track, more often than not dismounted, that led to Batak. I read the winged words which Gladstone addressed to the English Parliament and his clarion call to the slumbering churches as I followed in the path MacGahan had gone on his dangerous quest just thirteen years before. When he entered Batak the dogs were still gorging themselves with human flesh and the mountain village stank like a charnel-house. When I came the air was pure and sweet, the church where so many died was rebuilt, but before it stood a mound of skulls to remind the living of their martyred dead. Mac-Gahan speaks of a distraught woman who met him upon entering the ruined hamlet. Curiously enough, the same poor creature, or a sister in misfortune, greeted me upon my arrival and dogged our footsteps throughout my stay. Her cheeks were dry, she had no tears to shed, but always as she followed us she crooned a dirge which, with the help of Stoyanoff, I translated into the following doggerel:

> "I had shelter, now I have none,
> I had a man, now I'm alone,
> I had three sons, now I have none,
> I had five children, now I have one,
> She wears the Turkish veil,
> And serves the Pasha—his slave."

It was pleasant to learn that here in this, by us, forgotten hamlet the names of the men who had truthfully reported the story of their sufferings and tried to save other Christian villages from a similar fate were not forgotten. Even miles away from Batak scores came out to meet me and brought wreaths of wild flowers to the countrymen of their benefactors. One little girl took me by the hand and led me to the pyramid of skulls in her village. One of these, almost split in twain, she pointed out as the skull of her grandfather. When I forced upon her some of the flowers with which I was overburdened, she made of them a wreath and, placing it on the weather-beaten, fleshless skull, sank upon her knees in prayer. There can be little doubt that the people of Batak and of several of the adjacent villages were planning an uprising to take place in June or July of this year; and that, emboldened by the promises of help that were made by the leaders of the movement against Turkish domination, all of whom apparently remained at a safe distance in Bucharest, some hot heads among them fired upon minor Turkish officials and announced that for the last time they had paid taxes to the Turks. This was a sufficient pretext for the Sultan, Abdul Aziz (and not Abdul Hamid as generally stated), to let loose his Bashi-bazouks and to invite the mountain Pomaks to flesh their swords in the bodies of their Christian brethren.

When I entered the little church at Batak, thirteen years almost to a day after the massacre, it was but little changed from the day of MacGahan's visit five weeks after the atrocities had been committed. True, the mangled and disemboweled bodies that lay around when he came on the scene were gone, but on a great wooden platform in the middle of the church about a hundred skulls were arranged in pyramidal form. Some had been perforated by bullets, others slashed by *yataghans*. Each skull had preserved its identity, as it were. Those who accompanied us told us the name of this and that victim of Turkish fury and many placed flowers in the gaping clefts that revealed where the deadly wound had been inflicted.

An interesting character was the mayor of the village who, as soon as he heard of our arrival, insisted upon being our guide through the tragic scenes of which he was one of the few, the very few, survivors. He told me that he alone remained of the thirty-two souls that his family numbered at dawn on May 7, 1876. Shortly after sunrise the Agha and about a hundred of his men appeared on the outskirts of the village and demanded that the inhabitants give up their arms. This was an extraordinary request and filled the minds of the villagers with gloomy forebodings. While on several occasions during the long years of Turkish supremacy such a demand had been made, it was never enforced to the letter because the local Turkish officials recognized the necessity of having some rudimentary weapons for self-defense in a district that invited the lawless from many quarters. The Agha swore vengeance; but, for the time being, withdrew. This gave some of the villagers the opportunity to seek hiding places in the forests and to bury some of their most cherished possessions, sacred relics, church services, and family valuables in caves. But the great majority hastened to the church and to a rather substantial school house and prepared to defend their lives as best they could. Before noon the Agha was back, this time with five hundred well-armed men, and without further delay opened fire. As it was a shotgun battle against men with rifles, the result was a foregone conclusion. On the morning of the third day the villagers had lost half their number, and having nothing to eat or drink, they entered into a parley.

The mayor who took part in the negotiations claimed that the Agha swore the most solemn oaths, in both Christian and Moslem form, that if the besieged villagers would but give up their arms no harm should come to them. Once they were disarmed, however, the Pomaks demanded ransom money and to be led to the secret hiding-places of their treasures. A few of the villagers again seized what weapons they could lay hands on and, again taking refuge in the church, resumed the fight against fearful odds. Early in the second fight the mayor had been wounded and fell. Several dead men fell across him, and he could not extricate himself from the weight of their bodies. After some hours, with what ammunition they had exhausted, and also all hope of relief by the arrival of their own people or the coming of Turkish regulars from Philippopolis gone, the villagers entered into another parley with the murderous crew. Again they were promised their lives if they submitted, and again the Agha broke faith. As the survivors of the struggle, dazed and starving, came out of the darkened church they were cut down. The place was soon so cluttered up with corpses that at last the Agha ordered his men to lead their prisoners down to the little river and there on the bank they were beheaded. While a much higher figure is given in the Bulgarian accounts, I think it is conservative to say that on that fatal day five thousand men, women, and children perished in and around Batak. Toward sunset the Pomaks set fire to the church and, with the strength of despair, the man who was later to become mayor, and act as my guide, extricated himself from the corpses that had fallen across him and favored by darkness, crawling on hands and knees, made his way to a cave where several other villagers had taken refuge. There his wounds were dressed. Of the many thousands who died it was the boast of the Agha that he himself "executed" as he preferred to say, four hundred with his own sharp cutting knife.

There was at the time, at least, much uncertainty as to the relations between the Agha and the Turkish authorities of the day; and I cannot claim to have made clear where the responsibilities lie by my subsequent visit to the Pomak chieftain in his mountain fastness of Tomrush. One thing, however, is certain; for these mass murders Abdul Hamid who afterwards was given, and certainly deserved, the name of the "great Assassin" was not to blame. As a matter of fact, he did not ascend the throne until many months later and at the time they were planned, and ruthlessly executed, he was living under the restraint and in the dignified retirement from active affairs which during this period the rulers of Turkey generally imposed upon all kinsmen who were thought eligible to replace them in the case of a successful uprising.

It is not quite clear that even the Sultan of that day, Abdul Aziz, gave the orders for the destruction of the Christian villages, but he certainly rewarded those who carried them out. Chefket Pasha, who was in command of the Turkish forces in Roumelia, who presided over the burning of so many of the mountain hamlets and, without batting an eye, saw the slaughter of their inhabitants, while not present in person at the massacres in and around Batak, was a few weeks later given promotion and for the remainder of his days enjoyed high favor at the Imperial court.

Of course, the orders under which the Agha carried out his devilish work never saw the light of day and in all probability were never written. At the first signs of unrest, he was given command of the local Bashi-bazouks or irregulars in accordance with the custom of the War Office of placing responsibility for maintaining law and order upon the most powerful headman in the vicinity. Probably he was never told in so many words to murder ten thousand men, women, and children in Roumelia. What he did was doubtless his interpretation of the general orders that were given him to maintain the supremacy of the Crescent. Certainly later, when the Agha and his mountaineers saw red and advanced toward Philippopolis with the avowed purpose of burning the Roumelian capital and, of course, putting all its non-believing inhabitants to the sword, Chefket Pasha placed his regulars between the threatened town and the irregulars who were now running amok through the valley of the Maritza. On the other hand, it cannot be denied that the title of Pasha was given the Agha a few weeks after the massacres, and that he was rewarded for his fanatical loyalty with several high decorations. If anything could be amusing in regard to this dark episode, it would be the following incident. Faced by the remonstrance of the "Concert of Europe," which the Turkish government knew so well how to disconcert, the Sultan agreed to appoint a committee to investigate the outrages which had been committed, as he asserted, "by a few irregulars who had gotten out of hand," and the Agha was selected to head the committee! While the "Concert of Europe" was digesting this affront the Russians declared war and crossed the Danube.

And so began the Russo-Turkish War, the most righteous war of the century. It cost Russia a million men and the Concert of Europe remained passive until the bloody struggle was over. Then, incredible as it may seem, the Concert, under the leadership of England and Disraeli, intervened, robbed the victors of the fruits of their victory, and insisted upon millions of liberated Christians being restored to their former servitude under Turkish supremacy. Doubtless this just war would never have been undertaken but for the visit that was made to the scene of the massacres by MacGahan, the correspondent, and Eugene Schuyler, the secretary of the American Legation in Constantinople who accompanied him. Schuyler made his official report to Horace Maynard, our very able minister to Turkey at the time, and he, being more of a man than a diplomat, saw to it that the narrative was not put to sleep in archives. Together these two Americans followed the bloody trail of the Turks through the hills and the valleys of Roumelia and it was MacGahan's narrative, that he put on the wire in Bucharest on August 22, 1876, that inspired Mr. Gladstone's eloquent appeals to Christendom.

The truth about the massacres leaves Disraeli and Lord Salisbury in a very unenviable light before the bar of history, and it is only fair to say that their accredited representative in Turkey, the ambassador Elliot, was a very weak man, with, however, a keen appreciation of what his Foreign Office and his political leaders wished him to see and above all what to overlook. The massacres began on May 1st and continued for about ten days. No news reached Constantinople for a fortnight. The first fragmentary information came through official Turkish sources and this gave the Sublime Porte full opportunity to shape it, and full advantage was taken by the Turks to use Elliot as a cushion to minimize the terrible disclosures that could be delayed but not suppressed. From him came the reports that justified Disraeli in prating about the "gross exaggerations of the press," and the not over-subtle suggestion that the charges were largely Russian propaganda designed to justify the long-feared advance of the Tsar upon Constantinople. In any event, these reports satisfied Lord Salisbury with the result that, as he afterwards cynically admitted, he "put the English money on the wrong horse" and so thousands died who might have been saved and the well-deserved reputation of the English people as a bulwark of civilization in barbarous lands suffered an indelible stain.

I came back from my visit to Batak, and the other nearby scenes of racial and religious ferocity, determined that when there was a lull in what we correspondents called the higher politics of the Balkans I would visit the Agha in his mountain fastness and see how it had fared with the man who in that day was regarded as the outstanding mass murderer of modern times. Obviously my purpose was not easy of accomplishment, and the few to whom I dared broach the subject were most discouraging. And then as was so often the case I was called back to Belgrade where both Russian and Austrian intrigue had become more than usually rampant. The régime of the "tarnished generals" who composed the regency was tottering, and the ex-King Milan and the ex-Queen Nathalie were washing their dirty linen in public, apparently indifferent to the effect this would have upon the fortunes of their son, the little Alexander.

And so it was that three months elapsed before I was able to return to Roumelia and once again enter upon the negotiations which my darling project entailed. Fortunately I was now able to interest the elder Slaveikoff, the father of my friendly guide, in my plan. He tried to dissuade me but when his arguments failed he turned to and was of the greatest assistance. Slaveikoff was a poet of more than local renown; indeed he was often spoken of as the Victor Hugo of Bulgaria. I was not in a position to judge if his reputation was well-founded, but he was an interesting old gentleman with an immense amount of leisure and quite unconsciously, I think, he whetted my desire to visit the Pomaks who, after having provoked the Russo-Turkish War, had retired into the obscurity, and incidentally into the security, of their mountain villages. Slaveikoff regarded the followers of the Agha as scoundrels of the deepest dye, traitors to their race and their faith, but with all that he made them quite fascinating.

At the time when the Ottoman Turks spread over the peninsula these mountain people, like the great Bosnian *begs,* saved their property and doubtless their lives by changing their religion. As I was later to learn, the life-saving slogan of those turbulent days "where the sword is, there is also the Faith" was accepted and honored with the closest observance by almost all of them down to our day.

Of course the Bosnian *begs* or landowners despite their back-sliding, were squeezed a-plenty by the reigning pashas but the dwellers in the Rhodopian highlands were hard to get at and they were quite willing to pay for the more favorable treatment they received by services. The name Pomak with which they were baptized by the conquerors means, I understand, "helper or auxiliary soldier," and in payment of their devotion in many a foray into the Christian lands they acquired much booty and valuable privileges to which they clung tenaciously. Indeed under Sultan Mahomet the Fourth, a famous Nimrod who loved to hunt the bear in their wild country, they enjoyed rights and concessions which amounted to complete independence. They paid no taxes and lived under the rule of their own *beys* who were chosen from among the outstanding mountain men, and the Pasha of the Adrianople district always had the good sense to recognize this man as his *kaimakam* or prefect for the mountain region.

Gradually, according to Slaveikoff, the headship of the mountain clan remained with the members of one family. Hassan Agha, the hero of many legendary exploits, died with his boots on in 1860 and he was succeeded by his son, Akmet Agha, a man of great local fame and also of world-wide infamy and detestation of which, when I visited him some weeks later in his eyrie nest, I found he was entirely ignorant. Akmet had been quite successful in maintaining the independence of his people from the encroachments of both his Christian and his Moslem neighbors, and as a symbol of his sovereign rights he maintained an ambassador in Philippopolis. This extraordinary envoy was not lodged in a luxurious embassy and, as I later gathered, no funds for entertainment were at his disposal. Rain or shine, poorly garbed, he was to be found lounging on the front steps of the Ottoman Bank. Here the foreign affairs of the mountain satrapy were transacted before all men. Here as nowhere else in Europe at the time "open covenants" were "openly arrived at." Here men who would venture up in the highlands to buy skins or timber presented themselves for examination and scrutiny and here, when at last I decided upon the pilgrimage to the Great Assassin, I paid two pounds Turkish to have a traveling visa painted on my passport.

One afternoon while still in Philippopolis and only just getting on my legs again after another sharp attack of Vardar malaria, I fell in with a band of Pomaks who were coming into the Roumelian town, though at this time they were bent on trade and barter and not upon war. It was quite a caravan coming slowly down the rocky road that led into the city. Their horses, very diminutive creatures they were, but evidently sturdy, and the donkeys and oxen they convoyed were laden with timber and buckets of tar, and with skins they were planning to sell in the market. The men were tall and handsome, wore the *fez* or turban and, unlike the Bulgarians, most of them had beards. The fortune of war had gone against the mountain men but there was nothing obsequious in their bearing. They still took more than their fair share of the road and I noticed that the Bulgars only made slighting remarks about them when the Pomaks were out of hearing. These evidences of trade and commercial exchanges convinced me that the stories I had heard of the isolation of Pomak land had been exaggerated, to say the least. (I also learned that the Agha, whose lands had been handed back to the Sultan as a slight indemnity for his loss of the more fertile province of Eastern Roumelia by the Congress of Berlin, still tried to maintain the appearance of an independent sovereign although under the suzerainty of the Sultan.)

Then and there I determined to make the pilgrimage, and some days later I started on my journey. It might prove hazardous as Slaveikoff maintained, but on the other hand the mountain air would help me to get fit again. While sorely tempted, the younger Slaveikoff could not come with me, but he supplied a substitute and without this man the venture would have been a fiasco. He was a Spanish Jew, one of the thousands who had taken root in the Balkans after their expulsion by the Catholic kings and who, in my day at least, controlled all horse and mule transport throughout Roumelia.

While engaged in working out the time-taking arrangements for my visit to the Agha an incident occurred which would seem to indicate that I was not always such an alert newsgatherer as I have sought to make my readers believe. According to mythology even Jove nodded at times, and I can at least plead an extenuating circumstance. When caught napping I was in the throes of one of the attacks of the Vardar malaria which as a matter of fact continued to recur for several years.

One morning I was waited on in my inn by a strange, weird-looking man who, while he spoke English fluently, belonged to a race and a church that is most unpopular in Mohammedan countries. I shall not be more precise as to nationality and religion because while the Turks made strenuous efforts during the World War to exterminate these people quite a few scattered remnants still survive. My visitor told me that he and a group of his co-religionists were about to hold a meeting to discuss a very topical subject which was "The State of the World and What We Should Do to Improve it." He said he wanted me to be present, and as this was right up my alley I said I would be pleased to come. He seemed delighted and went away assuring me that shortly before the appointed hour he would call and lead me to the secret meeting-place.

The following day my visitor arrived and I had to receive him in my bedroom. I had had several chills and was dizzy from the quantity of quinine I had taken and I made it quite clear, indeed it was self-evident, that I could not attend the meeting.

"There is only one thing to be done," said my visitor. "We cannot go on without your advice and counsel so we shall assemble about midnight here in your bedroom. There are only five of us and as three of our number are staying in the caravansary adjoining your inn we can come in quite unobserved."

I acquiesced, and about midnight they were grouped about my bed. Two spoke excellent English and they started the proceedings. Their talk was discursive but I shall put the gist of the matter, as I digested it, rather briefly. For years they had been appealing to the conscience of the civilized world to put an end to the wrongs they suffered in the Turkish Empire. "But we have appealed in vain. Our prayers have gone unheeded. And now we have reached an important decision—we mean to take what was promised us at the Congress of Berlin."

I began to take notice. Ten eyes burning like coals were fixed upon me. In the darkness of the chamber, a darkness that was intensified by the faint flickering light of two candles, they were grouped about me like so many predatory animals of the jungle.

"We have decided—to strike," said the spokesman. "No longer will we be cajoled into silence while we are being killed off one by one."

My suggestions that they should petition the Pasha, send a protest to the Sultan, setting forth the details of their harsh treatment, and file copies with the embassies, were waved aside courteously but firmly.

"No—we are going to strike the Turk where he will feel it—in his pocket. We are going to destroy the great commercial city upon which he levies tribute and grows rich—"

I never was more wide awake than at this moment—as the plan came to me in sibilant whispers; I saw that fever or no fever I would have to think fast.

"We have decided to destroy the city of Salonica. We shall reduce it to ashes next week. The world will take notice, and even the Sublime Porte. The tobacco trade will be interrupted and the revenues will stop. As we know your paper supports the oppressed and the disinherited of the world we want you to come with us and see that we get fair play. In any event you can explain why we were driven to this step—"

I protested, as they could readily see, I was in no condition to go anywhere. But I insisted that I would not go with them even had I been in robust health. I explained what seemed to me the folly of their proposed action. To begin with, more than half the property and the wealth of Salonica was in the hands of the Spanish Jews, their companions in misfortune, their fellow-sufferers under Turkish oppression. They would be the greatest losers by such a conflagration as was proposed. Above all, while I admitted that the sympathy of the civilized world had not been very helpful, they would be poor indeed if they lost it and I concluded with the bromide of the day that political agitation should never depart from due processes of law.

The group listened patiently and the questions they put after my discourse was over were well considered and reasonable. When shortly before dawn they took their departure I thought that I had convinced them of the error of the plan and brought them back to a campaign within the limits of the law.

"You must keep within the bounds of legitimate political agitation," I insisted as they bowed themselves out and I sank back exhausted on my pillow.

I never saw my strange visitors again but a week later I heard from them and was compelled to revalue the effect of my oratory. Salonica was swept by a terrible conflagration, two thousand houses were reduced to ashes, tens of thousands became homeless although fortunately only a few of the bedridden and aged were roasted alive. It was found that combustibles had been placed in many quarters and the fire was undoubtedly of incendiary origin. Scores of suspects were arrested, not a few Armenians, Macedonians and Serbs. All representatives of the disaffected nationalities and minorities were lined up and shot while scores were sent to the convict stations in Tripoli where death came to them more slowly but no less surely. As it was quite clear to me that I had not handled this situation very intelligently, either as a newspaper correspondent or in any other capacity, I have never referred to it until the present writing. . . .

At last all difficulties had apparently been brushed away. Manuel Abeles had even paraded before me the horses with which the journey was to be attempted and I had approved of them. They were far from pleasing to the eye but they looked capable of making the mountain climb. Then suddenly, although I protested that he was paying me too much honor, the Ambassador of the Pomak King announced that he would accompany me on my mission. He would, he insisted, introduce me and vouch for me. I was getting along very well with Abeles and the archaic Spanish which his forbears had brought from Andalusia to the Balkans in the fifteenth century, and I feared, not without reason, that the injection of the Ambassador's Turco-Bulgarian would prove perplexing—and it certainly did.

I advanced a number of arguments, most convincing ones I thought, why the Ambassador should remain on the steps of the Ottoman Bank and there before all men attend to his important duties. But as Slaveikoff suspected from the very beginning, there was more to this move than at first met the eye. He learned that the Ambassador's appointments were in arrears and assumed that he wished to take this matter up with the King of the Rhodopians at the moment when the arrival of a representative of a rising power from across the great water would be pleasing to his vanity. The debate lasted for several days but in the end the stubborn diplomat prevailed and I thanked him for his courtesy when it became apparent that unless he accompanied us our permit to travel to Tomrushlu would be canceled. And then the Ambassador, man of infinite resource that he was, had another idea which Slaveikoff thought was inspired by a desire to strengthen his financial situation even before we left Philippopolis. As I ignored several hints, although they were quite broad, he finally came out with, "What presents do you propose bringing to my Lord?" I told him that this was not the custom in our world but I did toy with the idea, and thinking that I was a more promising prospect than I later proved to be the Ambassador led me to a shop where in a back room a very beautiful gold-hilted and bejeweled *yataghan* was produced. The Ambassador and the happy owner of this weapon seemed to be on the best of terms, and after an amusing parley the owner said that, while it could not be bought by lesser mortal for any price, in view of the fact that the Agha greatly desired to add it to his armory he would let me have it for the insignificant price of ten thousand *piasters!*

At this I hung back, I made it quite plain that such a present was not contemplated in my instructions from the American people. These would justify an exchange of compliments and good wishes but a present of such magnificence might, by the exercise of Oriental imagination, immediately put me in the category of tribute-bearers. And to this position I clung, even when the price asked for the gold-hilted *yataghan* was reduced fifty per cent . . .

At long last we got under way and, wrangling in many languages, we toiled for several hours across the fertile Maritza plain toward the purple mountains the view of which had always fascinated me. As we came out of the city we halted for a moment at the simple memorial of the victorious war of 1878 which cost Russia so many men. I asked the Ambassador what it commemorated and he said he had not the remotest idea. He was not strong on history, but straight Bulgar though he was, he held his own with Manuel Abeles the Sephardin Jew when it came to discussing the value of hides and timber in *kopecks* or any other coin.

Our horses proved to be much better than they looked, and in a few hours we reached the little town of Belovo which is half-Pomak and half-Bulgarian. Here and all along the road I had an excellent opportunity of seeing that generations of servitude and oppression are not to be wiped away in a day or a year by a victory however brilliant or thorough. The Christians hereabouts still bore the physical marks of slavery. They were just beginning to walk upright and hold themselves as free men. The doors of their hovels, as I had noted in other districts, were always turned away from the road and so low you would think that the dwellers therein would have to enter on hands and knees. When I asked an explanation of this Manuel said, "The Turkish *Effendi* makes free with other people's property—but he does not like to stoop."

We passed the night at a village famous for its medicinal springs, and the next morning started out through a great forest toward Tomrush, still the lair of Akmet Agha, the tiger of the Rhodopian hills. We passed through several villages of tiled roofed houses with limpid streams of water coursing down the streets. Everywhere elderly Turks were seated on well-worn carpets before their doors, sipping coffee and puffing at their long-stemmed pipes. Now and again we would meet a little caravan of Pomaks bringing timber down to the markets on the back of slow-moving oxen. Now and again we would see them shoeing their oxen with leather shoepads, a by no means easy job. All the oxen we fell in with seemed to have a decided preference for going barefoot.

A little before noon on the third day of our uphill journey we began to descend, and from now on our path was picketed by scouts who watched the intruders with unfriendly mien. They clutched at their guns and fingered their *yataghans* in a way that convinced me that but for the Ambassador the way would have been closed to us. Suddenly the valley narrowed and we were in Tomrush. I confess that the first view of the eagle's nest, the mountain eyrie of which I had heard so much, was disappointing. It was simply a wide place in a narrow trail. . . . And we certainly did not take the Lord of the Mountain by surprise; several runners had gone ahead announcing the strange visitor and when after a last steep and narrow ascent had been negotiated we came to the wide place in the road, there in front of a low stone-roofed house, by the side of a great ravine resounding with the rushing waters of a mountain stream, seated upon the stump of a tree, the Agha was awaiting us. Grouped behind him were four or five men with ancient muskets and belts bristling with *yataghans*.

They were smoking long cigarettes and looked quite nonchalant. And well they might, as I had ventured into the mountain lion's den quite unarmed—save for a swagger stick.

I had anticipated that the interview would not go off very smoothly. My brace of interpreters was not mutually helpful. Throughout the journey they had wrangled incessantly and their explanations often left me in great perplexity. It was natural that our conversation should limp a little, but I confess I was not prepared for the initial bombshell which put a quietus upon it for a minute or two. The Agha rose as I dismounted and drew near him, brought his right hand to his heart, then to his forehead in a gracious salute, and pointing to a vacant tree stump beside him resumed his seat.

Without awaiting any prompting from me, the Ambassador after a low bow opened up the conversation. It ran on for several minutes before I was taken into the inner circle. He was evidently explaining something and the Agha was receiving it with frank incredulity.

"Well! Well!" I exclaimed, in growing impatience.

"I have introduced you as the Envoy from America," at last the Ambassador explained. "Self-appointed," I insisted, and he nodded quick assent to my amendment. "But the Lord Agha says he has never heard of America. He says he has heard of Frankistan and has also received envoys from Nemski lands (the German countries)— but never has he heard of America."

When I recovered my aplomb, of course, I sailed right in and explained that America was many times as big as the little countries with which he seemed to be familiar, that its inhabitants were more numerous than the leaves on the forest trees and that it was reached by sailing across a great expanse of water that was several times as broad as the Maritza River was long. I got off what seemed to me a fairly impressive spread-eagle speech, but I am not at all sure it carried conviction. When I concluded the Agha said a few words and these were, according to the Ambassador, "It may be so, Allah is great and the world is big. Of course I do not know all the lands of black infidelity!"

This rather nettled the self-appointed envoy from the land the Agha was inclined to ignore, and so I went ahead without gloves, which I would not have presumed to do if perfectly cordial diplomatic relations had been established. I flattered myself that hereafter the Lord of the Mountain would have a pretty good idea of the great country that had swum so unceremoniously into his ken, and then I changed the subject. We were well past the middle of December and I noticed over the doorways of many of the houses little green trees and I asked if they advertised the wine that was sold within. This suggestion was denied with some heat and then came the explanation that filled me with amazement. The Mohammedan Pomaks were preparing to celebrate the Feast of the Nativity, in other words our Christmas!

"How can that be possible!" I exclaimed, "when you and your people . . . withdrew from our Church centuries ago."

"We honor all good men. We respect all strong men," came the answer.

I was quite reckless now so I said, "Tell me about the day when you entered the war under the Crescent and drew your sword upon your Bulgar brothers." With evident reluctance, the Ambassador passed this on.

"Brothers," repeated the Agha and then he spat out, "Dog-brothers."

"It happened in this way," he went on with perfect unconcern. "Our Sovereign Lord in Stamboul sent word that the dog-brothers of the plains and the valleys were waylaying his soldiers and he directed us to go down to their villages and quiet them."

"And you quieted them, ten thousand of them, men, women and children," I said bitterly. Now I knew I had burnt my bridges, but why should I dissemble when it was quite clear that the Lord of the Mountain would not enter into relations with a country he was confident did not exist?

"Yes, men, women and children," he answered softly. "The men were soldiers, the children were growing up, the women were the mothers of future soldiers. Yes, we killed them all. Where I was none escaped. Our Sovereign Lord was pleased. What happened would not have happened had not the One God approved."

I then, after a breathing spell, asked the Ambassador to draw the Agha out on the question as to which there has been so much dispute. Whether the people of Batak had been slaughtered after a promise had been given that their lives would be spared if they surrendered their arms; but here the good man refused. "These things happen in war—always," he affirmed. "There was and always is in battle much confusion. It is an unpleasant subject—let us not pursue it further. The Agha is a very old man—and doubtless he has forgotten much." And I agreed that this was the wisest course to follow.

Coffee, cakes, and long cigarettes were now brought by the heavily-armed serving men who had hovered about during our talk. It was soon apparent that the Agha was toothless but munching on his hard gums he seemed to enjoy the light refection. Then he and the Ambassador began to talk about the trade in timber and the barter of skins and tar, the realities of life for which, as with other countries in ages past, the Mission in Philoppopolis was maintained.

Soon I left them to their serious affairs and wandered about the village trying not to look crestfallen. But it was difficult, a strange role indeed was mine, that of ambassador from a country the receiving monarch had never heard of. Night fell, throwing a concealing mantle over my discomfiture, and suddenly it became bitterly cold. We were given comfortable, though by no means luxurious, quarters in an empty house. Nothing was said about supper, but fortunately some fragments of the provisions for the journey remained. I slept like a log on a skin-covered divan and at crack of dawn we, that is Abeles and myself, mounted our ponies and began the descent into the once blood-drenched valley. As we passed his house I caught my last glimpse of the man who enjoyed an unenviable fame in the land he had never heard of. He, too, lay on a skin-covered divan just outside his door. Two little boys with fly-swatters crouched beside him. On their hams the bodyguards formed a protective circle and apparently the Great Assassin was sleeping the sleep of the just. Nearby, crouching on his heels, like patience on an uneasy monument, the Ambassador awaited the awakening of the Lord of the Mountains. From his glum expression it was clear that the matter of his arrears in salary had not been satisfactorily arranged.

14. SERBIAN TRAGEDY—
MAGYAR DIVERTISSEMENT

IT MAY be helpful to the reader for me to explain at this point in my narrative that my Serbian experiences ran concurrently with the Bulgarian episodes which I have already described. Within a month after my first arrival in Sofia, and after making my bow to Prime Minister Stamboulöff in Sistova, I had steamed up the Danube through the Iron Gates of Orsova on an Austrian Lloyd vessel which carried excellent beer well-refrigerated, and landed in Belgrade, and this, with variations, was my procedure throughout the twenty exciting months that followed.

This river journey, although often repeated, never became monotonous. To get through the narrow Pass of Kasan we would often be compelled to transship to a smaller boat. The gorge through which we passed was immensely picturesque and only about a hundred and fifty yards broad, but the volume of water that rushed through it was nearly two hundred feet deep, and out of it rose a great rock (much feared of the pilots) around which swirls the famous whirlpool in which so many river craft have become involved with disastrous consequences. At Turnu Severin you could still see a few upstanding pillars of the great bridge the Roman Emperor built to carry on the war against the Dacians, and at Dubova we walked along the road which Trajan built with the avowed purpose of carrying the blessing of civilization to the outside barbarians. Only a goat track here and there indicates where the great military road ran, over which the legions and the cohorts marched in their invincible strength, but you can still see and, in part at least, decipher the arrogant memorial to the Roman conqueror inscribed

upon the granite wall of the great Pass. *"Imperator Caesar! Trajanus Augustus Germanicus! Pontifex Maximus! Pater Patriae."* *
He made this highway for all time. It was the vital artery of the
Empire upon which it was thought the sun would never set, but
today the bridge and the highway of conquest have disappeared
and the proud memorial is all but obliterated. On the deck of my
steamer the conquerors of the day, the Bulgars, the Serbs, and the
Macedonians, smiled with contempt at the ruins of the empire of
yesterday and, talking boastfully of their rising kingdoms and
principalities, ignored the handwriting on the wall of the Pass.

It may be recalled here that my only, but often repeated, instructions from the Commodore were, "Move about as you please,
but I shall expect you to be on hand when and wherever Hell
breaks loose." In these circumstances I could not remain long in
one place. A report of the *Agence Volcanique*, as we called it, would
send me hurtling from Bulgaria into Macedonia, or from Thrace
into Roumelia or Albania, and while my haphazard method of recounting these experiences may not result in a clear picture, when
in my notes I have followed the chronological sequence the result
has seemed to me something very like "confusion worse confounded."

I hope to disarm my critics by frankly admitting that what I
place before them is not history, but a staccato medley of news
alarms and breathless rumor chases, and that there are gaps in my
story. On the first day of my sojourn in the Serbian capital I heard
the Finance Minister of the day present his annual budget to the
deputies of the Skupshtina, or national assembly, in sonorous blank
verse. May I add that when, during a lull in the debates of the
Peace Conference in Paris, thirty years later, I sought to rescue this
poetical financier's name from oblivion by interrogating Prime
Minister Pashitch, that venerable statesman shrugged his shoulders and said, "In those Arcadian days it was our custom to break
out into verse on all occasions." And then with a gesture of contempt

---

* The inscription has recently been restored by the Serbian government, but
the text is still a subject of hot discussion between learned Latinists and archeologists. S.B.

he added, "Today the budget is presented by accountants and, of course, no Serbian can follow the stupid rows of ciphers."

The misery and squalor that prevailed at this time in the Serbian capital, so closely associated in the minds of Westerlings, at least, with Prince Eugene, the "noble knight," is indelibly impressed upon the tablets of my memory. While I was on quite intimate terms with all the members of the discordant royal family, I stopped at a tavern which was widely and most unfavorably known as the Inn of the Red Dog although I am not quite sure whether this was its official name or merely the sobriquet bestowed upon it by indignant guests.

At this time we had no permanent diplomatic representative in Serbia. There was, it is true, a peripatetic minister extraordinary from the United States accredited to Belgrade, Cettinje, and to Athens. The post was a party plum and the occupant, when not at home looking after his political "fences," wisely sojourned in Athens. The archives of the legation were in the keeping of an amusing Scot of the name of McClure. He also took his meals at the Red Dog Tavern and on more than one occasion he waxed indignant at my attitude toward the food that was served there. "With you it is only a matter of weeks or a couple of months," he explained, "but with me it looks like a life sentence." I asked for an explanation and it was promptly forthcoming. "No correspondent survives long in Belgrade. Sooner or later, and generally sooner, he is escorted across the river to Zemlin by the political police. There on Hungarian territory they live in a very comfortable hotel and their telegrams, as long as they are unfriendly to Serbia, are forwarded with the utmost dispatch. But they don't like it. They feel that they are lacking in prestige and then the news that dribbles across the river is fragmentary and unreliable. They find it difficult to interpret what is going on in a country from which they have been exiled."

When I asked McClure if his place were not also subject to the dangers that beset all political positions in the foreign service of that day, he assured me it was not. "You see, I'm a commercial vice-consul. I retain half the fees that are paid for invoices, but as there is no trade I never receive any. If I did—" Here McClure lapsed into eloquent silence, but it was quite clear that the moment he had the funds he would leave Belgrade.

The only thing that remains of the Belgrade I came to know so well in these years is its picturesque situation on the banks of the Save with the broad but never blue Danube flowing on in the near distance. The details of the picture have changed completely. In the Great War the city was bombarded and reduced to smoking ruins. When I came there after the Armistice of 1918 I lost my way in the still smouldering débris. This panorama of desolation by which I was bewildered was the handiwork of the Austrian monitors that came down the river and fired the first big guns that heralded the holocaust of disaster.

While the Turkish garrison had been withdrawn in 1867, or twenty years before I came this way, they left behind them many traces of their prolonged and heavy-handed domination. The streets were narrow and crooked and dusty or muddy, according to the season. The royal descendants of the swineherd Obrenovich housed higgledy-piggledy in the ancient *konak*, the new palace not having risen above ground in all its incredible ugliness. The Terasia, then as now the main street, was a popular pig-wallow, but through quagmires and filth it led into the street of Prince Michael the Liberator. From here you could climb up to the medieval fort that was for so long in the epic days the objective of Prince Eugene's artillery. From its dismantled battlements and crumbling walls there was unfolded a wonderful panorama which embraced a dozen battlefields where so often throughout the ages Christian and Moslem hosts had been locked in deadly struggle.

What the Turks had not been able to destroy on their enforced departure, though they tried to, was the deep cistern fed by springs within the walls of the fort which was, I dare say, its most valuable defensive arm during many a prolonged siege. You descended to it by four hundred steep stone steps worn away by the tread of the callous feet of many generations of thirsty, hard-pressed soldiery. Beyond the fort extended a rambling country road which later was given the name of Nathalie Boulevard in remembrance of the unhappy queen of my day. It led to Topchider or the vale of the Cannoneer. In its midst rose a simple country house where the boy king Alexander entertained his friends with sweets and delicious coffee during the hot weather. This royal retreat was surrounded by a forest of magnificent trees and an extensive deer park. Here after refreshments, in the cool of the evening, we often strolled about and frequently passed the spot where, as the memorial stone indicates, Prince Michael, the great-uncle of our host, was set upon and murdered. We little thought then that assassination had not been abandoned by the Serbs as a political weapon and that the little boy, who led us through the labyrinth of shrubbery, was destined, together with his wife, to die a violent death; or yet that the son of his successor, King Peter, another Alexander but of the Black George line, should come to his death at the hands apparently of one of his own people, although on foreign soil.

King Milan was in Vienna upon my arrival in Belgrade, but Queen Nathalie was present and living in a small private house not far from the ancient *konak*. With her was a charming lady-in-waiting, a bright vivacious creature who unhappily some years later was displaced by Draga Mashin, who brought about the downfall of the Obrenovich dynasty. My first contacts with Serbian royalty were with and through them, but I can say that what developed into an intimacy was in a manner forced upon me.

The leading Regent at this time, and for the period of the boy king's minority, was Jovan Ristich, an ancient war horse of Serbian politics. Serving with him as co-Regents were two military men, Protich and Belomarcovich, who were known throughout the Balkans as the "tarnished generals." I believe this unsavory appellation was bestowed because of their failure to distinguish themselves at the battle between the Serbs and the Bulgarians at Slivnitza four years before. But as I do not know whether these charges were well-founded or false, I should say that I use the uncomplimentary adjective that was always hitched on to their names merely for the purpose of identification.

I was pleased and I must confess somewhat surprised when upon my first call Ristich greeted me warmly, almost with enthusiasm;

indeed, when the bemedaled Belomarcovich was called into the conference, I was introduced to him as "a messenger from heaven." The explanation of this unusual welcome was not long delayed. It soon developed that two weeks before there had reached Belgrade an interview with Queen Nathalie written by a famous American newspaper correspondent who spent most of his time in London. In the course of the interview very unpleasant things were said about the Regents, and the situation in Serbia was depicted in most unflattering terms. Some of these strictures were said to be the very words of the Queen, others were admittedly the conclusions the writer reached after what, he claimed, was a careful survey of the Serbian situation. The Regents had ascertained that the writer in question had not been nearer to Belgrade than Munich, and I was informed that the Queen had never seen him and that she denounced the article as a fabrication. I had no particular interest in the matter; the correspondent, I knew, was a man of high standing, it seemed incredible that he should have perpetrated such a barefaced fake and, after all, it was water gone over the dam and did not concern me.

But, of course, it interested the Regents immensely and on the following day I was escorted to see the dark-eyed heroine of the interview whose status at the time was uncertain, for by all reports the church divorce that King Milan had secured from her through a corrupt bishop was wholly illegal. She was most gracious and we ate sweetmeats and drank tea for some time before I was able to fasten her attention on what was really the purpose of my visit and, indeed, its sole excuse.

"The Regents wish me to issue a denial of all this talk," she said, "and I can well understand their point of view." Here the dark-eyed woman laughed in a way that seemed to indicate that she had enjoyed the strictures on the great men of the moment—hugely. "And they have proved through the investigations of our consular officers that this newspaper Monsieur never came to Serbia, and I have not been away for years. This was very unchivalrous of him but, on the other hand, this newspaper Monsieur has penetrated into the inmost recesses of my soul; he has laid bare my secret thoughts and put them into words as I have never dared to do.

What a wonderful man he is! What a menace to society! Are all American journalists as able as this?"

I answered that while opinion was divided on this point, in my judgment they generally required some assistance from the person involved in reading secret thoughts, whereupon the Queen blushed and the lady-in-waiting had what she called a fit of coughing and had to leave the room for several minutes.

"No, I'm afraid to take any steps in this matter," said the Queen in conclusion. "Of course, as the Regents have proved, the interview never took place, but on the other hand here is a man who, while at a great distance, can read my thoughts. Why, he might, if I made him angry, fill another page of his paper with—well, things that the Regents would like even less than what has already been published." I told the Queen that I thought she was wise and, in parting, she gave me a very friendly shake of the hand. I was led back to the Regents and they were disgusted with me when I told them that, while the interview evidently had not taken place, the Queen had decided not to dignify the article with a formal denial. The fact that I had refused to play their game rankled, and two years later, when my position in Belgrade was shaken by an incident I shall in due season relate, the displeasure of the Regents weighed heavily against me.

I was convinced that in some clandestine way the Queen had furnished the correspondent in question with the information which, with or without authority, he had put in the form of an interview, and the Regents, though they tried cajolery and even veiled menace, were never able to induce me to enter into the controversy which was distinctly not my affair. And the Queen was grateful, and also the bright, vivacious lady-in-waiting.

In a few days, however, Milan appeared once more on the scene and became, as was apparent, an unwelcome guest at the Palace; but, as the jovial ex-monarch asserted when I waited on him, as in duty bound, "No man can allow his father to lack for food and shelter, be he prince or commoner." And if the boulevard sheets were to be believed at this time, his Paris creditors were constantly harassing the ex-King. It is, perhaps, advisable at this point to describe, as briefly as possible, the circumstances under which only six months before King Milan had joined the circle of kings in exile who were sojourning in the gay city on the banks of the Seine.

In January 1889, Milan, after having ruled the country most capriciously for a number of years, suddenly promulgated a liberal constitution and three months later, to the amazement of all, abdicated in favor of his son and, although the boy was only twelve years of age, had him proclaimed King. A Regency of three was constituted to rule the country until the boy came of age. At this late day it would be difficult for me to describe correctly the political situation by which, at the time, the country and I, as a political observer, were confronted. The *Skupshtina*, or national assembly, had a majority of Radicals, the Ministry claimed to be Liberal, and the Regents, whatever else they may have been, were certainly conservative in politics. In these circumstances the ordinary processes of administration were impeded and, as the political anarchy continued and increased, four years later the mechanics of government broke down. At this juncture young Alexander acted energetically. He dismissed the Regents, proclaimed himself King, although he was only seventeen, and then invited his father to return from exile and advise him out of his knowledge of men and affairs how to steer the ship of state away from the lee shores of bankruptcy and anarchy toward which it was drifting rapidly. The return of Milan to Belgrade, at least, proved a mistake. He had been formally exiled by the Regents for good and sufficient reasons, but I must not anticipate. In 1889, when I saw him for the first time, he was the guest of the nation and he had returned to his native land simply to explain that the prestige of their country, dear to all Serbians, would suffer if he were compelled to make both ends meet on the meager allowance which had been assigned to him on his departure.

In this the first of many talks which I had with the ex-King he dwelt at about equal length upon his financial and his matrimonial misfortunes. He asserted money was no object to him. He would gladly live upon a crust if by so doing he could enhance the prestige of his beloved country. But, unfortunately, the contrary was the case. The more he economized the more his people lost standing.

If they could not keep one former king in dignified affluence no one would believe that the Serbs were the coming people in the Balkans. Did I not see that? Here I, wisely I think, dodged the expression of an opinion upon a subject on which I, as a transatlantic democrat, had but little information.

Then the King, who spoke French rather badly (at least at this time) but with an amazing fluency, took up the subject of his marriage which he asserted had wrecked his career. His union with Nathalie had been a love match and it had turned out badly. He admitted he had turned a deaf ear to the counsels of his advisers who pointed out how advantageous it would have been for the dynasty and for him to marry into one of the royal or even into one of the old ducal families who would have welcomed such an alliance. "That is what I should have done," protested the repentant Lothario on more than one occasion. "I should have made an alliance that would have insured me and my family support in either Russia or Austria. But I was ensnared by those flashing black eyes, those billowy masses of jet black hair, and I married the Roumanian gentlewoman, or so she seemed."

This romantic comedian made no secret of the fact that the marriage was a failure from the very beginning, or that after the birth of the unfortunate pledge of the union the tie that bound the pair became merely nominal. Milan complained to all and sundry, and even to me, a wanderer from a strange land, in a way that was unusual in those reticent days, of the frigidity of his wife with the burning black eyes. He insisted that this revelation should be published (I never complied with his request), because this unhappy condition was in his judgment ample excuse for the constant, or inconstant, philanderings which lured him so often, and with such unpleasant results, far from home and fireside, first in Belgrade and, later, in Paris and Vienna.

Much that Milan said was doubtless true, and it is equally certain that the first announcement of the King's marriage to Mlle. Nathalie Kechko was a surprise and a rather unpleasant one to his people. Several Russian princesses had been thought of in connection with a suitable alliance that should not long be postponed, and indeed preliminary steps had already been taken, but Milan's

mother, Princess Helene Obrenovich, had selected the bride, Nathalie Kechko. It was she who brought about their meeting in Vienna,
which was represented as accidental, and, as he always admitted,
the King at first was delighted with his mother's choice. The Queen
must have been a very beautiful girl at this time when barely seventeen, and she was still a very handsome woman with wonderful
eyes and charming features when I met her fifteen years later.

As to who the Kechkos were many stories circulated. There was
a story that Nathalie's mother was a princess from the Caucasus,
and certainly the Queen looked like a Georgian. Only one thing is
certain—her father came from the lesser Moldavian nobility and
had served for many years in the Russian army as Colonel of a
crack cavalry regiment. The wedding day opened auspiciously and
the people of Belgrade were charmed as they saw the happy young
people driving to the cathedral where on a beautiful October morning the marriage was solemnized. By procuration the Great White
Tsar gave the bride away, and this added immensely to the éclat
of the brilliant ceremony. Then suddenly the omens became adverse. The horses of the wedding equipage balked for minutes as
they were driven away from the cathedral and a violent storm, at
the same time, burst suddenly over the so recently sunlit city, and
these things were regarded as of evil augury.

While all people are superstitious, none are more so than the
Serbians, and it was soon recognized that the young royal couple
had gotten off to a very bad start. The Serbians believe that a man's
fate is decided at his birth and that there is no way of escaping an
unfavorable destiny. The sequence of stark tragedy which followed,
which I shall briefly relate, had been foreseen by the famous seer of
the mountains, old Matche Krema, and his words of ill omen had
gone through the kingdom and were on many lips. The unfortunate thing about them was that, in the past, his predictions had
come true on many occasions. It was a pity that so bright a future
should be darkened by the presage of disaster, but—the swineherds
could only be sorry and shrug their shoulders; in the future, as in
the past, the powers of darkness would prevail. It was *kismet*.

As a matter of fact old Krema, the mountain bard, would have
ranked high as a seer even among a more prosaic people. Years be-

fore the murder took place, he had foretold in moving verse the assassination of Prince Michael that occurred in 1868. Long before the nuptials were celebrated, he had revealed that the marriage of Milan and Nathalie would prove unhappy, that only one child would be born to them and that he would be always beset by misfortune. He had forecast that Milan would live much abroad and die in a foreign land; that his son would marry a woman of the people and that with him the dynasty would perish. Even farther into the future penetrated his farseeing eyes. "A son of Black George will ascend the throne, a foreign army will invade and devastate our country. There will be starvation and suffering and the dead will outnumber the living, but after the years of sorrow by the aid of the blessed Virgin and of St. Michael, and all the angels, a Champion of God's people will appear; our enemies will be destroyed, and once again peace and happiness will descend from heaven upon all the Serbian lands."

These words of ill omen were given wide credence in the kingdom long before my arrival in Belgrade on my first visit. I would not venture to say that they sealed the fate of the Obrenovich family, but undoubtedly they exerted considerable influence in shaping the disastrous course of events. As the many dangers threatening the Obrenovich line became more apparent, even their loyal adherents confessed that they were powerless to combat fate while, on the other hand, its enemies were doubly armed by these words. Certain it is that in these circumstances the Black George conspiracy was hatched and many of the conspirators afterwards admitted they would not have had the courage to carry out their murderous plans but for the belief they had that the powers of darkness were on their side.

In this connection the vivacious lady-in-waiting, who was in attendance on Queen Nathalie when I first waited on her, in later years told me of an incident which would indicate that superstitious fears were not confined to the humble homes of the peasants. "For years the Queen would laugh to scorn the words of the Mountain Seer until one day in Paris," said the little lady, "she visited Mme. Thèbes, who was well-known then as the favorite *clairvoyante* of all the royal houses of Europe. She went incognito and quite alone and what was said to her she never told me. But from that day she was a changed woman, a very sad one, and the prey of many fears. Whenever anyone in her presence spoke of prophecy or mentioned the future she would always cross herself in the Russian fashion and become very pensive."

Rambles in the royal park were pleasant diversions to our humdrum existence in the close and humid atmosphere of the city. The little King often guided our steps. I say "we" advisedly, because we were generally accompanied, not only by one or more of the King's tutors, but by Douglas Dawson, a captain in one of the English Guard regiments, who at the time was serving as military attaché to the British legations in the Balkan States. Dawson * was as handsome as one of Ouida's guardsmen and in addition he was endowed with brains and with charm; the little King at whose birth so many fairies had been absent simply adored him and loved to walk hand in hand with him.

One day it chanced that we chatted about our swimming expeditions and our races in the great river below in which, among others, Pallavicini, who later during the Great War was saddled with the difficult role of Austro-Hungarian Ambassador to Turkey, took part. The little boy admitted that he had never been taught to swim and looked quite wistful when I told him that all boys in America had access to a swimming hole and that most of them could swim like fish. Dawson was indignant and announced that this flaw in his education should be remedied immediately. Under the shade of the great trees he found a dark forest pool, and while the tutor in attendance trembled nervously, we were soon stripped and Alexander was splashing about—not a little nervous, too. The tutor bleated out that the Regents should be informed, that perhaps they would not approve of the venture, but Dawson insisted the boy must learn to swim before he mounted the throne and that even the Regents must know that a king who could not swim would be under a heavy handicap.

Stripped, Dawson was the perfect figure of an Olympian athlete and his magnificent physique emphasized the strange and far from comely figure which naked and shivering little Alexander cut be-

* Later Controller of the Household of King George the Fifth.

fore our eyes. His head was much too heavy and he was terribly knock-kneed. His shoulders and arms were those of a man trained to carry heavy burdens, while his hips were weak and his shanks spindling and, indeed, none of his limbs matched up. It would seem that he had heired the physical discord that prevailed between his mismated parents. But he had a fine spirit and a stout courage and in a couple of weeks he could paddle across the pool dog-fashion. Dawson would start him from one bank with a vigorous shove and I would advance to meet him from the other side and hold him up when he sank. When he had accomplished the crossing, a distance of about thirty feet, the little chap was the happiest boy in the Balkans. "Now you need not tell the Regents that I'm being given swimming lessons by these gentlemen, my friends. You can tell them that I know how to swim." And so it was revealed, as I had long suspected, that the harassed tutor had not dared to mention to the Regents that the secret lessons were in progress.

In later years Dawson and I often plumed ourselves upon this exploit, but now that the chapter of his life is closed it may appear that in teaching the little King how to breast the waves (a manner of speaking!) we did him a disservice. Some years later when Queen Nathalie had definitely abandoned Belgrade and was living in Biarritz on the Gulf of Gascony, Alexander went to visit her as in duty bound, and here on the golden strand he loved to disport himself and face the surf as it dashed in upon the beach. In his water sports one of the ladies-in-waiting, according to court gossip, became interested and, finally, Alexander in his turn offered to teach her to swim. They became greatly attached to each other and despite the weighty reasons against the union, and apparently they were many and valid, Alexander married Draga Mashin.

No children were born to the union which was so unwise politically, as in other ways, and finally the enemies of the régime, and they had become quite numerous, as well as the adherents of the Black George family, started the rumor that recognizing that his wife would not or could not present the kingdom with an heir, the King was about to designate the younger brother of Draga as crown prince. There was probably no more in this story than in another also current at the time that in a very few days, when the Queen

had gone to Franzensbad where she had been ordered to take the
cure, the King proposed instituting divorce proceedings.

I was in Belgrade a few months after the tragic murder of this
luckless pair, in which also so many of their adherents lost their
lives, and while many tried to make me believe in the first story,
including the principal regicide, Colonel Mashin, who strangely
enough was the brother-in-law of Draga, I have always been convinced that it was a political fabrication of the adherents of Peter,
the king to come. And it was successful, for with Alexander died
the last legitimate scion of the Obrenovich family. And so ended
the feud between the Montague and the Capulets of the Balkans.

As they at this time exercised great influence on Serbian policy
and a little later destroyed the Obrenovich dynasty root and branch
it is necessary here to make a brief excursion, as brief as possible,
into the unpleasant realm of court scandals. And while I should
add that the events I am about to chronicle occurred some months
before my arrival in Belgrade, they are fully authenticated.

The most charming place in the environs of the Serbian capital,
especially in summer, is the Topchider Park. But to this pleasure
ground King Milan would never take his wife, explaining to her
that it was a place of evil omen to his family and that he could not
bear to see the spot where at least one of his predecessors had been
so foully murdered. For a long time the Queen did not question
the truthfulness of her husband's statements in this regard, but a
year or so later, doubtless primed by information from other
sources (the "affair" was an open secret to everyone in Belgrade),
the Queen penetrated one afternoon into the vale of Topchider and
there found the King walking arm in arm with Madame Christich,
the daughter of a Levantine lumber merchant of Constantinople
and the wife of a Serbian diplomat who was always somewhere else.
Madame Christich was at least ten years older than her admirer and
she was exceedingly ugly in a country where ugly women are rare.
But with all these handicaps she exercised a wonderful and certainly a most baleful influence over the King. Hers was not an easy
yoke either. And many who knew the King's dictatorial ways and
his love of creature comforts often wondered at the absolute control
which this exacting woman exerted over him. One of her favorite

forms of amusement was to summon Milan from the palace and order him to bring her to her house with his own hand, say, a bouquet of five hundred flowers. The King would be followed by a mob of curious idlers and not seldom he would be dismissed at the door of Madame Christich by a lackey, while those who lingered would see the flowers thrown out the window a moment later or deposited in a receptacle for garbage.

However, the King and Queen kept upon some sort of terms in public, at least until the high mass was celebrated in the Belgrade Cathedral on Easter morning in 1888. The Cathedral was crowded by the Court and by all the notables of the country, and after the ceremony they one and all filed past the King and Queen seated on their raised dais. It had been the immemorial custom for the ladies and gentlemen of the Court to say, as they passed before their sovereigns, "Christ is risen," and with the reply, "Of a truth Christ is risen," the King and Queen would kiss the cheek of each and every one of them, repeating the ceremony down to the end of the line. On this occasion Madame Christich had the audacity to place herself in the line but the Queen pretended not to see her and made no reply to her statement as to the Resurrection. King Milan was beside himself with rage. It is said he drew his sword, brandished it above his wife's head and shouted: "I order you to kiss her." When the Queen remained obdurate he attempted to strangle her, but the Court officers intervened and the ceremony ended in indescribable confusion.

While the sympathies of all Belgrade were with the Queen, Madame Christich left the Cathedral leaning on the King's arm and he tried to carry the affair off with a high hand. On the following day he announced to his amazed ministers that he proposed divorcing the Queen, and indeed an attempt to do so was made. Madame Christich was exceedingly extravagant and so was the King. They were always in money difficulties and soon Milan lost what little popularity he had hitherto enjoyed. It is to these days that one of his most despicable exploits dates. In a tight place financially he acquainted the Tsar of Russia with his embarrassment by telegram and, asking for a loan, offered certain estates of his as security. The Tsar helped him out of the unpleasant situation and a mortgage on the estates was duly executed in the Russian legation. But a few weeks later the Russian Minister M. Hitrovo found that the estates were already mortgaged up to their full value!

At this time politics in Serbia were at the very lowest ebb. This was not entirely due to King Milan, but he was certainly the largest contributing factor to a most unhappy state of affairs. There was corruption in the Court and there was corruption in the government everywhere. It was about this time that a tourist visiting the Skupshtina, or national assembly, was amazed to find all its members sitting upon one side of the house.

"Is there no opposition here?" he inquired.

"Oh yes," was the reply. "There are some opposition members but they find it safer to sit in the midst of the Ministerialists."

But there were many who had little confidence in parliamentary immunity, and of these quite a number were eating the bitter bread of exile. Among these was my wise friend M. Pashitch, who in happier days returned to Belgrade to serve as Prime Minister and to represent the heroic people of Serbia at the Versailles Peace Conference in 1919.

I had first and last many amusing experiences with King Milan, one of which at least it may be of interest to recall. He was a gambler and a spendthrift, and his word carried but little weight, either at home or abroad, but he had a rare and dangerous gift of eloquence that often, as in the instance I shall relate, stood him in good stead. At this time he had not been formally exiled, but certainly his repeated absences from Serbia were encouraged by the Regents and by all others in authority. He had gone abroad on what the government thought was a liberal allowance, but evidently the King thought differently. His overdrafts came pouring into the treasury from almost every reputable banker and also from every disreputable money-lender in western Europe, and at last they were formally dishonored by the government.

At this juncture Milan returned from Paris to lay his case before his friends and enemies alike, and I went to Nish where a party convention was being held. One of the announced purposes of this meeting was to denounce Milan for his reprehensible conduct and to support the government in its determination to dishonor the overdrafts. The convention was held in the garden of the one hotel of which this ancient city boasted, a hotel which for many reasons all travelers from the West who have entered its gates will long remember. I attended the session in the afternoon and was assured that if Milan appeared at the banquet that was to follow he would have a most unpleasant reception. It was even announced that plates would be thrown at the unwelcome guest, and that if he did not withdraw he would be forcibly removed.

Imagine my surprise, therefore, when as I watched the scene from my room window, I saw the King, quietly attired in civilian clothes, walk through the garden and take a vacant place at one of the tables for the humblest guests. Nobody threw a plate, nobody paid the least attention to the interloper, and the King sat pat and ate his swine flesh and drank his plum brandy in silence just like the other guests. But when the time for speech-making came he rose, and after overcoming some heckling he delivered an oration which demonstrated that, after all, speech is sometimes golden. He said that as for himself poverty had no horrors; he was willing to walk barefooted around the world and to wear threadbare clothes; but, he said, it was the nation and the prestige of his people which was lowered by such a situation. He then drew illustration after illustration of the unkingly plight to which he was reduced, how the other kings in exile looked down with contempt upon the head of the Obrenovich family; with the result that in about half an hour he had reduced many of his simple sheepskin-clad hearers to tears, and coaxed money out of their pockets. As he was escorted by a committee back to the hotel, he was assured that his drafts would be met and he was again hailed as "our stalwart alone-standing fighter, the conqueror of the Turks." Milan's words, unlike his paper promises to pay, were worth their weight in gold.

Perhaps the most inexplicable trait of the ex-King was his belief that he was lucky in war and that had his people but followed his leadership the "Great Serbian Idea" would long since have been realized. "Had they but followed their king who was lucky in war, today my son's kingdom would have embraced not only Bosnia and Herzegovina and Montenegro but also northern Macedonia and the Turkish sandjaks where, as you know, our musical language is spoken," he frequently asserted.

When I became more familiar with the details of recent Balkan wars I saw that the King's belief that he was fortunate in war was not without foundation. While he had been invariably defeated he had always been saved from the disastrous consequences of his foolhardy leadership. When the uprising took place in Bosnia (1877) he had thrown his ill-armed little host upon the Turks— and was only saved from destruction by the intervention of Russia. Again when he went off half-cocked in 1885 and threw his untrained men against the splendid little Bulgarian army which the Russians had trained to a high degree of efficiency, he was disastrously defeated at Slivnitza, and as the Bulgarians crossed the frontier and nothing stood between them and the Serbian capital but disorganized fugitives, they were stopped and Milan was saved by the appearance of the Austrian Minister who announced that if the Bulgarians advanced another step they would be met by Austrian troops. Nevertheless (or perhaps on this account) Milan was always planning new wars and dreaming of new Balkan lands to conquer!

I would not relate even in an expurgated form the terrible fate that overtook my little friend of the Topchider swimming pool, were it not for the sequel that I think important and which I believe leaves it without a parallel in the long roll of Court murders. It also reveals, as nothing else could, the anarchic conditions prevailing at the time in Serbia. I was in western Europe when the tragedy took place and did not return to Belgrade until some months later (March 1904). Pashitch was in control although he chose not to become Prime Minister immediately. King Peter was installed in the Palace and the old Turkish *konak* was still reeking with blood and sinister crime.

The Serbian capital was at last awakening to the fact, the very disagreeable fact, that it had been placed under a rigid boycott by the civilized powers, a movement which, be it said to his credit, had been inaugurated by King Edward of England. As I recall, at the time, the diplomatic corps in Belgrade was reduced to the agent of King Nicholas of Montenegro, whose daughter had married Peter and so became the mother of King Alexander (later to be assassinated in France) and a strange enigmatic creature who claimed to represent Prince Dadian of Mingrelia, a constant aspirant for any old Balkan throne.

The National Assembly had by unanimous resolution thanked the regicides, although it is only fair to say that many of its members acted from fear and under duress rather than from conviction. But among the people a more creditable attitude was becoming apparent. They had at last been impressed by the almost unanimous decision of the civilized powers to sever diplomatic relations. They had begun to look askance at the regicides and their puppet the unfortunate Peter who now sat on the blood-stained throne. Pashitch now in power, subject however to the dictates of the regicides, asked me to call upon Peter, but I declined and only listened, perfunctorily I fear, as he pictured the benefits that would accrue to the Serbian people as the first result of the new economic era that was about to dawn.

After months of terrified silence those who knew what had happened began to talk rather hysterically. They were generally of the opinion that while Peter had been conspiring all his life against the Obrenovich dynasty he had not advised the barbarous methods by which its overthrow, and indeed its extinction (for there were left no members of the family in the legitimate line), had been accomplished. In these circumstances it was doubtless wise to carry on as best one could with the Black Georges, and this with ability and persistence Pashitch set out to do.

Whenever I called, Pashitch rambled along for hours. To me, at least, it was not a surprise when fifteen years later in Paris he was unanimously recognized as easily the champion of all the long-winded ramblers who came to the Peace Conference. At times he placed responsibility for the tragedy that had in the eyes of the world disgraced his people, upon the Russians, and then only a few minutes later he would put the Austrians in the pillory. Of course, he absolved his party, composed of the Radical groups, of all guilt, and then again he begged me to call at the Palace and have a talk with "gentle" King Peter. This request I again declined, feeling that a correspondent, though he must be more catholic in his associations than most men, was entitled to draw the line somewhere.

Among the officers with whom I renewed acquaintance was one I would like to name were it not for the pledge of absolute secrecy which I gave at the time. In the Great War he died a gallant death, and if he was, as many thought, a leader of the regicides, at least in some measure his soul was purged of his guilt by a noble end. Of course, I should say that I had declined to meet any of the notorious regicides, the murderers of my poor little friend of the Topchider swimming pool, who were now in the saddle and riding King Peter with a cruel bit. But this man was different, and I came to spend many evenings with him. He admitted that he had gone to the Palace with the regicides, but he protested he went in the hope of restraining the band from carrying out what he suspected was their fiendish purpose.

"I was quite willing that they should force Alexander to give his kingly word of honor that he would not designate Draga's brother as his successor, and I must tell you that there were at least three or four other officers who went along with this purpose. But, maddened by drink and by the delay in finding the concealed pair, fearful of a rescuing party whose approach from the barracks was announced by the firing that had sprung up, the conspirators went ahead and in a general way you know what they did, and how we failed.

"But there are many mistakes in the accepted story. One is to the effect that the King was alive when thrown out of the Palace window, and that when he hung on tenaciously to the window sill, his fingers were chopped off by one of the brutes. This is absolutely untrue. He was quite dead, and as a matter of fact his body, and that of his wife, were thrown out of the window with a laudable purpose—to save further bloodshed."

"But how can that be?" I gasped.

"You see, soldiers were coming from several quarters who were not in the conspiracy. They were partisans of the Obrenovich clan, or police, who only knew that a group of strange men had taken possession of the Palace, and by throwing out the bodies, that ended the fighting at the Palace, at least, because there was not left a single member of the family to fight for, no descendant of the great Milosh—except Milan's bastard son."

"It was also a measure for the preservation of the conspirators against counter-attack, as I see it."

"Perhaps, but it ended the greater bloodshed. But what I really wanted to tell you was this. Both the King and his Prime Minister died under a wholly mistaken impression—"

"In other words, they died as most politicians live," I suggested. Paying no attention to this remark, the officer continued. "Only a few hours before the midnight murders the King and his Prime Minister, General Tsintsar Marcovich, had a long and unsatisfactory conference. Marcovich had been ruling the country at the King's command, but he had little popular support and but few adherents in the chamber and he, on this evening, asked to be relieved of his responsibilities. He admitted that his task was hopeless. This statement angered the King, but finally he asked Marcovich to remain on at least for a few days longer so that he might look the political field over for a suitable successor.

"Now the King, when he was shot down trying to shield the Queen, fell crying 'Mito, Mito! (The given name of Marcovich was Demeter, and this the affectionate diminutive.) How could you do this thing to me? What of your oath of fidelity?'

"An hour later I went with a company of soldiers to the nearby house of the Prime Minister. Captain Radokovich was in command, and what his real instructions were from the ringleaders I had no idea. Ostensibly he was sent to bring General Marcovich to the Palace to turn over the seals of office. The General we found working in his study, though it now must have been after two o'clock in the morning. The Captain said very politely, as he confronted us, 'I am ordered to place you under arrest and to guard you in your own house—until further orders.'

" 'I will endeavor to make your duty as pleasant as possible,' said the General, who was apparently entirely ignorant of what had happened at the Palace. We sat and smoked for a time and then the General said, 'Let's have some coffee.' He rose to give the order, and as he turned his back Captain Radokovich drew his revolver and fired three times. He then turned upon me and said sternly, 'Of course, you understand these were my orders from the Regents who will rule until King Peter arrives.'

"I lifted up the poor man's head. 'Sire, Sire,' he exclaimed, 'I have been faithful, I have not deserved that this thing should be done to me.' Then there came a choking sound, a rush of blood from his mouth, and the General moved no more. I closed his eyes and covered his body with a cloak."

Strange as it may seem, I found this description of what occurred on that dark night rather comforting. Men who escaped from the atmosphere of distrust and suspicion which reigned in the royal circle at this time could hardly be regarded as victims. They were lucky to get away from such a world by almost any exit. For me, for a season now, Belgrade was peopled by strange pitiful figures, some living and some dead, and I shuddered whenever I came upon poor little Sandra's swimming hole, nothing like as good a swimming hole as is the birthright of every American boy. I was happy, indeed, when a few days later orders came sending me to Constantinople to sojourn for a season among the "unspeakable Turks."

I would be remiss and indeed ungrateful if in this chronicle of my days in southeastern Europe I neglected to mention the many happy weeks I spent in Budapest as the guest of the chivalrous and horse-loving Magyars. While, of course, this magnificent city, so long held and always coveted by the Ottoman Turks, was well within my newsgathering "beat," it was a "quiet sector" and my repeated visits had the added charm that always goes with the enjoyment of forbidden fruit. While the Magyars had, and seemed to enjoy, many and distinct grievances as a result of the *Ausgleich* or Composition with Austria (in 1867), still the interest in these matters as far as America was concerned was slight, and I cannot recall that any of my dispatches from here reached the bulletin board in New York or were blazoned to the world by impressive headlines except when I described the passing of the great Andrássy who, after having been outlawed and condemned to death *in contumaciam* because of his allegiance to Kossuth, became the most substantial pillar of the Dual Monarchy and was followed to his grave not only by the people he loved so well but by a score, at least, of Austrian archdukes.

Of course, my undoubted unpopularity in the official circles of Sofia and Stamboul was an excellent foil and did emphasize my appreciation of the hospitality of a warm-hearted people that was so generously extended here. The morning after my arrival on my first visit (in 1888) there came to me, carried by a gorgeously attired messenger, a note in the trembling hand of an evidently aged writer, which read, "For forty years, until I reached the age of seventy, I have always called immediately upon everyone who came to our city from dear America. Now I'm seventy-six and I hope you will call upon me, Ferencz Pulszky."

Pulszky! Pulszky! The name was familiar, but for the life of me I could not recall where or in what connection I had heard it. But I was not left long in my ignorance. From my hotel, throughout the city, the news traveled with the speed of a prairie fire that the young American had received a note from Pulszky, the glory of Hungary, past and present, the trusted companion of Kossuth and Deák, the historian of the Magyar Revolution, the custodian of the patriotic archives in the Royal Library!

Within the hour I was at his desk and confronted by a handsome man with a hawklike face and a piercing eye, who talked about Webster and Clay as familiarly as we were accustomed to discuss Cleveland and Blaine. With great modesty he said that in the capacity of secretary he had accompanied Kossuth during his historic tour of America. It is unfortunate that I can only recall in a general way his impressions of our country, but they were all appreciative. He said he well understood the reasons why in that far-off day we could only give our moral support to the Hungarian insurgents, but he was quite confident that the time was near when America would gladly accept its responsibilities and perform its duties as the great liberty-loving world power. I do recall, however, a family anecdote of my own which amused the old gentleman immensely and the substantial accuracy of which he admitted. My father, at the time a young man, was a member of the very large reception committee in charge of arrangements during the visit of the Hungarian Revolutionist in Baltimore. There was much oratory and many ovations were showered upon him and lectures were given by the visitor. The ovations were participated in by thousands, but the lectures for which an admission charge was made were not so numerously attended. When the proceeds were turned over to him Kossuth accepted gratefully, but he was disappointed as to the amount and my father heard him say *sotto voce,* "Too much committee, too little money."

Pulszky laughed quietly and said this was not an isolated experience; then he added most charmingly, "But you were all so far away from the political conflagration in Europe! The Liberator thought, and I thought, it was wonderful how much you did in the circumstances. Others talked, but you sent a man of war to save us when the Turks were about to deliver us to the Austro-Russians. The Liberator always said, 'America is the hope of the world.'"

More, much more I fear than the diplomatic discussions with Count Albert Apponyi, the Tiszas and the other men of mark with whom I foregathered in the Hungarian capital, or even the long stories about the lost cause of Kossuth and the heroism of Klapka and Görgei (how like they were to the memories of Lee and Jackson which I listened to at my mother's knee!) I enjoyed the frequent excursions we made to the great stud farms and the race meetings which my horse-loving friends would there improvise. I recall with particular pleasure a frolic at Totis, one of the Esterházy estates. We went down by train and were met at some way station by box wagons filled with straw and painted all the colors of the rainbow. In these we shook down and were driven along the heavy mud roads to the large but by no means imposing castle. It had been well described to me as a horseman's paradise. While our quarters lacked much that we were used to and considered indispensable, the stables left nothing to be desired.

On the following morning we entered the paddock where some twenty horses were on display, and each of us chose his mount for the coming contest. Despite the warning of his three white feet, I picked out a bay horse that seemed very fit and up and coming. Six other guests entered the race, as did two of the horse-herders who enjoyed fraternal relations with the territorial lords present that were altogether charming. It was agreed that we were to race twice around a one-mile track with about a dozen low bush hurdles, which any horse that knew his business could take in his stride. Several things which happened before we were started led me to think that while it was not arranged everybody wanted to see the stranger from America win the race.

After the first mile was completed I saw that my most danger-ous opponent was a gray mare (most unusual color in Hungary) ridden by "Rudi" Kinsky, the famous gentleman jockey. I would not venture to say that Kinsky did anything so disgraceful as to pull the mare, to realize the hospitable plan, but before and since I have seen him ride in the Freudenau and at Baden and never have I seen him in the role of a passenger on his mount as he was this day. However, the gray mare was not as chivalrous as her rider and she won by a short but undeniable head.

And then occurred an incident that revealed that life even in Hungary was not all beer and skittles. In the evening we were at a country dance at a nearby *czarda*. During a lull in the dancing several stern-looking men approached and quickly roped a dancer, one of the herders who had ridden in the race. At first I thought it was a practical joke, but I soon learned that these were the men of the county draft and that when called the youngster had not presented himself for military duty.

But the interruption to the dance turned out more pleasantly than I had anticipated. The herder asserted that he had not the most remote wish to escape army duty but he did not want to be "unhorsed." Some of the other boys of the county had been drafted into infantry regiments and this was a humiliation that he could not face. His words were so sincere and his point of view so convincing to horse-lovers that even the agents of the draft were moved and they assured the boy he would go to the hussars. They then unbound the prisoner who became the hero of the evening. All the girls danced about him flapping their many-colored skirts and shouting "Hussar! Hussar!" and presenting goblets of the muddy red wine of the country. Then Kinsky assured him that he knew very intimately the Colonel of the Radetsky Hussars, the crack regiment of the Hungarian cavalry, and would see to it that he serve his time with these famous riders. This, or the muddy red wine, well named "bull's blood," was too much for the boy and an hour later we had to carry him into the inn and put him away in one of the strange and almost suffocating box beds of the country.

I fear that in those days we paid little attention to the submerged nationalities, later on to play such an important role in the history of the Balkan peninsula—indeed of the world. I was, of course, pro-Christian, and when Tashin Pasha, the "burden-bearer" of the Red Sultan, accused me of being a Gladstonian in my attitude toward Turkey, I could not deny it, but I do not think I differentiated between the Christian tribes, or was greatly concerned as to the outcome of the church rows or the language troubles. And doubtless this is why, when years later, in August 1918 to be exact, I was called upon to represent the United States in their congress to concert war measures, I presented myself at the Palais Bourbon, where the delegates of the Submerged Nationalities assembled, with an uncomfortable feeling. After all, I had had the opportunity nearly thirty years before to lay bare the wrongs of many of these unfortunate people and had failed to do so.

I confess that I do not remember having, at this time, even heard of the Slovaks, as a people quite distinct from the Hungarians, although I often went shooting in their districts north of Pressburg. But I did try to break a lance for the downtrodden Croats even when I was completely under the charm of the horse-loving Magyars. I suggested that their treatment in Parliament did not square with my idea of what a fair deal should be. At this time it seems, as a compromise on the thorny language problem, the few, the very few, Croat delegates were allowed to open their remarks with a sentence in the South-Slavic tongue, but then if they wanted to be listened to, or reported, they had to switch to Hungarian.

"But they are such insufferable swine," was the answer of an Erdödy or a Zichy to my mild reproof. "Now listen and you will understand the situation perfectly. Their Ban Jellachich helped the Russians to trample under foot the glorious republic of Kossuth—that, of course, we can understand, politics being what they are. But that was only the beginning. Only when the un-equal struggle was over and the Russians and their allies marched into our capital did we realize what Slav blood and Slav breed-ing is and can't help being. They tore down our flags which in war they had been unable to capture, and tried to steal the crown and the precious regalia of St. Stephen, but these, of course, we had hidden away. And then what do you think they did? You could not guess in a hundred years so I may as well tell you right away. Those Russian brutes dragged the Princess Batthyany from her palace out into the market-place and there spanked her publicly because, forsooth, her sons like all true Magyars had fought in Kossuth's army. You remember the little Prince, her youngest son who still races in England?—"

"Well, but the Croats," I inquired, "where do they come in?"

"Ban Jellachich and his men stood guard while the spanking of a lady—all of whose forbears had sat at the table of Magnats—went on! Now I think you will agree with me, we treat the Croats too gently. They should be hung to trees with their own cravats!* Fortunately, there are not so many of these vile people as there were. They are going to America in great numbers to work in the coal mines. Believe me, my dear friend, they are a bad lot. I advise you to keep them underground." That was the only lance I broke for the Croats in those days, and a feeble one it was. I am glad to say I have done better since.

It had been decided by my generous friends that I should be given a dinner, or as they called it a banquet, of welcome during my last stay of any length in the Magyar capital. While the preparations were under way there came a telegram from the Argus-eyed Commodore in Paris telling me, as so often before, "Return to Macedonia—outlook stormy." It had the effect of hurrying up the dinner date and changing it to a ceremony of farewell rather than one of welcome; Jókai threw himself into

---

* When the Croatian Lancers came to Paris with the allied armies in 1815 they introduced to the Western world their choking neckwear, and it was in their honor baptized "cravat" by the haberdashers.

the affair with energy and zest. It was to be an important occasion and I must make a speech that would be equal to it. Fearing that my unaided efforts would result in a jumble of drab words he wrote out the peroration himself. He liked it and so did I. When shown to Vámbéry he agreed that this speech would go far and be long remembered. There was still another surprise for me and for the guests at the banquet. My mentors decided that I was to recite at the conclusion of my remarks the first five lines and the last two of Petöfi's wonderful war song of the Magyars, the *Talpra Magyar*, the call to arms of 1848 which cost the inspired singer his life and gave him immortality.

I, of course, agreed. There was really nothing short of murder I would not have done to spend the magic hours that now were mine in Jókai's little study where he could weave better stories than I could find though I ransacked the world in search of them.

Often in the midst of the sing-song lessons that followed Jókai would embrace me and assert, so boundless was his imagination, that my Magyar accent demonstrated clearly what he had often suspected, that the Americans were a Turanian people. And then the stay-at-home romancer would sigh,

"How beautiful is your life! Here today and gone tomorrow —before stagnation follows. Always romance, always in action— while I sit here and dream of people and places I have never seen."

Vámbéry who often dropped in would join in the praise of my vagrant career and at times he would grow tearful as he realized what he had been and what he had become. With rapture he described the years he had spent as a beggar and a prayer-brother on the Central Asian plains—with no thought of the morrow— "when my only care was to secure my daily bread," he said. Then with sudden earnestness, "Young man, never settle down. That was the mistake of my life, but you see they tempted me so cunningly. Five hundred golden dollars a year they gave me, the beggar-man, to lay aside his pilgrim staff and become the professor of Oriental languages in the Royal University. I listened and

succumbed. I shall regret it always. Always I would leave the
bleak halls of learning and return to the living world."

In view of the very different feelings which my arrivals and
my departures from some of the Balkan capitals, notably Sofia
and Stamboul, had excited, the kindly sentiments expressed on
this evening were most pleasant to hear. It was a gorgeous hour
and I enjoyed every minute of it. The elder Pulszky, the companion of Kossuth, was ill and could not come but he sent his
charming son with his regrets and a message so flattering that I
dare not repeat it. Count Apponyi presided and the Erdödys, the
Zichys, and the Bornemizas were there in full force, all the rough
riders of the Hungarian plain, and not a few who had the right to
sit at the table of the Magnats and wear the leopard-skin dolman of
the Royal bodyguard.

Jókai, of course, made an impassioned speech and so did
Vámbéry, but the words of the great Orientalist ended in a warning, almost a menace. He evidently had a suspicion that would
not be quieted, that in my heart there was a dream of a placid
future and a farm, somewhere between the Susquehanna and the
Potomac, in the land where I was at home, and so he shouted,
"You must come to the Magyar land at least once a year and if
you ever settle down, I, and all the evil *djinns*, will haunt your
pillow."

The *Pesti Hirlap*, the old Kossuth organ, devoted much space
to the occasion and dwelt upon the real feeling I displayed in
reciting Petöfi's patriotic words. It was very pleasant and, of
course, I had not the remotest idea that a few months later when
the Pig War was on and the relations between Hungary and
Serbia had become more than usually embittered, my recitation
would be seized upon by my enemies, "the tarnished generals
of Belgrade," as proof positive that I had departed from the
neutral attitude which an American journalist should maintain in
European affairs. Then as always, fortunately, the future was a
closed book and I enjoyed a happy cloudless evening.

15. ABDUL HAMID—
THE GREAT ASSASSIN

I now come to the strange story of Tashin Pasha and the prisoner of Yildiz, the self-made Pasha of Seven Tails, and his slave, Abdul Hamid, "the Damned." When in the spring of 1932 I read a short and little-noticed press dispatch announcing that an aged man found dead of starvation in a Stamboul sewer had on investigation proved to be Tashin Pasha, so long the ruler of Turkey and the master of its Sultan, I was filled with an admiration that was surprising to my friends. After all, they asserted, this unsettled world is surfeited with the news of men, once powerful and affluent, dying in loneliness and want, and to emphasize their point of view they told the story of the Croatian General Boroevich, who during the Great War served out daily four million rations and yet in 1922, as his autopsy disclosed, died with undigested chunks of grass and straw in his stomach!

But my critics missed the point of this casualty. They did not know of the gallows which the Young Turks had erected for Tashin or the innumerable firing squads which the men of Union and Progress, as they called themselves, when they overthrew Tashin and Abdul Hamid, his slave, had told off to give him his quietus with a short, sharp volley. It was natural and fully in accordance with the custom of the country that the men of the Revolution should have felt this way about their relentless enemy who was at once the brains of the Old Turks and the sword and buckler of Abdul Hamid whom he enslaved.

Of course it may be pointed out that Machiavelli, Fouché, Talleyrand, and indeed many other masters of lawless intrigue died more or less quietly in their beds, but of them it perhaps cannot be said that they deserved to be hanged higher than Haman, and that would have been the fate of Tashin had he met with his deserts. Dying as he did in the gutter after reaching his eightieth year, with his boots on and unmolested except by the sewer rats, the once mighty Pasha demonstrated that he had lost none of his skill and cunning, and takes high rank in the category of great intriguers who triumphed over all their enemies except death, the final conqueror. Whatever else he may have been, this man of lowly birth who rose to be a Pasha of Seven Tails, who, not caring to command armies in person, was content to have their commanders cringe before him, who, in the name of the Sultan, ruled Turkey in Asia and Turkey in Europe as well, according to his own will, was, if not a personage, distinctly a somebody.

His origin, and even his nationality, was shrouded in mystery. Some said he was a Turk, true born; others maintained that he was an Armenian or a Greek or an Assyrian, a waif of the races he delighted to persecute. I think he was a Turk born in Syria but certainly a racial "sport." He was of less than medium height but was strongly built and always held himself very erect. He had a full chest and his energetic carriage breathed vitality. He never seemed to rest or lounge as did so many of his colleagues. Under their breaths his enemies would whisper that he never tired of evil-doing. By all accounts Tashin began as an office boy in the Press Bureau, which early in Abdul Hamid's reign was instituted under the supervision of Pangiris Bey, that fascinating Greek who figures so largely in Marion Crawford's Turkish novel, *Paul Patoff*. When Tashin had worked his way up to be second man in the Bureau, he very gracefully insisted upon his chief being made Turkish Minister in Rome, and that was the end of Pangiris as far as Stamboul was concerned, and the beginning of Tashin's greater career.

From these lowly beginnings Tashin gradually became the great power in the land of the Crescent and as the Bash Kiatib, or first secretary, consolidated his position; the former influence of the Grand Vizierate waned and those unfortunate officials who as of old sat in the gateway of the Sublime Porte became more and more ridiculous. It was not long before the Ambassadors who represented the West in Stamboul, at least those who were worth their keep, learned of the new power that had arisen beside rather than behind the throne. Not seldom they had thought to settle a vexatious question with the traditional *masbate* from the Council of Ministers, only to find out that it had rather less value than the peculiar parchment paper it was written on. What was really needed and what was so difficult to secure was an *Iradeh* which carried with it Imperial sanction but only when Tashin's sign manual was attached. And so it was that the Ambassador of England, with his fear of trouble with the Mohammedans on the northwest frontier of India, and the French Ambassador who had to keep an alert eye on the turbulent tribes along the Tripolitan-Tunisian border, were always angling to have a talk over coffee and cigarettes with Tashin the "Sphinx."

I shall not list the dead Pasha's high crimes or the low ones (they will not escape history) but content myself with a few snapshots of himself and his Imperial Master as I saw them at intervals during a period of fifteen years. I shall set down nought in malice and I shall even recall at the outset one of his good deeds which for some years made me feel under a very definite obligation to the strange man who was so long Grand Vizier of the Empire in everything save name and title. At my insistent request he brought back from the desert convict station at Insalah in southern Tripoli two Macedonian rebels, mere boys who had been caught red-handed and whose lives according to the rough war code of the day were forfeit. He restored them to their families and homes; brought them back from what was worse than death. And then, when the World War came, these boys, boys no longer, to my amazement marched shoulder to shoulder with their oppressors and against what I thought were the forces of civilization and humanity. This may have been an instance when Tashin's foresight was clearer than mine, as it often was. But it also left me with the impression that the saving of life is quite a gamble.

My first talk with Abdul Hamid took place before he was infamous or even famous. It was in the summer of 1889 or 1890.

My recollection of the details is not very vivid, but I recall that I was favorably impressed and enjoyed the experience. I was taken across the dancing waters in a galley rowed by many oarsmen to the Dolma Bagtsche Palace. And of course the glistening whiteness of the palace, the great marble quay on which we landed, and the flowering gardens through which I was escorted by an adjutant, were altogether enchanting.

Here, there, and everywhere the stalwart Albanian foot soldiers, with their hard-bitten features and their swishing skirts, were on guard. But the military precautions were far from excessive and as the talk went on we drank tea and ate the sweet preserves that were brought in, with no more pomp and ceremony than when a few weeks before I had been received by King Milan in Nish or by Edhem Pasha, the conqueror of Macedonia, in Usküb.

I had been escorted through the hall of the throne into a little room, or really a balcony, jutting out over the sparkling waters. As I saw him first Abdul was a slender, alert man some years under forty, with a slight but not ungraceful stoop in his carriage. There were present Tashin, who, as he had not yet emerged from insignificance, hovered in the background, unless called, and Tewfik Pasha, a handsome, stately figure, just what a Grand Vizier should look like, the very best picture that I can recall of the Old Turk. Opening the conversation, which was in French and consequently creaked a good deal, the Sultan spoke of the power of the press and the value he placed upon the friendship of my chief, James Gordon Bennett.

"How enlightening it all is," exclaimed the Sultan, "and some day we will have papers, great newspapers in Turkey, but they will come gradually."

This reached me through Tewfik though I was not long in making up my mind that the Sultan understood French better than his chosen interpreter, but for reasons of punctilio preferred to have his thoughts reach me by indirection. It wasn't so very easy and perhaps much was lost because neither the French of Tewfik nor mine smacked of Frankistan!

"The power of the press with us will have to be developed gradually," insisted the Sultan, "because among us so few people know how to read." "But," explained Tewfik, "so many know so many verses of the *Koran* by heart and that fills their lives with wisdom and beauty. They have world knowledge and do not need to follow current events."

When the talk hobbled along in short and simple sentences, Tewfik translated. Now and again his translation would be vetoed by His Majesty and then Tashin would be brought forward. And this was the first time I ever saw the great man who rose from obscurity to such heights. He was shabbily dressed, and his eyes were fixed meekly upon his well-worn gaiters. Time and again the Sultan discoursed at great length upon the world trend, time and again he talked of modernizing Turkey, but always he gave the assurance that he must proceed slowly, that there were dangerous elements that had to be held in check until the mass of the people became enlightened.

In a general way he showered nosegays upon the great American editors and asked me to repeat their names. Then suddenly he said: "Your greatest man is Edison. Tell me all you know about Edison."

I told him what I knew and perhaps a great deal more. I had at this time never seen the wizard, having lived abroad during the struggling years of the incandescent lamp, and at this the Sultan was greatly disappointed. But what I lacked in intimate knowledge I made up in enthusiasm. And the Sultan was pleased.

"Surely the greatest of men, the greatest of Americans," he declared, "Yes, surely, for he—he has brought light into the darkest places."

Eighteen months later my reports upon the first Armenian massacres (of the decade, at least) which were insignificant affairs indeed when compared with what happened in 1895, gave great offense at the Palace, and Tashin wrote a very severe letter to the Commodore which wound up with the request for my removal or at least my transfer to scenes that I would find more congenial. "Your representative always holds with the Schismatics and the enemies of the Padishah. He will not believe a Turkish official even when he swears by the beard of the Prophet." The Commodore forwarded the letter to me and asked for comment and he got it. I admitted that there was much truth in the accusation and that if his representative was expected to believe a Turkish official on oath, when the matter under investigation was the welfare or the fate of the Christian minorities, then I should be removed. Nothing further came to me on the subject although Mr. Bennett on several occasions remarked that on the Eastern question I was a Gladstonian, and this remark was not intended to be complimentary. Tashin soon recovered from his ill-humor. Doubtless he concluded that my successor might prove an even more active crusader, and after a few weeks his occasional offerings of the fragrant apples from Amasia came to me again.

Of the interviews that took place between my first and my last talk with the Sultan, it is only necessary to note one because this interview was requested and granted for a specific purpose. There had been terrible massacres in the Armenian villages in and around Erivan. Some of these atrocities the Turkish government frankly admitted, but they tried to place the responsibility upon Bashi-bazouks or irregular troops who had gotten out of hand. Further, the government advanced extenuating circumstances. These irregular troops had been provoked to bloody reprisals by the arrogance of Armenian patriots. And I believe there was some evidence, though not much, in support of this contention.

The Commodore, as they called him in Turkey, as well as in Europe, wished to have the matter investigated and thrashed out. Very properly he eliminated me from the list of those who were suitable to make the investigation. If I had come to Turkey with an open mind years before, and I think he had some doubt of this, he asserted that I could not claim to be in that position now. And, of course, he was right. My sympathies were entirely on the side of the oppressed Christian populations. I had indeed become a Gladstonian. I knew of no way the international scandal and disgrace to civilization could be terminated except by relegating the Ottoman Turk back to Asia, the farther back the better.

I freely admitted all this and welcomed the plan which Mr. Bennett now proposed. The situation required new eyes and a new reviewer. The churches in America were at last aroused and agitation could not be stilled in one sense or the other unless decisive evidence was produced by good churchmen. I was in Vienna at the time and the Commodore instructed me to run down to Stamboul and arrange through Tashin for a passport, which would permit the Reverend Doctor George Hepworth to visit the scene of the disturbances, investigate and report. I thought the idea was an excellent one, though rough on the Doctor. Doctor Hepworth had given up his ministry and for some years had been writing with considerable success the only kind of editorials which were permitted to appear in the *Herald* when, as was almost always the case, the Commodore was abroad. They were editorials which ran to many words, said nothing and got nowhere.

Tashin was perplexed by the proposal and showed much hesitation as to the course he should pursue. Finally, he took the matter up with the Sultan and as he was clearly, and not unwisely, shirking all responsibility in the matter, he arranged an interview at Yildiz, in which I must confess that I was very sharply cross-examined, both by the Sultan and the now powerful Pasha. I asserted, and with perfect truth, that I had never talked the matter over with the Doctor, that he was of full age, considerably over sixty, and would not be unduly influenced by anything I had written. I was sure he had an open mind and that owing to his standing in the church whatever conclusions he reached would carry great weight with the members of the congregations. Then the Sultan, who had listened for a long time to the by no means veiled allusions that Tashin permitted himself to make about my "wrong-headedness" on the subject under discussion, made the only bright remark of the conference.

"But suppose the Reverend Mullah falls into the hands of the unbelievers and schismatics, and is enmeshed in their wiles and lies, as so many have been, would not his opinions and his reports have very great weight with the churches and tend further to weaken the ties of friendship that today bind our countries but loosely?"

I admitted this was so. I had to. But I protested that unless they feared the verdict of a fair-minded observer they had better issue the passport. This, at long last, they agreed to do, and having wired Bennett that everything had been arranged, I returned to my post.

Some months later the good Doctor, a patient sufferer from acute rheumatism, and carrying the burden of more than two hundred pounds of tender flesh, came across the seas and ambled about the disturbed regions on a sumpter mule for some weeks. He saw and heard as much as was permitted and, of course, this was very little. He returned home and wrote a very fair report. To me he said, "You cannot believe anyone in these districts. For the most part the Christians and the Moslems alike are liars and the sons of long lines of liars. Conditions are impossible, for the upper dog as well as for the under dog. Armenians and Moslems could not live together in harmony—not even in Paradise," and without venturing an opinion as to who was primarily at fault for the pitiless warfare, the Doctor asserted that the combatants should be separated. No one offered to carry out this excellent plan and so the good Doctor's report, like so many of a similar nature, was filed away and all his pains and aches and discomfort had been suffered in vain.

The last and the most interesting of my talks with the Sultan took place in 1904, in early spring, I think. The war was raging in the Far East and the Commodore came nearer to giving me definite and full instructions in sending me to Constantinople than ever before. I did not have to tell him, though I could not forego the pleasure, that his Russian friends were in for a bad quarter of an hour, indeed for a bad year, at least. He knew all that and his instructions to me were "to keep the Balkans quiet"—a large order surely. Above all, to keep Turkey quiet, and if possible, to get the Turks to pay some of the long delayed war indemnities resulting from the Russo-Turkish War of the late 70's.

I was told to impress upon the Sultan how chivalrous the Russians were, how grateful they would be for payment now even though it was not as large as the obligation. A ruble now would be more appreciated than a Turkish pound later on, and

I was told to say that Turkey had at the moment a chance to make Russia her friend and that this might well prove her salvation.

"You will find things greatly changed," explained the Commodore. "In fear of his life the Sultan is living in complete seclusion. When I put in last spring with the *Lysistrata* I had to wait forty-eight hours for an audience. Of course, I would not have waited only the Duc de Gramont was my guest and he had been dreaming of the promised presentation for months."

As the Commodore warned me, I came to a greatly changed Turkey. Not wishing to leave my wife without official papers even in Vienna, I had turned over to her our joint passport and traversed the frontiers of Serbia and Bulgaria with only a life insurance policy which was blithely accepted and covered with official visas! But when, in the night, I came to the Turkish border at Mustapha Pasha the officials made a tremendous row and, while I was not stopped, I was accompanied to Constantinople by two gendarmes who stayed with me for several days until the matter was cleared up. The Ottoman Turks had been aroused from the sleep of centuries. The old loyalties had vanished. Foreign intrigues, working from within as well as from without, had undermined the Sultan's power. Secretly anti-dynastic committees were being enrolled and there was talk in the coffee houses and bazaars of popular representation! Traitors had been found even in the Albanian bodyguard, and it had been suggested that it would be wise for the Sultan to take refuge in the midst of his army. As this would not have looked well to foreign observers a compromise had been effected by having the greater part of the army camp around the palace, and every penny that could be extracted from the Thracian and Anatolian peasants went for maintaining this vast host. The money-lenders at home and abroad were refusing supplies, and as a result of the recent bold attempt to murder him at the very gate of the holy of holies, during the ceremony of the *Selamlik*, the Sultan had lost his nerve and lived on behind barred gates in fear and trembling.

So I soon found out that the Commodore had not exaggerated the changes that had come over the Constantinople scene since my last visit. Tashin was cordial but said nothing about an audience with the All Highest. After my second visit he sent apples, the fragrant fruit of Amasia, the usual offering, and said that at the next *Selamlik* a court carriage would await me and that afterwards he would take me to the palace. There was a possibility, but no assurance, that on this tour or later I might be received. But on the following Friday there was no *Selamlik*, the Commander of the Faithful paid his devotions, if at all, in a private mosque within the walls of Yildiz, and of course no court equipage came.

A day or two later there reached me a suggestion—how it came I do not recall—that there had been a complete readjustment of duties and of procedure, and for the purpose I had in view it would be wise for me to address myself to the Sublime Porte. I did look in upon this famous circumlocution office where foreign affairs were supposed to be transacted but never were.

Naoum Pasha was in charge, an old friend, and very considerate. He urged me to keep on my overcoat as I sat before him shivering with the cold. He himself was all trussed up in waistcoats and sweaters, and the March winds howled down the Bosphorus through the ill-fitting window sashes, and the cast-iron stoves that lay around, mostly crippled as to their feet, gave forth nothing more serviceable than smoke and smells.

He made a few vague remarks in regard to the Bagdad Railway and then, "And now tell me what news do you bring from Frankistan?" That was that.

True he did arrange for my reception by old Tewfik, the former Grand Vizier, who had also been side-tracked and who knew it. He was living in a great empty palace not far from the German Embassy, and whether it was from age or from fear of his powerful and somewhat arrogant neighbor, Marschall von Bieberstein, the new Ambassador from Berlin, he talked to me about nothing in a quavering whisper, and then offered tea and preserves.

In a day or two the reason of the delay was apparent. The British lion blocked my path. Sir Nicholas Dominick O'Connor, the British Ambassador Extraordinary, stood in the path leading to the "Palace of the Stars" where the Sultan now cowered in fear of his enemies. Many years before, when O'Connor was the diplomatic agent of his country in Bulgaria, he had in my presence compared Stambouloff, then ruling the unfortunate land in a most tyrannical manner, to George Washington, and I had in my indignation, which was righteous, countered with a remark that, while absolutely correct, was clothed in unseemly language. O'Connor's cynicism, the lesson he taught the Bulgars, that they were under no obligations, not even those of civility, to the Russians who at the cost of a million men had liberated them from the Turkish yoke, was the first step in the path of ingratitude which led them to bite the hand that had fed them and to fight against their benefactors, perhaps the most revolting mass-incident of the World War.

However, O'Connor's influence only brought about a delay of three days and one clear, cold morning, a rare day for the Constantinople March, the court carriage came, and also a brightly uniformed adjutant or official of the household who, as we drove along, was both indiscreet and amusing.

I recall particularly an incident that related to my distinguished chief with which he regaled me. Some months before he had been sent out to fetch to the palace Bennett and some Duke or other, who were on board the yacht anchored in the Golden Horn.

"When they were all ready to disembark I noticed," said the adjutant, "that the Commodore was not wearing his Turkish orders, and you know His Imperial Majesty has conferred all of them upon his distinguished friend, the 'sailor prince' from America. He should have been wearing the Order of the Osmanieh and the Medal of Mahomet, the Conqueror, and of Suleiman, the Magnificent (I may have some of these names wrong!), but as a matter of fact your Commodore wore none of them. I was greatly perplexed, particularly because the Duke was plastered with orders and medals and decorations although, as I noticed, his Turkish decoration was most insignificant. Oh, if your Commodore had had a secretary, that would have simplified matters, but he hadn't."

"That's an idiosyncrasy of his," I explained. "He maintains he will not have a secretary until he is eighty." I did not add that there were two or three unfortunate men who performed as well as they could these secretarial duties, but clandestinely; they were never allowed to come out into the open.

"There was no help for it, no secretary to break the news, to serve as intermediary, so I told the Commodore about the missing decorations and he ejaculated, 'Bless my soul! I wonder what has become of them.' He went into his cabin and must have been away ten minutes. When he came back his face was flushed and he was just a little embarrassed. 'I can't find them,' he admitted. 'I have hidden them away so carefully that no one can find them.' Seeing that my spirits sank, he added cheerfully, 'But, of course, His Imperial Majesty will not notice their absence.'

" 'Perhaps, but Tashin will and then what a wigging I will get.'

"Sure enough, Tashin met us at the Outer Gate, not at the gate of the Inner Pavilion, where perhaps he may meet you (I bowed; I was being put in my place, and that is so helpful in court life).

"I had made no mistake. There at the Outer Gate was Tashin. One side of his face was all smiles for your Commodore, the other was dark and full of menace for me. In the very midst of his words of greeting he growled out of the side of his mouth, 'Where are his decorations, the Turkish ones?' I explained and Tashin gave a short quick order and several lackeys darted off at great speed while we moved on in the direction of the Audience Pavilion at a snail's pace. Before we got there one of the lackeys had overtaken us with a velvet bag out of which Tashin took duplicates of the missing decorations and pinned them on your Commodore's coat. I would have given a good deal to laugh. Your Commodore was blushing like a débutante getting a bouquet from her best young man."

While the story ran along we had come to the Outer Gate of Yildiz and here we were halted, but most courteously, by the guard. A soldier messenger was dispatched and in about two minutes an officer appeared who saluted my escort respectfully and motioned the coachman to proceed. Through a labyrinth of narrow tree-planted roads we ambled along for five or ten minutes. Now and again it seemed to me we passed a shabby pavilion or villa that

I had seen before, but perhaps this was only because they all looked alike. What the purpose of the swing-around was I did not know, but if it was to bewilder me to the point that I could never again unaided return to the place of audience, it was most successful. At last we halted before a two-storied building, part brick and part wood, almost concealed by trees and shrubbery, but quite as shabby as any of the rest. Here in a narrow gateway Tashin stood and here he dismissed the voluble adjutant with a curt nod.

He led me up a narrow, rickety stair and along a narrow hall, the floor of which creaked under our feet. In all the corners and crevices were cast-iron stoves about which lounged and smoked groups of soldiers who paid no attention at all to the great man as he passed. They were all apparently hardy Albanians with magnificent figures, but with surly faces, and all were smoking the fat cigarettes I had learned to love during my journey in Higher Albania years before.

Finally, the narrow passageway widened out into a hall where there was a strange-looking coat and umbrella rack, and here Tashin insisted upon helping me off with my coat.

"How clumsy I am," he said. Perhaps he was and perhaps he was not. Some hours later, however, when another incident had aroused my suspicions, I came to the conclusion that he had not been clumsy but that very deftly he had felt my pockets and satisfied himself that I had neither a bomb nor a pistol concealed on my person. He was not taking chances even with an old acquaintance!

From the hall we entered Tashin's office. I must here confess that in our long drive and walk in and out of the Palace precincts I had not even caught a glimpse of the beautiful houris of the Turkish paradise peeping at me from behind curtains, nor had I come across any of those amazing dwarfs and deaf mutes who are always stumbled upon by more fortunate travelers. I had come across a few African eunuchs, or at least I thought so. Of course, you can never be certain. It was a huge room where we tarried now, with a low ceiling, and made even more gloomy by heavy, half-drawn curtains. Under foot were modern carpets of unspeakable ugliness. Tashin seated himself at a great desk, lit a cigarette and began to toy with some papers. Slippered messengers came in and out, sometimes passing through the room without halting, but always with an obsequious bow in the direction of the desk at which the great man sat.

Things had been in this static condition for about ten minutes, when one of the many doors that opened into the room was drawn back and a man appeared whose face was very familiar, but whom at first I could not place. He gave a quick glance at me, nodded to Tashin, and then backed out through another door. Suddenly an idea came to me, and Tashin with his eyes fixed upon me read it telepathically, I am sure. He knew what it was in my mind to say and what I concluded on short reflection had better be left unsaid. Surely this was not Munir Bey, that magnificent creature, the "glass of fashion and the mold of form," the Ambassador of Turkey to France, who sat on the Commodore's right hand at so many of the drag meets? This man wore a shiny coat and his shoes were cracked and run down at the heels and the bottoms of his trousers were frayed, and yet Tashin's black beady eyes fixed upon me were not to be denied.

"If I did not know he was in Paris," I said, "I would take that man to be Munir Bey."

"It is Munir," said Tashin. "You have a good memory for faces." He smiled coldly. The appealing poverty of the get-up in which the Turkish Ambassador in Paris was masquerading had not made a sympathetic impression. "It is Munir," he repeated. "The Ambassador is here asking for more pay. He says life is becoming so expensive in Paris that he cannot live on his appointments." I, of course, said a word for the down-at-heels Ambassador, thinking that we salaried men who had to live in Paris must stand together. I insisted that all the necessities of life had gone up and how inaccessible were the luxuries, save for a few millionaires—

I was interrupted by the sudden opening of one of the many doors, through which someone, invisible to me, apparently made a sign to Tashin that was perfectly comprehensible to him. He rose. "His Imperial Majesty awaits us," and led me through the same door into a narrow corridor along which we continued for about a hundred feet. It was bare of furniture and of people.

Suddenly Tashin opened a slit of a door which I never would
have noticed, passing into a little ante-chamber, where two black
soldiers sat like ebony statues on a divan with a pyramid of cigarette butts before them. Pushing aside a curtain we entered a larger
room and there, on a great sofa, half-sitting and half-reclining
upon cushions, was Abdul Hamid. Seeing him, as I saw him here,
there could be no doubt about it, but had I met him anywhere else
I would not have recognized in him the attractive and rather
romantic-looking figure I had first seen fifteen years before. The
bright, intelligent eyes that had then charmed me were dead. His
cheeks were fallen in. There was a furtive expression in his eyes,
that were never still, but always moving about, prying into corners
and then coming back to me with an uneasy, startled expression.
Most disastrous of all the changes that time had wrought was that
in his nose. It had broadened, and hung over his mouth like an
arched beak. Behind the mask of dignity which he sought to maintain you could read the never-ending anxieties of a hunted man.

Tashin apparently primed him about our previous talks and the
Sultan said graciously he remembered them distinctly. I referred
to Edison and our talk regarding him of years ago, but this did
not register. He had apparently some difficulty in recalling Edison,
and as to light in the dark places, well, evidently that was no longer
his great preoccupation.

I had made a deep bow as Tashin had suggested I should when
we were face to face, and the Sultan half rose and then fell back
into the cushions without extending his hand. I, too, sank down in
a low chair, and while Tashin was drinking in the Turkish words
that were later conveyed to me in creaking French, I had a chance
to look the strange creature over very closely. There was today
no suggestion of the Field Marshal's uniform he had worn on the
previous occasions; he was distinctly in négligé. He wore a gabar-
dine of some dark blue cloth, and under it was a tunic of lighter
blue which buttoned closely right up to his now very prominent
Adam's apple. His shoes were loose-fitting gaiters and his baggy
trousers flowed over them. He wore his fez, very dark red, so dark
it seemed almost black, and altogether the appearance of the Sultan was rather sepulchral.

As they gabbled on I turned away, and was glad to catch a glimpse, through a slit in the curtains, out through the window over the harbor where ships were coming and going and there was promise of contact with the living world. When I came back to the business in hand, I found that I was being cross-examined as to my movements since my arrival, and soon it was apparent that my answers which were rather vague were far from satisfactory. Suddenly I was brought to book. "His Imperial Majesty would like to know where you spent yesterday."

"I visited Robert College up the Bosphorus at Roumeli Hissar," I replied. Then, for the first time, there was a light in the Sultan's eyes that recalled the intelligent expression that had often shone there in former days. "Did the Commodore order you to go there?" "No," I answered, "he rarely gives detailed instructions. He doubtless assumed that I would know that a survey of a school for the Balkan peoples, founded by a merchant prince of New York, should interest the readers of the paper. I always go there—when I come to Stamboul," I concluded.

There followed a long hissing sibilant conversation between the Sultan and Tashin that quite escaped my wayfaring Turkish. I knew, however, it would be wise to get off this topic as soon as possible. Apparently Tashin thought the same, but in answer to an insistent nod from his master he said:

"His Majesty begs me to say that Roumeli Hissar is a place that is hallowed in the history of the Ottoman Turks. There it was that his mighty ancestors crossed from Asia into Europe and there began the conquests which reached to Buda and brought under the Crescent an expanse of territory four times as great as that of the Turkish Empire today. In those days, the path of the Conqueror led by Roumeli Hissar—" Here he paused and only continued in obedience to an insistent gesture from the Sultan. "His Majesty begs me to inquire whether you think, as he does, that at a no very distant day another conqueror will pass through Roumeli Hissar, but coming from the West, not from the East. And then our Empire—" Tashin stopped short and the Sultan fixed his eyes upon me. I was certainly in a predicament, but I did the best I could.

"Politics are not taught at Robert College," I asserted. "The good men who teach there pray daily for His Majesty and for the President of the United States—and for all in authority." Then, thinking to see an avenue of escape, I grasped it. "But now I see what your Majesty has in mind. True, education is the modern Conqueror. It is sweeping over America and Europe alike. Everywhere it is bringing light into the dark places." As Tashin translated, the Sultan who had risen for an alert moment sank back into his cushions. Light in the dark places! That was certainly not his objective today.

The Sultan after a pause dropped the dangerous topic and expressed his appreciation of the constant friendship of Commodore Bennett. This was my opening.

"The Commodore has instructed me to say that in his judgment this is a crucial moment in your relations with Russia." Smiling for once almost brightly the Sultan countered, "The relations of Russia with Japan seem to be more important just now." Evidently Abdul Hamid was shedding no tears over the defeat of the Russian armies on the Manchurian plains.

"Precisely," I commented. "It will require a second, perhaps a third campaign before Russia gets the upper hand. In the meantime, deserted by false or short-sighted friends, she needs support and, above all, money. The Commodore thinks that this is the moment when you can end the ancient feud and bind Russia to you in the bonds of a lasting friendship."

"And how, pray?" This from the Sultan direct, without awaiting the creaking translation.

"By making a payment, as considerable as possible, upon the long delayed war debts." *

At this the Sultan became greatly excited. His words to Tashin were vehement and he accompanied them with emphatic gestures. Doubtless they were toned down before they reached me. "It is a

* At the Congress of Berlin, Turkey agreed to pay Russia the sum of three hundred million gold rubles as war indemnity, but as appears above the payments were not made and the arrears came to assume what were then considered astronomical proportions. The question lay dormant until 1909 when an arrangement was made by which Bulgaria agreed to pay Russia the tribute money which by the Treaty of Berlin it had agreed to pay to the ex-suzerain, the Sultan of Turkey, but which was also in default.

just debt," began Tashin, "at least, it has been admitted and ratified in several treaties and some day it will be paid—praise God—but His Majesty asserts and quite correctly that it is impossible to pay the debt today, or any part of it or even the interest that is overdue. The revenues of the Empire have fallen off and continue to fall. We have the greatest difficulty in finding the money to feed and clothe the thousands of soldiers who are camped about Yildiz." Here a conference took place between master and interpreter and then Tashin continued while Abdul Hamid smiled, almost beamed approval. "It is not only important for His Majesty to have one hundred thousand men camped about Yildiz; it is important for the Empire if it is to survive, and more, these men are indispensable for the maintenance of the peace of southeastern Europe."

"The peace of all Europe," corrected the Sultan sharply. "If this army should be disbanded, the result would be disastrous to Turkey and even to the Russian Empire. Public Law would disappear from the councils of the nations. Europe would—" Suddenly the Sultan half-rose, lifted his arms and flapped them as though they were wings. "There would be anarchy here and everywhere," he shouted in a strange guttural French, and then sank back on his cushions exhausted by the effort, but still repeating half to himself, and half to me, *"Anarchie! Anarchie!"* Obviously there was nothing further to be said about the payment of the ancient war debt, and I was looking anxiously toward Tashin for the signal to go, when the Sultan asked, "And in what other way can I serve my good friend, the Commodore?"

"In no way," I answered, "except perhaps by charging me with the assurance of your continued friendship and esteem." Again a long and confidential confab took place between the Sultan and Tashin which I could not follow, but something was said about cigarettes and there was almost a dispute as to figures. Finally Tashin turned to me and said with the air of a man who had been defeated in argument but was of his own opinion still:

"His Imperial Majesty requests you to convey to the Commodore the assurance of his unfailing friendship. He will also commit to your care, for the Commodore, a present of the Giubec cigarettes which, as rolled for my Imperial Master, we know that he highly esteems." "Five thousand of them," interrupted the Sultan sharply. "Five thousand," repeated Tashin glumly. Then the Sultan half-rose and extended his hand which I took, and I followed the Pasha as he backed his way to the door by which we had entered.

Back in Pera, I spent some time and thought in drawing up a cable with the secret key word address which was the guarantee that wherever the Commodore might be, whether off the Spanish Main or in Samarkand, wherever he might be and regardless of expense, the message would reach him. The European situation as it appeared to the man shut in at Yildiz I put quite briefly. Also, I did not dwell very long on the undoubted *impasse* in regard to the war debt payments. I emphasized the hundred and fifty thousand men who were on guard around the palace gates and the amount of money they ate up. By this time, I saw that the cable would have to go by messenger to our agent in Sofia for transmission and then I added, not the least important item, "He sends 5,000 Giubec cigarettes." But when I came to read over the dispatch I struck out the numerals and, for once, I was wise, for in the morning the cigarettes came and there were exactly 418 of them. Tashin, as so often in matters of greater import, had had the last word!

After the Young Turks had seized control and deposed Abdul Hamid in 1908 many things happened which optimists regarded as a general liquidation of Balkan problems. In October Austria-Hungary informed the signatory powers of the Treaty of Berlin that the annexation of Bosnia and Herzegovina which under mandate she had occupied for thirty years was necessary, and within a few days Bulgaria proclaimed her independence. Russia protested but Count Benckendorf, her Ambassador in London, was informed by Sir Edward Grey that while England favored the sanctity of treaties, the Balkans were far away—not near like Belgium, for instance, although the little, neutralized kingdom was not mentioned in the discussion.

And, of course, the Young Turks also protested, but being practical men they admitted they would accept financial compensation for their territorial losses. The new Ottoman Parliament was then offered and accepted twelve million dollars from Austria, and in a few days the independence of Bulgaria was recognized by the Porte.

There was then much discussion as to the compensation that Bulgaria should offer the revolutionary heirs of her former suzerain, but finally this was adjusted to the satisfaction of all—except the Turks. In a generous moment the Tsar turned over to the Bulgarian government the I.O.U.'s from Turkey which since 1878 the Russians had been unable to collect, and Bulgaria turned them back, or some of them, to the Turks in payment of the arrears of tribute money promised in the eastern Roumelia protocol and also to cancel the Turkish investment in the Bulgarian railways. It was a new way to pay old debts and it was not done with goods or services which economists insist is the only way it can be done. And, of course, no money passed and so there was no trouble with exchange! The Turks apparently were paid in their own coin—that is, with their own worthless notes!

16. BELGRADE AND THE PIG WAR

THE POLITICAL situation in Serbia at this time (mid-summer 1890) is difficult to describe and perhaps it would be futile to attempt it. Political morals were at a low ebb and the future seemed to depend upon the antics of ex-King Milan, the prodigal parent with his unfortunate homing instinct, and the success or failure of the deep-laid schemes of Monsieur Hitrovo, the Machiavellian minister from Russia. There were active in the political arena all the parties that I have previously mentioned, and a brand-new one besides. Its members were called the Possibilists and their policy was to keep the Balkans boiling and to get just as many rubles as they could out of the Pan-Slavs of Moscow without interrupting for a moment the flow of florins that came to them from Vienna, from the men who believed in the vital urge that lay behind Austria's historic advance toward the East and, to be specific, toward Salonica and the Aegean.

Serbia was very hard-up and the army was being starved. Try as they would to balance the budget the accounts were always upset by the arrival of Milan's overdrafts from Paris and other uncontrolled expenditures. In a fit of righteous anger the radical assembly not only dishonored the last flock of drafts but cancelled the King's allowance altogether. They soon had much reason to regret this natural but ill-considered action. Within the week Milan stepped jauntily off the Orient Express, drove to the palace and told his son, the unfortunate Sandra, that he had come to take refuge with him against the disloyal strokes of a cruel world. A very few hours later, he whispered to me that the boy king had called him home to take charge of the army which needed "jacking up."

It was soon evident that the relations between father and son were greatly strained. Milan, however, held his ground and maintained separate apartments in the palace from which his son could not expel him, much as he doubtless wanted to. Still the ship of state sailed on, although the waves of discontent were rising to formidable heights, and what was a source of constant surprise to McClure, and of indignation to my exiled colleagues across the river in Zemlin, despite cabals and backstairs gossip against me I maintained my position as the only correspondent in the capital with unhindered access to the wires.

Perhaps my attitude, however successful, was not very creditable, but as an extenuating circumstance may I stress the fact that there was being debated in the political arena no great question upon which, as a Jeffersonian democrat, I should have taken an appropriate stand. It seemed to me, rightly or wrongly, that I was not called upon here to suffer for a great political and moral principle as I had in Sofia, and so it came about that, in an academic way, at least, I conspired freely with all the conspirators (and heaven alone knows how many there were!) with but little or no regard to creed or political complexion. I played *tarok* with the Radicals in the morning and *tric-trac* with the Conservatives in the afternoon. I rambled through the forest and swam with little Sandra in the park of Topchider and ate the cloying sweets which Milan had served in that part of the palace where he had established himself. And I will confess that even when he gossiped about his expensive, and as some thought extravagant, *menus plaisirs* in Paris I did not feel called upon to interject a word about economy or the sanctity of the home.

Probably I was becoming Balkanized. This had happened to others before me, but the explanation of my attitude which I prefer is that I was increasingly anxious to return home. There were people I wanted to see again of whom I frequently thought during my lonely vigils. I had saved what seemed to me a great sum of money, particularly during the last two years in the Balkans where there was nothing, that money could buy, that I wanted. There it was

stacking up mountain high in the *Herald* office in Paris by reason
of my underdrafts for the salary account. It was not drawing interest, but it was growing rapidly because often I only drew half of
my salary and never more than three-quarters of it.

It was a pleasure to dream of what I would do with all this
money when my responsibilities for these turbulent regions ceased
and my Balkan assignment was at an end. I would, of course, replenish my wardrobe in London. I would discard those ill-fitting
Stamboul clothes which the Greek tailors on the Rue de Pera
turned out for me, and then with my hard-won prize money I
would buy a farm in Maryland, or at least I would make a partial
down payment on it, which would be in accordance with the custom of our county. I would plant tobacco and start my Diamond
Back terrapin breeding establishment. I would, equally of course,
acquire two or three brood mares and some day at Pimlico I might
see a colt carrying my colors pass the winning post in the four-
mile heats. Mine would be real horses, not the racing machines
for the short and silly dashes which, alas! were coming into
fashion.

This was the state of affairs and my frame of mind toward the
end of the fourth month of my longest sojourn in the Serbian capital. I had become there, or so it seemed to me, as stable as the town
pump. All the plots of my former colleagues, living in exile across
the river, had failed to shake my position. Now indeed they were
cringing before me, and I? Well, I was letting bygones be bygones.
Sometimes I even went to the extreme of generosity by furnishing
them with the news I had cabled the day before! Some of the local
papers spoke of my continued presence in Belgrade as one of the
more encouraging signs of the times, and I was several times referred to in editorials as a sympathetic colleague.

But from the American viewpoint, and I always clung tenaciously
to that, affairs in the Balkans were growing dull and, of course, we
from across the Atlantic were only interested in Balkan fireworks.
Every morning I expected to receive from the Commodore one of
his long telegrams, or one of his short letters, telling me to move
on to some more exciting front of world news, when suddenly out
of a clear sky there thundered the bolt which inaugurated the first

skirmish of the Balkan Pig War which, as all economists know, was the prelude to the great disaster of 1914–18.

How it happened was not clear then, and it is not much clearer now—and much less important. Perhaps, as rumored, the Austrian agents discovered that M. Hitrovo, the Russian Minister, was smuggling into the country by the way of Semendria hand grenades and bombs, indeed anything in the way of a weapon in any way suitable to block the progress of Felix Austria across Macedonia or Albania to the sea and so to strengthen the barricade the Pan-Slavs sought to erect against the German *Drang nach Osten*. Austria sulked and Berlin growled, but better than that someone in Vienna or in Budapest put on his thinking cap to good purpose. Who it was I have no idea. The clever Andrássy, who would have been immediately suspected, was dead, but whoever he may have been this great anonymous conceived a plan of economic boycott which brought Serbia low in a few days and perhaps laid the fuse for the terrible conflagration in the years to come.

This fulmination took the commonplace form of a telegram from Vienna to the effect that hog cholera having been discovered in many Serbian pigsties, no more Serbian pigs would be admitted into the Dual Monarchy. People who now, as then, are ignorant of the intimate relation between a prosperous budget and pigs in Serbia will hardly appreciate the force of this stroke. "How is that?" they inquired, "with all the pigs penned up at home, food, or at least pork, must have been plentiful and cheap—and certainly no fear of starvation."

But the people who indulge in such remarks merely show their ignorance of the idiosyncrasies of the Serbian pig. The pig in Serbia is not eatable. Upon his native heath he is wonderfully prolific, but still only skin and bone and bristles. The pigs are driven up to Belgrade from their inland swamps, lean as greyhounds and hungry as wolves. But once across the river in the green pastures of Hungary they fatten rapidly and are highly prized in the European markets. With Hungary closed, its lush fields embargoed, a tantalizing dream and yet one you could plainly see across the river with an ordinary field glass, there was nothing for the Serbian pigs and the Serbian swineherds to do but starve.

Perhaps I was incautious at this juncture. Frankly, as I have admitted, I was taken by surprise, and perhaps I did not appreciate the far-reaching consequences to myself as well as to Serbia of this new economic policy. But a man, certainly not a newspaper correspondent, cannot hold his tongue forever, and besides I recognized that the popularity in which I basked at the moment was not a permanent asset. I felt I must keep bidding for it and consolidating it all the time. So I bid. "That is not diplomacy," I said for publication. " 'Tis a disloyal stroke—a blow beneath the belt." And the next morning the *Male Novine*, the greatest of the Belgrade papers, hailed me as an outstanding friend of Serbia and a protector of the pigs.

Three days passed and the press of pigs in the Belgrade streets was so great that one found a place to put one's feet with difficulty. On the evening of the fourth day a famished drove broke into the restaurant of the Red Dog Tavern and ravenously devoured the crumbs that had fallen from our round table. Raskelvich, the Chief of Police, did what he could to protect me, as often before. But prestige, or even a Browning, are not effective weapons against famishing pigs. Raskelvich was a good friend of mine who had worked in an American packing establishment where he had acquired a taste for our dime novels. This taste of his I pandered to by securing for him copies of the *White Savage,* the *Wild Man of the West,* and above all, *Jack Harkaway in Search of a Mountain of Gold.* So that night Raskelvich sat late with me over his plum brandy, reflecting on and discussing the parlous state of the kingdom and how the white-coated, white-livered Austrians could be bested.

Suddenly an inspiration came to him. "You can do all kinds of things with pigs in America. In Chicago, I know, they put a pig in one end of a pipe and presto! he comes out at the other divided into a dozen neatly wrapped parcels. You lose nothing but the squeal."

Here I had my first inkling of what was coming—a presentiment of how near I—who had so long escaped the shoals and the whirlpools of Belgrade waters—was to shipwreck. Yet could I, merely to safeguard my personal position, forswear one of the most envied garlands in our commercial crown?

"Yes, they can do a lot with a pig in Chicago," I admitted. I was about to add—and self-preservation being the second if not the first law of nature it seemed only fair that I should—that we could, because of the tariff, only work these wonders with native-born pigs; but Raskelvich was gone with a ray of intelligence in his eyes which I could not ascribe wholly to the plum brandy.

The next morning, as I had anticipated, I was summoned to the Presidency. There sat Belomarcovich and the man who had taken the place of the late Protich. This substitute looked upon me with evident ill-will. When the vacancy occurred, the surviving Regents, who were very friendly and even deferential to me at this time, asked my opinion how to fill it and I had suggested Pashitch. They thought the man who had often eaten the bread of exile with me in Philippopolis and in Tsaribrod a bit too radical, and the clever fellow who in later years became the perennial Prime Minister was turned down. All I had really said was that often the wisest way to handle a radical was to draft him into a conservative administration and then he would probably hold his tongue; but these wise words had been distorted and the man who got the place, as I have said, on this notable occasion regarded me with ill-concealed dislike. However, Belomarcovich was, as usual, charming, and he "after compliments" got down to business even before I had eaten the customary sweet.

"You cannot ignore," he began, "the deplorable condition of the pig market, the principal product of our country, and our money crop?" I admitted that I was well aware that the pig market was—ahem—a little congested and then, foolishly enough, went on to say that with the greatest difficulty we had succeeded in keeping several droves of them out of the Red Dog Tavern on the previous evening. The man who had taken the place of Protich frowned at this and I was, or at least should have been, warned of his hostility. But, smiling amiably, Belomarcovich continued.

"You, Sir, as we all know, are an important man in your happy country. There are thousands there who hang upon your words."

Of course, I made a deprecating gesture such as modesty demanded, but the ranking Regent went on with a eulogy which, dared I recall it, would excite ribald laughter among even my friends—and how my enemies would enjoy it.

"As such, and in appreciation of your position, you have been received and honored by all those who move in court circles and also by the lowly. And therefore we frankly put our problem up to you, for you, and perhaps you alone, can save Serbia from bankruptcy, her people from starvation and Europe from the outbreak of war." Then he snatched up pen and paper and began to figure out the situation. The result he achieved was then communicated to me—in fact, to all of us, and I should add that at this time Raskelvich joined the group with an enigmatic smile upon his face. Well, the conclusion of the figuring was about this: With pigs selling in Belgrade—or as perhaps I should put it with pigs to be bought in Belgrade, for six cents apiece, there would be a handsome profit in importing them and distributing the bacon on the American market.

"Indeed," interrupted the new and junior Regent who so evidently did not like me, "you could send them first-class by the Cunard steamers from Trieste or Fiume and yet so dear is swine flesh in your country there would still be a handsome profit for the importers."

"True," I assented, "but there are difficulties. How could we get the pigs to the port of shipment? There stands the Dual Monarchy like a stone wall. They might not even let the pigs pass in bond and, of course, they would refuse to admit to bondage pigs of which it has been said, most falsely, I know, that they are tainted with hog cholera. Mine is a commercial not a warlike people. We don't want any trouble with the Austrians, and this is particularly true of our pork-packers because the Austrians are among their best customers."

"Fortunately, we can and shall avoid all those complications," asserted Belomarcovich, "although, I must say, in my judgment you magnify them somewhat. We'll raft the pigs down the Danube to the Black Sea. Thank God and Prince Michael, the Danube is an international river. Once on the Black Sea you can pick up the pigs with your cattle boats and shoot them to Chicago. It's easy." "It's easy," chimed in that devil Raskelvich with a wicked smile.

Strange as it may seem, at this time I did not know a single pork-packer in Chicago, or anywhere else for that matter, even by name, but I did know a Chicago grainman, the Caius Metellus of our day, the same who by his partisan contribution had made of me such a favorite in the Boulanger camp two years before. Surely he would have close relations with the pork-packers so I cabled him a statement of the situation in which I had become involved, and as I prepaid the answer I expected an early reply, but the eighth, ninth, and then even the tenth day of the Pig War came and went and still no answer. The explanation I made to Raskelvich, as sulky and alone, he sipped his plum brandy in a corner of the tavern, that perhaps the wires were down, was received in unbelieving silence.*

And then the unfriendly campaign in the press began. It opened with a squib in the *Male Novine* which read, "There was a man named Bonsaloff with the Bulgarian army at Slivnitza and Pirot. He glorified our enemies—was violently anti-Serbian. He claimed to be an American, but he came from the Ukraine."

"They are going to put you on the skids," commented the wise McClure. "You had better reserve a room in Zemlin. It's rather crowded, you know, with your colleagues."

On the following day, the disreputable but influential organ opened with heavy artillery. This announcement read, "Last year in Budapest at a Pan-Turanian banquet, to the delight of the Magyars, a certain alleged American, well-known here, truckled to our hereditary enemies by reciting Petöfi's infamous ballad calling upon the Huns to throw themselves upon the Slav world."

There was in this statement that mixture of truth and fiction which is so dangerous and often indeed convincing. There seemed nothing left for me to do but to pack up. Of course I had wanted to leave Belgrade, but certainly not in this way.

And then, almost miraculously, the atmosphere cleared, and I was in a position to snap my fingers at the Regents and my other false friends. Silvano, an Italian porter on the Orient Express with

* Later it developed that my good friend was in China. S.B.

whom I had long enjoyed confidential relations, slipped into the tavern and presented me with a magazine which he assured me I would find interesting reading. And indeed I did. Tucked away between the covers was a telegram from the Commodore ordering me to Vienna as fast as I could get there. I was half-packed already, but now in a triumphant mood I continued the operation. It was clear I could get away next day on the noon train. . . .

I can hardly blame my colleagues in exile at Zemlin for their misunderstanding of the situation that had so suddenly developed. Of course, in sending the news to western Europe that at last I had been toppled from the pinnacle of favor I had so long enjoyed, and other misinformation, they were simply running, and wiring, true to form. Indeed, even in Belgrade in high circles these absurd rumors were credited. While I was still packing my bags the adjutant of the King (that is of the ex-King Milan), sneaked into the Red Dog Tavern by the back door and I must add the cowardly fellow was in uncompromising mufti. "His Majesty charges me to say that his affectionate good wishes go with you. He knows you will understand that it was only because of those overdrafts he could not interfere." I was in a hurry so I simply thanked the adjutant and then added somewhat cynically, "Of course, I understand. Sooner or later overdrafts have to be met."

The incognito which marked the visit of the King's messenger was successful and so this timid gesture of friendship escaped the attention of my long-envious but now jubilant colleagues in Zemlin, but I must admit there were other circumstances attending my departure which lent a certain color of plausibility to their version of the event to which they gave the widest publicity in western Europe. At the station did appear both Raskelvich, the Police Chief, though in fatigue dress, and McClure, the Scot, who was substituting at our fee consulate where to his sorrow no fees came in. McClure presented himself in rather formal attire.

Naturally enough these, as always, ill-informed correspondents, felt justified, with these facts to go on, to announce that Raskelvich was there to see that I should not evade the expulsion order of the Regents, and they had the audacity to add "as I had so often before." The presence of McClure they chose to interpret in an equally unfriendly way. They asserted that while, of course, the Consul was convinced of the justice of the edict that sent me into exile, still he came to defend me against the indignation of the populace, righteous as this was, as the Consul well knew, in view of the articles that I had written—so misleading as to the actual situation in the kingdom. Reluctant as the Consul was to become mixed up in the matter, and while he made no secret of where his sympathies lay, still his sense of duty had brought him to the station to see that such rights and privileges as an American citizen I had not forfeited, were safeguarded by his presence.

Of course I did not condescend to answer the ravings of these fellows. It would have been but a waste of my valuable time, and indeed I regarded the abuse they heaped upon my head as the inevitable reward of anyone who pursued higher politics in the Balkans in the conscientious way that had always characterized my activities. But today I see no reason why I should not reveal the real purpose of these gentlemen as they came to salute me at the moment when I hoped that I was saying goodbye to Belgrade forever. Raskelvich came to beg, indeed to beseech me not to allow anything to interfere in the future with the flow of dime novels with which for so long I had been furnishing him. He admitted this had become his necessary mental pabulum. I gave him my solemn promise to continue these favors and I kept it, too, as far as my vagrant career permitted. I could not have done this, of course, had Raskelvich been a party to my mythical expulsion. As a matter of fact, I harbored no ill-feeling against him and should not have done so even had the blessed letter of release from Mr. Bennett not come and things gone on to what seemed, only twenty-four hours before, to be the logical conclusion. In this case I was enough of a philosopher to recognize that we would both have been the helpless victims of an economic revolution. I personally have been inclined to think, when similar disaster has overtaken me in other parts of the world, that it was the appearance of spots in the glorious orb that should give light to all, but doesn't, that was responsible, and not the machinations of mere men.

And McClure? Well, he was there because he was my faithful friend and then he was completely possessed by a financial project which he wished to lay before me. He was confident that if I could only get the right people interested it would make me immensely rich and also furnish him with the funds necessary to effect his escape from Serbia which was his ardent wish.

"The fact that pigs are a drug on the market today in Belgrade," he explained, "should not blind us to the fact that the market furnishes other short-cuts to fortune. For instance, look at kids. They practically have no value at all. Have you not heard them bleating in shame and despair over by Bulova and Krushevatz the live-long day?" Indeed I had noticed their complaints though the kids were not so intrusive as the pigs. And so I listened patiently to McClure's get-rich-quick scheme as I have to many another, to the plan for a salmon cannery on the banks of the Amoor, so dear to the hearts of the Cossacks in that lonely stanitza, to the opportunity which the Paraguayans on the banks of the Paraná gave me to become the maté millionaire. But I did not have the Midas touch, and fortunately knew it.

"Just as soon as you reach civilization," was McClure's plan, "get in touch with a glover. I mean, of course, a large-scale manufacturer of gloves. With a thousand dollars in hand I can control the kid market here which is capable of expansion—if necessary. I will draw up iron-clad contracts and not a single kid shall escape us. All the goats, billies as well as nannies, will be working for us and our fortune will be assured, and further, and this is most desirable, kid gloves will be within the reach of the underprivileged— which is not the case today."

I thanked McClure for letting me in on this Pactolian project and promised to lay the matter before the next glover I came across. I mean, of course, a glove man on a large scale, but as such a one never presented himself I never did. So far as I know the field is still open to pioneers who may wish to try their luck in foreign fields. As for myself, I can only list it as another one of the golden opportunities which came my way and which I missed because— well, because I was predestined to the pursuit of higher politics for all time, from its enticing beginning to the ragged out-at-the-elbow end.

Other and not a few less compromising friends were on hand at this trying moment and we had a stirrup cup, in fact several of them, in the dining car as the train was shunted about and the wheels well greased before it began the run in the blessed westerly direction.

"*Shogum! Shogum!* Go with God and may He accompany you," was the heartfelt prayer of this faithful group. Of all save Pope Gregori, the sophisticated chaplain of Milan, who had accompanied the ex-King on many European tours and seen things. Hearing these pious wishes he raised his arms in holy horror and shouted in his great bass voice, "No! A thousand times no! Wishing our friend Stefan Stefanovich a pleasant journey is one thing, but calling upon God to accompany him is quite another. Dullards and swineherds; have you forgotten that Stefan Stefanovich is going to Paris?" And in a moment I was gone—but as a matter of fact I did not know where I was going—I only knew that definite instructions were awaiting me in Vienna at the Imperial Hotel.

As is often the case when you return to a place of happy memories, the few days I now spent in Vienna were disappointing. I was hungry for human conversation; I wanted to hear words that had no bearing whatsoever upon South-Slav problems. But it was Sunday when I arrived and most of my friends had gone up to the Semmering or were sojourning at Baden or somewhere under the trees of the Wiener-wald. In our corner of the Imperial Café I came upon Theodore Herzl and he was friendly and charming as always. But he was very busy; with muddy ink and sputtering pen, all that the café afforded, he was driving along upon his weekly feuilleton for the *Neue Freie Presse*. Perhaps he was working on that epoch-making and possibly war-breeding article in which for the first time he outlined his dream of the Zionist State, a national home for the Jews in Palestine.

I have another memory of those days in Vienna which, though it seemed trivial at the time, has grown in importance with the passing of the years. It comes back to me very clearly whenever I have heard the cannon roar and failed to locate the responsible battery—and heaven only knows how often that has happened. It is my recollection of a Legation dinner that was not boring and where the conversation was not banal. That would mark it as epoch-making in diplomatic circles, but it was even more remarkable than that. Our Minister at the time was Colonel Fred Grant, a son of the Great Commander whom I was to know better years later in the Philippines where he commanded a division. Here in Vienna he had nothing to do and did it very well, and he was ably supported by his gracious lady who had both tact and brains. The dinner was a small affair, half a dozen members of the corps and a Prince Schwarzenberg, the descendant of the sluggish Austrian General whose tactics Bonaparte found so amusing in the Napoleonic Wars. Another guest, obviously a misfit, although he did not seem to know it, was introduced as Mr. Hiram Maxim from Maine. "A remarkable inventor," whispered Mrs. Grant to me.

I came to the conclusion that Maxim must be the inventor of the machine gun in which so much interest and so much ignorance was being displayed in the military journals. He was a tall, powerfully built man with a ruddy complexion and a great upstanding shock of iron-gray hair. His expression was kindly, his eyes friendly —almost meek. It was hard to believe that such a benevolent figure had produced the new and terrible instrument of warfare. He was silent for a long time, but when he began to talk he monopolized the attention of all.

"I was a barefoot boy in Maine," he said, "and I hoped to become a tinker. That is, I was always tinkering with pots and pans and thought that some day I could make a living by mending them for the housewives of our village. Then suddenly an idea came to me. I saw I had hit upon something that seemed important, at least to me. It was a mechanical device which once attached to the sewing machine would save the seamstress all her tiresome treadling. But it didn't go at all. No one seemed to want to relieve the sewing mothers from their treadmill, and so I adjusted my device to a gun and people began to take notice. With this device attached to his rifle a soldier can continue firing incessantly. He will not have to lift a finger. He will only have to keep his finger on the trigger and his fusillade will continue indefinitely or as long as his ammunition lasts."

We all expressed interest in this new and terrible weapon—all except the Schwarzenberg Prince. He registered dissent by saying

that nothing mechanical would displace the regularity and the reliability of the trained soldier, at least not if he had been trained
in the school of the late Archduke Charles. The inventor smiled
courteously. "Perhaps you are right—only time will tell." And
then, after a pause, "But I have in my pocket something that will
change the whole aspect of warfare, indeed revolutionize it." We
sat up at this—even the Schwarzenberg Prince opened wide his
sleepy eyes. And as he began to talk Maxim turned deferentially
to the grandson of the man who was great, at least in the number
of troops he trained in the wrong way.

"Do you officers of the army not say 'A battery discovered is a
battery destroyed?'" The Prince nodded assent and the inventor
went on, "Well, with my new powder, maximite I call it, it will
be almost impossible to locate a battery. It is smokeless. Battalions
will be mowed down and black powder guns in battery will be dismounted and no one will be able to say from whence the destructive fire comes." All expressed interest and while he tried to conceal it even the Prince betrayed a certain amount of curiosity, so
Maxim bowing to our hostess said, "If you will let me have a deep
plate—but not a valuable one—I will show you how it works."

The deep plate was forthcoming and Maxim produced an envelope from which he poured a gray powder. He lit it with a match
and it burnt for several minutes with a clear bright flame until
the powder was consumed without even a wisp of smoke arising
from the fire.

It developed in the following days that the inventor was in
Austria to push his new-style munitions which he had just patented,
but he was getting nowhere. The vested interests in black powder
were up in arms and then his Old Testament name of Hiram was
a heavy handicap to a fair consideration of his remarkable discovery.
At the War Office Hiram Maxim was ticketed as a Jew and that
was that. On the following day, at the suggestion of Colonel Grant,
I called at the Ministry and told my friends there that far from
being Semitic, Hiram Maxim was of straight Aryan descent, although I did not then misuse that term as we do so frequently
today.

Nevertheless the school of Schwarzenberg and the ideas of the late Archduke Charles prevailed, and in Vienna the American inventor was rebuffed. He soon went to England and there maximite was quickly appreciated. The inventions of the kindly old man from Maine, and those that have followed upon them, ushered in a new era of carnage in comparison with which the wars of the Middle Ages were milk and water affairs. The smokeless powder and the concealed batteries helped to extend the rule of Britain in many lands and over many savage peoples who were brought to heel. And in the end the tinker from Maine grew immensely wealthy and King Edward raised him to knighthood!

In those last hectic days in Belgrade there came to me the sad news of the death of my dear friend P.G. . . . and his passing requires more than perfunctory notice because of his charming personality and also because he was, it seems to me, the last of the old-school correspondents. As the typos tell me that initials followed by the dotted lines disfigure the printed page, I shall now speak of him as Peter Grant although that was not his name as the few who enjoyed his friendship and still survive, will recall. There it stood in black and white, a little item in the old *London Standard*, at that time the English paper of largest circulation in the Balkans and, as a matter of fact, in Europe generally. It read, "We regret to announce the death of Mr. Peter Grant, an American gentleman of independent means. It occurred last evening in Brighton at the Queen's private hotel after a paroxysm of coughing. Mr. Grant was a great traveler and was leaving in a few days for Asia Minor on holiday."

Some eighteen months before, Peter had been sent to Russia by the *Herald* to interview Tschaikowsky, and according to some accounts he had made quite a mess of it. The music editor said that Peter had gotten the Sleeping Beauty Waltz and the famous Scherzo, *presto ma non assai,* all mixed up. I do not know the truth about this because the Commodore dropped the article into his capacious wastepaper basket and sacked the unfortunate writer by wire. Peter went to London to work with Labouchère and write pungent paragraphs for *Truth,* then in the zenith of its power and renown. But the racking cough he had brought back from Russia bore him down and soon Peter became a charge on the men of the London Bureau and upon those of us who were willing to contribute something weekly to defray his expenses at a little hotel in Brighton where the doctor had ordered him. The report of this medico was far from encouraging. It read: "One of his lungs is gone. He may last six months and he may go off suddenly."

The London staff and the rest of us stood up fairly well under this burden for four or five months, and then there began to appear unmistakable signs of restiveness among the contributors. Certain friends and distant kinsfolk of Peter in Philadelphia were apprised of the situation, but, while sympathetic, owing to recent financial reverses one and all protested they were unable to help out. At this time the Commodore was cruising off Anatolian shores and it was surmised by the men in London that after taking his friends to visit the "ringing plains of windy Troy" he would stop at some Dalmatian port and order me to report to him there, as he frequently did when he came anywhere near my territory.

This surmise, very unwelcome to me, proved to be correct, and the men in London now served a pretty stiff memorandum upon me. I was called upon in no uncertain words to place the Peter Grant situation frankly before the Commodore. Hal had taken to himself a new wife—and she was thrifty. Jack had a new mistress and she was most extravagant. As far as they were concerned, there was an end to the subsidies and they insisted that I should appeal, as they put it, "to the Commodore's better nature." In due season the expected instructions came and once again I hastened across the wildest sections of the Balkan countries, at times on horseback and then again in the springless carriage called a *paitan*, but I was fortunate and made good time which permitted me two days of rest in Cettinje, the eagle nest of the Montenegrins. On the morning of the second day Prince Nikita, that charming old buccaneer of the Black Mountain country, waited upon me, supported by his stalwart henchmen, and asked me to sit with him upon his "bed of Justice" outside his lilliputian palace and watch him as like Ulysses of old he dealt "unequal laws unto a savage race." And he did it very fairly, it seemed to me, and certainly in the patriarchal manner. I little thought then I should, twenty-nine years later, see the handsome old man as a suppliant in Paris before the world "bed of Justice" and hear his sentence of deposition, a very unfair one I have always thought. That afternoon I coasted down the steep descent to the Bocche di Cattaro and an hour later the *Namouna* steamed into the picturesque port.

But for the unpleasant task that my colleagues, and also my conscience, imposed upon me, I would at this time, as always, have enjoyed my stay on the yacht. The Commodore was busy with a number of things, including particularly the electric mechanism with which the cows that always sailed with him were milked, so for several days I did not find an opening for the plea that sooner or later I would have to make. In all conscience indeed I was forced to concede that my dear friend did not have a very strong claim on the Commodore's bounty, but on the other hand, I argued, so many people without better claims, and indeed many with no claim at all, were living more or less comfortably upon him, why should I not slip Peter into the company of these countless pensioners? And then, as the doctor indicated, it would not be for long.

After a short stay in Ragusa and an amusing visit to the white monks of the island of Lacroma, who were also pensioners (and these were grateful ones—even in his life time they erected a memorial in marble to their American patron), I thought I had found the Commodore in a mellow moment and so began my sad story, but evidently I was woefully mistaken. He stopped me before I had finished my plea with the round statement, "I owe that man nothing, *bien au contraire,* and I want you and the men in the London Bureau to understand once and for all that the *Herald* is no poorhouse."

From Trieste, where I was landed with no particular honors, I sent on to the men in London my discouraging report, and then tried to forget the distressing matter and had, I have no doubt, succeeded in doing so when about a month later an answering letter from London overtook me in Salonica. It reported, "Miracle, but perfectly good money has come to Peter from somewhere and where it comes from we do not care as long as it keeps coming," and then a few days later a charming grateful letter from the dear old boy himself. He thanked me for all I had tried to do and then went on to say, "My friends in Philadelphia are having

quite a run of luck and they have kindly arranged a weekly re-
mittance of ten pounds which, of course, I shall repay very soon—
the moment I am in the saddle again." How the miracle money
was minted Peter was never to know and I was only to learn its
mechanism many months later, as in due season I shall relate.

17. VON MOLTKE
AND THE MEN OF MARX

THE INSTRUCTIONS that I picked up in Vienna were more definite than any I had ever received from the Commodore, and strange to relate they were typed on one of the new-fangled writing machines which at the time were banned from the editorial rooms of the *Herald*. Although drawn up by an alien hand the instructions were plastered over by remarks and commands in French (so I knew he was interested!) scrawled by the Commodore himself with the famous blue pencil. I read them and re-read them, time and again, as I rolled along the road that was to become so familiar in later years, the road to Berlin by the way of beautiful Prague. "*Vous, mettez vous en campagne,*" he adjured me. "Go underground if necessary. Saturate yourself with all possible information as to the purpose and the goal of the Social-Democratic party. Ascertain what the development of this movement means for the Empire, the Emperor and the dynasty.

"Germany is the greatest field for news in the world today," he continued. "The growth of the Social-Democratic party is a portent and it may well become a great power for good or evil. Get at the bottom of this new movement. Go underground, live with the leaders, and when you are ready, send your reports to me personally and not to the paper. Not a word to any of your associates as to your whereabouts. On this occasion you must be, as a special correspondent always should be, half-detective and half-diplomat."

I had fortunately met Liebknecht in America and he made easy the first steps of my mission. He brought me into contact with the great Bebel and Singer and with many of the other leaders whose names I have forgotten. I was admitted to their meetings, public as well as private, and, as far as I could see, my investigation of their activities was warmly welcomed.

At this time Liebknecht was chief editor of *Vorwärts*, the party organ. After many years in prison and in exile, upon the fall of Bismarck he had returned a few weeks before to Berlin as the anointed of the Master, the prophet of Marx. He was also a staunch admirer of Mazzini with whom he had become very intimate during their long years of joint exile in Geneva and London.

I have a vivid recollection of an afternoon when we were closeted in the editorial sanctum talking about the things that were to come. An eager-faced boy of sixteen came in. He wore heavy boots and his school books were strapped on his back. The tired editor ran his fingers through the boy's fair hair and then presented him to me. It was his son, Karl, for whom a sad fate was reserved. Grown to manhood in 1914 the boy headed the small group in the Reichstag that voted against the war credits. He formed the Spartacus party, advocated the free Socialist Republic in the last months of the war, and in January 1919, on his way to prison was brutally murdered with Rosa Luxemburg—their bodies were thrown into the canal.*

At my first meeting with Bebel, as indeed many times afterwards, the leader pointed out that Socialism was an old, old story in Germany. "It is born in the blood and bred in the bone of the old Germanen," was an expression he was fond of repeating. "Our party program is but a modern manifestation of our old creed." For the sake of brevity in his historical sketch of the background of the movement, he would only go back to the Peasant Wars of the sixteenth century and then he would hasten on to the yesterday of Lassalle.

"Nothing that Lassalle ever said or wrote, urged, or even contemplated, implied revolution," he asserted. "Lasalle was simply

* When I was in Berlin, after the Great War, in September 1919 I often heard the "comrades" in the *kneipen* of the Moabit quarter intoning their dolorous chant, *"Es liegt eine Leiche in dem Landwehr Kanal."* ("There floats a corpse in the Landwehr Canal.") When I came back in 1925 the singers, too, had been done to death or driven underground by Noske and his men, who doubtless had not the remotest idea that they were making the way smooth for Hitler!

a state socialist and, as you know, while later he broke with him, for a time Bismarck was quite enamored of his simple schemes. Had they been put in force they would have gotten us nowhere, but in another sense his agitation was valuable because he awakened in the people of Germany a keen appreciation of their wrongs. So in a way it is proper to regard Lassalle as the accelerator of our awakening movement, although undoubtedly he would not approve many of its developments. Fichte, like so many others, helped better than he knew, and I have decided that his wonderful sentence shall be emblazoned on the banner which will fly over the first permitted meeting of our party for many decades, which will assemble in Halle next month. It reads, 'No one should be permitted to enjoy superfluities whilst many lack the necessities of life.' "

The situation which caught and held the Commodore's attention at this time was an interesting one, although at this late day it would be futile to go into all its details. Bismarck and the then young Emperor had views on foreign policy which clashed, particularly with regard to relations with Russia and the secret reinsurance treaty with the Tsar. But openly, at least, the break came over the proposed social legislation and the repeal of the repressive laws designed to hamper the socialistic agitation. The Emperor was undoubtedly persuaded by his new advisers that the movement that had flourished under persecution would languish, if not die out entirely, when given a free rein.

Certainly, under the so-called laws of repression, the Social-Democrats had won a large number of seats in the Reichstag, and here they enjoyed an open forum and could not be silenced as they had been on the street corners and in the *kneipen*. Bismarck was so closely identified with the repressive laws that had failed of their purpose that in abrogating them the Emperor doubtless had the secondary purpose at least of smashing the Bismarck legend of wisdom and omnipotence. The "New Course" was decried by the bankers and the industrial magnates and, of course, most roundly abused by the Junker land-owning class who, as never before, now came to the support of Bismarck or rather to uphold his policies. On the other hand the "New Course" received the approval of classes that had hitherto been somewhat lukewarm to the throne.

And of course, while still, and not without reason, suspicious of their new friends, the Social-Democrats were loud in praise of Von Caprivi, the new Chancellor, although he too belonged to the hated militaristic class. Indeed at a meeting held in Brunswick, at this time, even the hitherto unreconcilable Liebknecht went so far in welcoming the "New Course" as to say that the projects and plans of the Emperor enjoyed the unqualified approval of one million and a half Socialist voters. At the time, Bebel told me that he endorsed this statement but was convinced that the figure of the voters mentioned was a gross underestimate. In about a month I made a preliminary report on the situation in which I hazarded the belief, and it was by no means venturesome, that there was no immediate danger to the dynasty from the movement. What the Commodore did with my report I do not know with any certainty, but I did hear later that through his good friend, Prince Max Fürstenberg, it found its way back to Berlin, and for all I know to the contrary into the hands of the All-Highest.

Bennett made several favorable comments on the report, and told me to cover the news from Berlin, not the routine news but every now and then to emphasize a feature, but under no circumstances to allow these new duties to interfere with the paramount purpose of my stay in Germany, which was to live with and to keep in closest touch and understanding with the leaders of the Social-Democratic movement. In view of these instructions I assumed that the veil of secrecy had been removed from my mission, and that I would soon hear from the business office and that the weekly remittances, long interrupted, would be resumed.

All these new contacts were very interesting, or should have been, but I found my mind wandering to other fields. I could not keep my eyes on the rolling ball, and that, I knew, was a dangerous situation for a special correspondent to find himself in. Certainly I was not keen for a prolonged stay in Berlin. I had been there before and my experience had confirmed the statement that the great de Blowitz once made to me. "In Paris," he said, "even the fish talk, but in Berlin the parrots hold their tongues," and, of course, talk and sometimes even twaddle is the very life-blood of special correspondence.

Of course, I was not severely critical of the frame of mind in which I found myself. It was, to me, at least, comprehensible, and there were attenuating circumstances. My *wanderjahre* had lasted longer than I or anyone else had anticipated. I was entering upon the fourth year of my absence from the "Right Bank of the Susquehanna" where increasingly often I longed to be. How to get home was my problem. Of course, I had only to be caught napping in some emergency or to infringe upon one of the Commodore's unwritten and somewhat capricious orders, and then I could count upon getting my walking papers by cable.

But truth to tell this was not what I wanted; my problem was more complicated. I wanted to go home, but in circumstances that would make my recall in a very few months to one of the world's exciting fronts a foregone conclusion. To the solution of the problem I devoted much thought and many hours of plotting which, as the sequel soon demonstrated, I might well have spared myself. Sharply the good-luck gods who had showered so many undeserved favors upon me were turning against me. In the immediate future I was to take the direction I wanted to go, but I was not to go in triumph and, as it seemed, irrevocably the favor of our extravagant "money boss" as Stanley called him, the lynx-eyed Argus of Paris who moved us about as his pawns in the world game, was to be withdrawn.

The hardships as well as the sensational surprises of life in southeastern Europe had begun to pall. For one thing, I was only twenty-four, I wanted to wear a well-fitting suit of clothes again, and I had lost my taste for Macedonian tobacco. How was I to manage my recall? That was the rub. It was well known to all of us that in the eyes of Mr. Bennett the unpardonable offense was to get wounded at the front. "I have spent ten thousand dollars putting you in a place of vantage, and all you make out of it is to stop a bullet," is the legendary cable he was reported to have sent to some luckless wight who was wounded in the first skirmish of the war he had been sent to describe. Only second to this offense was the development of homesickness which the Commodore, however, called "growing stale." Unless you were captivated by life in Philippopolis or Teheran and neighed with joy over your unexpected transfer to Asia Minor, the dancing girls of Basra, and all that sort of thing, you were "getting stale." In the eyes of Mr. Bennett you had outlived your usefulness and you had better get off the paper, or of a certainty you would be put off in short order.

While alert to the possibilities of my position and not blind to the dangers of the plans that I secretly cherished, these last weeks in Berlin were filled with contrasting experiences which are the very spice of a correspondent's life. Never had my duties served up such a mixed dish of pickles as on this occasion. As ordered, I went underground with the leaders of the Social-Democratic party, who were to transform Germany for a season, but who soon bobbed up again, as under Chancellor Caprivi their activities became open and aboveboard. I hobnobbed with Bebel and Liebknecht at Halle where the first International Congress of working men proclaimed the Marxist doctrine in the light of day. I sat at the feet of Field-Marshal Helmuth Von Moltke and so became fairly familiar with the views of a War Lord of the old school. Most interesting and certainly more valuable for the future was my contact with Dr. Koch, that prince of science who, notwithstanding his aversion to what he called with a curl of the lip *"die politische Presse,"* did what he could do make plain to me both the scope and the limitations of his great tuberculine discovery. Viewing the havoc which so often strews the path of the "special," I today experience not a little satisfaction from the fact that to Dr. Koch, at least, I was of service, and through him to the suffering world. But now I will pick up again the thread of my story.

While the apostles of the new era were straining every nerve and sparing no effort to avail themselves of the liberty of speech and freedom of action which had been so long denied them, it should not be thought for a moment that the "old guard" had surrendered. Thousands and indeed millions of Germans were looking backwards and, intent upon recalling the glories of yesterday, were preparing a spectacle which was certainly the most notable that took place in the Fatherland for many decades. While Bebel and his followers talked of the brotherhood of man and sought to present to the astonished gaze of their fellow countrymen the vision of universal peace and world brotherhood, the beat of the drum was heard even more loudly than usual throughout the Fatherland, and in the barracks there was bustle and stir. In sober Berlin from morning until night men were raising scaffoldings and decorating public and private buildings. Old soldiers, the veterans of what was then the "great War," were everywhere stringing many-colored lanterns upon public buildings and young girls were preparing to cover that grim granite pile which is the Brandenburg Gate with the hero's crown of laurels. This was happening about the middle of October 1890, and the city and all the people of the land were getting ready to give Field-Marshal Von Moltke a royal welcome when he came to spend his ninetieth birthday with his pupil, the German Emperor, the King of Prussia.

As my "life underground" had become merely a figure of the Harun al-Rashid speech in which my chief delighted, I was fortunate at this time to meet at our Legation, as it was then,* the Countess Waldersee, an American girl from New York who after the unusual experience, in those days at least, of being the wife of one of the Hessian Princes, was happily married to General Count Waldersee, who a few months before had succeeded Von Moltke, the man of the hour, in the onerous duties of Chief of Staff of the Imperial armies. We talked, of course, of the great man. Everyone, great and small alike, was bringing his nosegay in the hope that it might be entwined in some way with the tribute of a people who loved war and had no thought of disarming. With the regret that I expressed, because in my visits to Berlin I had only caught the most hasty and unsatisfactory glimpses of the Prussian Paladin, the Countess was sympathetic. Once in my student days I had indeed ventured to follow him as he dropped into the shabby little *wein-stube* near the gorgeous Café Bauer where over a glass of wine he was accustomed to meet some of his cronies of the never-to-be-forgotten war, and talk over the battles that were so fresh in their memories. And unforgettable indeed was the fugitive glance I had had of the tall spare figure of the Great Commander as in 1888 he followed his Imperial Master out of the city through the driving snow toward his last resting-place in the Charlottenburg mausoleum.

* It became an Embassy only many years later.

"Yes," prattled the Countess, "but that was a meager harvest indeed. A war correspondent could learn much from our Chief—if he would talk." And then, without thought and certainly without guile on my part, I took a line which proved most fortunate in the sequel.

"Even if the opportunity presented," I said, "I would not try to draw out the Great Commander upon the strategy of war, because these are things I know nothing about and would not understand." The Countess was evidently nonplussed so I went on to explain, "You see, unlike Forbes and your own Von Huhn of the Cologne *Gazette*, I have never been a soldier and know nothing about the technical side of war. I am sent to these scenes of slaughter because of the human interest they should inspire. I am sent to emphasize the pity of the thing, the waste, the futility of it."

"Unfortunately only in faraway America," interrupted the Countess, "can sane people dream of a world without war."

"I would like, however," I continued, "to talk to the Field-Marshal about the descriptive writings of his early years. His pictures of Turkey when he served the Sultan and kept his eyes open. His vivid letters from Russia when he witnessed the barbaric splendor with which Tsar Alexander the Second was crowned. I came across those rare volumes years ago in Constantinople and I carried them with me all through my Balkan travels. What limpid prose! Not a word too many, not a word that could be spared. What a correspondent your Great Commander would have made. It was a crime against literature when your Great War Staff drafted Von Moltke and then locked up all his writings in their secret archives."

The Countess laughed heartily and then suddenly became serious.

"Well, certainly, that is a new point of view. It should please him and then, the great *Schweiger*, the man who is silent in six languages, might talk."

"He ought to talk on his Jubilee," I suggested, "and that is only three weeks off. All the world would hang upon his words."

"When I see him I will tell the Field-Marshal what you have said. It would please him, I know, and he might relent—after holding his tongue for all the sixty years he has served the King.

You see, most of your colleagues want to talk to him about Alsace-Lorraine. What even the papers in America sometimes still speak of as the outstanding 'crime of the century.' " Laughing again, the Countess moved away, repeating my phrase which she found so droll, "Der Moltke, War correspondent." I laughed, too, and as I never heard from the Countess on the subject I concluded that she had given the matter no further thought, even less than I did, which was very little.

But a few days later, while I listened to the men of the future, to Bebel, Liebknecht, and to Guesde of France as, assembled in the great Congress of Socialists, gathered together from all over the world in Halle, they drew glowing pictures of the Marxian world that was to come, I decided, once the Congress adjourned, to make an attempt to see as "plain" as I could this great figure of a past upon which the curtain was being definitely drawn. I planned to run down to Silesia where the great warrior was awaiting the coming of his ninetieth birthday on the Creisau estate which had been presented to him by the German people. While they were far from hopeful of the outcome, the Wilhelmstrasse people gave me a letter which they thought might smooth my path. "In any case, keep the letter," said one of the assistant secretaries of the Foreign Office hopefully. "In the event that the police arrest you, it will prove that you are not an anarchist."

The people of the old university town, where the Congress assembled, or at least large numbers of them, were none too pleased that the ancient seat of learning, now being fast converted into a manufacturing center of importance, should have been chosen as the forum of the Marxists as they came up from underground. As I wandered about the narrow streets with the delegates, groups of long-haired men and a few short-haired women, I often overheard remarks that were far from complimentary to the visitors. There were several clashes in the shadow of the Red Tower and by the Handel statue, but as the police were vigilant, nothing very serious happened. Of course, *Die liebe Jugend* could not be prevented from holding their noses and shouting, "*Käfer* (cockroaches)," as the followers of the new gospel passed, and equally, of course, the delegates did not take this in silence but retaliated with a song which, as I remember, ran about in this way.

> *In Halle, In Halle*
> *Da gibts's so viel Jungfrauen*
> *Wie Wallfisch im Saale.*

Or, in plain prose, "There are just as many whales in the Saale river as there are virgins in Halle."

One of the important industries of Halle is or was the output of the brine springs. These are monopolized by Wendish workers who, wearing a strange medieval garb, often sat in the galleries listening intently to the proceedings and making their comments in Wendish or in a German which I could not understand.

The only really discordant voice that was heard during the Congress came from George Vollmar. Earnestly and very eloquently he sought a change of policy in party tactics. But it was more a matter of detail than a change in objective. He wanted the party to concentrate on possible things that were, he thought, quickly and easily attainable, and not to continue grasping for what was obviously beyond reach. He asked that the executive committee be empowered (1) to enlarge and broaden the scope of the laws protecting workers; (2) he demanded a complete recognition of the right of workers to organize; (3) he urged that the committee should insist upon the removal of all taxes and duties upon foodstuffs and the necessities of life; and concluded his impassioned speech with these words, "To those of good will I offer the hand of friendship, but to our irreconcilable enemies I present my clenched fist." And as he spoke he did so.

This was, of course, frank disapproval of the parliamentary activities of the party leaders, particularly of Bebel and Liebknecht. They were not slow in answering the outspoken rebel, but their words were conciliatory. They admitted that since the fall of Bismarck they, too, had anxiously scanned the horizon for signs of good will but had discovered few or none in the ruling classes; they further admitted that Chancellor Caprivi enforced the food taxes as drastically as had Bismarck and that the undoubted right of working men to organize, while conceded and even guaranteed by law, was hampered in every possible way. But they urged patience and asked that parliamentary agitation be not discarded until it had been fairly tried out.

Vollmar's criticism and the resolution in which it was embodied were voted down, a defeat which he took in good part, and at the Congress in Erfurt in the following year he expressed approval of the course pursued and was taken into the inner council again. While the debates that lasted five full days were lively, the conclusions reached were practically unanimous. The program drawn up by Auer, Bebel, and Liebknecht to replace the manifesto issued many years before at Gotha was ratified. And it was a party program based on Marxian principles—but sugar-coated.

During the week of the Congress when for the first time in several decades the Social-Democrats were basking in an atmosphere of legality, I saw much of both Bebel and Liebknecht, the Elder. They were an interesting pair and complemented each other in a remarkable manner. Liebknecht was a widely read man and, even at this time when he must have been over sixty, a tireless student. He was an orthodox Marxist, or so it seemed to me, while Bebel was rather an opportunist, thinking it wise to shape dogma to existing circumstances. The relations between the two men were ideal and the not infrequent disagreements as to tactics did not disturb the harmony of their close personal relations. Bebel, much younger, was an impressive speaker, tactful and resourceful in debate. Liebknecht was his teacher, but he would not always follow the indicated path.

At the beginning of the repressive legislation under Bismarck they had been imprisoned together both at Hubertusburg and Zwickau. The jailors, however, had been kindly and all the books they wanted were made available. "The prison was my University," said Bebel. Here Liebknecht taught him French and some English and many things even more valuable, and in this way his fragmentary education had been supplemented without impairing the native force of this remarkable man. Here at Halle both leaders were patient under criticism and it was only a year later at Erfurt that stark Marxism was insisted upon and the few dissidents were expelled. The phenomenal growth of the party continued until in 1903 it polled three million votes. Then it was apparent that the conciliatory policy had failed in its purpose as signally as had the repressive laws. It was doubtless only the general prosperity of Germany that marked this period and the increasing world trade that retarded the crusade for a more equal distribution of the products of labor.

More than the formal debates in the Congress I enjoyed the frank and, at times, unruly discussions which took place every evening at the *Stammtisch* in the ancient inn of the Golden Bullet when, as was frequently the case, the inquiring stranger from the then distant America was admitted to hear the apostles explain the problem which, it seems to me, is still unsolved as to what Marx, the Master, really meant. Then, as now, fiery debates ensued and then, as now, the disciples were as far apart as the poles. Mischievously, perhaps, I added to the confusion of the debate by quoting a letter from the Master to Lassalle or to someone else but recently published, in which he said, "Thank God, I am not a Marxist." Of course, the great teacher merely intended to disassociate himself from the aberrations of many of his professed followers, but much discussion ensued before this point was cleared up.

Often we talked about the wars of the past and the wars to come, but this ticklish topic was tactfully avoided when Jules Guesde, who represented France at the Congress, was present. When this distinguished son-in-law of Marx, the Master, sat with us, only the economic aspects of socialistic policies were discussed. I have, however, a very vivid remembrance of a prophecy which Bebel made, though as he died in 1913 he did not live to see its partial fulfillment.

"In the future," he said, "wars will come and they will continue their destructive course until the prevailing capitalistic system is destroyed. But they will not be as in the past duels between two nations, France against Germany, or Russia against Turkey. Today the interests of all peoples are inextricably intertwined. No, all nations will be drawn in. It will be horrible, but out of this universal disaster I am convinced good will come, indeed a lasting peace which the long-suffering peoples of the world will impose. Only then will it be possible for the working classes to begin their historic task which is to secure the greatest possible welfare for all through the socialization of the means of production and exchange."

Bebel was an outspoken advocate of Woman Suffrage when many of his party lieutenants wished that he would hold his tongue on this topic. He frequently in my presence denounced the saying, that was indeed in Germany at the time a political slogan, to the effect, "Man's place is in the factory; woman's in the home." He frequently expressed the hope that women would be called upon to share with men all their civic duties and responsibilities, but he admitted it would be an uphill fight.

To many it has seemed odd that as I listened to the debates of Socialists in Halle and heard the programs of the New World era explained, my determination to visit Creisau and, if possible, to talk with Field-Marshal Von Moltke grew stronger. Several candid friends have suggested that my attitude on this occasion indicates that I was lacking in appreciation of the men that were coming to the fore, and indeed that I failed to recognize the importance of the new day that was dawning, of which the Congress was the harbinger. Of course, I do not think so. I recognized that the scenes I witnessed in Halle were the prelude to world-shaking changes. But they would take some time to materialize, and I in all probability would be there to see, but with the Prussian Paladin there was no time to lose. He was in his ninetieth year, the last great figure of a generation upon which the curtain was falling, and so while the still hoped-for letter from the Countess failed to come, I started for Silesia several hours after the Congress adjourned.* It was a cold and dreary journey and my optimism departed when in the midst of a driving rain I was turned out on the platform of the Schweidnitz station and informed that the remainder

* An account of my visit to Creisau was published in the *New York Herald* in October, 1890, but at the Field-Marshal's request, I omitted from the article the references he made to the Alsace-Lorraine question and, also, his views as to the relative merits of the great Civil War leaders, Grant and Lee.

"I have always sought and generally succeeded in avoiding fruitless controversies," he explained, "and now with one foot in the grave it would be unseemly for me to do so, and quite unfair to those who may differ from me. They might say we respect old Moltke's age more than we do his brains," he added with a quiet chuckle. S.B.

of the journey would have to be made on foot. Apparently, the fields and the roads around the station were several feet under water. It was too deep to wade through and too shallow for swimming, so I sat down on a wet bench to await the dawn and the coming of *menschen,* for at this hour I was evidently the only human being about the station, all others I surmised having been taken off in life boats.

Finally people did come and also the light of a dark day, and I was guided to an inn just as the station and everything connected with it seemed to be on the point of floating away. Here there were many refugees from the rising waters. Some had evidently been there all night and were singing songs in praise of Silesian wine. Over and over again they roared, "*Auf Schlesiens Bergen da wächst ein Wein.*" And who was I to gainsay them? Indeed, after several liters had been disposed of, I joined loyally in the chorus. But though restored and comforted I did not allow anyone to forget the hardships and the discomforts I had undergone. "But all will be forgotten," I assured my listeners, an ever-increasing number, "if I succeed in getting but a glimpse of 'Der Moltke,' The Lord of War."

As it turned out, it was not a bad move, this putting my cards face-up on the table. As the legend ran through the town that I had come all the way from America to visit Count Von Moltke, "His Old Excellency" as they called him with an amusing mingling of familiarity and respect, the delight of the inhabitants knew no bounds, and on all sides were heard proffers of assistance and *prosits* followed by the genial jingle of glasses. It was suggested that I had better wait a day or two until the country dried up a bit, but after one look upon the dreary prospect of the town and with the thought of the intoxicating hospitality of the City Council which had been proffered, I determined to set out immediately for Creisau, even if I had to swim.

My new-found friends finally discovered a man who had a horse which was certainly web-footed and was said to swim. So we toiled through the flood and the mud for two hours until at last the village of Creisau, looking like a floating island, came in sight. We dropped anchor at the Inn to the Crown where, after we had taken something stronger, my guide and driver regaled his amphibious steed with a bucket of *stoff* or unfermented beer before we continued on our way.

"And the castle?"

The driver pointed down the valley to a great square house almost concealed by magnificent oaks. Three stories were of sandstone, the fourth and the mansard of wood and painted black, while from the flagstaff floated a standard which, as I heard, was borne to the wars when "Old Fritz" was King, and Silesia an Austrian Crown land.

Another short turn in the road, and the bronze cannon taken at Metz and given to the Marshal by the old Emperor William frowned upon us, and the clanging of a quaint triangle indicated that we were "observed." When I made known the mission with which I had been entrusted to Major Helmuth Von Moltke, the nephew of the Paladin, and himself one of the most distinguished strategists among the younger members of the General Staff, he threw every door of the castle open to me, but held out, however, very little hope of my seeing and speaking with his distinguished uncle. Count Waldersee was visiting him. The new and the old generation were fighting over again the battles of the past and planning those of the future. So, for the day, the Marshal's time was fully taken up.

We went up the broad stone steps, festooned with Virginia creeper, and entered the reception hall. Here we were confronted with the famous equestrian statue of Emperor William I, which the members of the General Staff presented their chief after the French campaigns. Here also were busts and portraits of nearly all the autonomous German Kings and Princes; also, one of Victor Emmanuel. The gift and the bust which I heard he treasured most was a small bronze statuette of the young Emperor, William the Second, which His Majesty brought with him and personally presented to the Field-Marshal on the then recent occasion of the maneuvers near Schweidnitz and his memorable visit to the old warrior's home (1887). Through a half-open door I was allowed a hasty glance at the bedroom of the great General. It was a little cabinet of about twenty feet by twelve in dimensions, and contained a narrow soldier's bed, a washstand, a table, a photograph, faded and dim, of his so greatly loved and so sincerely lamented wife. There was something touching in the simplicity and modest appearance of the place, and there one seemed to breathe a fresher and a purer atmosphere than in the world beyond.

Indeed the visit to Creisau was distinctly encouraging to a hero-worshiper who, as a correspondent, had suffered many sharp and sad disillusions. After thanking Major Von Moltke for his kindness, and receiving from him the courteous permission to visit Creisau as often as I wished and to make as many sketches as I cared to, I turned my back upon the Prussian Valhalla. I followed the path which the peasants told me led to the grave of the Silent Thinker's wife, a simple vault made into the hillside, about fifteen minutes' walk from the Schloss. The little chapel was overshadowed by a copy of Thorwaldsen's "Christ" with the Biblical saying engraved on the pedestal, *Die Liebe ist des Gesetzes Erfüllung*," or "Love is the fulfillment of the law." To the memory of his so dearly loved companion in life, Von Moltke had remained constant and true for twenty-two years, and not a day passed, as the peasants told me, but what he visited the chapel, to which he alone possessed the key, and remained there often an hour in silent communion with his beloved dead. The fresh-cut violets which lay strewn upon the cold stone were culled on the hillside and placed there not an hour before by the man who passed in the world as being "of blood and iron."

I turned away from the spot hallowed by so many years of devotion and, following the course of the Peille, a little stream full of sportive trout, approached once again the mansion through the park. About two hundred yards from the castle, seated on a bench, I perceived the object of my quest. It was Von Moltke. There could be no mistake, though a frieze jacket, such as foresters wear, had taken the place of the military mantle which he wore when I last saw his tall figure following with sad step the remains of his Emperor from the Dom to the Brandenburger Thor, through all the snow and ice which on that memorable day gave the lindens such an Arctic appearance. He was very gentle and courteous as I told him with some diffidence how much the *Herald* would esteem on the occasion of his Jubilee a few words from him to the address of the new generation. "I am very happy to welcome you to Creisau," said the Marshal, "but everything I have had to say I have said years ago. Here surrounded by my family and happy in the consciousness of having tried to do my duty to King and country in the stormy times in which my generation was called upon to live, I, in the evening of life, am awaiting the things that are to come. If you think that it would give pleasure, or imagine that in young and bustling America there are people who still remember 'Old Moltke,' why, I beg you to be so kind as to say that entering on my ninetieth year I wish their country well; and especially I would send my good wishes to those of our *Alte Krieger* (veterans) who, after having done their duty to their Vaterland, have gone out into the New World seeking and finding new homes and hospitable reception. Tell them never to forget the Vaterland, as the Vaterland will never fail to remember its worthy sons." With that and a friendly shake of the hand, he turned and entered the house.

I had planned to return to Berlin that night. It was certainly high time. I had been away from my post for ten days and things might happen, doubtless were happening, but then the weather had cleared and I wanted to see the man whom I fatuously regarded as the last of the War Lords again and under more favorable circumstances. True, the Field-Marshal had said nothing about the Waldersee letter and it was quite possible that the charming Countess had desisted from her audacious plan and, of course, there was the chance that she had overestimated her influence with Von Moltke and that her letter had landed in the wastepaper basket. Be this as it may, the fact is that the little I had seen of the great man had only served to whet my appetite, and bright and early the next morning I found myself again on the way to Creisau. I met the Herr Major as I entered the garden, and he gave me a pleasant nod and went about his business. Some minutes later, I saw coming toward me the Field-Marshal himself. I can see now that consciously or unconsciously I had returned to the castle in the hope of having a real talk with the great War Lord, but with the opportunity in my grasp, my courage failed me. Would he not consider me a frightful nuisance? And, if he did, would he be far wrong? With a turn of direction which I sought to make as dignified as possible I tried to escape by a path that ran off obliquely. But he would have none of that! I can, at least, protest that this second confrontation was forced upon me and not the other way about—as is more usual in similar circumstances. "*Heyda*," he shouted, "not so fast. Are you the young man who told the Countess Waldersee that I might have been a great correspondent had I not been confined by Staff work?"

"No," I answered; being cornered I grew bold; "but I did tell the Countess that you were a great correspondent and, Herr Graf, that is what you are!" The stern face relaxed and a flush of pleasure gave color to the leathery cheeks of the veteran. He took me firmly by the hand and led me to a garden seat. Fortunately my memory at the time was good and I was able to quote both chapter and verse of striking pictures from his Russian Letters and episodes from his Turkish Campaigns. And the great War Lord listened with evident pleasure. He interviewed me for about ten minutes and then began to give me my reward.

"It is strange that you should think that," he began. "The political press of all countries, particularly the American papers, describes me as a man of blood and iron, and the caricaturists present me to their public as a war-dragon breathing fire and flame. I am what the world has made me, but when I was young and could dream—well, I aspired to wield the pen—gently and so earn my living without doing harm to anyone. I even wrote a novel." * And here the Lord of War smiled broadly. It was funny, but I kept a straight face. "But what a hard life it is, or at any rate it was. For five years every night I worked upon a translation of Gibbon's *Decline and Fall of the Roman Empire*. What a task and what a pleasure it was! I had finished nine volumes when the publisher failed, and I only received five hundred marks. But my labor and my time was not a total loss, and I fear that is what the poor publisher suffered for I, at least, had gained a working knowledge of Roman history, which was world history, rather unusual for one who at the time was merely a sub-

* This charming production of the Field-Marshal's youthful pen, entitled *Die Beiden Freunde—Eine Erzahlung*, was at long last published in New York in 1907.

altern in what you would call a marching regiment. And that knowledge stood me in good stead many a time and, especially, years later when I had my little talks with Count Bismarck and the statesmen." In retrospect these talks must have been very amusing. The Field-Marshal chuckled on for almost a minute, but alas! he did not give me the chance to share his amusement. Then he led me into Macedonia and put many searching questions as to Edhem Pasha's campaigns of which I had seen a little. He knew the Turkish general as a subaltern and thought well of him but, doubtless fathoming the shallowness of my military knowledge, we were soon back again on the American front.

"Do they still speak of me over there as a man of blood and iron?" he inquired.

"Yes," I admitted frankly, "and our papers tell a story of how you acted in your great moment."

"Tell me that," said the War Lord.

"Well, it runs in this way," I went on. "While the Emperor was signing the declaration of war against France all you had to do was to send a two word telegram to the Corps commanders, 'Krieg mobil—mobilize for war,' and then you, carefree, went to bed."

The War Lord laughed almost loudly. Certainly it was the only laugh that came from him that was not quite noiseless. "That is a stretcher—worthy of the political papers. Our war machine was not as well oiled as that. Indeed it creaked for weeks. After the order was issued I did not sleep for forty-eight hours and I did not get to bed for four nights." I had thought as much but, of course, regretted having to place our stock anecdote in the category of the ben trovato.

Suddenly it began to rain, indeed to pour, and the Field-Marshal rose from the bench and, in doing so, for the first time he confessed his age and his slim figure trembled and for a moment tottered. As he led the way to the castle, he asked me where I was staying and then, without more ado, ordered a servant who rushed out to meet him with a greatcoat to go to the inn and get my bag. As we entered the house he said, "I wrote the Countess that I would be glad to see you and, of course, I hoped you would stay with me—if you could put up with a soldier's rations and our Silesian wine which is bitter, but I like it above all other vintages." * He led the way through a large library filled with books and overflow stacks on which, as I examined them later in the day, I found quite as many gems of world literature as military treatises and books on strategy. He pushed open a heavy door and soon we were seated in his gloomy little study, adorned by an almost life-size photograph of the late Emperor with an affectionate inscription in his bold handwriting. On the floor was a huge bearskin rug which Von Moltke admitted he had long cherished as a trophy of a memorable hunt in the Rhodopian Mountains. He offered me a black cigar which I took with many misgivings. The Field-Marshal did not smoke himself, and soon he was getting me way beyond my depth talking about strategy and Alexander and the great Swedish King when, suddenly, I brought matters nearer to date by saying that as a boy in the border state of Maryland I had been brought up on Civil War stories and that at the age of five I had seen General Lee— that I had played truant from school so that I might walk down Charles Street in Baltimore behind the great soldier.

This gave our conversation an almost topical turn and while I have often delighted Confederate veterans with Von Moltke's praise of their great leader, this was one of the subjects that he requested me to leave out of my account of my visit which appeared in the *New York Herald* on the birthday of the Prussian Paladin in October 1890. As Von Moltke began to talk about Lee it seemed to me that the fact of my presence passed entirely out of his mind. He seemed to be jotting down the salient points of the great Southerner's career as though he were preparing a lecture to be delivered

---

* What became of this letter is a mystery. Later, in Berlin, the Countess told me it had never reached her. How I would have treasured it! Of course, at the time I suspected that the Herr Major, the somewhat pompous *Neffe* of the War Lord, had suppressed it, undoubtedly with the best motives in the world, but his want of confidence in me was not justified.

However, at this late day, I shall not throw a stone—no, not even a pebble, at this unfortunate man who lived to point a moral and to become one of the outstanding victims of that holocaust of disaster that marked the terrible year 1914. It was he who directed the German invasion of Belgium and France in 1914. Was it wise to change the Schlieffen plan, and who was responsible for doing it? Time may tell, but today only one thing is certain and that is very certain. It is a terrible thing to be given a world-conquering name unless the brains that made it what it was come with it—and, also, the favor of the gods.

at the Great War School, and once he got going I was not so foolish as to interrupt him with questions. I contented myself with writing down, even before I left the castle, the Prussian General's opinion of the great Virginian.

"Lee," he began, "had a full understanding of the unfavorable position of the Southern states when the issue was joined. He grasped from the first the unalterable conditions by which he was confronted. He knew how best to adapt the slender means he disposed of to the end he sought. It was unattainable, but he was not defeated for four years. Particularly remarkable was Lee's success in separating his divisions on the march and concentrating them at the decisive moment, on the eve of battle. Von Borcke, when he returned to Germany, invalided after his service with the Confederate cavalry, insisted that this feat, always difficult, was little short of magical in view of the condition of the Virginia roads at that time. When Sheridan was at our headquarters in 1870 he told me that Grant always had as many as ten thousand men working on the roads in front of his army, if possible, and always behind it, on the line of supply, but of course Lee could not spare men in any considerable numbers, even for this vital purpose, from his always thin and depleted fighting lines.

"There have been many critics of Lee's offensives, the Antietam and the Gettysburg campaigns. I think they indicate complete ignorance of the existing circumstances, the conditions under which Lee had to fight. From the very beginning, the North had a strong hold on the life-line of the South. I refer to the control of the seas. When Lee took command the South was being choked to death. Was it enough for him to try and keep his windpipe open? No, certainly not. He had to strike out to relieve, if he could not remove, the pressure, and that is what Lee did and with considerable temporary, if not permanent, success. The supply services of the army of northern Virginia were undoubtedly faulty, and this handicapped its resistance. But who was to blame? Certainly not Lee. Behind him he found a wretched railway system and he was absolutely without the material to improve it. Behind Grant was an excellent railway system and everything that was necessary to keep it going and to improve it. His line of supply led to the richest regions of the country and, indeed, over it he was able to draw men and material from the whole world. But, of course, Grant was a great commander, too. That is, if my definition of a great commander is correct. It is that a great commander is one who brings into action all the means at his disposal and uses them to best advantage.

"Now Grant, though slowly and reluctantly, did find out that he could not compete with the Southern leader in strategy or in tactics. He also must have recognized that his troops were not as homogeneous as were those of Lee and that his generals, some of whom were political, could not be compared with Lee's lieutenants and then, of course, Lee had the considerable advantage of the inner line and the more unfaltering support and confidence of his civil authorities.

"After being worsted a number of times, Grant had the great good sense to see that his defeats that were depleting the forces of the victors opened to him the only possible avenue of success and he kept right at it hammer and tongs. Yes, we must not neglect Grant. His simple tactics can be studied to great advantage because, after all, a man of genius is required to carry out the campaign plans of Lee and he would have to be backed by an exceptional army with an unusually high morale."

Then, without the slightest encouragement from me, the Field-Marshal broached another highly contentious subject. It was doubtless suggested by current debates in the German Reichstag and in the French Chamber as to the racial stock of the people of Alsace who had been incorporated in the Empire as a result of the successful war.

"When this question arose I most certainly never told the Emperor, my August Master, that the Alsatians were our long lost brothers, or even that they were nearer to us ethnically than they are to the Gauls. In fact, I have never expressed an opinion on this subject. Unlike Herr von Bismarck I have always stuck to my last. (This was not by any means the only dig that the Field-Marshal gave to his great contemporary in the course of the day!) When the matter came up the Emperor asked my opinion on strategic grounds, and it was on these grounds alone that my opinion was based and determined. Our decision was incorporated in the annexation clause of the Treaty of Frankfort, but our position was taken up long before that. Let me read you the letter which my August Master wrote to the Empress Eugénie as early as October, 1870, a month after Sedan. In courteous language it sets forth our views at the time and we have never deviated from them and I am sure we would not even if the *fachmaenner* should develop the fact, let us say, that the Alsatians, charming people that they are, really belong to the Ibernian or Lombardian tribes. This letter, which expresses the unanimous opinion of our General Staff and also that of all the army commanders in the field—who had been in one way or another consulted—reads—I will show it you."

With but a moment's delay the Field-Marshal drew out from his orderly archives the famous document that has had such far-reaching consequences upon the course of events. It was in his hand-writing and may have been the original draft placed before the Emperor for his signature, although the Field-Marshal did not say so. It read:

"I love my country, as you love yours, and so I can well understand the sorrow and the bitterness that at this moment fills the heart of your Majesty. But after having made immense sacrifices for her defense Germany wishes to be assured that the next war will find her better prepared for defense and to repel aggression than in the recent past. Such attacks we have every reason to expect the moment France shall have regained her strength and secured alliances. It is this consideration alone and not in the least a desire to increase the territory of the Fatherland which compels me to insist upon cessions of territory which have no other purpose than to push back the points of departure, and attack, of the French armies."

For a moment the Field-Marshal paused. His thoughts evidently went back to the epic days, and then he added with a smile, "You see, the remote origin or even the present sympathies of the Alsatians did not enter into our thoughts. We were convinced that as long as the French were in possession of Alsace-Lorraine the Fatherland was open to attack, indeed invited it. I recognize that this question, as it stands today, may provoke war but, if it does, it will find us better prepared than if this essential defensive step had been neglected." Carefully, methodically, the Field-Marshal folded the historic paper and filed it away. As far as he was concerned, the question was settled and would not be reopened and, indeed, it was not in his lifetime.

At this very moment a newspaper controversy in regard to a minor frontier incident had once again brought the Alsace question on the carpet. The Paris papers were accusing the Imperial Statt-halter of dragooning the unfortunate people who had been torn away from their natural allegiance, and the Abbé Wetterlé had even ventured to bring the matter up in the German Reichstag. It was whispered about that Bismarck in his wisdom had opposed the annexation of the disputed province, but that the views of Von Moltke and other militarists had prevailed. I, of course, referred to this.

"The press is not well-informed on this subject, if you will allow me to say so," he added graciously. "When the question arose I had only one thing in mind, and that was the lay of the land. Of course, I do not mean to say that the reasons of civilian *fachmaenner* who looked into the matter were not valid, though I do believe that my August Master, the Emperor, acted solely on the basis of the facts I submitted to him." Then, with a charming smile, "I like the Al-satians. I am sorry they occupy such an unfortunate geographical position. I do not think they are French and I do not think they are German. They are men apart; unfortunately for them, they are placed between two races who are naturally pugnacious and have much to fight over."

Though the Herr Major, *Der Neffe,* as everyone in Silesia called the young officer who, twenty-four years later, weighted down by a great name and lacking the qualities that in the day of his uncle had gone with it, headed the German armies that were stopped at the battle of the Marne, evidently did not approve of the way the great *Schweiger* was talking to me on the last afternoon of my stay, while the Field-Marshal was taking his nap, he told me an amusing anecdote of the great man's peculiarities which are, I think, often shared by many others who have been long in the public eye.

"The Field-Marshal thinks he would like to live and move about incognito, and he often complained rather bitterly of the pub-

licity which attended all his movements. So when a year ago he retired, unloading most of his duties on the shoulders of Count
Waldersee, he said to me, 'I want to forget it all and, above all, I
want the people to forget me. I want to taste the sweets of life—
privacy such as every ordinary *mensch* enjoys.' So we started for a
little village in the Thuringian forest and I told the inn-keeper that
he must not reveal the Field-Marshal's identity and warned him
that if he did so we would leave immediately. The inn-keeper was
most dejected and bowed down under the mighty secret, and soon
I noticed that my uncle was not enjoying himself. He wandered
about a bit, asked for the newspapers, threw them away and, finally,
spent most of his time twiddling his thumbs and yawning. On the
evening of the third day of this isolation, he said to me, 'This is the
dullest place I have ever been in and the people of a stupidity!'
And then he added, 'We shall move on at daybreak. Order the
horses.' Now I did not want to move on. I had found an excellent
trout stream and I thought I knew what was the matter with the
Field-Marshal. He was tired of his incognito. He hated being out
of touch with the people. So I slipped downstairs and told the
Wirth that he had overdone his discreet role and now he should
reveal the name of his guest. He gave a shriek of delight and was
off like an arrow and in five minutes all the villagers and many
from the countryside had gathered about the inn and were shouting,
'Der Moltke! Der Moltke! We must see our great Lord of War.'
I rushed into my uncle's room and found that he had been disturbed
as he read his Bible by the light of a single candle dip. 'Don't blame
the *Wirth*,' I said, 'I suppose some old soldier recognized you. At
least, you have enjoyed your incognito for three days.'

"'I don't blame the *Wirth*—I don't blame anybody,' answered
the Field-Marshal. 'I think they are all *liebe leut* and I shall get up
and tell them how I appreciate their hearty welcome.' He got out
of bed and as there were no curtains in the room the villagers had
the rare pleasure of seeing the Field-Marshal draw on his boots and
hosen before he appeared at the window to thank them for disturbing his rest. We stayed on for another week. I caught two hundred
trout and in the end I had difficulty getting my uncle to go back to

Silesia. He was having such a splendid time telling the old veterans and their grandchildren war stories."

That night I could not sleep. I do not think it was the hard camp bed upon which I lay, for that was almost luxurious after my Balkan experiences, nor had anything that the great War Lord said proved especially electrifying. But around my pillow came trooping figures from the historic past, conjured out of oblivion by this long-desired but unexpected contact with the Master of Creisau. There was the old Emperor and Bismarck, the Iron Chancellor, and Prince Anton Radziwill, the Emperor's closest friend whom I had last seen a gaunt wolflike figure of a man at the Imperial funeral, standing with drawn sword by the catafalque crowned with garlands and war medals, and there was the pale figure of the last Napoleon who lost all at Sedan. To Radziwill my thoughts returned most frequently. I could not get away from him. He was present at that fatal conversation on the Promenade at Ems, the sequel of which was war and the ghastly battlefields of 1870. He was the only ear-witness to the words that were spoken there. He knew what was said and how it was said, and yet there never came from him a word of disclosure much less of indiscretion in life or from his tomb after death. Radziwill was indeed a servant of the old school that has vanished from the world scene. *"Ein treuer Diener seines Herrn."*

On the afternoon of the next day I left the castle, and the War Lord was gracious enough to see me off at the door and wave me a courteous farewell. He sent me to the station in a muddy country carriage. "But it is the best we have," he protested modestly, "and I did not have that until two years ago when I had to give up riding." And even the *Neffe* was amiable. The fact was, and he dwelt upon it continually, I had not harassed the War Lord with a single leading question, and this negligence or self-control on my part had, at last, allayed his distrust. He even accompanied me to the village, but I must not boast of that. He went there in an attempt to sell some of the rye from the estate which I gathered was not going off like hot cakes.

On my way back to Berlin I had to *umsteigen* or transfer from

388 HEYDAY IN A VANISHED WORLD

one train to another in Breslau, and there was quite a wait but I enjoyed every minute of the delay. There was a large gathering of people from all over Silesia to commemorate the anniversary of some victory in the French War, and the Platz by the station was filled with far from sober veterans of the war that had come to an end nearly two decades before. They were singing and indeed often screaming out ditties, such as *"Das Vaterland muss Grosser sein"* (The Fatherland must be larger), or *"Der Moltke—Dass ist ein Kerl,"* and, as often as any of them, Arndt's inflammatory song about the Rhine being a German stream and "German it must remain."

Suddenly, out of a narrow *gasse* from some hall where they had been engaged in ratifying the resolutions passed at Halle, came marching in stern, undeviating columns a large number of Social-Democrats. And as they marched, they sang their ominous chant:

> *In Breslau, ein Friedhof, ein Grab,*
> *Da lieght ja begraben*
> *Wer Schwerter uns gab.*

Which roughly Englished, reads:

> "In Breslau there's a cemetery and a grave.
> There lies buried the man who
> Put swords in our hands."

In the clash that ensued bitter words and even fisticuffs were exchanged, but nothing more serious followed. Even the police, generally so officious, merely looked on and tittered. The men of the dawn, confident that they were marching toward the rising sun, seemed more inclined merely to brush the old war-bitten veterans aside than to fight them. Yet, from that moment, and in later years with increasing frequency, it has seemed to me that on that day the sword of Lassalle was drawn and the battle on—that I had witnessed the opening skirmish of a war that was to topple over proud empires and reduce prosperous nations to beggary. True, all that came later, much later. It was a generation of victors and vanquished alike, at that time unborn, who were called upon to share almost equally the shame, the suffering, and the humiliation that followed in its baleful train.

A week later when Von Moltke came up to Berlin to be the guest of a grateful Emperor and to be fêted by his idolatrous fellow-countrymen, a patriotic holiday was proclaimed. With much grace and dignity, the Field-Marshal submitted to it. Forty thousand Berliners marched from the Spree to the Column of Victory, loudly calling on Moltke to live forever. Unter den Linden was illuminated and draped with Prussian and Imperial flags, with their parti-colored ribbons. The march was opened by veterans from all over the Empire. Then came the great bulk of Berliners divided into brigades from the various electoral districts, with all political differences for the moment forgotten in paying honor to the great soldier. Among the torch-bearers were every sort and condition of man—and Berlinese youth. The students of the Art Academy, however, succeeded in presenting, as was natural, the artistic success of the celebration. They had copied from historic tomes the costumes of twenty centuries and came marching by in detachments, amidst enthusiastic plaudits, representing, as they did with great accuracy, warriors of every era in German history. They were all there, from Tacitus' brave barbarians down to amusing caricatures of Major von Wissmann's Zanzibari troops who formed the entering wedge of Germany's short-lived East African Empire.

On reaching the building of the General Staff, where the Field-Marshal, surrounded by every Corps Commander in the Empire and a great number of superior officers, stood with uncovered head, the committee of art students presented the Count with a laurel wreath made of solid silver, for which he spoke a few words of thanks.

But the scene in the Koenigsplatz was even more interesting. Throughout the two hours it took the procession to pass, Von Moltke stood bareheaded and smiling on the balcony, saluting the enthusiastic thousands to the end, though Count Waldersee made many attempts to bring him indoors out of the cold, damp atmosphere. On the day following the parade Von Moltke received all who called in the building of the War School, the notables of the land as well as the obscure veterans who had followed him across the frontier to victory. I was so fortunate as to obtain access to the Kriegschule before the general public. The Kaiser was the first caller. He brought with him the young Crown Prince, aged eight, and his second son, Eitel Fritz, a scant year younger. They were very simply dressed in sailor suits, and after having delivered the military salute they approached the Prussian Paladin and kissed the withered hand that had dealt such sturdy blows to the enemies of the Vaterland.

And now, while the circle was formed, and surrounded by his brilliant staff of officers and guests, among whom were many sovereigns of the German States, the young Emperor discussed questions of strategy in a loud voice, Von Moltke stole away from the group and taking each of the little Princes by the hand led them around the great galleries in which are hung the captured banners and the remnants of the standards which were shot to pieces in what was their "last war." Before these memorials of the great conflict the Field-Marshal would pause and his great eagle eyes would blaze again for a moment with war-like fire as he told the young Princes how the banner had been captured and how the battle was won and lost.

So, to the open-eyed delight of the boy Princes, Von Moltke continued to guide them through the building and the great reception was half over before he, in whose honor it was held, returned to his post and submitted to the innumerable handshakings and congratulations of the notables of the Empire.

Six months later the aged warrior followed his venerable Emperor to the tomb. The eldest of the youngsters, the afterwards famous Crown Prince, had at this time a grave and interesting face, but his brother, Eitel Fritz, was the handsomest boy of seven or eight that I have ever seen. Twenty-five years later, almost to the day, as I left the headquarters of Field-Marshal Von Hindenburg at Lyck on the Eastern front an armored car drove up, and as the drums beat and the guard turned out two officers descended.

"Who are these notables?" I inquired of my escort, a reserve officer from the Foreign Office. He stood as if transfixed, at *stramm* salute, and only when the new arrivals had disappeared did he relax and answer, "The stout one—the majestic one—is Eitel Fritz; the slight one, Prince Joachim." The stout one! Heavens, he looked like a hog trussed up in uniform; from his sleek featureless face porcine eyes glinted and several chins drooped on his chest. It was into this that war and self-indulgence had transformed the handsome boy, the *wunder-knabe* as they called him at Potsdam! Poor Joachim, who at least was not gun-shy, shed the only Hohenzollern blood that was spilled during the war at Tauroggen a few days later. Several months after the war was over, for reasons and in circumstances that were never cleared up, he committed suicide.

18. AN IMPERIAL PUBLICITY
STUNT

AND SUDDENLY bourgeois and rather beery Berlin became the scene of a stark tragedy which made me, for a time, forget my personal problems. Under my eyes scenes of suffering and misery were enacted more poignant indeed than any I had witnessed in the wound hospitals of the Turkish troops, or in the smallpox-ridden camps of Macedonian refugees. At first the rumor was whispered about that Dr. Koch had made a discovery that would revolutionize the health of the world. My early information came from Professor Virchow, the friend of Bismarck, a politician as well as a pathologist, a great man so supreme in his sphere and so big-hearted that there was not a particle of jealousy in his makeup.

The elderly professor admired, and indeed as he told me, loved his young colleague, Robert Koch, who, sent out to Egypt in 1882, had identified the comma bacillus as the special organism of Asiatic cholera. On his return from Africa, Koch had turned his attention to tuberculosis and had been successful in preparing a lymph, afterward to be known as tuberculine, of which great things were expected in some quarters. In the fall of 1890, much to his dismay, the searching light of publicity was turned on the Charité Hospital in Berlin where Koch and his trusted assistants were treating with the new and admittedly mysterious serum about threescore patients suffering from tubercular troubles. From this searchlight there was no escape for the modest doctor, for it was held in the hand and projected upon him by no less a personage than Emperor William II who was entering upon the third year of his reign and was very desirous indeed of some *action d'éclat* that would add

luster to the throne and convince the stupid burghers that everything was going on well—even if the "old pilot," Bismarck, had
been thrown overboard.

Some busybody evidently had brought the news of what was
happening in the laboratory to the Emperor. He immediately intervened and thereby became responsible for as many shocking
deaths as usually resulted from the little wars of the generation
that was on its last legs. Poor Professor Koch was summoned to the
Palace, given the Red Eagle or some other high order, and told
that he must immediately proclaim his discovery to the city and to
the world. It was pointed out to him what a magnificent opportunity was presented of justifying before the whole world the proud
slogan of *"Deutschland über alles"* and the Emperor, with a majestic
gesture, silenced the unfortunate scientist when he explained that
the experiments had only been under way a few weeks and that
while the results were encouraging it was far too soon to claim
definitive curative results or future immunity from the white
plague. The Emperor, so far from heeding these words of wisdom,
publicly announced, and who dared gainsay him? that the "miracle-
working remedy of Herr Professor Koch was a boon to long-
suffering humanity and that the thanks of the world were due him.
Germany is indeed proud of her distinguished son."

The great scientist, suddenly brought face to face with the propaganda machine in its kindergarten stage, took to his bed and for
some days was no more seen of men. It is true that he was completely exhausted by his labors of eighteen hours a day in his clinic
or in his laboratory on the Klosterstrasse and, perhaps, the Imperial
interference was but the last straw. This, however, soon took an
official form. Herr von Gossler, the Minister of Public Instruction,
announced in the official gazette that Herr Professor Koch had consented to explain to the medical men of the world who, most op-
portunely, to the number of three thousand were shortly to convene
in Berlin for the purpose of holding their biennial Congress, all the
details of his epoch-making discovery. Then the official press announced, and this time quite correctly, that in addition to the selected delegates at least four thousand more distinguished doctors
were coming to Berlin to listen to the first exposition of the re-

markable discovery. Of course, the Minister would not have dared to make this announcement except at the Emperor's command and equally, of course, Doctor Koch had to obey.

The interest aroused was world-wide and inquiries for detailed information came pouring in from all quarters. Armed with a card from Professor Virchow I was received by Dr. Koch in his laboratory, and also given the run of the clinic where the patients were being treated. The doctor was a small man, hardly five feet four, I should say, but strongly built. He had been described to me as having sharp and penetrating eyes of great beauty, but the incessant labor at the microscope for the last few months had robbed them of their brightness and their power. During the weeks in which I saw him frequently Koch wore spectacles of triple glass, and without them he was almost blind.

At this, our first talk, I showed the professor a sheaf of telegrams that had reached me listing the names of the distinguished medical men who, dropping all other matters, had sailed from America and would soon reach Berlin. Rather ruefully the professor said, "Of course, I shall be glad to see them." But when I showed him the other telegrams with graphic accounts of the hordes of "lungers" who were pulling up stakes at Davos Platz, Algiers, the Riviera resorts, and even faraway Arizona and starting for Berlin, Koch nearly collapsed.

"Do all you can to stop these unfortunate people," he pled. "We are far, very far, from being prepared to take care of them. We are still groping, though we think we see a little light. We are engaged in scientific experimentation of the most delicate description. We are not offering a cure-all and we are not even sure that we are on the right track. But if we were sure, we are certainly not able to care for more patients than those at present under treatment. The preparation of the lymph demands great care and is a slow process and must remain, for the present, a secret one. Not, of course, with the remotest idea of commercializing it, but because we are well aware that it may not prove helpful in many advanced cases of the disease and also because, not without reason, in view of past experiences, we fear that it may be exploited by charlatans and be improperly and unskillfully applied."

At first off the unfortunate scientist's words of reason and remonstrance went unheeded. Many of the unfortunates, recognizing that the clinical capacity of the hospitals would soon be overtaxed, only hastened on the faster in the hope of being among the fortunate few who would not have to wait for treatment, and, of course, quacks sprang up on every side who claimed to have stocks of the lymph or something else as good or better. This last development gave Dr. Koch, however regrettable it was in other respects, his cue by which without openly betraying the Emperor he extricated himself from a false position for which the "All Highest" was alone responsible.

In the address to the Medical Congress, which was, of course, cabled to the farthest ends of the earth, Professor Koch stated that it had been his purpose to withhold information as to the course of his experiments until the lymph had given decisive, unmistakable results and clinical experience had justified its wider preparation and use. "I can only say now that by our treatment we have arrested tubercular disease in animals, and that in certain forms of tubercular disease in men the treatment seems to have a beneficial effect. I am not definitely settled as to the best ingredients of the lymph and as to the best method of production. All this may have to be changed in the light of the experiments we are making every day. In the circumstances, I am sure my distinguished colleagues from all over the world will agree with me it is wiser to withhold details for the present." The secrecy of the process by which the tuberculine was obtained was found to be the vulnerable joint in the scientist's armor in the world-wide battle that now ensued, although Koch's explanation of why frankness at this early stage would be unwise and even dangerous seemed quite sound to me.

Yet nothing could stem the mad rush of consumptives from all over the world. For this, in part, at least, the official German telegraph agencies were to blame. They emphasized the claims of the unscientific observers, and the disclaimers of Koch himself, when not suppressed, they ascribed to his native modesty. Within the week as many as ten thousand tubercular patients from foreign lands, many of them in advanced stages of the dread disease, were dumped out at the railway stations, and probably double that number arrived from the German States. Many came with little or no money, and even those with ample means had difficulty in securing suitable lodgings. I saw hundreds of them stretched out on hard tables in the corridors of hotels, and not a few were even less comfortably housed.

When the sufferers dragged themselves, or were carried on stretchers, to the hospital, there was no lymph available and little in prospect for weeks to come. Then there came a cold douche for the unfortunates with the statement that Koch and his assistants were not confident that good results would follow the injections in all cases, and that they were determined to study each case individually. Even when the tuberculine was as plentiful as beer there would be no inoculation *en masse;* each case would be treated after careful and, perhaps, prolonged examination. As a consequence of this decision, however wise it may have been, many patients whose waning strength had been overtaxed by the long journeys they had made, died in sight of what they had thought would prove the promised land.

On several occasions I was permitted to accompany the harassed scientist on his rounds in the hospital wards, and I also witnessed a number of inoculations; generally the brown transparent fluid was injected between the shoulder blades of the sufferers and, even during the few days in which I observed the treatment, marvelous results were apparent when the diseased tissues were on the surface; i. e., tuberculosis of the skin. However, the appeals of many in the last throes of the malady were so piteous they could not be resisted. Several of these unfortunates were undoubtedly on their death beds, they were doomed, so why not take a chance? Listening to the dictates of his heart rather than of his head, Koch inoculated a number of these people, and in several instances with disastrous results. When they died a hue and cry was raised, particularly in some of the foreign medical papers which had been skeptical from the first. This was in the day before the invaluable X-ray had been brought into general application, and only the post-mortems revealed that the lung tissues of these unfortunate people had been destroyed long before the treatment was applied.

I saw the unfortunate doctor the day before I left Berlin. The

Commodore had returned and a telegram, more laconic than usual, came, ordering me to report immediately in Paris. Probably because he was a cable magnate his telegrams were, as a rule, as diffuse as his letters were terse. The change in the great scientist's appearance was at once startling and shocking. Von Bergman, his assistant, told me he feared that his chief, who had lived so many months in an atmosphere impregnated with the bacilli, was about to become a victim of the scourge he had sought so valiantly to combat. As a matter of fact, it was the campaign against him, in what he called with the scorn natural to a scientist "the political press," that was wearing him down. As we shook hands for the last time he said rather plaintively, "Of course, I may be groping in the dark, but I do think I see a little light ahead. I was trying to do what good I could and now I find," he added bitterly, "I am regarded as a mass-murderer." As a matter of fact, these outrageous charges had no basis in fact, and in time justice was done the great bacteriologist and when, in 1905, several years before his lamented death, Koch was awarded the Nobel Prize for his services to humanity, not a dissenting voice was raised.

From several personal experiences I have learned how dangerous it is for a man of science to open his heart and explain the achievement of his brain to a newspaper correspondent not technically trained, but in this instance, at least, I had the good fortune to ward off a blow directed at Koch, indeed one from a very high quarter which he would have felt deeply. A few hours after my arrival in Paris, I called up a good friend, Dr. Eugène Dupuy, as famous in America as in Paris. For years he had practiced medicine in San Francisco and had been so fortunate as to save the lives of several of the most prominent dwellers on Nob Hill. Having amassed a small fortune, he returned to Paris and devoted his life, which was fortunately prolonged, to scientific research. He made me lunch with him, became interested in what I had to say, and insisted that I accompany him to a meeting of leading medical men at the Académie de Médecine that afternoon, where he said he feared Koch was to be denounced—though he hoped in measured terms.

When the great men were assembled in the amphitheater, Dupuy introduced me, and in exceedingly bad medical French, helped out now and again by Dupuy who had an enviable mastery of both languages, I reported exactly what I had seen and heard in Berlin. I, of course, insisted that Koch had been the victim of circumstances, all powerful in Court circles, which we as good Republicans found it difficult to understand. I was also wise enough to recall the homage which Koch had on several occasions in my presence paid to Pasteur, the great pioneer in bacteriology. As a result, a resolution of censure, which Dupuy thought would have passed unanimously, was dropped, and, after thanking me for my information, the Dean of the Faculty announced that the French men of science would wait and see the results of the important discoveries of their German colleague, and that in the meantime they wished Dr. Koch all the good fortune in the world.

I wish I could let the foregoing stand as a complete account of the circumstances attending my arrival in Paris and how, in my humble way, I had struck a blow for the great apostle of pure science. But truth compels me to complete the record and so make it quite clear that I reached the capital on the Seine greatly depressed in mind, body, and estate. The hope that I had expressed some weeks before in a communication to the office that now the necessity for secrecy covering my German activities having been removed, my weekly stipend would be resumed and some attention be paid to my long-neglected expense account, had not been realized. After patient waiting I sent on duplicates of my accounts, and in the covering letter I expressed the fear that unless they were attended to at an early day the work of the *Herald* correspondent in Berlin would be embarrassed, perhaps even crippled.

This appeal drew an answer from the man to whom it was addressed, unfortunately not directly from Mr. Bennett as I had hoped. He explained that the Commodore was cruising in Spanish waters and that, before his departure, he had decided upon a radical change in the management of the paper and the Paris office. Control and responsibility had been lodged in the hands of a committee of three and, while it would be premature to express a definite judgment on the change, certain inconveniences were already quite apparent. One of these was the extreme difficulty in having a meeting of the committee at which all the committeemen, vested as they were with equal powers, could be present. Their personal duties were very burdensome and their working hours were not susceptible of synchronization. In view of these difficulties, that could not well have been foreseen, they had written the Commodore, not favoring the abandonment of the system, which as yet had obviously not been given a fair trial, but venturing to suggest the introduction of the panel system in the arrangement. It would work out in this way: Smith would be in charge of the paper on Monday, Jones on Tuesday, Robinson on Wednesday, and so on around the calendar. And there was a postscript to the effect that all the members of the committee found it baffling that the Balkan correspondent, whose work they so greatly admired, should request that funds be sent him to Berlin, and they must add that the memoranda which the Commodore, on sailing, had left with them for their guidance shed no light on this situation. The communication closed on an optimistic strain; solution of my problem could not be long delayed as the Commodore would be back in Paris in a few weeks.

In a few weeks! When in the matter of finances I was nearing the end of my "iron portion!" Kempinski was showing reluctance in accepting my signature in lieu of cash payment for meals and my landlady was grumbling. However, as I had been wise and thrifty, there was really no need to tighten my belt. Sooner or later the situation would be clarified and all I had to do was to ask the cashier at the Paris office to send me five hundred dollars and charge it to my savings account. The answer to this letter was prompt, but by no means helpful. M. Le P. . . . wrote in French that he did not understand my extraordinary request and would I be so good as to favor him with further particulars.

On this same dark day I received a rasping cable signed "Bennett," pointing out that I had been "beaten" on what I considered a most trivial item of news, if news it was, and also that several papers in Paris, including *L'Illustration*, had published a photograph of the two Emperors in shooting togs which should, of course, have been first published in the *Herald*. While this impertinence was signed Bennett, I knew full well it had not been written by the Commodore. His telegraphic style was unmistakable and inimitable. I also knew, of course, that from time to time he

conferred upon one or another of his temporary favorites the dangerous privilege of signing his name, and indeed I knew who had
written it as though I had seen him at his desk, pen in hand. I cordially disliked this man, a feeling which he reciprocated with equal
cordiality, but today I shall not hold up his name to public obloquy,
for now that the hot fit is over I admit that his punishment in this
world has been greater than his deserts, immeasurable as they
seemed at the time.

If I had any doubt as to the real author of the reprimand it
would have been cleared up by an item in the *Figaro*, which, confirming the statement of the hydra-headed steering committee unhappily in control of the paper, was to the effect that "M. Gordon-
Bennett" with the many distinguished lords and beautiful ladies
who were his guests, had, disembarking from the *Namouna*, spent
a delightful day viewing the famous palm trees of Elche in Spain.

The weather in Berlin was depressing and I had a very lively
memory of what had happened according to Stanley to the "forgotten" correspondent in Teheran. True, I was not so far away, but
he certainly had the advantage of climate. I dipped my pen in ink
mixed with vitriol and determined to teach this fellow a lesson, he
who had never written a printable dispatch in his life, but never let
a day go by without sending a fulsome letter of adulation to our
chief who was extremely susceptible to flattery—who could take it
in spoon—nay, in shovel fulls! And I wrote, and alas! cabled, that
the *Herald* correspondent in Berlin had not the wherewithal to pay
for his meals much less to purchase photographs. If ordinary intelligence had characterized the examination of the photo—I went
on to say—it would have been noted that it was taken and printed
in Vienna and that even had there been funds at his disposal it
would have been most improper for the Berlin correspondent to
trespass on the territory of his able Austrian colleague. The item
referred to? Well, I was glad I had not sent it. It was not worthy of
publication in a reputable paper!

Well, my guess as to who had written the provocative telegram
was quite correct. It was true that our roving editor had visited the
palm trees at Elche, but what I had in my anger overlooked was
that he might immediately afterwards have abandoned the yacht

and made one of those "surprise" visits to the office where, thinking him far away, the steering committee might well have been celebrating the absence of their chief by lolling about and taking things easy—as those office folk were only too prone to do. He did, alas! this very thing, received the intemperate telegram which I had sent to the private reserved address at the moment of his arrival and, without a second's hesitation, he had sent me the orders to return and bring my baggage and settle my accounts. There was not the least room for doubt as to the authorship of this command. It had all the earmarks of authenticity and while the subject of funds, which a few hours before had been all-important, was not touched upon, I had not the least difficulty in complying. Within twelve hours I was on the way.

Only some days after my financial dilemma had reached an acute stage did it suddenly occur to me that I had another account in Paris, although in my Balkan wanderings I had lost the bankbook and had not the remotest idea what my balance, if any, would be. Incredible as it sounds, I suddenly remembered that I had money on deposit with the House of Rothschild, and this astonishing thing happened in this wise. Three years before, Baron Gustave de Rothschild, a partner in the Paris firm, less in the news but more attentive to affairs than his society-minded brother Baron Alphonse, had taken refuge in the inn at Blida on the border of the African desert from a blinding sandstorm which for three days without interruption blew from the Sahara. I, too, was weather-bound there, and in the limited quarters that have now been replaced by a palace hotel we were soon jostled together. With the Baron was his kindly wife and two children, Juliette of the flashing eyes, a daring horsewoman who a few years later met with a tragic death in the hunting field, and her much younger brother, Robert, a quiet, studious child.

Quite possibly it was due to the tedium that we all suffered from during our enforced confinement in the stuffy public hall, and perhaps the Baron was naturally curious. In any case it is true that in these long days he asked me as many questions as ever did in later years that famous inquirer after personal details, Li Hung Chang, and by the third day when the winds abated there were few chapters in my vagrant life that he had not unveiled. As he listened to them, this thrifty banker was evidently torn by feelings of both dis-approval and of amusement. He thought that Mr. Bennett paid me far too large a salary and he had a low opinion of newspaper work. He added that the Commodore was "a great spendthrift and that some day—" But here professional etiquette intervened, for as the Baron admitted, my boss banked with him.

Then the great financier wanted to know what I did with my weekly stipend when in Paris, and this I explained with *force dé-tails*. In the form of a draft or a check it came to me on Fridays, either from the Paris or the London office. This paying procedure varied owing to circumstances of which we were not advised. "With us Friday is not black—but the brightest day in the week," I ex-plained. "Then I sally out and sell my draft to the first exchange establishment I come across on the Boulevard. The fluctuations in exchange are so slight it is not worth my valuable time to shop around and sell my paper to the highest bidder." Then I added proudly, "I distribute the proceeds of the sale, at least as far as they go, to the deserving people who have trusted me in the last seven days." This simple, but I fear rather unctuous, statement quite upset the Baron's keen sense of finance.

"Don't you know," he said, "that money breeds money and that you are not giving your dollars a chance? You should deposit your checks and drafts in a reliable and conservative bank where your account would grow—if you only drew upon it when you were ab-solutely compelled to do so."

I yielded to the old financier's grim insistence and upon my re-turn to Paris I deposited one, perhaps even two, salary checks in the shabby banking house in the Rue Lafitte (or was it the Rue Tait-bout?) from where the astute brothers ruled the finances of two hemispheres. In this way I opened what I venture to say was the most inactive account that was ever saddled on the House of Roths-child. My money did not breed very fast but the fact that it was there was the source of much amusement to me and to my friends, and later on as I shall now relate, it saved me from—well, I shall simply say, great inconvenience.

As one confidence deserved another, I asked the Baron to explain (the subject at this time had not become threadbare) how the House of Rothschild had achieved its present power and fame. I suggested that, as that smacked of war correspondence, I would like to know all about those couriers from the *morne plaine* of Waterloo who brought the first news of the decisive battle and helped them to make a great "killing" in English consols which rose as Napoleon fell.

"I haven't the slightest doubt that we got early news as to what was happening in Belgium and converted it into a substantial profit," explained the Baron. "Then, as now, we did not depend upon the newspapers for our serious information. But I will say that in my judgment the most profitable business we have ever enjoyed, and the one from which we have derived our greatest profit, is our management of the fiscal affairs of Brazil. For one hundred years the people of Brazil sent us all they produced. We marketed for them and opened credits for them. For one hundred and fifty years we have looked after the fiscal affairs of the Brazilian government, first as a colony, second as an empire, and at last as a Republic. That business has been very profitable to us—" and after a pause he added, "and to the Brazilians."

Most apropos in these my days of need in Berlin I recalled this long idle account. I immediately presented myself at the grim battlemented bank of the Bleichroeders and acquainted the very austere-looking cashier that I had a small deposit with the Rothschilds of Paris which I wished to draw out to meet an unexpected demand. As I had no documents he suggested that I make out a draft for the amount I needed which they would send on to Paris and, if it was honored, they would pay me the amount minus the small charge they would have to make for their services. I made out the draft and I did more. I wrote Messrs. Rothschild explaining that owing to the loss of my bankbook perhaps my draft exceeded my balance. If this was the case, I would make up the overdraft very shortly. The money came and also a very civil letter. I had, it seemed, overdrawn my balance—slightly—but they were glad to await my convenience in settling it. This highly creditable behavior eased my departure from Berlin and facilitated my trip to Paris. The old Baron was quite right. It is great to have a bank account.

It was certainly great good luck that on my arrival I found Reick in Paris on one of his flying visits from New York. I knew that he would do what he could to straighten out my tangled affairs, and for the moment I chose to forget that he could do very little. At first off he took an optimistic view of the situation. The Commodore was quick to anger, it was true, but he would cool off quickly. We must wait and give him time, he assured me. And it seemed to me after recent experiences there was no more pleasant place to wait than Paris. But on the following day when Reick looked me up at my hotel his face was serious. "I'm afraid," he began, "this is not a tea-pot tempest—not by a long shot. Only once before have I seen the Commodore so angry. That was years ago when R.R., one of his prime favorites, who turned out to be such a scamp, traveled all over Europe impersonating the Khedive of Egypt, or his Grand Vizier, running up tremendous bills in Vienna and Baden-Baden which in the end the paper had to pay.

"Your telegram, he says, was simply a slap in the face and it reached him just as the Grand Duchess Wladimir and some other important people were sitting down to lunch with him. In fact to enjoy their company he had cut short his cruise and returned so suddenly, and he says it was your telegram that converted what should have been a most enjoyable affair into a complete fiasco.

" 'Charley Christianson (the confidential cabin boy now brought on from the yacht), who was lowering in the background, says this is not quite correct—but I'm afraid it is, if the Commodore thinks so. Christianson says the Grand Duchess was in a bad humor right at the start and gave the Commodore a terrible wigging even before the cocktails were served. And when *they* came, the oyster crabs the Commodore had had brought from the Chesapeake by special messenger, she said in a deep bass voice, 'Take 'em away—to me they look like deep sea vermin.' But worse was yet to come. When the Diamond Back terrapin à la Maryland Club were served, she said (Charley says she yelled), 'It looks to me as if the claws of pygmy monkeys were swimming around in that messy dish. No, I wouldn't feed it to my dogs.' It may have been the unusual seafood or maybe the Grand Duchess Marie Paulovna was in one of her tantrums, but the fact is the luncheon was a dreary failure and the Commodore makes you the scapegoat. He says your telegram completely destroyed his appetite—"

"Many a time in Berlin," I interrupted, "I wished the Commodore would send me a telegram to take my appetite away. In fact, that was all I asked for."

Reick thought my crack amusing, and with the very best intentions in the world on the following day he repeated it to the Commodore, but his attempt to turn the affair into a laughing matter was a complete failure.

"That young man has been riding a high horse too long. Of course, I have spoiled him, but—I'll send him back to New York where there may be, and where there may not be, work for him to do. Le P. . . . reports he has the audacity to assert he has on deposit with the *Herald* something like four thousand dollars. Of course, I knew I was paying him more, much more, than he is worth, but that sum is simply fantastic!"

Then came the business of going over the accounts with the French cashier in whom the Commodore, as well as I myself, had every confidence at the time. He certainly was hard driven, and how he could keep books in the circumstances was a marvel to me, and the answer probably is that he did not do it. We would settle down to our task about ten in the morning, and then would come in quick succession innumerable interruptions. A strange-looking sailor would appear, with an order from Mr. Bennett on his unmistakable robin's-egg writing paper, which would often read, "Give bearer one thousand francs and charge same to cable account." Then perhaps a fluffy young lady would appear with an order written out on the same undeniable paper, in the same unmistakable handwriting. "Mademoiselle Dorada tells me her scholarship money has failed to come. Advance her five thousand francs and charge to insurance." And so on throughout the live-long day.

I was amazed at these notations, but soon their purpose was made clear to me by the cashier. "Of course, as M. Gordon-Bennett is the sole owner of the *Herald*, it makes no manner of difference how these expenditures are charged. But we do it in this way to keep the books ship-shape, especially when we know, and we generally do, when the *fiscal* is coming around." And the *fiscal*, I learned later, was the advance agent of the income tax people.

But in all this confusion the muddle as to my Balkan accounts was by far the most involved. And in part, at least, this was the fault of nobody in particular. Much of it was clearly unavoidable. The drafts on Paris as they reached me in Belgrade or in Sofia and sometimes in even more outlandish places such as Scopia or Samokoff, I had sold to anyone who would buy them for what they would bring, often to hotel-keepers and to Greek restaurant keepers. Often I had made no records of these transactions (and why should I? The net was so simple I could carry it easily in my head) and of the records I had made, unfortunately not all had been preserved. I had begun working back from the books of 1890 and was making slow progress when the cashier cheered me with the remark, "Of course, as soon as my books for 1888 and 1889 were balanced, I destroyed the item entries."

Well, that was done and there was no use crying about it. In any event the thing would be over sooner than I had expected, and so I concentrated on the ledger for 1890. We explored these accounts intermittently for ten days, and I used the word intermittently advisedly, for there were interruptions and postponements almost every hour. And during these days, for reasons that I never sought to fathom, Mr. Bennett did not come near the business office, but his robin's-egg blue chits and orders to pay, to pay, came frequently.

I was not on a salary basis now, and as I knew that this pleasant relation would not be resumed until I reached New York, if then, I had this reason added to many others for wishing to return home. The Commodore, as I say, did not come near the office, but the cashier received frequent messages from him and quite often stepped out to consult the "money-boss" at Cuvillier's, which was then a small grocery store just around the corner on the Rue de la Paix. In the front of the store luxurious groceries and delicacies were exposed, but behind this there was a small pleasant room where Mr. Bennett and his particular pals would often meet to sip a special sherry from Jerez and munch caviar sandwiches. When called in consultation to this unusual meeting-place, the perplexed and puzzled cashier would, I must admit, leave me alone with the confusing records which he called his books, in the most confiding manner, but I should say I profited little by the opportunities that he gave me.

It would have been wise if at this moment I had consulted a lawyer or for that matter a level-headed business man or, perhaps, even had managed a personal interview with my dread boss for which he was evidently none too eager, but I was never wise and at this moment I was very angry, though truth to tell I was not more angry with my chief than I was with myself. Banking with the *Herald!* Placing my savings in the hands of M. Le P. . . . ! Well, it was clear that I had done it—incredible as it seemed in the cold light of the morning after.

And perhaps I was riding a high horse. I certainly had an exaggerated idea of the services I had rendered in southeastern Europe. But the Commodore shared responsibility for this! How he had slathered me with praise and how I had loved it! And, in any event, I spurned the strategic move which Reick now suggested. I would not, I simply would not, drop in at Cuvillier *frères*, much less loiter about the place in the hope of bumping into Mr. Bennett in a mellow moment when in a flash all might be forgotten, or at least forgiven. Had he not called me in a staccato telegram "his young Murat"? Well, I would teach him a lesson; and he would find out in his sad future that Murats, young or old, do not grow on every bush. "If he wants to see me, he will have to summon me," that was my last word. Apparently he did not want to see me; the summons never came.

But I did go to the rather down-at-heels bank in the Rue Taîtbout to assure the House of Rothschild that they would not lose by reason of their considerate treatment of me, and to settle the small overdraft or rather to assure them that the settlement would now not long be delayed. The cashier was charming. I should not give myself the least trouble. When convenient— I told him it would be convenient in two weeks and that I would insist upon paying interest! Touched to the quick by my noble attitude, the cashier said that the Baron was always interested in my travels and experiences, that he was even then in his office and would not be pleased unless I asked to see him. My card went in, and in a few moments I was explaining the German situation to the great man, and being invited to join him, Madame la Baronne and charming Mlle. Juliette, in his box at the Comédie Française that evening. The matter of my little overdraft was dismissed as a mere bagatelle, and then suddenly a change came over the great financier's countenance and his voice, that had been so soft and silken, sounded almost dictatorial.

"Your overdraft is perfectly all right, and I understand how it happened. We are here to serve the convenience of our customers; but—" and his eyes flashed, "but, I wish that at the next opportunity you will tell Mr. Bennett that should he again overdraw his account by one hundred thousand dollars, well—we shall not honor his signature."

This was indeed a bolt from the blue. I never had an opportunity of taking up the matter with Mr. Bennett, and I would not have done so had the opportunity presented itself, but if the Baron's statement were true, and how could I doubt it? it certainly explained the Commodore's peevishness at the suggestion I had made to the effect that I had on deposit with the business office a credit of nearly four thousand dollars. It seemed incredible, but as a matter of fact, with an income from his newspaper, and from his New York real estate, of close to a million dollars a year at this time, the Commodore was often in as dire financial straits as were the extravagant young men who were working for him on salaries they considered wholly inadequate.

As I continued to delve into the confusing array of figures which the always amiable cashier shoveled out to me, suddenly, under some telepathic influence, I began to wonder who the good people were who had come to the rescue of Peter Grant in his hour of need and seen to it that his last days were not without some of the luxuries which he so thoroughly appreciated. Six months before, I confess, I had not given the matter much thought. It was enough to know that the blessed Philadelphia remittances had come and that Peter was pleased at the thought he had not been forgotten by old friends. Confident that the remittances would long continue, we

Herald men had addressed ourselves to other and more pressing problems. Of course, as always, we were very busy. Unlike Atlas, perhaps, we did not carry the world on our shoulders, but we did carry Europe, and with the Commodore perched upon the top of that continent it made altogether quite a heavy load. And then one day, still in pursuit of my missing assets, I came across a series of weekly entries in the ledger before me that were so simple even I could understand them. They read, "Ten pounds to be remitted to Philadelphia Bureau—to be forwarded through First National Bank, to Peter Grant, Brighton, England. No acknowledgment required except from head of Bureau. Charge to entertainment fund."

And so the dry records revealed without the peradventure of a doubt how and by whom the comparative comfort in which our friend had ended his days had been provided. How like "Tiger Jim" it was, or at least I chose to think so. How he would insist upon pitiless publicity being meted out to him when he was in an unamiable mood, and here I was by the purest accident detecting him doing good by stealth! How particularly thoughtful and kind it was for the Commodore to let Peter Grant live and die under the illusion that his old friends in Philadelphia were willing and able to lend a helping hand. Of course I recognized that in view of the mess over my accounts with the cashier I, too, was contributing to the charitable fund, but the discovery left me with a very warm feeling toward the "money-boss" and with a readiness to accept a compromise on my claim which I had some reason to know was soon to be offered.

One day the cashier informed me that he had told "M. Gordon-Bennett" that the books plainly showed a balance in my favor, although it was nothing like the amount I was inclined to claim. On the following day he announced that "M. Bennett is getting impatient, he wants you to report to New York. I have told him that about three hundred pounds is owing you. Would you accept that in settlement?" I told him I would, and the next day I signed a receipt, the welcome money was forthcoming, and in the evening I crossed the Channel to London. In the Balkans it had been impossible to replenish my wardrobe. I was quite shabby, and hungry for good clothes. I spent almost the entire amount of my prize money, that is, all that I had been able to salvage, in Saville Row and in Bond Street.

Of course the dream of the Maryland farm had been shattered and I had been punished for my thrifty practices, but on the other hand I had contributed more to the comfort of Peter Grant's last days than I had at first off, in my meanness, thought I could afford. So with a clear conscience I spent two delightful weeks in London, renewing old friendships and making new acquaintances. I was on my own and spending my own hard-earned money, or rather what was left of it. And delay was perhaps excellent strategy; even Reick had suggested the advisability of postponing my arrival across the water. "It will give the Commodore more time to cool off," he had said.

In this moment of perplexity I had hoped to consult Henry M. Stanley who, back from rescuing Emin Pasha, the eccentric governor of Equatorial Africa who did not want to be rescued, was supposedly recruiting his shattered health and writing his travel epic in the Swiss Alps; but when I learned that the man who had so long ignored women had married and was on his honeymoon with the charming artist, Dorothy Tennant, I desisted.

Mr. Stanley was the greatest glory of the *Herald* staff and he always treated us youngsters in the kindest, indeed in an almost paternal manner. I had first approached him with my personal problems in 1885, during one of his rare visits to New York. Then as later in London he had given me good advice, all of which I treasured and some of which I followed. True, the jolt administered to me at this time by our roving sea-lord had been severe but—

"We must give our 'money-boss' (as he always called Mr. Bennett) a little, quite a little leeway," said Stanley. "Because? Well, stop and think what a dull drab place our world would be without him. I advise you to grin and bear it and above all to hang on. I can assure you he never forgets a piece of good work or the man who did it—although he tries to. Perhaps it will help you if I tell the story of my own first experience with our chief. You may remember I went to Magdala with Lord Napier, and had a good deal of luck in sending in the first news of the fall and death of Theodore, King of Kings."

"That's the first thing every cub reporter learns when he gets on the *Herald,*" I blurted out. "And it was particularly lucky—that break in the cable after your story had passed and the official dispatches were delayed."

But Stanley was not going to tell the story of how the cable "got broken," of which so many versions were current. He only smiled and said:

"Yes, that was lucky too. I thought Mr. Bennett would be pleased, but I did not hear from him, and when I reached Paris he had gone to the ends of the earth, somewhere, I forget where. But he had not forgotten me; there was a memo which read 'Tell "Dick" Stanley to report to New York as soon as possible.' Now I didn't like that. He might at least have gotten my name right. When I reached New York the city editor told me that I was to cover the Tombs Police Court, and I didn't like that at all. I thought of resigning just as you are doing now. But I hung on, as I hope you will, and soon I was glad I did. The people I met at the Police Court were interesting. They widened my world knowledge, indeed they were far more interesting than the people I had met in Abyssinia. A few months later I was called to Madrid and later to Paris, and together with our great boss I planned finding Livingstone, long lost in darkest Africa. And then Bennett referred casually to my Police Court assignment.

" 'Stanley,' he said, 'I was afraid you were getting in a rut, running 'round with generals and Kings of Kings and all that. I'm glad you hung on, however, and now I think you are just the man I want to go and find Livingstone.' "

I thanked the great explorer for his story and I too decided to hang on.

Naturally, as in my stay in England three years before, I cultivated the great war correspondents who survived from the previous generation, in whose footsteps I hoped to follow, and again Archibald Forbes was particularly kind, probably because of the fact that at the age of twelve, many years before in Washington, I had served as a sort of usher at his impromptu wedding to an American army girl, which had turned out very happily.

But in other respects Forbes was not happy. He had begun to feel the weight of years and his iron constitution was undermined by years of exposure. Often rheumatism laid him low for weeks at a time, and confessedly he could no longer follow the bugle calls or gallop to the sound of the guns. When I called at his invitation he said, "I am writing now what you call in the States a 'second day' story. I am writing the life of Julius Caesar—not because he is Caesar or was Emperor and for a time ruled the world, but because he was and is the greatest war correspondent who ever lived." I confess I gasped at this statement. During my arduous bouts with the *Commentaries* in school days this thought had never occurred to me, but I looked into the matter, as Forbes suggested I should, and when next I saw him I signified my complete agreement—but I added, pertly, "In our day he would not go far. His prose is plain and unadorned. He pronounces no slogans. Pictures he paints, it is true, but only in sub-tones."

"What would they do with Caesar on the *Herald* today?" asked Forbes quizzically.

"Well, I will tell you. He would be immediately withdrawn from the field. He might be given a job on the copy desk as a great condenser—a man who can reduce five columns to two 'sticks' and not leave out an essential fact."

"You are right," agreed Forbes, smiling now rather sadly. "To-day I fear Caesar could not hold a job even on the *Times* or the *Standard*, but the fact remains that he was the greatest of military writers and that we are not worthy to buckle on his sandals."

With his soldierly figure racked with rheumatic pains, and with new names holding the attention of the public, it was natural that Forbes should view the outlook with bitter forebodings and think that the profession he had so long adorned was going to the dogs. The speed of transmission which the editors and the public insisted upon was the factor that in his judgment had absolutely ruined the game. "And it was one of your men, and your present boss Bennett, who started us down the road to ruin," he asserted. In answer to my request for details he explained how it was MacGahan of the

Herald with whom he first came in contact during the Russo-Turkish War, who speeded up the profession.

"In the Franco-Prussian War while we were given no facilities, and indeed sought for none, things went along in this way. We would get as near the fighting as was permitted, or as was safe, and then when the fighting was over we would try to complete the picture by talks with the commanders of the units most closely engaged, then we would hustle around to get something to eat, and then we, or at least I, would begin to write my account of what had taken place. I always finished my yarn when once I began it and then I filed it away."

"At the telegraph office?" I inquired. "No, in my sabretache," he answered. "Then I had a smoke and a sleep. In the morning I would read my dispatch over and if on second thoughts it seemed all right I would roam about until I found a field postbox and drop it in. I was lucky when my letters reached London under a week. Then came MacGahan, wonderful, wonderful man that he was and Good Lord! how he jolted us. He had at his beck and call a corps of gallopers and he sent bulletins from the battlefields in Roumelia or Thrace every twenty minutes or so, and then before the fight was well over, or at least before we slow-thinking and slow-moving folk knew that it was, he was off to the nearest cable or telegraph station and he would not let the Kalmuck operator eat or sleep until his narrative was off (and what a narrative it was!) on the wings of speed to the Western world. He seemed to have lightning flashes at his command and I have heard, while I do not vouch for it, that once when he was campaigning with Skobeleff on the Oxus his account of one of the great battles with the Turcomans, owing to the difference in time and benefiting from it, was published in a late afternoon edition of a San Francisco paper on the evening before the battle was fought!"

I added to the veteran's horror by telling him of what the Commodore was planning to do with that then new-fangled gadget, the telephone—as soon as it was practical. All the European news was to come to Paris by telephone. The Constantinople man was to communicate with his colleague in Sofia. He in turn was to relay on to Belgrade, and so on *viva voce* to Pest, Vienna, Berlin, Cologne and then to Paris. At this revelation poor Forbes' scanty gray hair stood on end. "My God! What would Herodotus say to this," was his comment.

As a matter of fact, while the plan was greatly delayed Mr. Bennett did attempt his international telephone service in 1903. I fortunately escaped the coils of this network and, as it proved mechanically premature, and the leased wires very expensive, in a few months the experiment was abandoned and at this time telegraphy resumed an almost undisputed sway in the world of communications. I have often wondered what the comment of Forbes would have been had he lived to see the news services of the Great War period, when a word was often sent around the world in a fraction of a minute.

I had also met "Bull Run" Russell three years before, but unfortunately only on formal and very stodgy occasions. But now I was to have better luck and even enjoy an intimate view of the man who was certainly the father of war correspondence in its modern phase. Some of my old colleagues and some of the new ones were good enough to celebrate my return from the boisterous Balkans with a gay dinner at the Café Royal. Frank White, who had succeeded Brisbane on the *Sun*, presided and Harold Frederic of the *Times*, Poultney Bigelow of the *Critic*, Williams of the *London Chronicle*, and several others, whose names I do not recall, were present. As the dinner came to an end Bigelow had an idea. "This is 'Bull Run' Russell's birthday," he announced, "and no one has taken any notice of it. Let us drop in on the old man, bring him the news from the Balkans and let him see that he is not entirely forgotten." Some made objections because of the lateness of the hour, but soon five or six of us were jammed in a four-wheeler bound for Victoria Street where, in an apartment that the elder Bigelows occupied the year before, the Father Anchises of our craft now lived.

We had some difficulty getting in, and while "Bull Run" was wide awake when he greeted us, it was quite evident that a few minutes before he had been sound asleep. I had pictured him as old as Methusaleh but as a matter of fact he had been "caught young" and was at this time, with a great career behind him, only in the late sixties, and his complexion was ruddy, his step quick and his eyes bright. When we reminded him of the day we had come to celebrate, he roared with laughter and shouted that everyone else had forgotten his birthday and he was trying to. It was not difficult to see that the charming old boy was touched with our remembrance of him, at the end of what had been a lonely evening. It was different, very different, from the day forty years before when he brought to England the news from Sebastapol, and his disclosures overthrew the ministry of Lord Aberdeen and all England hung upon his every word. It was very different from the day thirty-five years before when he brought the news from Richmond where, according to Gladstone, Jefferson Davis had called a nation into being.

Now he was quite alone and our tribute brought tears to his eyes. He mixed us acceptable hot drinks and it was long after midnight when the stories of forgotten wars died away and he sent us out into the night with a "God bless you, and thank you." To me, in one of the asides, he had poured out a long yarn about his newspaper controversy with Burton Harrison, the talented Secretary of the Confederate President, but I cannot trust my fallible memory to repeat what Russell said. As the controverted points, in the opinion of Russell, marked the turn of the tide in the fortunes of the Southern states, it might be well for some industrious historian of the new school to look up in the yellowing newspaper files the letters that were then exchanged.

19. HOME—DEFEAT AND VICTORY

I WAS indeed a very resplendent person, or at least I thought so, when two weeks later I arrived in New York with exactly fifty dollars in my pocketbook, a sum rather smaller than that I was possessed of when I set out upon my adventures three years and six months before. Though I had been so long away there still survived not a few landmarks of my New York. The first and certainly the most famous of these was the St. James Hotel on Broadway at Twenty-sixth Street, then and for many years later the rendezvous of race-horse men. There, as of old, Captain Connor presided in the lobby and held circle while Ed Hill, the affable clerk, a walking directory of all the men, and women too for that matter, who followed the horses, stood behind the desk. John McCullagh, the actor, and Colonel Tom Ochiltree, the wit, were having a violent quarrel as I entered to the amusement of quite a number of the survivors of the '49 gold rush who together with old sports of other days sat in the capacious armchairs along the wall. They were talking about the great race years before at Pimlico between Parole and Ten Broeck and the four-legged Tom Ochiltree, but what the two-legged Tom was talking about we could not make out. There he was in his flashy waistcoat and red tie shouting at the top of his voice:

> "I know! I know!
> The big black man
> Wot picked de lock
> Ob de hen house do'."

"There is here a veiled innuendo which I fail to understand," said one of the side-liners in courtly language, "but McCullagh evi-

dently does." There could be little doubt of that. Finally McCullagh hurled a spittoon at the merry Texan and then Captain Con-
ner intervened. "Lead the gentlemen to their quarters," he said to
bell boys who were built on the scale of bouncers, and things quieted
down.

Ed Hill remembered me—faintly, and noted that I had been
absent from the race meetings for some time. "Hoped I would do
better now." After I had registered he said in a low voice, he was
evidently not proud of it, "The Percheron people are holding a
convention and the house is full. But you shall have a room tomorrow. In the meantime Brady will wheel your things down to
the overflow house we favor. It's on Twenty-sixth Street, just past
the Lambs and right opposite the Racquet Club." I was there very
soon but I did not unpack. I wanted to see people and places that
had been dear to me. The landlady had given me a latchkey and
there was no reason why I should not return late, and as a matter
of fact I did. Then it seemed to me the room did not look quite as
I left it. "I suppose they have unpacked and put my things away—
as they do in London lodgings," I surmised, and tumbled into bed.

But the clear light of a late morning awakening disclosed another
scene. The trunks had been unpacked, indeed they had been gutted.
The landlady, as she insisted when summoned, could not believe
her eyes and I had difficulty in crediting mine. I went to the
Twenty-ninth Street precinct station but the famous Captain "Alec"
Williams was away on important business and the sergeant put
me in charge of a ward detective. "Evidently a professional job,"
was his verdict. Then shuffling from one leg to another the detective
sighed, "To me it looks like Finnegan—and I could get him if they
would let me have the time off." I slipped the ingenious fellow a
tenner, one of the very few remaining in my wallet, and he said he
would leave no stone unturned to bring the sneak thief to justice,
"and the return of my clothes," I cried. "I have nothing but what I
stand up in."

The ward detective wanted to talk although I urged him to be up
and doing. He found it simply flabbergasting that I should have
lived for three years among low-class Europeans, "practically
savages" as he put it, without missing anything more valuable than

a scarf pin, and now "my first night home from a foreign shore 'the boys' should rob me of every stitch of clothing that I possessed." He said it was baffling, and that the Captain would be mad as hops because of it happening to one of the *Herald* boys of whom he was particularly fond. He talked in this strain for so long that I had to remind him that the trail was getting cold. Then and then only he was off.

To my amazement there was not the slightest difficulty in re-plenishing my wardrobe, and first off it did not cost me a cent. On the corner of Ann and Nassau Streets there did business at this time a tailor who prided himself upon "dressing" the *Herald* men. I wish I could recall the name of this patient fellow but I cannot. Those who would seek further will doubtless find it in the Golden Book where are inscribed the names of all those who loved their fellow men, and also I fear in the archives of the bankruptcy court. This philanthropist, his tribe did not increase, was not at all inter-ested in your banking standing but if you were on the paper he would dress you from crown to toe, and while this man's courage, and above all his patience, was often sorely tried, it was a point of honor with all of us that in the end he should not be defrauded of his just dues. While as works of art these garments could not be mentioned in the same breath with those that the master tailors of Saville Row had turned out, they were probably more fitting to the role which I was now called upon to play which was, it seemed, that of "emergency man" on the city staff.

While humiliating to a degree for a man who had walked with kings, and held converse with great civic leaders and the captains of mighty hosts, this new duty was simply fascinating. I had to confess that—although of course under my breath. As I afterwards learned I was even an interloper in this humble job. The Commodore had not deigned to announce my arrival to his New York authorities and Reick, as always friendly, had decided not to mention my name until we had given the Commodore ample time to "cool off," as we called it.

Two or three days after my arrival, Morgan, our most trusted stableboy of the racing days, appeared at my door with a broad grin of welcome. I was pleased at his affectionate greeting and again absolved him of any responsibility for the disaster at Sheepshead Bay which had turned me adrift on the sea of journalism.

"It want Liz's fault nuther," he protested loyally. "She had the race in hand and I stood at the head of the stretch to give the old gal her cue. I yelled 'Come on, Lizzie Preston, show 'em your heels.' But that track ain't quiet like Timonium and the waves on the shore mixed up in it too, making a terrible fuss. She never heard me. Ef she had of heard me things would have been different, a mighty sight different," continued Morgan in mournful tones. "Yer could have jest been loafing along with yer horse and yer dorg and yer gun—and livin like a gentleman—"

"But it has been great fun, Morgan," I said. "I have had better luck than the other boys." This pretense he brushed away curtly, "Yer right—Mr. Steenie it ain't no use hollerin, hollerin never did help nobody." "I'm not hollerin, Morgan; I've seen the world and a lot of interesting people."

"I hears very few on 'em speaks our language as we does and most of 'em are onnery critters—them Vulcans."

"Not at all, Morgan," I said, "they are mostly fine fellows but every now and then you do run against one who is pizen bad."

"Why then they are jest like the folks at home," commented Morgan in astonishment. And his last word on the Balkans was not a bad summing up of a situation upon which so many more learned men have discoursed.

I knew Morgan would not leave me without picturing a rainbow on our rather dark horizon, and now he set to work upon it in low confidential tones as became a racing man who knew full well that walls have ears. "We 'ave bred Liz to Jonesboro. He stands at Dr. Thom's place on the Rolling Road and she has thrown the likeliest colt I ever sot my eyes on. Mr. Steenie, I declare that rompety colt will put us all on easy street some day. Last month I took old Martin out to see him and he sez, 'Morgan, that's a good one. He's a born lepper.' But that boy wasn't born no lepper. I'se trained him to be one. Ebery day he jumps for his breakfast, his dinner, and his supper, and them brush hurdles are getting pretty high now and when he jumps 'em clean, and he most allays does, he gets a carrot or a turnip extra. Don't tell ole Martin. Those Irish foreigners are getting a lot of horse jobs away from us American boys."

"Mum's the word, Morgan."

Though very hard-up as a result of financing the researches of the ward detective, who had touched me again the evening before, it was clear to me that I should pay Morgan's return fare to Baltimore, indeed if I could manage it, his round trip. It was undoubtedly a case of *noblesse oblige*, but when I delicately broached the subject Morgan burst out laughing. "Why, Mr. Steenie, I don't need no ticket on no train—that is if they runs a Pullman and where I wants to go they generally does. I jes' put on my little white jacket, mix up with the other boys and travels free. I don't give up any of my money, but of course I don't beat my way nuther. If it's a sporty crew on the diner I gives 'em tips on the races. If they are no-count niggers, why I helps 'em wash up the dishes."

No one, not even Reick at this time, unless mercifully he suppressed it, had any idea of what my actual status was, but very soon it developed that there was no salary attached to it. I was "on space" and very little encouragement to "grab it" was given me by the men at the desk. Doubtless the intelligent thing to do would have been to have left the paper and made a fresh start elsewhere. Brisbane offered to pave my way to a place on the *Sun*, where he was all powerful, but I hung on and gradually I became, not the permanent (no such luck as that!) but rather the extra or occasional "emergency man" on the night staff.

Fascinating as it undoubtedly was, I must make it quite plain that emergency duty was not sought after by trained men. It was generally reserved for some fledgling favored by a man higher up, "downstairs," who was determined that his protégé should be given a chance to show the stuff that was in him or for a man "who was destined to walk the plank." I never was quite certain as to which of these categories I had been placed in.

In my humble capacity I reported to the night city editor every afternoon at five o'clock and remained on guard until five the next morning, and indeed often later when something "big" loomed, something big enough to justify a postscript to the city edition.

For these long hours the "emergency man" received three dollars and his expenses of transportation—but even his carfares were closely scrutinized and food and refreshments came out of his own pocket. But these three dollars were safe from the arrogant man at the desk and the cheese-paring activities of the condensing men who sat at the copy desk. Whether you turned in a "sweet and startling story" of two or three columns or merely a few city items you got the three dollars. That was money in the bank that could not be taken from you, but how little it was, especially in comparison with the long stories I had handed in and the "big" bills I had made in the happy days before the lightning of the Commodore's favor had struck me and I was ordered abroad!

The "turn over" in the city rooms of a metropolitan newspaper is very rapid and many of my good friends were gone. Most of all I missed "Jim F. . . ." who was dead, as the saying was—not literally correct—he had gone to the well once too often. The attitude of my new colleagues was generally marked by complete indifference. I once heard a youngster who had just arrived from Dublin by the way of Castle Garden say to a new arrival with college paper experience, with unmistakable reference to me, "Well, he went up like a rocket—and he came down like a stick." "How I would like to have his chance," sighed the college man. "Some get it and some don't," commented an old-timer of twenty summers, "but when the Boss is through with you—he's through."

Dear old H. . . . with his Civil War stories had taken refuge with a proud daughter who ran a dairy farm in Connecticut. No longer would he delight us with his graphic account of the charge of Pickett's men up the slope at Gettysburg. Most depressing of all was the reappearance on the scene of "Modoc" Smith, the man who in his brave youth had tracked "Captain Jack" to the Lava Beds, interviewed him exclusively for the *Herald* and who told such wonderful stories of "Scarred Face Charley," the lieutenant of the great Indian chief. "Modoc" as he admitted had counted too confidently upon the appreciation of his abilities by a Tammany sachem who had now left him in the lurch. Panting and puffing the old boy climbed up the four flights of steep steps that led to the city rooms and told me that financial stringency compelled him to stage a "comeback." "Fortunately I have not lost my nose for news," he asserted, and then in a confidential whisper he added, "I have downstairs at Sandy's the only genuine Simon pure Tichborne claimant. I have primed him with liquor and he has agreed to spill his story—to me exclusively, and I'll pass it on to you exclusive—but on one condition. I'm to be paid for any space you get out of it." That seemed fair enough to me, but of course such an agreement required the sanction of the man in charge. When I broke it to X. . . . he howled, "Tichborne claimant! 'Modoc' Smith? Why he's in his dotage. Always bringing in old stuff! Throw him out." I could not bring myself to do that; in fact I went downstairs and blew them both to supper. "Modoc" had overdone the priming and the only genuine Simon pure Tichborne claimant was too full for utterance. But as I saw him plain I read the handwriting on the wall. Perhaps my stories were old stuff. I, too, was an old-timer—of twenty-four!

So the nights rolled on, and while I had every confidence that Reick was doing all he could to help me retrieve my fortunes, there was as yet no perceptible break in the dark clouds overhead. Once I cornered him but in answer to my inquiries he only gave me a significant wink. It was all very perplexing. The nights rolled on and truly an infinite variety of emergencies arose. A murder "broke" and you were sent to reinforce the mighty men at police headquarters. Or the man in charge of City Hall stuttered in over the new-fangled telephone in a way that indicated to the night editor that he was in no condition to write his story, and you were sent to extract it from him. A pestilence would be reported on a ship off quarantine and in defiance of all regulations you were sent to get it—the story, not the pestilence. Then a perfectly inadequate yarn would drift in from a rural correspondent upstate or down in Jersey and you were sent to grab it. It meant "hopping" the milk train on your homeward journey, or sitting in the caboose with the kindly crew, and the moment you reached the terminal, to catch the last edition, you had to shout your news over the telephone to the night man who was invariably hard of hearing.

One night a seedy-looking doctor wandered into the office with what he said was an important communication to the American people. "It has long, too long, been withheld, but now my conscience forces me to speak." The man in charge sent him over to my desk. The visitor could not have walked a tight rope, or even a chalk line, but when he began to talk his language was surprisingly coherent.

"Young man," he began, "Edgar Allan Poe, our peerless poet, died in these very arms. I supported him in his last moments. I sought to ease his agony. I, I alone, heard his last words."

"What were they?" I inquired eagerly.

"He was very weak—as you know those ruffianly 'plug-uglies' in Baltimore had been carrying him from poll to poll and voting him in the name of reputable citizens long dead, and all the time very inadequately clad he was exposed to wind and weather. When brought into the hospital he seemed so faint I offered him a sip of brandy, not a gulp mind you but just a medicinal and tonic sip, as was our practice in similar emergencies; but he waved it aside and said, 'Not that, not that, I would not touch it if thereby I secured an eternity of happy days.' Young man, Mr. Poe then went softly to sleep and he never awoke in this world—these were his last words." Of course, I rushed over to the desk of X. . . ., who was in charge that night, and advised him of the wonderful story that had dropped into our laps, but X. . . . took a different view of it. "I don't think we had oughter print that," he snarled. "It's a libel on Mr. Poe. Whiskey has helped a lot of men and even a sip of brandy has saved many a life. We'll make a 'stick' of it and I'll see later."

Later I saw him "kill" it. X. . . . drank a lot that night; the office boys were quite worn out bringing him up hot toddies from Sandy Spencer's—in coffee cups, of course. He was a staunch friend of John Barleycorn both in theory and in practice and toward morning he announced that he was "all in" and wanted to be taken to St. Vincent's where the Sisters understood his "trouble" as nobody else did. As day dawned those who still lingered in the city room scraped together their available cash, hired a shabby barouche that stood in Fulton Street, and escorted X. . . . to the hospital, where he was received as an old friend without the least formality. The four days he now passed in the padded room were, as we learned to our sorrow, not spent in idleness. On the morning of the fifth day he was back on his job. With him he brought heavily blue-penciled copies of every issue of the *Herald* since he had been placed in safe refuge. Every one of the contributors to the life-saving ride to the hospital was fined for some slip or error in his copy. What were the offenses of the other men I do not remember but my own dereliction I shall never forget. I had misspelled the name of the late A. T. Stewart, the merchant prince. That cost me two dollars. X. . . . 's boast was that he played no favorites, even-handed justice to all was his motto, to all except the Irish and why did he favor the Irish? Well, it was a divine command, "God loves the Irish," and this at least was a heavenly command he never failed to obey. But he taught me a lot; the most valuable lesson I ever learned came from observing his way of life. He took his pleasures so sadly and on my next visit to Maryland old friends found me changed. Singularly, surprisingly abstemious was the way they put it. I owed a lot to the ungrateful old reprobate. Peace to his ashes!

One evening as I came on duty I found the city room charged with mystery. The cynical, devil-may-care atmosphere was gone and this was perfectly understandable to me when I learned that X. . . . 's new sojourn at St. Vincent's was being prolonged and that the romantic Frank N. . . . was in charge. He was a long-haired sentimental soul, kindly to all, but a perfect tiger for "scoops and beats" as he called exclusive stories. He was also something of a mystic and when in doubt he was known to consult a spiritualistic medium for crime solutions which baffled the men at Police Headquarters.

And it was at this moment that for the first time O'Rorke's "flimsy," abominable innovation! later to become so disastrous to space men, dawned on my horizon. Our great crime story man was reeling off the yellow pages and several of his jackals who had been sent out on the side issues were feeding him obsequiously with the details they had brought to light. Suddenly Frank sprang from his desk, and with flaming eyes bulging from their sockets, joined the busy group. In his hand, trembling with emotion, he held a sheet of "flimsy." "This completes our story," he announced. "The murderer has executed himself. He lies at the morgue. My God! We've a beat. This supplies the missing link to the sweetest murder story

I have ever handled." With a nod of approval the great crime writer drove on furiously, covering more of the yellow sheets which, indorsed in blue-penciled hieroglyphics, Frank would send up the whistling pipe to the composing room.

Then he came over to me. "The missing man is without doubt lying on a slab at the morgue. Examine him carefully but in a nonchalant manner, for we all know that Luke, the keeper, leaks to the *Sun*. Look him over casually, pass the time of night with Luke and then—disgusted-like—you leave; but once you are clear of the morgue run like the devil and report to me. Of course it's our man, but to make assurance doubly sure here's our description. He's well over six feet, the type of a desperado, evidently a man of Herculean strength; clean-shaven, but with a lot of close cropped hair. One finger is missing. I'm sorry we are not quite certain whether it is from the right or the left hand."

I hurried through the dark and dreary night to our street of Sorrows, and finally landed at the foot of Twenty-sixth Street and the East River at the miserable hovel where in those days New York's nameless dead were exhibited while awaiting recognition.

Old Luke was as usual at the door, smoking his pipe and nursing his wooden leg, and to him I said, a great improvement on Frank's suggestion I flattered myself, "I'm covering the East Side police stations tonight, old man, and so I thought I'd drop in to see if anything is doing." "Nope," he answered, "only one pore stiff. River's frozen—not givin 'em up 'spose."

Doing the honors of his gruesome establishment, in the atmosphere of the charnel house through which even his villainous tobacco could not cut its way, stumbling with his wooden limb over the sanded floor, Luke led me down the dark passage and then threw the light of his flickering lantern upon his only guest. And what a disappointment it was. The unfortunate man was the perfect physical antithesis of the missing link that was needed to complete the story that Frank and the crime expert were weaving. . . .

It was just too bad for Frank and it was none too good for me. It was no feather in your cap to come back to the office and smash a "scoop" that had looked as promising as this. You soon got the reputation of being unlucky, and that was no help to a man in the news-gathering business. So once out in the snow again I slowed down and took counsel with myself. Of course, I was not for a moment tempted to wander from the narrow path of virtue and accuracy. Not even a *Morning Journal* reporter could rise to the imaginative height, or sink to the depths of depravity that would be required to pretend that this poor inoffensive "floater" was all that remained of the desperate murderer that was required to round out our exclusive crime story. No, I was not tempted, but I was kind. I would not hurry back to the office. I would let Frank and the others involved enjoy their dream of a scoop for another half hour or so.

In this mood of mercy and charitable delay I wandered about in the snow drifts for several minutes, expanding my lungs in the cold bracing air of the winter night and expelling that breath of the dead house that still clung to me.

Suddenly I was confronted by a great pyramid, not as high as Cheops but still reaching heavenward, which closer examination revealed as a monumental heap of horse dung and stable bedding. That was a strange sight, but stranger still were the lights that flickered rather than flashed from it and the gay voices speaking in a strange tongue that came from it. I could hardly believe my ears, and as is axiomatic with a newshawk, when in doubt I appealed for light and leading to the nearest bar-keep, and he was not far away. "It's a lot of Eyetalians, the filthy beasts. It's wops and guineas who have broken in there and made themselves very much at home. I have told the cop about it, as any decent man would, but he only twirls his stick and laughs. But what can you expect? The force is going to the dogs—and naturally since not more than half of them wuz born in Ireland."

I thanked the indignant bar-keep, paid for my drink and his, and was about to proceed on my way when an idea which in the sequel turned out not to be a bad one occurred to me. Often when one story fizzles out you stumble upon another. I worked around three sides of the Gargantuan manure pile before I came, not to a door, but to an alley which gave access to the interior. From it strayed feeble beams of light and sounds of music. Someone was playing a

love song on a guitar and someone was accompanying on the con-
certina. Softly the romance died away and half a dozen musical
voices joined in a cheerful marching song.

> *Corraggio, Corraggio!*
> *Macaroni con Formaggio!*

were it seemed to me the simple words. When that too died away,
giving way to the clinking of glasses, I pushed my way along the
narrow passage which, after penetrating for about ten feet through
a solid wall of manure, broadened out into a great hall about thirty
feet square. Here seated around a piano packing case, upon little
soap boxes, were half a dozen men and women, evidently Italians,
engaged in cheerful converse and in drinking a muddy red wine
out of goblets. The hall was lighted by two or three battered carriage lanterns and the four or five galleries which led from it were
also dimly lighted. While I was pleasantly and even effusively
greeted, my presence was evidently embarrassing to the cheerful
folk who were having such a merry time when I disturbed them,
but this soon passed when I assured them that I was not a ward
detective and rather admired their housing scheme.

As I had to put the crime story men out of their suspense my first
visit was short, but when the next evening, being absolutely master
of my time, I returned, these Italians seemed glad to see me and
throwing caution to the winds I sipped of their wine and found it
far from bad. Some three or four of the dung heap denizens were
organ-grinders, but most of them were skilled timbermen working
in a new railway tunnel. The skill they possessed was demonstrated
by the way they had shored up the walls of the rooms and galleries
in their unusual home with odds and ends of planks and beams.
The little galleries from the social hall led to the sleeping alcoves
of the married couples and to a larger dormitory for the single men.
This was fairly close, but beyond was a kitchen furnished with a
charcoal stove. The kitchen was better ventilated than any of the
other apartments by the ingenious device of an old stove pipe thrust
through the roof of dung and straw. There was a pungent odor of

urine-soaked straw about the social hall, but it was not particularly disagreeable to an almost professional horse lover who now seemed to be definitely dismounted.

The colony numbered thirty and they all came from adjacent villages in the Abruzzi district. They explained that early in November they had learned of this mountain of dung from several of their fellow countrymen who were city scavengers. Down in Mulberry Street, the tenement where they lived was damp and dark and the rents were high "and so cold. And here we are quite warm and have no fires to keep up. But when the *primavera* comes—" Well—that reference to spring with a sad grimace from one of the girls I did not understand until later.

Some of the girls worked long hours in an artificial flower factory on Bleecker Street. One stayed at home and she, by far the prettiest, was about to have a baby, and an old woman presided over the community kitchen and, as far as I could see, never emerged from it. It was not long before I had organized the colony into an Organ-Grinders Club and soon this social organization found its way into the feature pages of our Sunday edition. There must have been intrinsic merit in these stories because while still a member of the staff, in a way of speaking, I was clearly a man who "was on his way out," and the Sunday editor would have rejected these contributions, as he had so many others, but for the fact that they simply forced their way into his columns.

Here in March, without medical assistance of any kind (I heard that the old woman, who stayed so persistently in the kitchen that I never saw her, came out and lent a hand), the pretty girl gave birth to a man child and no under-privileged American citizen ever came into the world in more singular surroundings than did he. A few days later the comely mother and the robust child were sunning themselves outside the entrance gallery. She was combing out her heavy black hair, that had become sadly tangled during her hour of travail, and the baby with a rather wry face was sucking his big toe while awaiting something more nourishing. I remarked that both were enjoying the more clement weather, but the Abruzzi girl answered sadly, "*Si, Si, primavera* is coming," and then she explained what spring meant to the happy dwellers inside the mountain of dung. "Santa Madonna, in the spring come many boats and many, very many, big shovel men will dig our house down and pile it on scows—and then up the river to manure the farm lands. So speaks my brother the scavenger, he says he has seen it happen already two years."

And true enough, as I passed that way a short week later I saw that the palace of dung,* so dear to these hardy people, had disappeared like the fabric of a dream. A string of scows was still visible, being towed up the river. The mighty shovelers were resting from their labors on the soap boxes, and only the pungent odor remained. The Organ-Grinders Club had been forced back to Mulberry Street and into the clutches of the grasping landlords until the blessed winter time when it does not pay to transport manure, and dung heaps rise (or did) mountain high along the East River. I would have followed my interesting friends to their new quarters but by a sudden turn in the wheel of fortune my daily life was now directed into other channels. This experiment in housing had helped the gay settlers through a hard winter, and to me their acquaintance had been profitable, indeed, without exaggeration, it had been a lifesaver.

While things were apparently improving I was not out of the woods yet. When Reick was absent, or away on a vacation, my assignments even to emergency duty became few and far between. On one of these evenings of enforced leisure which were so frequent I picked up Brisbane in the cubby hole office in the Sun Building from which he was running the afternoon edition. Small as was his den, the young and ardent editor had installed a cot where from time to time he hoped to get a few winks of sleep; but as a matter of fact, like the great presses that rumbled down below, he never closed an eye. We ran into Billy Harper, the most genial member of the famous publishing firm, and with Frank Millet, who had retired from war correspondence and was painting portraits, we wound up a gay evening in the new (it is a Victorian antique now!) and splendiferous apartment house where Harper and Brisbane lived (at 247 Fifth Avenue, I think).

Other amusements having been exhausted we began matching

* It stood on the present site of the landing stage of the N.Y. Yacht Club.

quarters. Mine were soon lost and I was about to start home when Brisbane insisted that I should go to bed in his apartment down below. He knew from long experience how hard I was to move in the morning and we had planned to go at crack of dawn to meet at quarantine the divine and adorable Sarah Bernhardt. We had both learned to admire and to love her in Paris, and were determined to extend a welcoming hand on this, perhaps the first of a long series of farewell tours in America. Millet left, insisting that since he had gray hair he slept in his own bed, so Brisbane installed me in his apartment and returned to Harper's where now, matching dollars, they fought with each other for the spoils of the long evening.

I had but just gotten to sleep when someone aroused me by pulling my big toe—not roughly, to be sure, indeed as deferentially as it can be done. And then I heard, "I'm sorry to wake you up, Briz —but it is a case of must. I'm going down to Lakewood by the first train. It's just the sweetest story you ever heard of and I think it will be a 'scoop.' I shall try to be back at eleven but hold the forms as long as you can and set aside at least two columns—and let me have a little more leeway if you can."

My deferential awakener poured out more details of his prospective scoop, all of which I have forgotten, but never shall I forget the ingratiating voice with which he spoke. "So long Briz," he added but I called him back and informed him that he had not been talking with his chief but with a *Herald* man! The young reporter was quite agitated but I assured him I would not take advantage of his mistake in toes, and so began the most pleasant friendship of my life. This eager news-gatherer and stormer of the night was no other than Richard Harding Davis. While he was a year or two older than I, at this time Dick had only been abroad a few weeks when he acted as the chronicler of the doings of a Philadelphia cricket eleven touring England. My experiences, which I was by no means loathe to relate—in Europe, Asia and Africa—filled him with admiration and envy of a rare generous quality. He was infatuated with what he called my Balkan background and he hailed me as a superman.

In a few weeks Dick grew so enthusiastic that he shared me with his friends. He took me to not a few houses where he was cherished and so persuasive was he that in many of them he succeeded in having me accepted at the very high value he placed upon me. One afternoon by arrangement he took me to the Early-General-Grant brownstone house on Madison Avenue where in the active retirement he enjoyed between his two presidential terms, President Cleveland and his charming wife were living. Both of them loved Dick whom they had known since earliest boyhood. *Gallegher and Other Stories* had just appeared, and its early sales were flattering. Three or four charming young ladies came in and surrounded Dick with an admiring circle which he enjoyed. With the deference which from my larger experience I knew was pleasing to the great ones of the earth, especially to those who are temporarily in eclipse, I sat in a corner with our recent Chief Magistrate and listened to the rather commonplace remarks he was making.

But it was hard, very hard, and often my attention wandered to the gay group being regaled by one of Dick's stories. Well, shame on me—and an original Cleveland man, too!, at last, I turned a deaf ear to the great man and listened in on Dick's amusing anecdote. He was describing his first visit to the Philadelphia newspaper office after the appearance of the notable story in which he praised the office boy Gallegher "for beating the town." He was surprised by the cold aloofness of his hero and only with difficulty drew from him the explanation, "You see, Mr. Davis, you have gone and spelled my name wrong. My mother says we Gallaghers are big people in Galway—while the Galleghers are quite a common sort from Roscommon. She do take on awful like about the mistake and she do say she 'opes you will give credit where it is due."

Well, I got most of the yarn but, of course, I cannot reproduce Dick's inimitable mimicry. The peals of laughter that followed completely drowned out what the ex-President was saying. He flushed scarlet and banging the table before him until the teacups rattled he shouted, half in earnest and half in jest, "Of course, I admit I didn't write Gallegher or any other stories, but I have been President of these United States and some of you have got to listen to me!" Led by Mrs. Cleveland the bevy of charming young ladies crowded around the great man and soon he was amiable again.

But now too late I realized that I had been ambushed. Dick, accompanied by Mrs. Cleveland, sang *Little Annie Rooney* and *Sweet Rosie O'Grady* and then announced, "We have with us the greatest living war correspondent—just back from the cockpit of Europe, and he will now oblige with *Shumi Maritza,* the war song of the Bulgarians." I prayed that as of old some pitying goddess would envelop me with a protective cloud and so conceal my embarrassment, but I had no such luck. I stood stock still and blushed scarlet. The prettiest of the young ladies tapped the floor petulantly and said scornfully, "I don't believe he knows it." "You are right," I admitted, and fled—not the only time I fear that I failed absolutely to live up to Dick's glowing announcements.

For many obvious reasons the subject of my Balkan accounts was distasteful to me, and back in New York I was careful not to refer to the matter. I had learned my lesson and I would never again bank with the business office, and that was all there was to it. But some rumors had come from Paris and one day Judson Brown, the treasurer, whom we all loved (and with much reason, for while he safeguarded the interests of his spendthrift boss, he also looked after ours) called me in. I told him that as far as I was concerned the chapter was closed, but I did express the opinion that if an accountant went over the Paris *Herald* books, interesting things would come to light. Brown made a suggestion to this effect and was snubbed for his pains, but as so often happened, while the Commodore snubbed the man who made it, he accepted the suggestion.

Famous and sworn accountants were brought over from London and they discovered incredible irregularities, and my antagonist in the Balkan accounts was arrested. The London firm charged that four hundred thousand dollars had been stolen but the Commodore, who did not want his business brought into court, or his accounts publicly aired, contented himself with an indictment charging the embezzlement of eighty thousand francs. And as a matter of fact, even the bringing of this minor charge he lived to regret. M. Le P. . . . the cashier, having plenty of money, secured a very able lawyer who rang the changes on the fact that while M. Bennett had an income of five million a year he only paid his cashier five hundred a month. Even I, who had suffered from his depredations, had a certain amount of sympathy with the fellow who while he stood by in shabby clothing and enjoying but meager fare saw all the play boys and play girls of Paris, indeed of the world, put their predatory hands into the *Herald* till. In the end he got two years in prison and several years later, having completed his sentence, M. Le P. . . . opened a bank in Shanghai where in the French Concession he grew to be quite a power. If there was ever any re-adjustment of my Balkan accounts the news of it never reached me.

Brisbane thought that Mr. Bennett had treated me shamefully but that I also was to blame for my wasted years. He would con-done the months I had spent in western Europe but the two years lost in the Balkans was an unforgivable offense against any future I might possibly have had. "It's the men who have stayed at home that have gotten the plums," he asserted. "Now there's Speer. He's not a better man than you, but see how he's gone ahead. He dubbed Fred Gibbs the 'Wicked Senator' and the town still rings with it. Why a thing like that is an annuity; without doubt when a vacancy occurs he will just naturally be sent to Albany as our cor-respondent. Now, what have you brought back from the Balkans?"

That was a leading question and hard to answer, but I did the best I could. "Well, I am probably the only man on the New York papers who knows how to spell Stambouloff."

"Much good that will do you," snorted Brisbane.

"How right you are," I admitted. "I never can get it printed right in the paper. Jack Henderson the foreman of the pressroom tells me that the chapel of Typographical Union No. 6 have de-cided to spell it the wrong way and that their decision is irrevoca-ble."

But Brisbane did not stop at mere criticism. He tried to be help-ful, and with this purpose in view brought me into contact with William Laffan who had recently made him editor of the *Evening Sun*. Laffan was a wise and somewhat taciturn Irishman who had made his debut on the *Sun* a few years before writing art and liter-ary notes, but soon by favor of Dana, and through his ability, ac-quired complete control of the paper. We lunched together at Mou-quin's and Laffan was at first far from enthusiastic on the subject of my employment, but finally made me a proposition and said that

I could begin work on the following day. He admitted that the salary he mentioned was probably considerably less than I received on the *Herald*, but he dwelt with emphasis upon the stability that went with my new position and also the honor of being enrolled on the staff of the *Sun*.

I conceded all these advantages but I asked for a delay of twenty-four hours in which to consider his offer. They were restless, sleepless hours, but on the following morning I reached a firm decision and declined the new opening. Of course, I was well aware that I had fallen from favor. Everyone on the *Herald* staff was aware of that, and not a few of those in positions of power showed their knowledge of it in unpleasant ways. On the other hand, the field of the *Herald* was world-wide, while that of the *Sun* was purely local. I had visited many strange countries and consorted with many wild tribes; at times the Commodore had been generous in his praise and he might forget what he had called my outbreak of impertinence. And then I liked the man and so, wisely or unwisely, I stayed on the *Herald*.

When Minister Beltcheff was assassinated, as the cables from Sofia briefly reported, I was sorry it was not Petroff, the chief of the "stick-men" who had so often harassed me, but still I recognized it was a step in the right direction and Bulgaria might yet be free. Beltcheff was also a rather unscrupulous individual and he was not the first or the last to die, of the thick-set beetle-browed individuals with whom Stambouloff surrounded himself in the hope of misleading his would-be murderers. The cable was so laconic that I could not control my desire to enlighten the readers of the *Herald* as to what the news meant in the actual situation in southeastern Europe. So I wrote an article with, as I thought, the descriptive title of "The European Powder Mine." I introduced it with the suggestion that an explosion was in order, and concluded it with the remark, which was our ritual, that the *Herald* with its Argus eyes and warning voice should and undoubtedly would be on the scene first.

Unfortunate for all concerned, and particularly unfortunate for me, was the fact that at this moment Reick was away in the South on a brief vacation. The article would have to be passed upon by

Flynn, and I had abundant reason to know what his attitude was on news from the Balkans, however thrilling it might seem to me. But here was an opportunity for him to reverse himself, not only to the advantage of the paper, but to my own. Indeed I was probably driven to the bold steps I now took by the financial stringency in which I was involved. For whenever Reick went away the sterling qualities of my work were overlooked; quite frequently the night city editor would say, "There will be nothing for you to-night." Not even the poorly paid but fascinating emergency duty!

So while I had nothing else I had a lot of time on my hands, and I devoted many hours of it to this picture of a situation with which I was so familiar. As in this busy world no one will have either the leisure or the inclination to look more closely into the subject, I venture to say that it was an excellent article and that the moral responsibility of the European powers in permitting the continuance of conditions that were leading inevitably to a European war was made quite plain. I emphasized the title "The European Powder Mine," and was quite confident an explosion would follow upon its publication.

But with Reick away how to get it published was a problem. Finally I decided to turn it over to "Jimmy" Williams to be placed on Flynn's desk with any recommendation he might decide to bestow upon it. I knew—we all knew—that "Jimmy" was the chartered libertine of the *Herald* staff and certainly he was the only one who ever enjoyed this enviable position for any length of time. He or his father, upon this point there was hot dispute, had been the favorite bootblack of the Elder Bennett. When the founder of the paper died James Jr. made "Jimmy" his valet although he was ignorant of the A.B.C. of valeting, but from this humble station he had worked his way up to the proud but altogether mysterious position he occupied in the Herald Building when I returned from abroad.

"He worked his way up" is a figure of speech which will, I fear, be contested by any of the old-timers who may survive. "Jimmy" was the laziest of colored boys and certainly no one ever detected him at work. He had charge of the bedroom adjoining the impressive reception hall on the first floor of the building where the Commodore was supposed to sleep after performing the arduous duty of "putting the paper to press," which, of course, he never performed, even on the rare occasions when he came to New York. The *Herald* was at this time published from the old Herald Building on the corner of Broadway and Ann Street, the once famous site of Barnum's Museum. Those who did not admire the paper, and their name was legion, maintained that the paper was staffed by the freaks that Barnum had left behind when he moved his show uptown.

According to the office tradition which I would not vouch for (but it does indicate the strength of "Jimmy's" position in our estimation) on the occasion of one of Bennett Junior's surprise visits to New York (he had a habit of bringing his yacht into Charleston or Hampton Roads where the ship news reporters were napping and so taking his editors by surprise!) he found "Jimmy" shaving with his own private and personal mother-of-pearl-handled razors and, as the old-timers asserted, "said nothing—but just gave 'Jimmy' the razors."

But the other story as to where and how "Jimmy" spent his few working hours I can vouch for. Indeed when I decided to enlist his good offices I found him stretched out on the canopied bed in the famous sleeping chamber to which he alone, while the Commodore was away, had free access. Here with natural trepidation I had tiptoed my way, and here as he looked up I asked him to bring my article to Ed Flynn's attention. "Of course I will," replied the good-natured fellow, "I like your stuff, Bonsal."

But even his powerful support did not put over the article. A few hours later he sought me out and surreptitiously, so that no one else could see my discomfiture, slipped me the rejected manuscript and saying in a low voice, "Flynn says he can't use it. Sorry—you see, he's agin the Balkans," turned and retired to the state apartments down below.

An hour later Dick Davis appeared in a state of high excitement. "Bill Harper came to see me last night," he announced, "and at noon I'm to take charge of the *Weekly*. I want to wake up the sleepers of Franklin Square with a great big bang and to begin with I want you to write me an article about the Balkans. That will make the folks sit up," he added confidently. "Here it is," I said, and the article passed on to its new destination. It appeared in due course wonderfully illustrated and impressively featured, but if it made people outside sit up as warm-hearted Dick assured me it did, it apparently attracted no attention in the *Herald* office where the *Journal of Civilization* was not required reading. But someone must have noticed it, no well-wisher of mine I fear, and this someone must have sent it on to the Commodore who outside of his beloved *Herald* was not an omnivorous reader of American publications.

Two or three weeks passed and I still sat in the frigid atmosphere of the city room that had not been thawed out in the least by Dick's warm-hearted praise of the Balkan article. Then one morning Reick came prancing in from his New Jersey home, as always full of ideas and vibrant with energy. After looking over the telegrams and the papers that had accumulated on his desk, with a grave face he signaled me to approach. "I'm sorry I must tell you the Commodore has cabled me to fire you. He asks me to show you the cable and here it is." I read, "Tell Bonsal he will write for the *Herald* again—when Hell freezes over." "He makes himself perfectly clear," I said, "but what is it all about?" "Well, he did not tell me to show you the other cable that came yesterday—so I will not do it— You most certainly would not like it. It is all about an article he says you have written for Harper's recounting all the news and all the experiences you acquired in the Balkans at his expense. He says it is an unexampled case of base ingratitude and want of loyalty—even in his long and sad experience."

"But while you were away Flynn rejected the article, as he has so many others about southeastern Europe, damned gibberish he calls them. I'm writing on space, why shouldn't I sell it to Harper's?"

"No reason that I can see. I shall cable the Commodore and hold up his discharge order until I hear from him."

Strange as it may seem, I felt quite nervous about the outcome. The Chief rarely reversed himself and then there was nothing on paper as to what had happened. It was simply my word against Flynn's, for "Jimmy" Williams was famous for keeping his skirts clear of all office controversies. But my anxiety did injustice to Flynn. Whatever else he may have been he was an honest man. Two days later "Jimmy" tapped me on the shoulder in the passageway and said almost deferentially, "Flynn would like to speak to you if you've got the time." There was nothing so much I had as time, so in a few minutes I descended to the lower regions where the non-writing editor sat all day smoking his villainous cigars.

"Ah, young man," he barked as he caught sight of me, "I'm indebted to you for the most complete dressing down I have ever received from that man. Of course, I told him when he put me on the mat that I had refused your blankety blank stories and that I could see no reason in God's world why you should not sell them to Harper's—if you can. I then suggested that he make you foreign editor and that I would welcome that—our contacts would be few. I could tell you how many columns of outlandish stuff I would allot you every day and within those limits you could hash it up to suit yourself. But he said no—you had too many ideas. Then he told me to reinstate you at your former salary."

I thought that was all and was turning to go when Flynn added, "Another thing—he has cabled Nordhoff of the Washington Bureau to have you appear before the Senate Foreign Relations Committee—to tell them all you know about the Macedonian outrages and the Bulgarian atrocities. And that's all right with me. That's where all this gibberish belongs but not in the columns of the *New York Herald*."

And so we parted, but I must admit Flynn was not revengeful. He greeted me thereafter with acidulous amiability. For my activities which he always viewed with a pitying smile, he blamed the Commodore—not me.

On my return from Washington I found myself in affluent circumstances, and quite a different atmosphere prevailed in the office. Not that I had accomplished anything at the national capital; still the grave senators had listened patiently to what I had to say and Cushman Davis seemed impressed.

"Why do not the people of Macedonia and of the Balkans generally," he inquired, "leave off killing one another, burning down each others' houses, and do what is right?"

"Unfortunately," I answered, "they are convinced that they are doing what is right. The blows they strike they believe are struck in the most righteous of causes. If they could only be inoculated with the virus of modern skepticism and leave off doing right so fervently, there might come about an era of peace in the Balkans—and certainly the population would increase. As full warrant and justification of their merciless warfare, the Christians point to Joshua the Conqueror of the land of Canaan, the Turks to Mahomet. The war of extermination is in large measure inspired by their spiritual advisers, and the luckless contestants find full warrant for it in Scriptures which they accept as Holy Writ."

I then made it quite plain that the conditions prevailing in the Balkans were leading to war, that unless they were adjusted a world conflagration was inevitable and that we could not escape the consequences. We, like the other powers, would be involved. After I had described, at considerable length I fear, the regrettable situation in which all the unfortunate people of southeastern Europe were involved, old Senator Shelby Cullom, an impressive figure with a hawk-like face, shook his gray head and said, "Young man we must not go too fast. The time is not yet. But you may live to see the day when we, having gained strength, and the power that comes with it, will arise in our might and set the world in order."

The venerable Nordhoff having been under the weather, I was escorted to the hearing by one of his assistants, who delighted me by saying that my talk had been a notable success. But when, hungry for the details upon which his flattering opinion was based, I insisted that he be more explicit, he simply said, "Well at least none of the senators went to sleep on you." So I was forced to the conclusion that after all success is relative.

H. C. Bunner, the famous editor of *Puck,* wrote some amusing verses about the Washington foray in which he poked good-natured fun at "Bonsal of the Balkans." He suggested, however, that I was not a little mad, and boldly asserted that the great American people would only become interested in the Balkans when happenings there affected Wall Street. "And that will never be," he concluded. When the shot that was fired at Sarajevo put Wall Street out of business for months and the American nation, along with the rest of the world, into a plight from which as yet it has not recovered, I had forgotten all about it. I was so busy during the first world war that some years elapsed before I recalled that at least, in this venture into prophecy, I had scored a bull's eye.

While I enjoyed the appreciative atmosphere and the enviable position to which I now returned, I cherished no illusions as to the future or as to the hard road that was opening before me, but I liked the Commodore for all his faults, perhaps because of some of them, and that helped me to travel over the rough places to which he sent me and also to bear up under the rude jolts he often gave me as I traveled over them. After all, as they sing in the old hunting song, I had had a "rattlin' day" and more of them might dawn for me.

My hopes were realized sooner than I had anticipated. After but a few humdrum weeks there came a cable from our vagrant chief who was cruising off the Somali coast in the *Namouna* that read:

"Last month French Premier Ribot was cheered to the echo in the Chamber when he announced that at any moment the armed intervention of the Republic in Morocco might become necessary. Bismarck knew what he was talking about when recently from Varzin he pointed to the menacing war clouds which are gathering over the western entrance to the Mediterranean. The future of Morocco is, as I have every reason to know, causing the statesmen of Europe many anxious hours. The struggle for power in the Balkans has reached a stalemate, the Eastern Question although unsolved is in abeyance and the problem of Turkey for the moment is side-tracked, but the Western Question is charged with dynamite and peace or war in Europe hangs by a thread. Send Bonsal to Fez— immediately." In a few hours I was on my way.

INDEX